MW00787187

Mometrix
TEST PREPARATION

SCAN HERE

FREE Study Skills Videos/DVD Offer

Dear Customer,

Thank you for your purchase from Mometrix! We consider it an honor and a privilege that you have purchased our product and we want to ensure your satisfaction.

As part of our ongoing effort to meet the needs of test takers, we have developed a set of Study Skills Videos that we would like to give you for FREE. These videos cover our *best practices* for getting ready for your exam, from how to use our study materials to how to best prepare for the day of the test.

All that we ask is that you email us with feedback that would describe your experience so far with our product. Good, bad, or indifferent, we want to know what you think!

To get your FREE Study Skills Videos, you can use the **QR code** below, or send us an **email** at studyvideos@mometrix.com with *FREE VIDEOS* in the subject line and the following information in the body of the email:

- The name of the product you purchased.
- Your product rating on a scale of 1-5, with 5 being the highest rating.
- Your feedback. It can be long, short, or anything in between. We just want to know your impressions and experience so far with our product. (Good feedback might include how our study material met your needs and ways we might be able to make it even better. You could highlight features that you found helpful or features that you think we should add.)

If you have any questions or concerns, please don't hesitate to contact me directly.

Thanks again!

Sincerely,

Jay Willis
Vice President
jay.willis@mometrix.com
1-800-673-8175

NYSTCE

EAS Educating All Students Test (201) Secrets Study Guide

NYSTCE Exam Review for the New York State Teacher Certification Examinations

Written and edited by Mometrix Test Prep

Printed in the United States of America

This paper meets the requirements of ANSI/NISO Z39.48-1992 (Permanence of Paper).

Paperback
ISBN 13: 978-1-5167-0606-8
ISBN 10: 1-5167-0606-4

Ebook
ISBN 13: 978-1-5167-0881-9
ISBN 10: 1-5167-0881-4

DEAR FUTURE EXAM SUCCESS STORY

First of all, **THANK YOU** for purchasing Mometrix study materials!

Second, congratulations! You are one of the few determined test-takers who are committed to doing whatever it takes to excel on your exam. **You have come to the right place.** We developed these study materials with one goal in mind: to deliver you the information you need in a format that's concise and easy to use.

In addition to optimizing your guide for the content of the test, we've outlined our recommended steps for breaking down the preparation process into small, attainable goals so you can make sure you stay on track.

We've also analyzed the entire test-taking process, identifying the most common pitfalls and showing how you can overcome them and be ready for any curveball the test throws you.

Standardized testing is one of the biggest obstacles on your road to success, which only increases the importance of doing well in the high-pressure, high-stakes environment of test day. Your results on this test could have a significant impact on your future, and this guide provides the information and practical advice to help you achieve your full potential on test day.

Your success is our success

We would love to hear from you! If you would like to share the story of your exam success or if you have any questions or comments in regard to our products, please contact us at **800-673-8175** or **support@mometrix.com**.

Thanks again for your business and we wish you continued success!

Sincerely,
The Mometrix Test Preparation Team

Need more help? Check out our flashcards at:
http://mometrixflashcards.com/NYSTCE

Written and edited by the Mometrix Exam Secrets Test Prep Team
Printed in the United States of America

TABLE OF CONTENTS

Introduction

Thank you for purchasing this resource! You have made the choice to prepare yourself for a test that could have a huge impact on your future, and this guide is designed to help you be fully ready for test day. Obviously, it's important to have a solid understanding of the test material, but you also need to be prepared for the unique environment and stressors of the test, so that you can perform to the best of your abilities.

For this purpose, the first section that appears in this guide is the **Secret Keys**. We've devoted countless hours to meticulously researching what works and what doesn't, and we've boiled down our findings to the five most impactful steps you can take to improve your performance on the test. We start at the beginning with study planning and move through the preparation process, all the way to the testing strategies that will help you get the most out of what you know when you're finally sitting in front of the test.

We recommend that you start preparing for your test as far in advance as possible. However, if you've bought this guide as a last-minute study resource and only have a few days before your test, we recommend that you skip over the first two Secret Keys since they address a long-term study plan.

If you struggle with **test anxiety**, we strongly encourage you to check out our recommendations for how you can overcome it. Test anxiety is a formidable foe, but it can be beaten, and we want to make sure you have the tools you need to defeat it.

Review Video Directory

As you work your way through this guide, you will see numerous review video links interspersed with the written content. If you would like to access all of these review videos in one place, click on the video directory link found on the bonus page: **mometrix.com/bonus948/nystceeas**

Secret Key #1 – Plan Big, Study Small

There's a lot riding on your performance. If you want to ace this test, you're going to need to keep your skills sharp and the material fresh in your mind. You need a plan that lets you review everything you need to know while still fitting in your schedule. We'll break this strategy down into three categories.

Information Organization

Start with the information you already have: the official test outline. From this, you can make a complete list of all the concepts you need to cover before the test. Organize these concepts into groups that can be studied together, and create a list of any related vocabulary you need to learn so you can brush up on any difficult terms. You'll want to keep this vocabulary list handy once you actually start studying since you may need to add to it along the way.

Time Management

Once you have your set of study concepts, decide how to spread them out over the time you have left before the test. Break your study plan into small, clear goals so you have a manageable task for each day and know exactly what you're doing. Then just focus on one small step at a time. When you manage your time this way, you don't need to spend hours at a time studying. Studying a small block of content for a short period each day helps you retain information better and avoid stressing over how much you have left to do. You can relax knowing that you have a plan to cover everything in time. In order for this strategy to be effective though, you have to start studying early and stick to your schedule. Avoid the exhaustion and futility that comes from last-minute cramming!

Study Environment

The environment you study in has a big impact on your learning. Studying in a coffee shop, while probably more enjoyable, is not likely to be as fruitful as studying in a quiet room. It's important to keep distractions to a minimum. You're only planning to study for a short block of time, so make the most of it. Don't pause to check your phone or get up to find a snack. It's also important to **avoid multitasking**. Research has consistently shown that multitasking will make your studying dramatically less effective. Your study area should also be comfortable and well-lit so you don't have the distraction of straining your eyes or sitting on an uncomfortable chair.

The time of day you study is also important. You want to be rested and alert. Don't wait until just before bedtime. Study when you'll be most likely to comprehend and remember. Even better, if you know what time of day your test will be, set that time aside for study. That way your brain will be used to working on that subject at that specific time and you'll have a better chance of recalling information.

Finally, it can be helpful to team up with others who are studying for the same test. Your actual studying should be done in as isolated an environment as possible, but the work of organizing the information and setting up the study plan can be divided up. In between study sessions, you can discuss with your teammates the concepts that you're all studying and quiz each other on the details. Just be sure that your teammates are as serious about the test as you are. If you find that your study time is being replaced with social time, you might need to find a new team.

Secret Key #2 – Make Your Studying Count

You're devoting a lot of time and effort to preparing for this test, so you want to be absolutely certain it will pay off. This means doing more than just reading the content and hoping you can remember it on test day. It's important to make every minute of study count. There are two main areas you can focus on to make your studying count.

Retention

It doesn't matter how much time you study if you can't remember the material. You need to make sure you are retaining the concepts. To check your retention of the information you're learning, try recalling it at later times with minimal prompting. Try carrying around flashcards and glance at one or two from time to time or ask a friend who's also studying for the test to quiz you.

To enhance your retention, look for ways to put the information into practice so that you can apply it rather than simply recalling it. If you're using the information in practical ways, it will be much easier to remember. Similarly, it helps to solidify a concept in your mind if you're not only reading it to yourself but also explaining it to someone else. Ask a friend to let you teach them about a concept you're a little shaky on (or speak aloud to an imaginary audience if necessary). As you try to summarize, define, give examples, and answer your friend's questions, you'll understand the concepts better and they will stay with you longer. Finally, step back for a big picture view and ask yourself how each piece of information fits with the whole subject. When you link the different concepts together and see them working together as a whole, it's easier to remember the individual components.

Finally, practice showing your work on any multi-step problems, even if you're just studying. Writing out each step you take to solve a problem will help solidify the process in your mind, and you'll be more likely to remember it during the test.

Modality

Modality simply refers to the means or method by which you study. Choosing a study modality that fits your own individual learning style is crucial. No two people learn best in exactly the same way, so it's important to know your strengths and use them to your advantage.

For example, if you learn best by visualization, focus on visualizing a concept in your mind and draw an image or a diagram. Try color-coding your notes, illustrating them, or creating symbols that will trigger your mind to recall a learned concept. If you learn best by hearing or discussing information, find a study partner who learns the same way or read aloud to yourself. Think about how to put the information in your own words. Imagine that you are giving a lecture on the topic and record yourself so you can listen to it later.

For any learning style, flashcards can be helpful. Organize the information so you can take advantage of spare moments to review. Underline key words or phrases. Use different colors for different categories. Mnemonic devices (such as creating a short list in which every item starts with the same letter) can also help with retention. Find what works best for you and use it to store the information in your mind most effectively and easily.

Secret Key #3 – Practice the Right Way

Your success on test day depends not only on how many hours you put into preparing, but also on whether you prepared the right way. It's good to check along the way to see if your studying is paying off. One of the most effective ways to do this is by taking practice tests to evaluate your progress. Practice tests are useful because they show exactly where you need to improve. Every time you take a practice test, pay special attention to these three groups of questions:

- The questions you got wrong
- The questions you had to guess on, even if you guessed right
- The questions you found difficult or slow to work through

This will show you exactly what your weak areas are, and where you need to devote more study time. Ask yourself why each of these questions gave you trouble. Was it because you didn't understand the material? Was it because you didn't remember the vocabulary? Do you need more repetitions on this type of question to build speed and confidence? Dig into those questions and figure out how you can strengthen your weak areas as you go back to review the material.

Additionally, many practice tests have a section explaining the answer choices. It can be tempting to read the explanation and think that you now have a good understanding of the concept. However, an explanation likely only covers part of the question's broader context. Even if the explanation makes perfect sense, **go back and investigate** every concept related to the question until you're positive you have a thorough understanding.

As you go along, keep in mind that the practice test is just that: practice. Memorizing these questions and answers will not be very helpful on the actual test because it is unlikely to have any of the same exact questions. If you only know the right answers to the sample questions, you won't be prepared for the real thing. **Study the concepts** until you understand them fully, and then you'll be able to answer any question that shows up on the test.

It's important to wait on the practice tests until you're ready. If you take a test on your first day of study, you may be overwhelmed by the amount of material covered and how much you need to learn. Work up to it gradually.

On test day, you'll need to be prepared for answering questions, managing your time, and using the test-taking strategies you've learned. It's a lot to balance, like a mental marathon that will have a big impact on your future. Like training for a marathon, you'll need to start slowly and work your way up. When test day arrives, you'll be ready.

Start with the strategies you've read in the first two Secret Keys—plan your course and study in the way that works best for you. If you have time, consider using multiple study resources to get different approaches to the same concepts. It can be helpful to see difficult concepts from more than one angle. Then find a good source for practice tests. Many times, the test website will suggest potential study resources or provide sample tests.

Practice Test Strategy

If you're able to find at least three practice tests, we recommend this strategy:

Untimed and Open-Book Practice

Take the first test with no time constraints and with your notes and study guide handy. Take your time and focus on applying the strategies you've learned.

Timed and Open-Book Practice

Take the second practice test open-book as well, but set a timer and practice pacing yourself to finish in time.

Timed and Closed-Book Practice

Take any other practice tests as if it were test day. Set a timer and put away your study materials. Sit at a table or desk in a quiet room, imagine yourself at the testing center, and answer questions as quickly and accurately as possible.

Keep repeating timed and closed-book tests on a regular basis until you run out of practice tests or it's time for the actual test. Your mind will be ready for the schedule and stress of test day, and you'll be able to focus on recalling the material you've learned.

Secret Key #4 – Pace Yourself

Once you're fully prepared for the material on the test, your biggest challenge on test day will be managing your time. Just knowing that the clock is ticking can make you panic even if you have plenty of time left. Work on pacing yourself so you can build confidence against the time constraints of the exam. Pacing is a difficult skill to master, especially in a high-pressure environment, so **practice is vital**.

Set time expectations for your pace based on how much time is available. For example, if a section has 60 questions and the time limit is 30 minutes, you know you have to average 30 seconds or less per question in order to answer them all. Although 30 seconds is the hard limit, set 25 seconds per question as your goal, so you reserve extra time to spend on harder questions. When you budget extra time for the harder questions, you no longer have any reason to stress when those questions take longer to answer.

Don't let this time expectation distract you from working through the test at a calm, steady pace, but keep it in mind so you don't spend too much time on any one question. Recognize that taking extra time on one question you don't understand may keep you from answering two that you do understand later in the test. If your time limit for a question is up and you're still not sure of the answer, mark it and move on, and come back to it later if the time and the test format allow. If the testing format doesn't allow you to return to earlier questions, just make an educated guess; then put it out of your mind and move on.

On the easier questions, be careful not to rush. It may seem wise to hurry through them so you have more time for the challenging ones, but it's not worth missing one if you know the concept and just didn't take the time to read the question fully. Work efficiently but make sure you understand the question and have looked at all of the answer choices, since more than one may seem right at first.

Even if you're paying attention to the time, you may find yourself a little behind at some point. You should speed up to get back on track, but do so wisely. Don't panic; just take a few seconds less on each question until you're caught up. Don't guess without thinking, but do look through the answer choices and eliminate any you know are wrong. If you can get down to two choices, it is often worthwhile to guess from those. Once you've chosen an answer, move on and don't dwell on any that you skipped or had to hurry through. If a question was taking too long, chances are it was one of the harder ones, so you weren't as likely to get it right anyway.

On the other hand, if you find yourself getting ahead of schedule, it may be beneficial to slow down a little. The more quickly you work, the more likely you are to make a careless mistake that will affect your score. You've budgeted time for each question, so don't be afraid to spend that time. Practice an efficient but careful pace to get the most out of the time you have.

Secret Key #5 – Have a Plan for Guessing

When you're taking the test, you may find yourself stuck on a question. Some of the answer choices seem better than others, but you don't see the one answer choice that is obviously correct. What do you do?

The scenario described above is very common, yet most test takers have not effectively prepared for it. Developing and practicing a plan for guessing may be one of the single most effective uses of your time as you get ready for the exam.

In developing your plan for guessing, there are three questions to address:

- When should you start the guessing process?
- How should you narrow down the choices?
- Which answer should you choose?

When to Start the Guessing Process

Unless your plan for guessing is to select C every time (which, despite its merits, is not what we recommend), you need to leave yourself enough time to apply your answer elimination strategies. Since you have a limited amount of time for each question, that means that if you're going to give yourself the best shot at guessing correctly, you have to decide quickly whether or not you will guess.

Of course, the best-case scenario is that you don't have to guess at all, so first, see if you can answer the question based on your knowledge of the subject and basic reasoning skills. Focus on the key words in the question and try to jog your memory of related topics. Give yourself a chance to bring the knowledge to mind, but once you realize that you don't have (or you can't access) the knowledge you need to answer the question, it's time to start the guessing process.

It's almost always better to start the guessing process too early than too late. It only takes a few seconds to remember something and answer the question from knowledge. Carefully eliminating wrong answer choices takes longer. Plus, going through the process of eliminating answer choices can actually help jog your memory.

Summary: Start the guessing process as soon as you decide that you can't answer the question based on your knowledge.

How to Narrow Down the Choices

The next chapter in this book (**Test-Taking Strategies**) includes a wide range of strategies for how to approach questions and how to look for answer choices to eliminate. You will definitely want to read those carefully, practice them, and figure out which ones work best for you. Here though, we're going to address a mindset rather than a particular strategy.

Your odds of guessing an answer correctly depend on how many options you are choosing from.

Number of options left	5	4	3	2	1
Odds of guessing correctly	20%	25%	33%	50%	100%

You can see from this chart just how valuable it is to be able to eliminate incorrect answers and make an educated guess, but there are two things that many test takers do that cause them to miss out on the benefits of guessing:

- Accidentally eliminating the correct answer
- Selecting an answer based on an impression

We'll look at the first one here, and the second one in the next section.

To avoid accidentally eliminating the correct answer, we recommend a thought exercise called **the $5 challenge**. In this challenge, you only eliminate an answer choice from contention if you are willing to bet $5 on it being wrong. Why $5? Five dollars is a small but not insignificant amount of money. It's an amount you could afford to lose but wouldn't want to throw away. And while losing $5 once might not hurt too much, doing it twenty times will set you back $100. In the same way, each small decision you make—eliminating a choice here, guessing on a question there—won't by itself impact your score very much, but when you put them all together, they can make a big difference. By holding each answer choice elimination decision to a higher standard, you can reduce the risk of accidentally eliminating the correct answer.

The $5 challenge can also be applied in a positive sense: If you are willing to bet $5 that an answer choice *is* correct, go ahead and mark it as correct.

Summary: Only eliminate an answer choice if you are willing to bet $5 that it is wrong.

Which Answer to Choose

You're taking the test. You've run into a hard question and decided you'll have to guess. You've eliminated all the answer choices you're willing to bet $5 on. Now you have to pick an answer. Why do we even need to talk about this? Why can't you just pick whichever one you feel like when the time comes?

The answer to these questions is that if you don't come into the test with a plan, you'll rely on your impression to select an answer choice, and if you do that, you risk falling into a trap. The test writers know that everyone who takes their test will be guessing on some of the questions, so they intentionally write wrong answer choices to seem plausible. You still have to pick an answer though, and if the wrong answer choices are designed to look right, how can you ever be sure that you're not falling for their trap? The best solution we've found to this dilemma is to take the decision out of your hands entirely. Here is the process we recommend:

Once you've eliminated any choices that you are confident (willing to bet $5) are wrong, select the first remaining choice as your answer.

Whether you choose to select the first remaining choice, the second, or the last, the important thing is that you use some preselected standard. Using this approach guarantees that you will not be enticed into selecting an answer choice that looks right, because you are not basing your decision on how the answer choices look.

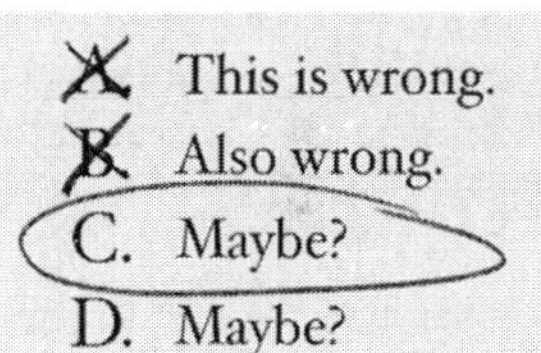

This is not meant to make you question your knowledge. Instead, it is to help you recognize the difference between your knowledge and your impressions. There's a huge difference between thinking an answer is right because of what you know, and thinking an answer is right because it looks or sounds like it should be right.

Summary: To ensure that your selection is appropriately random, make a predetermined selection from among all answer choices you have not eliminated.

Test-Taking Strategies

This section contains a list of test-taking strategies that you may find helpful as you work through the test. By taking what you know and applying logical thought, you can maximize your chances of answering any question correctly!

It is very important to realize that every question is different and every person is different: no single strategy will work on every question, and no single strategy will work for every person. That's why we've included all of them here, so you can try them out and determine which ones work best for different types of questions and which ones work best for you.

Question Strategies

✓ Read Carefully

Read the question and the answer choices carefully. Don't miss the question because you misread the terms. You have plenty of time to read each question thoroughly and make sure you understand what is being asked. Yet a happy medium must be attained, so don't waste too much time. You must read carefully and efficiently.

✓ Contextual Clues

Look for contextual clues. If the question includes a word you are not familiar with, look at the immediate context for some indication of what the word might mean. Contextual clues can often give you all the information you need to decipher the meaning of an unfamiliar word. Even if you can't determine the meaning, you may be able to narrow down the possibilities enough to make a solid guess at the answer to the question.

✓ Prefixes

If you're having trouble with a word in the question or answer choices, try dissecting it. Take advantage of every clue that the word might include. Prefixes can be a huge help. Usually, they allow you to determine a basic meaning. *Pre-* means before, *post-* means after, *pro-* is positive, *de-* is negative. From prefixes, you can get an idea of the general meaning of the word and try to put it into context.

✓ Hedge Words

Watch out for critical hedge words, such as *likely, may, can, sometimes, often, almost, mostly, usually, generally, rarely,* and *sometimes.* Question writers insert these hedge phrases to cover every possibility. Often an answer choice will be wrong simply because it leaves no room for exception. Be on guard for answer choices that have definitive words such as *exactly* and *always.*

✓ Switchback Words

Stay alert for *switchbacks.* These are the words and phrases frequently used to alert you to shifts in thought. The most common switchback words are *but, although,* and *however.* Others include *nevertheless, on the other hand, even though, while, in spite of, despite,* and *regardless of.* Switchback words are important to catch because they can change the direction of the question or an answer choice.

☑ Face Value

When in doubt, use common sense. Accept the situation in the problem at face value. Don't read too much into it. These problems will not require you to make wild assumptions. If you have to go beyond creativity and warp time or space in order to have an answer choice fit the question, then you should move on and consider the other answer choices. These are normal problems rooted in reality. The applicable relationship or explanation may not be readily apparent, but it is there for you to figure out. Use your common sense to interpret anything that isn't clear.

Answer Choice Strategies

☑ Answer Selection

The most thorough way to pick an answer choice is to identify and eliminate wrong answers until only one is left, then confirm it is the correct answer. Sometimes an answer choice may immediately seem right, but be careful. The test writers will usually put more than one reasonable answer choice on each question, so take a second to read all of them and make sure that the other choices are not equally obvious. As long as you have time left, it is better to read every answer choice than to pick the first one that looks right without checking the others.

☑ Answer Choice Families

An answer choice family consists of two (in rare cases, three) answer choices that are very similar in construction and cannot all be true at the same time. If you see two answer choices that are direct opposites or parallels, one of them is usually the correct answer. For instance, if one answer choice says that quantity x increases and another either says that quantity x decreases (opposite) or says that quantity y increases (parallel), then those answer choices would fall into the same family. An answer choice that doesn't match the construction of the answer choice family is more likely to be incorrect. Most questions will not have answer choice families, but when they do appear, you should be prepared to recognize them.

☑ Eliminate Answers

Eliminate answer choices as soon as you realize they are wrong, but make sure you consider all possibilities. If you are eliminating answer choices and realize that the last one you are left with is also wrong, don't panic. Start over and consider each choice again. There may be something you missed the first time that you will realize on the second pass.

☑ Avoid Fact Traps

Don't be distracted by an answer choice that is factually true but doesn't answer the question. You are looking for the choice that answers the question. Stay focused on what the question is asking for so you don't accidentally pick an answer that is true but incorrect. Always go back to the question and make sure the answer choice you've selected actually answers the question and is not merely a true statement.

☑ Extreme Statements

In general, you should avoid answers that put forth extreme actions as standard practice or proclaim controversial ideas as established fact. An answer choice that states the "process should be used in certain situations, if..." is much more likely to be correct than one that states the "process should be discontinued completely." The first is a calm rational statement and doesn't even make a definitive, uncompromising stance, using a hedge word *if* to provide wiggle room, whereas the second choice is far more extreme.

✓ BENCHMARK

As you read through the answer choices and you come across one that seems to answer the question well, mentally select that answer choice. This is not your final answer, but it's the one that will help you evaluate the other answer choices. The one that you selected is your benchmark or standard for judging each of the other answer choices. Every other answer choice must be compared to your benchmark. That choice is correct until proven otherwise by another answer choice beating it. If you find a better answer, then that one becomes your new benchmark. Once you've decided that no other choice answers the question as well as your benchmark, you have your final answer.

✓ PREDICT THE ANSWER

Before you even start looking at the answer choices, it is often best to try to predict the answer. When you come up with the answer on your own, it is easier to avoid distractions and traps because you will know exactly what to look for. The right answer choice is unlikely to be word-for-word what you came up with, but it should be a close match. Even if you are confident that you have the right answer, you should still take the time to read each option before moving on.

General Strategies

✓ TOUGH QUESTIONS

If you are stumped on a problem or it appears too hard or too difficult, don't waste time. Move on! Remember though, if you can quickly check for obviously incorrect answer choices, your chances of guessing correctly are greatly improved. Before you completely give up, at least try to knock out a couple of possible answers. Eliminate what you can and then guess at the remaining answer choices before moving on.

✓ CHECK YOUR WORK

Since you will probably not know every term listed and the answer to every question, it is important that you get credit for the ones that you do know. Don't miss any questions through careless mistakes. If at all possible, try to take a second to look back over your answer selection and make sure you've selected the correct answer choice and haven't made a costly careless mistake (such as marking an answer choice that you didn't mean to mark). This quick double check should more than pay for itself in caught mistakes for the time it costs.

✓ PACE YOURSELF

It's easy to be overwhelmed when you're looking at a page full of questions; your mind is confused and full of random thoughts, and the clock is ticking down faster than you would like. Calm down and maintain the pace that you have set for yourself. Especially as you get down to the last few minutes of the test, don't let the small numbers on the clock make you panic. As long as you are on track by monitoring your pace, you are guaranteed to have time for each question.

✓ DON'T RUSH

It is very easy to make errors when you are in a hurry. Maintaining a fast pace in answering questions is pointless if it makes you miss questions that you would have gotten right otherwise. Test writers like to include distracting information and wrong answers that seem right. Taking a little extra time to avoid careless mistakes can make all the difference in your test score. Find a pace that allows you to be confident in the answers that you select.

⊘ KEEP MOVING

Panicking will not help you pass the test, so do your best to stay calm and keep moving. Taking deep breaths and going through the answer elimination steps you practiced can help to break through a stress barrier and keep your pace.

Final Notes

The combination of a solid foundation of content knowledge and the confidence that comes from practicing your plan for applying that knowledge is the key to maximizing your performance on test day. As your foundation of content knowledge is built up and strengthened, you'll find that the strategies included in this chapter become more and more effective in helping you quickly sift through the distractions and traps of the test to isolate the correct answer.

Now that you're preparing to move forward into the test content chapters of this book, be sure to keep your goal in mind. As you read, think about how you will be able to apply this information on the test. If you've already seen sample questions for the test and you have an idea of the question format and style, try to come up with questions of your own that you can answer based on what you're reading. This will give you valuable practice applying your knowledge in the same ways you can expect to on test day.

Good luck and good studying!

Diverse Student Populations

Transform passive reading into active learning! After immersing yourself in this chapter, put your comprehension to the test by taking a quiz. The insights you gained will stay with you longer this way. Scan the QR code to go directly to the chapter quiz interface for this study guide. If you're using a computer, simply visit the bonus page at **mometrix.com/bonus948/nystceeas** and click the Chapter Quizzes link.

Diverse Student Populations

Understanding Students' Diverse Backgrounds and Needs

Self-Education

Educating oneself on students' diverse backgrounds and needs enhances one's overall understanding of their students and creates a culturally sensitive, accepting classroom environment tailored to students' individual needs. There are several avenues through which teachers should educate themselves in an effort to build an accepting and respectful classroom climate. Communication is key for learning about diversities; thus, it is important for teachers to foster and maintain positive communications with students' families to deepen understanding of cultures, beliefs, lifestyles, and needs that exist within their classroom. This could include learning some language of students with different cultural backgrounds, attending family nights at school, or participating in social events within their students' communities to integrate themselves into the culture. Furthermore, teachers can learn more about their students' backgrounds and needs through gaining an understanding of student differences, incorporating these diversities into the curriculum, and encouraging students to participate in learning by sharing aspects of their lives with the class.

Teaching, Learning, and Classroom Climate Benefits

A deep understanding of students' diverse backgrounds and needs provides multiple benefits for teaching, learning, and overall classroom climate. Knowledge of students' diversities allows teachers to understand the individual needs and abilities of their students, and tailor instruction accordingly to maximize student development and achievement. Additionally, it allows teachers to know which authentic materials to incorporate in lessons and instructions to best create an engaging, relevant, and respectful learning experience that fosters student interest in learning and promotes success. Furthermore, by enhancing understanding of students' diverse backgrounds and needs, teachers consequently begin to model an attitude of inclusivity, acceptance, and respect for differences, which is then reflected by students and achieves a positive, welcoming classroom climate that promotes diversity.

Implications for Teaching, Learning, and Assessment in Diverse Classrooms

In any classroom, a teacher will encounter a wide range of variances among individual students that inevitably will influence teaching, learning, and assessment. Diversities in ethnicity, gender, language background, and learning exceptionality will likely exist simultaneously in a single classroom. Educators must be prepared to teach to these diversities while concurrently teaching students the value and importance of diversity. The curriculum and classroom environment must be adjusted to meet individual student needs and create an **inclusive**, **respectful**, and **equitable** environment that welcomes differences and allows for success in learning. This begins with the teacher developing an understanding of the unique diversities that exist within their students and using this knowledge to **differentiate** curriculum, materials, activities, and assessments in such a way that students of all needs, interests, backgrounds, and abilities feel encouraged and included. Furthermore, the teacher must understand how to instill appropriate supports to accommodate the diverse needs of students, as well as how to modify the classroom environment in such a way that is reflective of the diversity of the students.

Considerations for Teaching in Diverse Classrooms

Ethnically-Diverse Classrooms

As society becomes increasingly diverse, teachers will certainly encounter classrooms with students of multiple ethnicities. Thus, to create an accepting and respectful classroom environment that allows for success in learning for all students, there are several factors to consider. Teachers must educate themselves on the various ethnicities within their classroom. This includes being mindful of **social norms, values, beliefs, traditions,** and **lifestyles** of different ethnic groups, and learning to communicate with students and families in a respectful, culturally sensitive manner. Additionally, the teacher must make a conscious effort to incorporate aspects of each ethnicity into the curriculum, activities, and classroom environment to create an inclusive atmosphere that teaches the acceptance, respect for, and celebration of differences. Teachers must be **culturally competent** and ensure that all materials are accurate, relevant, authentic, and portray the different ethnicities within the classroom in a respectful, unbiased manner. Furthermore, teachers must consider how their own ethnicity impacts their teaching style and interactions with students, how they may be perceived by other ethnic groups, and how to respond in a manner that fosters respect and inclusivity.

Gender-Diverse Classrooms

When approaching a gender-diverse classroom, teachers need to consider their perceptions, interactions with, and expectations of different genders, as well as how the classroom environment and materials portray gender differences. Teachers must work to eliminate possible stereotypical beliefs so all students feel respected, accepted, and encouraged to participate. Furthermore, teachers must consider how their behavior acts as a model for how students perceive gender roles and should act in a way that eliminates gender divisiveness. Teachers should use gender-neutral language when addressing students and ensure that all students receive equal attention. Teachers must maintain equal academic and behavioral expectations between genders and be sure to equally praise and discipline students so that neither gender feels superior or inferior to another. Regarding curriculum and classroom materials, teachers must ensure that the classroom environment encourages equal participation in, access to, and choice of all activities and procedures. Activities and materials should provide equal opportunities and foster collaboration between genders. Furthermore, teachers must ensure that curriculum materials avoid gender stereotypes, and highlight each gender equally in order to create an accepting and respectful learning environment that provides equal opportunities for students of all genders to develop their individual identities and abilities.

Linguistically Diverse Classrooms

In a **linguistically diverse** classroom, teachers must consider how to effectively demonstrate value for students' native languages while simultaneously supporting the development of necessary language skills to thrive in the school setting. By accepting and encouraging students to use their native languages, teachers can establish an inclusive learning environment that celebrates linguistic differences, and therefore, encourages students to want to build upon their language skills. Through this, teachers create an equitable learning environment that allows for academic success. To develop English language skills, the teacher must first consider each students' language ability and level of exposure to English prior to entering the classroom, as well as the level of language learning support each student has at home. Teachers can then implement effective instructional strategies and supports to modify curriculum in a way that addresses students' language needs. Teachers must also consider the implications of the classroom environment on language acquisition. By creating an atmosphere that encourages language acquisition through **literacy-rich resources** and **cooperative learning**, teachers promote the use of language skills and ultimately provide opportunities for success for all students.

Linguistic Supports and Instructional Strategies Promoting English Language Proficiency

Incorporating a variety of linguistic aids and instructional strategies is beneficial in supporting ELL students of varying levels of English language proficiency. **Visual representations** to accompany instruction, such as posters, charts, pictures, slide shows, videos, tables, or anchor charts, are valuable in providing clarification and reference while promoting vocabulary acquisition. When delivering instruction, **body language** such as hand gestures, eye contact, and movement to mimic verbal directions and explanations can provide clarification to enhance understanding. These students may also require **translation devices** for clarification, an interpreter to help with understanding instructions and new concepts, alternate assignments with simplified language, or **individualized instruction** from an ESL teacher. Frequently checking for understanding and providing clarification as necessary throughout instruction are necessary to ensuring ELL students understand learning materials, instructions, and assessments. In addition, creating a print and literacy-rich environment by including word walls for new vocabulary, reading materials that vary in complexity, labels, and opportunities for speaking, reading, and writing within instruction are valuable in promoting English language acquisition.

Learning Disabilities and Other Exceptionalities

In a classroom where learning disabilities and exceptionalities are present, teachers must consider accommodations for students of various learning needs while fostering an atmosphere of respect and acceptance. Teachers must understand the individual learning needs of each student and differentiate instruction accordingly to create an equitable and inclusive learning atmosphere. For **learning disabled** students, teachers must consider accommodations that allow for inclusion in all areas of curriculum and instruction. Such considerations may include extended work time, individualized instruction, and cooperative learning activities to ensure that learning disabled students are provided the necessary supports to achieve academic success. For students with other exceptionalities, such as **gifted and talented** students, teachers need to consider ways to provide challenging and stimulating opportunities for expansion and enrichment of curriculum. Furthermore, the teacher must be aware of their own interactions with students in order to demonstrate and encourage respect and acceptance among students. By providing supports for individual student success, teachers can effectively highlight students' strengths and therefore, teach students to accept and celebrate differences in learning abilities.

Educating Students about Diversity

Goals of Teaching Diversity in the Classroom

Teaching diversity in the classroom aims to establish a welcoming and inclusive classroom environment that encourages academic achievement and whole-child development. Diversity education works to develop students' understanding, acceptance, and respect for others' perspectives while instilling the concept that people are ultimately more alike than different, and that diversities should be celebrated. Teaching the importance of differences creates a positive, inclusive classroom atmosphere in which all students feel respected, safe, and valued by their teacher and peers. Such an environment promotes academic achievement among students in that it encourages participation in learning and builds the self-esteem necessary for positive growth and development. Furthermore, teaching diversity has a significant role in **whole-child development** in that it instills the ability to understand and respect multiple frames of reference, thus increasing their ability to problem solve, cooperate with others, and develop a broader global perspective. Additionally, it allows for the development of cultural competency and ultimately creates accepting and respectful contributors to society.

Review Video: Multiculturalism/Celebrating All Cultures
Visit mometrix.com/academy and enter code: 708545

Recognizing and Eliminating Personal Biases

Personal biases are often subtle and unconscious, yet it is essential that teachers work to recognize and eliminate them to create an accepting and respectful classroom environment. Personal biases may negatively impact teaching style, interactions with students, and ultimately, student learning and self-esteem. In eliminating personal bias, teachers ensure that they establish an inclusive classroom environment where each student is treated fairly. Furthermore, students' beliefs toward diversity are influenced by the attitudes and behaviors modeled by their teacher, and therefore, eradicating personal bias is vital in positively influencing students to accept and respect differences. To eliminate personal bias, teachers must **reflect** on their own culture's attitudes toward diversity, as well as how these attitudes influence their interactions toward other groups, and work to make positive changes. Teachers must **educate** themselves on the diversities among their students and work to deepen their understanding of different groups through **communicating** with families, **integrating** themselves into students' communities, and participating in **professional development** that focuses on **cultural competency** and the importance of teaching diversity. Through making positive changes against personal biases, teachers foster a classroom environment that promotes diversity and empowers all students to be successful.

Impact of Diverse Cultural Climate in the Classroom

Creating a diverse cultural climate in the classroom results in an empowering and engaging learning environment that facilitates academic success. An atmosphere that respects and accepts differences fosters a sense of inclusivity and welcoming among teachers and students, which allows students to feel comfortable with differences, safe in their own identities, and consequently, comfortable to engage in learning. This fosters a positive attitude toward learning that promotes academic achievement. Additionally, when students accept one another's differences in a diverse cultural climate, they are better able to work together and adopt creative problem-solving solutions through others' perspectives, which results in success in learning. Furthermore, a successfully diverse cultural climate reflects the diversity of the students within it, which ultimately creates a more engaging and relevant academic environment that sparks motivation and curiosity toward learning. Learning environments that reflect students' diversity create a sense of unity and belonging in the classroom and positively contribute to success in learning through building students' self-esteem and self-concept to empower them in believing they can achieve academic success.

Authentic Classroom Materials

Authentic classroom materials are artifacts from various cultures, events, or periods of time. These items enhance the relevancy of instruction by promoting students' real-world connection to learning and may also be used to incorporate students' backgrounds and experiences into the classroom to increase engagement. Such materials include magazines, newspapers, advertisements, restaurant menus, and recipes. In addition, resources such as video clips, films, television shows, documentaries, news segments, and music serve as authentic media sources to incorporate into instruction. Original works or documents, including art pieces, literature, poetry, maps, or historical records, are also valuable authentic resources for providing students with a real-world learning experience.

Locating and Implementing

Authentic classroom materials and resources are integral in creating a classroom environment that fosters engaging, relevant, and positive learning experiences. Teachers must work to develop an understanding of the diversities among their students and use this knowledge to locate and implement authentic classroom materials into daily instruction. In doing so, teachers create a positive learning environment that accepts and respects differences through incorporating **relevant** and **familiar** materials that make students from all backgrounds feel valued and included in instruction. When students can see aspects of their culture reflected in authentic learning materials, they can make **personal connections** between what they are learning and their own lives, and learning becomes more valuable, engaging, and relevant, thereby promoting success in learning.

Incorporating Diversity Education into the Classroom

Incorporating diversity into the classroom maximizes student opportunities for academic success through creating a welcoming, empowering, and inclusive atmosphere. Teachers can implement multiple strategies to incorporate **diversity education** into the curriculum both as its own unit and woven into content instruction once they develop an understanding of the diversities among their own students. Through **building relationships** with students, teachers can use their knowledge of students' lives to incorporate aspects of their backgrounds into the curriculum by creating specific **cultural lessons** on food, music, language, art, and history. Additionally, **cultural comparison** studies are an effective method of teaching students the value of diversity, as well as highlighting the fact that people from different backgrounds often have more similarities than differences. Teachers can further implement diversity education by encouraging students to participate in learning through having them share elements of their culture and background with the class through activities such as show and tell or hosting family nights. Furthermore, integrating **cooperative learning** activities into instruction allow and encourage students from different backgrounds to work together and gain an understanding of the perspectives and backgrounds of others.

Incorporating Diversity in the Curriculum

Incorporating diversity into the curriculum is vital for teaching the value and importance of differences and for contributing to a respectful and accepting environment. Additionally, it is imperative that diversity education extend from the curriculum to the entire classroom environment to maximize student growth and opportunity to reach potential. When students learn in an atmosphere that celebrates diversity and identifies strengths in differences, they feel a sense of belonging and confidence that encourages them to engage in learning, thus maximizing the potential for academic success. Teachers can effectively integrate diversity into the classroom environment through making authentic cultural materials such as texts, music, and art readily accessible for students. Additionally, providing several opportunities for students to collaborate and socialize in a natural setting allows them to gain an understanding and respect for their peers' backgrounds. By encouraging students to share aspects of their own lives and backgrounds with the class through cultural activities, teachers facilitate a diverse climate that celebrates differences.

Culturally Responsive Teaching

Culturally responsive teaching is an instructional approach in which the teacher practices awareness, inclusivity, and sensitivity regarding the social and cultural diversities that are present within the classroom. With this awareness in mind, the culturally responsive teacher designs curriculum, instruction, activities, and assessments that are inclusive and reflective of students' social and cultural backgrounds and experiences. When planning instruction and learning experiences, the teacher can demonstrate awareness of social and cultural norms through consciously educating themselves on the beliefs, values, and norms of their students. This is achieved through connecting with students and building positive relationships to learn about their individual backgrounds and locate authentic learning materials that are reflective of their experiences. Through communicating with students' parents, family members, and members of the community, the teacher can practice and build awareness of the diverse social and cultural norms of their students to gain an understanding of how to design culturally responsive instruction. By educating themselves on the social and cultural norms of their students, the teacher can effectively ensure that students' diversities are reflected in all areas of instruction in a culturally sensitive manner to create an empowering learning environment that engages all students.

Practices for Culturally Responsive Teaching	
1	Create an inclusive classroom environment
2	Recognize personal biases and work to eliminate them
3	Self-educate on the community and students' social and cultural backgrounds
4	Use curriculum that reflects students' diversities using authentic materials
5	Frequently communicate with students' families
6	Build positive interpersonal relationships with students
7	Be involved in the community

Supporting Students with Varied Learning Needs

Planning and Adapting Lessons to Address Students' Needs

Varied Backgrounds

Effectively planning lessons and adapting instruction to address students' varied backgrounds requires teachers to gain an understanding of individual students, and educate themselves on **customs, norms**, and **values** of the cultures in their classroom. This allows teachers to effectively plan **culturally responsive** lessons with **authentic materials** to make learning valuable, interesting, relevant, and allow students to feel included. Understanding students' backgrounds means teachers recognize variances in their knowledge and experiences on different topics and can effectively plan engaging and inclusive lessons that build upon it. Teachers must assess students' knowledge on material prior to creating lessons to effectively plan instruction that adapts to the needs of students' varied backgrounds and reflects students' experiences. Teachers must plan lesson materials such as texts, art, music, and language that accurately and sensitively reflect students' diverse backgrounds. Cooperative learning strategies should be incorporated to facilitate communication among students with varying backgrounds, as it helps them build knowledge from others' experiences, as well as teaches them to respect and value differences among their peers. Teachers must plan instruction that communicates high academic expectations for all students and adapt instruction as necessary by implementing supports to create equity and address the needs of varying backgrounds.

Review Video: Adapting and Modifying Lessons or Activities
Visit mometrix.com/academy and enter code: 834946

Differences in Individual Students' Skills

Teachers must use their knowledge of differences in students' skills to plan multifaceted, adaptable lessons that highlight students' strengths while providing instructional supports where needed based on individual skill level. To effectively plan, teachers must incorporate multiple strategies and mediums for instruction, activities, and assessments to allow students of all skill levels equitable and enriching access to content material. This includes allowing multiple opportunities for **student choice** in learning and demonstration of understanding through such strategies as choice boards, learning centers, project menus, and digital resources that allow students to approach content in multiple ways. In doing so, teachers effectively plan instruction that allows students to grasp new material and demonstrate learning in a way that best suits their skill level. Additionally, teachers must plan to incorporate **scaffolds** into their lessons and plan to adapt instruction as needed through continuous **formative assessments** to provide additional support for students of lower skill levels, while adding opportunities for enrichment and acceleration for gifted students. Supports can also be effectively planned into lessons through providing several opportunities for small-group activities in which students of various skill levels can work together, provide peer tutoring, and build upon one another's knowledge.

Differences in Students' Individual Interests

In order to plan engaging instruction that fosters success in learning, teachers must plan lessons and adapt instruction to address differences in students' individual interests. To accomplish this, teachers first need to work to build relationships with students and develop an understanding of their unique interests to effectively tailor instruction that taps into these interests. Through **differentiated instruction** and the incorporation of **student-choice** opportunities for learning and assessment, teachers can effectively plan **student-centered** lessons that teach content in multiple ways that appeal to varying interests. Additionally, interest centers in the classroom foster engagement in learning, are easily adaptable, and can be planned into daily instruction. By frequently conducting **formative assessments**, teachers can gauge student interest in activities and adjust as necessary. This ultimately promotes self-direction, motivation, and curiosity in learning through providing students the opportunity to build content knowledge based on their individual interests.

Differences in Students' Individual Learning Needs

Differences in backgrounds, abilities, skills, and interests results in a wide spectrum of student learning needs that must be addressed when planning effective and adaptable instruction. Teachers must recognize the individual learning needs of students to plan lessons that are accommodating, equitable, and promote success in learning. Through **student-centered** and **differentiated** instruction, teachers can effectively provide multiple avenues for content instruction, learning, and assessment based on individual need. Planning for **student-choice** and **self-directed learning** allows teachers to successfully address all learning styles and needs. Additionally, teachers must incorporate scaffolds into their lessons to adapt instruction. This can be done through incorporating such supports as graphic organizers, outlines, charts, and visuals, as well as planning for small, mixed-ability group instruction based on learning needs to provide scaffolding. Teachers should plan to check frequently for understanding during instruction in order to adapt activities and adjust instruction to meet individual learning needs.

ELL Students

English language learners (ELLs) need support in both understanding content material and building their English proficiency levels. To effectively plan and adapt instruction to accommodate them and facilitate success in learning, it is important that teachers demonstrate respect for the student's native language while encouraging the acquisition of English language skills. Teachers should plan for some content instruction to be in the student's native language to begin to build knowledge. To effectively assist ELLs in building vocabulary on specific content areas, lessons should be planned around **themed units**. Additionally, planning multiple cooperative learning and peer-tutoring activities allows ELLs to practice and develop their English skills in a natural setting, as well provides support for understanding new instructional concepts. Teachers must plan to scaffold content material, texts, and writing assignments to align with students' proficiency levels through adding such supports as graphic organizers, labels, and charts. Incorporating **linguistic aids** such as verbal cues, gestures, pictures, and digital resources allow teachers to effectively adapt instruction as necessary to support understanding and develop English language skills.

Students with Disabilities

Students with disabilities may require **instructional or physical supports** in order to have an equitable learning experience that facilitates their academic success. Teachers must be cognizant of any student disabilities and work to effectively plan instruction in a subtle, sensitive, and inclusive manner. Students with learning disabilities may require the planning of supports such as preferential seating, extra time for work and assessments, graphic organizers, and shorter or chunked assignments. These students may need to be paired with others that can provide scaffolding and peer-tutoring or may require individualized instruction or small focused groups. Students with physical disabilities may require such supports as a modified classroom environment to address their physical needs, audiovisual supplements, enlarged font, or braille texts. Teachers must work to incorporate these supports into their lesson planning to ensure that all students are included and empowered to learn, while allowing for flexibility in their lesson plans to allow for necessary adaptations.

Cultural and Socioeconomic Differences

Addressing Differences in an Inclusive and Equitable Classroom Environment

In a **culturally responsive** classroom, the teacher recognizes and is sensitive to the importance of planning instruction that addresses cultural and socioeconomic differences among students for creating an **inclusive** and **equitable** learning environment. The teacher responds to differences in norms, values, interests, and lifestyles through designing relevant instruction that builds on students' experiences and facilitates personal connections that foster engagement in learning. This is important in conveying to students the value of their diverse experiences and highlighting their strengths in a manner that empowers them to achieve academic success while providing support where needed. It is important that the teacher incorporate supports in instructional planning to address academic, social, behavioral, and emotional needs of students from different cultural and socioeconomic backgrounds to provide all students an equitable opportunity for success in learning while maintaining high academic expectations.

Possible Impacts on Academic Achievement

If not properly addressed, cultural and socioeconomic differences among students pose potentially negative impacts on academic achievement. It is vital that teachers recognize and accommodate these differences to instill the proper supports for engagement and success in learning. Students from different cultural or socioeconomic backgrounds may feel excluded from curriculum and instruction, which may result in lowered self-concept, self-esteem, and ultimately, disengagement toward learning. Thus, teachers must practice **culturally responsive teaching** to create instruction in which all students feel valued and included. These students may lack the support or resources for education at home due to various cultural and social challenges, and students from low socioeconomic backgrounds may face health, behavioral, or emotional challenges that impact their development and ability to learn. It is important that the teacher recognize these challenges and subtly address them in the classroom to establish an inclusive, equitable, and empowering environment that fosters engagement in learning. Some strategies for addressing these differences include providing community classroom materials, extra time for tutoring and assistance outside of classroom hours, individualized instruction, or opportunities to use the internet at school for students who lack access at home.

Significance of Varied Student Learning Needs and Preferences

Implications on Instruction

Variances in students' learning needs and preferences implies that instruction must be **differentiated**, flexible, and allow for adaptations as necessary to accommodate students' individual needs, abilities, and interests. Furthermore, it means that teachers must work to build relationships with their students to develop an understanding of their different needs and preferences. This allows teachers to design instruction that emphasizes individual strengths while challenging students academically based on their abilities and providing instructional supports where necessary to ensure student success. To accomplish this, teachers must plan and deliver instructional material in multiple ways to address differences in learning needs and preferences, as well as allow for student choice in learning, processing, and demonstrating understanding of content.

Possible Variances That May Be Encountered

Teachers will inevitably encounter an array of learning needs and preferences among their students. As students have varying **learning styles**, including but not limited to visual, auditory, or kinesthetic, their methods for acquiring, processing, and retaining information will differ, as well as their **preferred modalities** for doing so. Some students may prefer written assignments in which they work independently, while others may prefer activities that involve active movement within a group. Similarly, some students require more individualized attention, while others may function better in a small group or whole-class setting. Students will also come to the classroom with differing **academic abilities**, and therefore, will require varying levels of assistance, support, and guidance to facilitate their success in learning. In addition, students may have specific learning, physical, social, or emotional **disabilities**, and as such, will need varying degrees of supports and accommodations to support their ability to learn effectively.

Importance of Tailoring Curriculum, Instruction, and Assessments

Through tailoring curriculum, instruction, and assessments according to student learning needs and preferences, teachers create a **student-centered** learning environment. This motivates and empowers students to take ownership of their learning and allows every student an equal opportunity to achieve academic success. By creating a flexible curriculum and presenting instruction through multiple methods, teachers ensure that the learning needs and preferences of all students are met by facilitating a dynamic and engaging learning environment in which students can learn in the way that best suits their needs. Furthermore, in adapting assessments based upon students' learning needs and preferences by allowing **student choice**, teachers maximize student understanding of content material, allowing them to demonstrate learning according to their interests and abilities.

Teaching English Language Learners

English Language Learners

Characteristics and Needs of Language Proficiency Levels

The term ***English language learner*** **(ELL)** refers to students acquiring English as a second language, and consists of beginner, intermediate, and advanced levels of English language proficiency. Each proficiency level is determined by specific characteristics and requires differing linguistic supports across listening, speaking, reading, and writing domains. **Beginning** ELLs have little or no ability to understand the English language across domains and rely heavily on linguistic aids such as visual representations, gestures, verbal cues, and environmental print. These students communicate through memorized high-frequency words or phrases and often require individualized instruction. **Intermediate** ELLs have acquired some foundational knowledge on the English language and can communicate with increasing complexity. They are generally able to understand, speak, read, and write in short, simple sentences and follow clear, routine directions. These students are able to seek clarification for misunderstandings but continue to require linguistic supports such as repetition, slowed speech, visual representations, and body language. **Advanced** ELL students are generally able to understand and utilize the English language with minimal error and often do not require extensive linguistic support outside of occasional repetition or clarification. Their proficiency is comparable to that of their native English-speaking peers.

Acquiring Listening and Speaking Skills

The acquisition of **listening** and **speaking** skills are interrelated and often are the first two domains in which English language proficiency is developed. As the ELL hears and observes the teacher modeling proper speech and active listening, they begin acquiring listening skills. Additionally, listening to and observing classmates is integral for the development of listening and speaking skills. By watching and imitating their peers, ELLs build understanding of the nuances of the English language in different settings. When words and phrases heard are linked to a particular action or event, the ELL derives meaning and can utilize the newly acquired vocabulary, thus developing listening and speaking skills simultaneously. The development of listening and speaking skills is enhanced in a **language-rich environment** in which students are provided multiple opportunities to practice and develop their skills in a natural setting. Therefore, the teacher must include opportunities for ELLs to speak, actively listen, and work collaboratively. Incorporating materials such as songs, games, stories, and digital media further immerse the ELL in a language-rich environment and allow them to attach meaning to new vocabulary to build proficiency.

Acquiring Reading and Writing Skills

The acquisition of listening and speaking skills in English provides the foundation for developing **reading** and **writing** skills. Reading and writing abilities develop in relation to one another, as when students begin acquiring reading skills, they learn to attach meaning to vocabulary and texts that enable them to express themselves in writing. The development of reading skills begins with understanding simple, high-frequency vocabulary and simple sentence structures as a foundation, building upon this knowledge with increasingly complex vocabulary and sentence structures. Similarly, writing ability increases in complexity from basic labels, lists, and copying and develops into expression though simple sentences on familiar topics, and ultimately, complex writing abilities that employ higher-order thinking on abstract concepts. Reading and writing skill development is enhanced through consistent practice in a **print** and **literacy-rich** environment. Students should be provided with multiple opportunities for reading and expressing themselves through writing throughout instruction. Reading materials with varying levels of complexity should be readily available for students, and literacy development must be incorporated into all subject areas to build vocabulary and comprehension.

Review Video: Stages of Reading Development
Visit mometrix.com/academy and enter code: 121184

Review Video: The Link Between Grammar Skills and Reading Comprehension
Visit mometrix.com/academy and enter code: 411287

Print and Literacy-Rich Learning Environment

A print and literacy-rich learning environment is beneficial for providing an **immersive** experience that promotes the development of students' reading, writing, speaking, and listening skills. Such an environment typically incorporates a variety of learning resources and strategies to encourage literacy. The walls are often decorated with a variety of print materials, such as posters, captions, word walls with high-frequency or thematic vocabulary words, signs, labels, bulletin boards, and anchor charts. Students are provided with authentic printed and digital literacy materials, such as newspapers, magazines, shopping advertisements, video clips, songs, and documentaries to increase relevancy and personal connections. A print and literacy-rich classroom also includes a class library that offers texts of varying genres, formats, and levels of complexity. Learning activities provide multiple opportunities to develop literacy skills in a natural setting, such as opportunities for collaborative learning, self-selected reading, and free-write sessions.

Review Video: Print Awareness and Alphabet Knowledge
Visit mometrix.com/academy and enter code: 541069

Components of Language

All languages are comprised of syntax, semantics, morphology, phonology, and pragmatics.

- **Syntax** refers to the structure and arrangement of words within a sentence, which controls the functions of grammar.
- **Semantics** refers to how language conveys meaning.
- **Morphology** refers to how words are constructed of smaller parts, such as root words, prefixes, and suffixes.
- **Phonology** refers to how words are pronounced.
- **Pragmatics** refers to the practical, social applications of language and its use in the real world, including non-verbal communication.

These components heavily overlap with one another. For instance, morphology is heavily involved in constructing the meaning of a word, which largely falls under the category of semantics and without a logical ordering of the words in a sentence (syntax), the sentence could mean something completely different, or be altogether incoherent. Each of these systems needs to be well-established for communication in English or any other language. Some of these components, such as morphology, can be particularly targeted to support content-based instruction. For instance, a teacher might work on prefixes and root words that commonly occur in science, such as bio-, geo-, tele-, -logy, -scope, and -graphy.

English Language Proficiency for Listening and Speaking

Descriptors for English Language Proficiency for Each Ability Level

Development of English language proficiency is marked by descriptors for each ability level in listening and speaking. **Beginner** ELLs are highly limited or unable to understand or speak English in any setting. They have difficulty understanding and using simple vocabulary even with the help of linguistic aids and rely on single words for basic communication. Grammatically, they are unable to construct full sentences. **Intermediate** ELLs understand and speak using high-frequency English vocabulary on familiar topics and settings. They speak and understand short sentences and demonstrate a basic understanding of English grammatical patterns for constructing simple sentences but need linguistic aids for unfamiliar vocabulary. Additionally, they make several errors when communicating, but can ask in English for clarification, and are usually understood by those familiar with working with ELLs. **Advanced** ELLs can speak and understand grade-appropriate English with linguistic supports. They understand and participate in longer conversations about familiar and unfamiliar topics, but may rely on linguistic aids, repetition, or clarification. These students still make some errors in communication but are often understood by people unfamiliar with working with ELLs. **Advanced high** ELLs require minimal linguistic support and can understand and speak English at a similar level to native English-speaking peers.

Teaching Students at Different Proficiency Levels

Teaching students with different proficiency levels for listening and speaking English implies that students will require varying degrees of linguistic support to develop their skills and provide them with an equitable learning environment. Specifically, students with lower proficiency levels in these areas will rely more on linguistic accommodations than students with more developed abilities. Teachers must be knowledgeable of the descriptors for each proficiency level to implement the proper supports and instructional strategies to address individual learning needs for developing listening and speaking skills in English. Instructional strategies should aim to promote the acquisition of skills through building background knowledge and providing context in multiple ways. This includes modeling proper speaking and listening skills, accompanying instruction with verbal cues, slower speech, repetition, gestures, and visual aids to improve student comprehension and build vocabulary. Additionally, incorporating several cooperative learning opportunities provides scaffolding and opportunities to practice and build upon listening and speaking abilities. Content instruction can be supported with the implementation of digital resources that promote the acquisition and development of listening and speaking skills and can be tailored to students' individual abilities.

> **Review Video: ESL/ESOL/Second Language Learning**
> Visit mometrix.com/academy and enter code: 795047

English Language Proficiency for Reading and Writing

Descriptors for English Language Proficiency at Each Ability Level

English language proficiency for ELLs is determined by descriptors for each ability level in reading and writing. **Beginning** ELLs possess little or no ability to read, understand, or write in English. Comprehension is restricted to single, familiar vocabulary words, and writing is limited to lists, labels, and vocabulary accompanied by pictures. These students rely heavily on linguistic supports for understanding, and their writing is unclear to those unfamiliar with working with ELLs. **Intermediate** ELLs can read, understand, and write short sentences and simple language structures on familiar material with the help of linguistic aids. They engage in writing assignments, but their writing contains errors and is unclear to those unfamiliar with working with ELLs. **Advanced** ELLs read, understand, and write using more expansive vocabulary and sentence structures with the help of linguistic accommodations. They may have difficulty with unfamiliar vocabulary but can read and write at a faster pace with increased accuracy. These students demonstrate more complex writing abilities, and their writing is usually understood by those unfamiliar with working with ELLs. **Advanced high** ELLs can read, understand, and write using grade-appropriate English with minimal linguistic support at a level similar to native English-speaking peers.

Teaching Students at Different Proficiency Levels

Teaching students with different proficiency levels for reading and writing English means linguistic accommodations in the classroom will need to be scaffolded to address the needs and abilities of individual students and promote the development of skills in these areas. Students with lower proficiency levels in reading and writing will require more linguistic aids than students with more developed abilities. Thus, the teacher must have a deep understanding both of individual student needs and of descriptors for proficiency at each level to effectively support students in their acquisition of reading and writing skills. Instructional strategies should foster the acquisition of these skills through providing several ways to allow students to build background knowledge and context to increase understanding. This includes creating a language-rich classroom environment that emphasizes the development of literacy skills in the form of environmental print, word walls and charts for new vocabulary and high-frequency words, labels, and visual aids. Reading materials on subject content should be available at each reading level. Additionally, the use of graphic organizers and outlines increases comprehension and writing ability through breaking information into smaller portions to provide scaffolding.

Creating Equitable Learning Environment for ELLs Using Linguistic Supports

To create an equitable learning environment, ELL students must be provided with linguistic supports that are applicable across content areas in order to ensure they are provided with an equal opportunity for success in learning. Teachers can implement varying supports appropriate to students' levels of English language proficiency that are beneficial in facilitating both English language and content-specific learning. Such supports include incorporating verbal cues, gestures, and visual representations into instruction to provide context and build background knowledge. The use of environmental print, word walls, and labels are also effective in supporting English language skills while simultaneously providing context for facilitating learning in the content area. Teachers should model speaking and listening skills, and practice slow speech or repetition when necessary to ensure understanding. Scaffolding instruction and activities across content areas through such supports as graphic organizers, outlines, and cooperative learning opportunities serve to assist ELL students in building English language proficiency skills across content areas at a pace appropriate for their ability level. By implementing the proper supports, teachers can effectively foster English language learning in all subject areas while ensuring that students simultaneously learn content-specific material.

Instructional Strategies for English Language Learning in All Subject Areas

Language acquisition occurs across content areas for ELL students, as each subject is comprised of different vocabulary, grammatical patterns, and methods of expressing ideas. Thus, it is important that teachers provide these students with learning strategies that are applicable in all subject areas in order to effectively support English language acquisition and content-specific learning. Through a metacognitive approach, teachers can facilitate ELL students in thinking about how they learn, reflecting on their strengths and weaknesses, and applying useful learning strategies from one content area to another to develop their English language skills in all subjects. This strategy enhances learning through teaching students how to apply learning strategies from one instructional context to another when developing language skills. By activating students' prior knowledge when introducing new material in a given subject area, teachers promote English language learning through providing context and encouraging students to consider what they may already know about a new concept. Such methods as pre-teaching, anticipatory guides, graphic organizers, and brainstorming allow ELL students to make connections that build their language abilities across content areas.

Adapting Instruction for Varying Levels of English Language Proficiency

When encountering ELL students with varying English language skills, it is imperative to adapt instruction to accommodate these differences and ensure that all students receive appropriate linguistic support. Instruction must be communicated, sequenced, and scaffolded to support learners with different English proficiency abilities. The teacher must communicate instruction clearly while allowing time for repetition or slowed speech as necessary. In addition, teachers must supplement instruction with linguistic supports such as verbal cues, gestures, and visual representations as needed to provide assistance and context appropriate to individual ability levels. Instruction must also be sequenced logically and clearly communicate the expectations and steps of learning experiences. This is achieved by indicating an explicit beginning, middle, and end to activities through transition words and actions appropriate to students' levels of English proficiency. Teachers must scaffold instruction, activities, and assessments to meet individual students' language learning needs. Supports such as word walls, graphic organizers, charts, labels, and pairing students with others who can provide assistance are effective means of scaffolding learning to accommodate varying ability. By communicating, sequencing, and scaffolding instruction in a way that is tailored to ELL students' individual language needs, teachers effectively foster an equitable environment that promotes success in learning.

Chapter Quiz

Ready to see how well you retained what you just read? Scan the QR code to go directly to the chapter quiz interface for this study guide. If you're using a computer, simply visit the bonus page at **mometrix.com/bonus948/nystceeas** and click the Chapter Quizzes link.

English Language Learners

Transform passive reading into active learning! After immersing yourself in this chapter, put your comprehension to the test by taking a quiz. The insights you gained will stay with you longer this way. Scan the QR code to go directly to the chapter quiz interface for this study guide. If you're using a computer, simply visit the bonus page at **mometrix.com/bonus948/nystceeas** and click the Chapter Quizzes link.

General Language Acquisition Theory

Krashen's Monitor Hypothesis

Stephen Krashen argues that individuals who acquire languages know inherently what is correct in that language, even if they have not formally studied the grammatical or syntactical rules of that language. However, learning continues to play a role even for individuals who have acquired a language: once they learn explicit rules, they can use them to **monitor** and correct their language use. Monitoring one's language, however, takes time and conscious attention and, thus, is more feasible when writing than speaking. As Krashen points out, it is difficult to speak fluently and simultaneously attend to what one is saying—attempting to do so usually leads to interrupted speech. Critics of the monitor hypothesis include both those who argue that children may monitor their speech before they have learned language rules and those who argue that, as defined, the hypothesis does not apply to the vast majority of speech and thus is of limited use.

Krashen's Acquisition/Learning Hypothesis

Stephen Krashen distinguishes between acquiring a language and learning a language. **Acquisition** is an unconscious, natural process that occurs when a learner uses the language for a variety of real-life purposes and interacts extensively with native speakers. **Learning**, by contrast, is a conscious process during which a student is likely to study parts of a language in sequence, as when they study vocabulary lists or learn to conjugate verbs. Krashen argues that only acquisition leads to fluency, and he further claims that learning cannot be transformed into acquisition. Unlike some theorists, Krashen does not deny that adults can acquire (rather than learn) a new language but argues that doing so would require them to immerse themselves in that language. Krashen's distinction is widely used in language theory. Critics, however, have disputed his claim that learned languages cannot subsequently be acquired and say that the distinction is difficult to define in some contexts.

Krashen's Natural Order

Stephen Krashen argues that people acquire aspects of language in a **natural order**, regardless of which language they are acquiring or which language is their primary language. That is, certain grammatical structures are acquired early in the language process and others later. For example, research shows that individuals acquiring English will master the use of the "-ing" form of verbs before they learn to add an "-s" to the third person singular form of regular verbs. Research since Krashen's formulation of the hypothesis has weakened his findings but not overturned them. Critics have argued that, in fact, one's first language does influence the order in which elements of a second language are acquired.

Krashen's Input Hypothesis

Stephen Krashen argues that language acquisition takes place most efficiently when students are presented with **input** that is slightly beyond their current mastery level. In other words, students should be able to understand most of what they hear or read, but not all. If used correctly, students will be able to understand this **comprehensible input** through the use of context, their background knowledge, or non-linguistic cues. If comprehensible input is used effectively, it eliminates the need for explicit explanation of new structures or meanings; students will be able to deduce the meaning without explanation. Merrill Swain answered one of the principal criticisms of this hypothesis—that it only treated comprehension, not speech production—by coining the term "**output hypothesis.**" In Swain's view, students will be motivated to improve their speech production when they notice, in conversation, that they are unable to express themselves fully.

Krashen's Affective Filter Hypothesis

Stephen Krashen's affective filter hypothesis states that students learn most effectively in **low-stress learning environments**. Affective factors such as boredom or anxiety, Krashen argues, create **affective filters** that interfere with the learning process. Krashen and collaborator Tracy Terrell are credited with developing the natural approach to second-language learning around this idea. This approach emphasizes that students should not be forced to speak until they feel comfortable doing so, in order to avoid affective interference in the learning process. Krashen argued that children are less influenced by affective factors than adults, providing children with an advantage in language acquisition. This assertion has subsequently been challenged. Krashen's hypothesis remains useful, however, in drawing attention to the importance of non-linguistic factors in language acquisition.

Review Video: ESL/ESOL/Second Language Learning
Visit mometrix.com/academy and enter code: 795047

Sequential Bilingualism, Simultaneous Bilingualism, and Multilingualism

Bilingualism is the ability to use two languages fluently, while **multilingualism** is the ability to use more than one language fluently. **Simultaneous bilingualism** occurs when a child is raised bilingually from birth or is introduced to the second language before the age of three. **Sequential bilingualism** occurs when a child obtains fluency in a second language after the first language is well established—usually around the age of three.

Recent research has demonstrated that children can readily learn more than one language at a time. This research overturns the limited capacity hypothesis—the assertion that children exposed to more than one language at a time experience delayed and incomplete proficiency in either—that influenced the field for decades. Current research suggests bilingual learners may experience slight delays in speech production, but the variance is small and within the range of normal development. Further, bilingual children often possess smaller vocabularies in either language than their monolingual peers, but their combined vocabulary is on par with that of their peers.

Code-Switching

Code-switching is a phenomenon in which speakers switch from one language to another in the same conversation, often in the same sentence. **Code-switching** among bilingual Spanish-English speakers is so common that a name for it has been coined: "Spanglish." One reason people code-switch is that they are unable to think of a word in the language they are speaking, and so they resort to a word from their native language. However, in conversation with other bilinguals, code-switching may signal solidarity or familiarity, or it may be used to convey associative, technical, or figurative meanings not available in the primary language. Bilingual speakers often use their native language to talk about their daily life and use their learned language when discussing academic or job-related topics.

Code-switching can also refer to alterations in discourse undertaken in a single language—for example, when one speaker changes accent to match that of his or her interlocutor, or when an English speaker drops the final "-g" on progressive-tense verbs to project an informal, working-class form of speech.

Interlanguage

An interlanguage is the version of a learned language produced at any given moment by a language learner. An **interlanguage** contains elements and structures of both L1 and L2 but may differ substantially from either, leading some linguists to refer to the interlanguage as an entirely separate language. Interlanguage is often referred to as a strategy adopted by a learner to compensate for his or her limited proficiency in L2. While interlanguage is considered a normal part of language learning, it risks becoming **fossilized** if a learner lacks the opportunity or motivation to improve upon it. Fossilization often occurs when a learner achieves a level of proficiency that allows for effective, albeit limited, communication.

Various **cognitive tendencies** contribute to the formation of an interlanguage. The linguist Larry Selinker, who first developed the concept of interlanguage in the 1970s, identified five such tendencies, including language transfer, which occurs when a learner applies knowledge or rules from L1 to L2. A second tendency, overgeneralization, occurs when a learner extends a language rule beyond its actual scope—for example, when an ELL universally adds "-ed" to create a past-tense verb, resulting in errors like "swimmed."

The Basic Word Order of English

The grammars of nearly all languages have **subjects** (S), **verbs** (V), and **objects** (O). This is an example of a non-absolute language universal. Of the possible ordering of those three components in a standard sentence, only three are frequently found—S-V-O (as in English), S-O-V (as in Japanese), and V-S-O (as in Malagasy).

Both Spanish and English rely overwhelmingly on the **S-V-O ordering**, though Spanish does allow for frequent subject-verb inversion in cases where English does not. Many Spanish sentences do not have a stated subject at all—because Spanish verbs are conjugated differently for each person (unlike in English), the subject of a sentence can be inferred from the verb. In English, adjectives typically precede nouns; in Spanish, the opposite is more common. In Spanish, nouns cannot modify nouns, so possession is indicated after an object, contrary to English: "John's car" versus "el coche de John" ("the car of John").

Universals

A language universal is a characteristic that is shared by all the world's languages. In 1966, the linguist Joseph Greenberg published a list of 45 allegedly universal characteristics of language, but modern linguists, with much more language data and computer analysis available to them, are much more cautious. The few agreed-upon **absolute universals** (those with no known exceptions) are relatively uninteresting—for example, all languages have syllables, consonants, and vowels. Linguists work more fruitfully with **non-absolute universals**—that is, features that are found with a high degree of statistical regularity but also have exceptions.

Implicational universals are language properties that occur together—in other words, they fit the logical form of "If a language has A, it will also have B." An example of a non-absolute implicational universal is "If verb-subject-object is the dominant syntax form in a language, the adjective will follow the noun."

First Language Acquisition Theory

Model of First-Language Acquisition

Developmental psychologists have created approximate timelines for both first-language acquisition and second-language learning. The following are typical stages and landmarks in first-language acquisition:

1. **Pre-speech stage (0-6 months)**: Babies may produce what are called comfort signs (grunts and sighs) while paying attention to spoken language and beginning to distinguish phonemes.
2. **Babbling stage (6-8 months)**: Babies begin to babble, or produce rhythmic sounds with syllable-like stops, often with repeated patterns. Babbling allows infants to practice essential motor skills and learn how to produce basic sounds.
3. **One-word stage (10-18 months)**: Children produce their first words, usually in reference to people, objects, or actions that produce desired outcomes. Overextension and underextension (using words too broadly or too narrowly) are common.
4. **Two-word or telegraphic stage (18-24 months)**: Children produce two-word phrases using lexical rather than functional or grammatical morphemes.
5. **Multiword stage (30 months)**: Children speak in complete sentences, adding functional and grammatical elements, though often making errors.

Pivot Grammar

The cognitive psychologist Martin Braine created the **pivot grammar model** in the 1960s to explain how children first structure language when moving from the one-word to the two-word speaking phase. Braine noticed children create many utterances anchored by a single word (the **pivot**) used in combination with a larger variety of words (which he termed **open-class words**). For example, children commonly use the anchor "all" to create oft-repeated variations: "all gone," "all done," "all eat," etc. "More" is another typical anchor: "more milk," "more TV," etc. Researchers noticed that children use certain pivot words first and others second, suggesting that in this phase they have begun to understand differences in word class and function. While some scholars suggest that pivot grammar is compatible with universal grammar (UG) models, others argue that with pivot grammars children are not building upon *syntactic* regularities, but rather upon *lexical* regularities—a direct challenge to the UG model of how children acquire languages.

Holophrase

A holophrase is a single word used to express complex thought. For example, a toddler who utters the **holophrase** "up" may be intending the more complex thought "pick me up." Consistent with the idea that children understand more language than they can produce, holophrastic conversations with adults often consist of the adult trying to interpret the meaning of a holophrastic phrase, offering alternatives to which the child responds with body-language affirmations or rejections. For example, a toddler may say "mommy," leaving the adult to guess "where's mommy?" or "you want mommy's bag?"—one of which will eventually trigger the toddler's assent.

Some holophrases may consist of unanalyzed combinations of two or more words—for example, "allgone." According to development theory, children pass into the subsequent, **telegraphic stage** of language development when they begin to produce two-word utterances, many of which are structured around pivot words as elaborated in the pivot grammar model.

The Behaviorist Theory of First-Language Acquisition

Behaviorist theories of language learning propose that humans learn language through a process of **reinforcement**. In response to a stimulus, children offer a spoken response, usually a repetition of something they've just heard, and then receive either positive or negative feedback. This feedback creates what founder B.F. Skinner (1904–1990) coined the term **operant conditioning**—a change in behavior in response to feedback. (In contrast, his so-called classical conditioning involves learning to associate two events but does not entail any behavioral change.) Through this back-and-forth inductive process, children learn the rules and patterns of language.

The behaviorist theory has intuitive appeal, as we often use variations of the repetition/feedback model in teaching. However, critics point out that the model completely excludes any **theory of the mind**, reducing the complexity of language to a rudimentary input-output model. Critics also challenged the behaviorists to explain how children could produce novel, and often complex, utterances that they had never heard—these utterances could not have been acquired through imitation, repetition, or reinforcement.

The Innate or Universal Grammar Theory of First-Language Acquisition

The universal grammar theory, developed by the linguist Noam Chomsky in the 1960s, posits that humans are born with **innate language abilities**, which include general grammatical categories and constraints that can be adapted to or activated by any language a child is exposed to. Chomsky gave the name "**language activation device**" to this hypothetical region of the brain devoted to language acquisition and production. Chomsky developed his theory in response to the behaviorists' suggestion that language competence is built through a process of trial and error.

The **universal grammar theory** helps explain several key features of languages and language learning: that all languages share certain properties; that children who are exposed to a common language will all converge in their competence, despite receiving different input; and that children will learn linguistic forms for which they have received no specific input. Chomsky also turned theoretical attention to the brain and its adaptive capacities. Critics of innateness theories suggest that it privileges syntax over semantics, pragmatics, and discourse and, further, that it focuses on developmental aspects of language acquisition at the expense of social and psychological aspects.

The Cognitive Constructivist Model of First-Language Acquisition

The cognitive constructivist model of L1 acquisition is derived from the work of the Swiss psychologist Jean Piaget (1896–1980). Piaget hypothesized that **cognitive development** (and thus language development) occurs in universal, identifiable stages. **Learning** occurs when a child's experiences challenge his or her current understanding of the world, driving the child to a new, more complex stage of cognitive/linguistic development. Thus, language learning is a form of adaptation to one's environment.

Proponents of cognitive models of language learning point to the fact that language learning does appear to proceed according to certain **stages of complexity**—for example, learners in all languages master functional morphemes in similar order. Critics argue that there is little merit in Piaget's four-stage model, as the stages themselves cannot be empirically identified. Further, critics argue that the theory undervalues the influence of both culture and social interaction on language development.

Cognitive constructivism differs from social constructivism in its suggestion that learners create representations of their world largely through their own inquiries and activities rather than through social interaction.

THE SOCIAL CONSTRUCTIVISM THEORY OF FIRST-LANGUAGE ACQUISITION

The social constructivism theory, attributed to the Soviet psychologist Lev Vygotsky (1896–1934), emphasizes the importance of social interaction in language theory. According to this model, children learn primarily from adults ("more experienced others" to Vygotsky) who model new language patterns and also correct errors. Vygotsky coined the influential term "**zone of proximal development**" to explain how learning occurs: according to Vygotsky, children best learn when presented with tasks or challenges that they can accomplish with the help of others but not alone. The set of challenges that a child can accomplish with assistance or scaffolding fall within his or her zone of proximal development.

Social constructivism theory is often credited with giving proper attention to **discourse**, or actual language use. In this view, language is developed in a specific context rather than in accordance with universal structures or dispositions. Critics point to the fact that not all cultures prioritize interaction between children and "more experienced others," and yet children in these cultures still become competent language users.

Review Video: Instructional Scaffolding
Visit mometrix.com/academy and enter code: 989759

Review Video: Zone of Proximal Development (ZPD)
Visit mometrix.com/academy and enter code: 555594

DISCOVERY LEARNING THEORY

Discovery learning theory posits that students learn best when they **construct their own knowledge** through a process of inquiry, investigation, and problem-solving ("discovery") rather than when a teacher or parent tells them explicitly what they are expected to know. Bruner's theory has been very influential in the modern movement away from lecture-based teaching and toward methods that guide students in various **inquiry-based activities**.

Like Piaget, Bruner argued that children learn in different ways as they develop, moving from mere physical manipulation of objects to the creation of mental images to the use of language. However, unlike Piaget, Bruner believed these stages to be continuous and that children can speed up their progression through the stages. He also theorized that it is language that causes cognitive development rather than vice versa. Like Piaget, Bruner is a **constructivist**, emphasizing the active role of the learner in building understanding through successively more complex engagements with the world. Chomsky, by contrast, prioritizes the importance of innate cognitive potentials.

THE CRITICAL PERIOD HYPOTHESIS

The critical period hypothesis argues that there is an **optimal age for learning a language** and that the ease with which a person can learn languages declines over time.

The hypothesis was first formulated by neurologist Wilder Penfield and then elaborated by Eric Lenneberg, who argued that language learning is dependent on **brain plasticity**, which in humans is at an optimal level for learning during a critical period extending from roughly age two until puberty.

The hypothesis has been extended to L2 learning based on the claim that adults rarely achieve full fluency in a second language learned later in life, failing most often to master complex grammatical structures or achieve a native accent. Critics of the hypothesis point to the fact that some adult learners do fully master a second language. They also point out that factors other than brain development could explain the difference in L2 learning, as adults and children learn in different motivational and social contexts.

The hypothesis privileges the explanatory framework of developmental biology by positing the existence of certain biological potentials for and limitations to language learning. It shares this orientation with Noam Chomsky and the universal grammar school of language acquisition.

Connectionist Theories of Language Acquisition

Connectionist theories attempt to apply insights from neuroscience and computer science to explain language acquisition. Proponents look to advances in knowledge of how neurons function in order to explain how learning occurs. For example, the more frequently a given set of neurons fires in tandem, the more established that neuron network becomes—a feature that helps explain memory and is seen as a mechanism by which a language learner comes to associate words with objects or events. In more general terms, learning is seen as the development of specific **connections** in an otherwise general network in response to environmental stimuli. Computer scientists working in the field of artificial intelligence attempt to build learning networks with silicon chips playing the role of simplified neurons. Computer scientists have built models that simulate many language-acquisition activities, including how to break a continuous auditory stream into words and how to correctly form both regular and irregular verbs. These models rely primarily on statistical, inferential learning rather than on the symbol- and rule-based learning typically advanced by non-computational models. Critics of the existing computational models point to their unrealistic initial assumptions and abstractions from human reality, whereas proponents see these as weaknesses that can be overcome in time.

The Emergentist Theory of Language Acquisition

The emergentist theory suggests that children learn language by using a simple but adaptable set of **neural networks** to process and understand the complex linguistic environment they are immersed in. The theory differs from the innate theories of scholars such as Noam Chomsky in that it doesn't suggest that children are born with an expansive universal grammar hard-wired in the brain—rather, children are born with a **pattern extraction ability** that arises from the growth and strengthening of neural networks. Emergentist theory shares with social constructivism the idea that social interaction is critical for language development but differs in its focus on the brain's ability to find patterns and extract meaning from what is potentially an overwhelming linguistic environment. The theory suggests that the brain narrows the field of possible meanings through the use of contextual, phonological, and morphological cues and by applying a type of statistical analysis of frequent language forms. While the brain is inherently capable of narrowing the field of possible meanings and finding patterns, parents and teachers can help the process by providing rich, structured, patterned linguistic input.

The Competition Model of Language Acquisition

The competition model of language learning or acquisition attributed to Brian MacWhinney and Elizabeth Bates argues that there is no fundamental difference in how people acquire a first language or learn subsequent languages—in both cases, various cognitive processes compete to offer the best **interpretation of the language cues** offered to the language learner by the surrounding environment. The cognitive processes that make the best interpretations of the language—those that lead to the learner having successful interactions and speech acts—are reinforced as neural networks eventually get consolidated as permanent features of the brain. With its focus on the development and consolidation of neural networks in the brain, the competition model is a type of connectionist theory of language learning.

The competition model rejects the idea of innate *linguistic* structures in the brain. Rather, it posits that language develops through the interaction of generalized *cognitive* structures in the brain (those responsible for all aspects of thought, not just language) with the environment.

Second Language Acquisition Theory

Acquisition of First and Second Languages

The following chart outlines some of the differences in the acquisition of first and second languages:

First Language	Second Language
Is acquired without conscious effort	Is acquired with conscious effort
Is a natural, integrated part of daily life	May be acquired primarily in a classroom
Is based on a universal grammar	Is affected by first-language grammar
Doesn't require instruction	Requires instruction
Needed to function in life and satisfy desires	May be acquired for various reasons
Is less influenced by cognitive and affective factors	Is critically influenced by cognitive and affective factors

There are many similarities in the acquisition of L1 and L2: both occur in predictable stages, mistakes are normal, learners of both rely heavily on context and cues, production is more difficult than comprehension, and learning occurs most rapidly with interaction and task-based instructional scenarios.

Model of Second-Language Acquisition

Researchers have found that second-language students progress through predictable stages as they advance from their first classroom encounters with a language to full proficiency. Recognizing which stage students are in will help ESOL teachers design appropriate learning activities.

1. **Silent period** (also called the preproduction stage): The learner knows around 500 words but is uncomfortable speaking. Teachers should allow the student to build receptive skills while gaining confidence.
2. **Private speech** (early production stage): The learner creates one- and two-word phrases using 1,000 words. Teachers should pose questions that allow abbreviated answers and scaffold their instruction.
3. **Lexical chunks** (speech emergence stage): The learner uses 3,000 words to form short phrases and sentences with frequent grammatical errors. Students are able to conduct short conversations with peers and read beginning stories.
4. **Formulaic speech** (intermediate language proficiency): The learner uses 6,000 words to make complex sentences, state opinions, and share thoughts. Learners can study content subjects in English. Teachers may shift the instructional focus to writing.
5. **Experimental or simplified speech** (advanced language proficiency stage): The learner approaches fluency and can make generalizations about grammar and semantics. The learner may exit the ESOL program but continue to receive assistance with writing and in the content areas.

Silent Period of Second-Language Development

The term "silent period" refers to a common first stage in language acquisition, during which a student speaks little while he or she gains confidence and consolidates comprehension of the spoken language. Experts agree that students at this stage should not be forced to speak. Teachers might elicit "yes" or "no" answers or head nods and shakes. They can also ask students at this stage to draw pictures that demonstrate their understanding or draw connections between pre-printed images. If a student is hesitating to speak due to a lack of confidence, the teacher can interact first with him or her in a one-on-one, protected environment, and generally strive to create a low-risk classroom environment.

Language Transfer

Language transfer is the influence of a native language (L1) on a learner's ability to learn a new language (L2). This influence can have either positive or negative effects—for example, the existence of cognates can help a learner understand L2, whereas the existence of false cognates can exert a negative influence. The term "**language interference**" is often used synonymously with "language transfer" but is also used to refer specifically to cases of negative influence.

Linguists often use **contrastive analysis**, or the comparison of two languages to identify similarities and differences, in order to determine whether language transfer is likely, and in which forms. In general, the more similar two languages are, the greater the likelihood of positive transfer.

Positive transfers often raise the confidence and spur the interest of language learners. Teachers can lessen the impact of negative transfers by becoming familiar with those most likely to arise from a given L1 and then explicitly teaching methods of overcoming those transfers.

Comprehension-Based Approaches to Second-Language Learning

Comprehension-based learning focuses on building students' **receptive skills** (listening and reading) before they are asked to produce the language (through speech or writing). Proponents argue that **listening comprehension** is the most fundamental linguistic skill and serves as a useful basis for the others. Listening is also viewed as the least stressful language skill and thus the one most likely to engage and encourage early learners. Students should not be forced to speak until they are ready, and an early silent period in which students listen to meaningful speech is expected. Stephen Krashen and Tracy Terrell's natural way methodology is a leading example of a comprehension-based approach to second-language learning.

Communicative Approaches to Second-Language Learning

Communicative approaches to second-language learning focus on providing students genuine, meaningful, experience-based interactions in the target language. Teachers spend little time talking about the target language or teaching grammar and instead focus on facilitating use of the **target-language**. Students often work in pairs or groups, role-playing or negotiating the transfer of information that one student has and another lacks. Unlike comprehension-based approaches, reading, writing, speaking, and listening are integrated from the beginning. Constructivist theories emphasize that learners don't acquire knowledge but construct it through their own experiences. Constructivists therefore seek to engage language students in as many reality-based participatory scenarios as possible.

As defined, communicative approaches are the most commonly used approaches in the modern classroom.

Grammar-Translation and Audio-Lingual Methods

The grammar-translation method relies on explanations in the students' native language of the grammatical structures of the target language. Students are challenged to read difficult texts in the target language and to translate sentences from L2 to L1. This model is based on the way Latin was traditionally taught: with a focus on verb declensions. Modern approaches focus on

communication rather than explicit knowledge of grammatical structures and favor sustained use of L2.

The **audio-lingual method** relies heavily on repetition and drills, with language skills built systematically from simple to complex structures. The focus is on accurate pronunciation and the minimization of errors. Oral exercises are designed to control the vocabulary and grammar structures in use rather than to reflect real-world communication. This method dominated in the US immediately after World War II but has since been replaced by methods that encourage dialogue in realistic settings and trust that learners will overcome most of their early errors in later stages of speech development.

Silent Way, Suggestopedia, and Total Physical Response

In silent way classrooms, teacher speech is minimized: after initially modeling an expression, the teacher uses a series of props, such as Cuisenaire rods (rods of different lengths and colors that can model both vocabulary and syntax), to help the students learn basic structures.

Suggestopedia relies on music and rhythm to reinforce language patterns. Students are given scripts of L2 to read aloud with games and music. Later in the lesson, they might elaborate on the script with their own inventions or compare the L2 script to an L1 translation before moving on to another script.

The **total physical response method** begins with the teacher giving elementary commands in L2 (e.g., "stand up!"). As students progress, the commands become more complex. Eventually, the students begin to give one another commands. This technique is still used in ESOL instruction today but is one of many teaching techniques rather than an exclusive approach to learning.

Michael Long's Interaction Hypothesis

Michael Long's interaction hypothesis is similar to Stephen Krashen's input hypothesis in emphasizing the importance of **comprehensible input**—language just beyond an ELL's mastery level—for language learning. Long, however, adds an emphasis on conversational interaction, suggesting that advances in language learning will occur most readily when conversation partners have to negotiate meaning to be understood—by paraphrasing, restating, asking for clarification, using context clues, etc. Proponents of the hypothesis often add the qualification that it helps if the conversation participants are of equal status or social position (peer conversations, for example, rather than student-teacher conversations) so that the conversational queries and negotiations can occur freely. Critics have pointed out that conversational clarifications are not always successful, particularly when conducted by non-proficient language speakers.

Cognitive Strategies in Second-Language Acquisition

Students use a variety of strategies in learning a second language, including cognitive strategies, social strategies, and communication strategies. **Cognitive strategies** are those that students employ to understand a task at hand and include such activities as memorizing, categorizing, summarizing, generalizing, deducing, and using inductive reasoning. Research has shown that students who use a variety of cognitive strategies are more successful in learning a second language.

The term "**metacognitive strategies**" refers to strategies that students use to improve their own learning process. Planning, self-monitoring, prioritizing, and setting goals are all examples of metacognitive strategies. The use of metacognitive strategies is highly correlated with language student success. Thus, an ESOL teacher should monitor and encourage the use of these strategies.

Robert De Keyser's Skill Acquisition Theory

The skill acquisition theory posits that individuals learn skills by gradually transforming **declarative knowledge** into **procedural knowledge** through meaningful use and practice. In this model, students learn declarative knowledge about a language through classroom instruction or observation—for example, they might be taught a specific grammatical form. They then begin to use it, ideally through contextualized practice. Repeated practice leads to automaticity marked by fluency and the absence of errors. The theory thus emphasizes that full competency requires processing of information by two representational systems of the mind—the declarative and the procedural—which reinforce one another in language learning. The distinction between declarative and procedural knowledge mirrors in some ways the distinction between learning and acquiring knowledge—the goal within De Keyser's framework is to move an ELL student toward further degrees of automaticity.

Contrastive Analysis

Contrastive analysis is the study of the similarities and differences between languages. Teachers can use the results of **contrastive analysis** to anticipate language transfer issues likely to be present in their student populations. One of the most common examples is the use in Spanish and French of the verb "to have" in many contexts in which English uses "to be"—for example, a translation of the English phrase "I am hungry" becomes "I have hunger" in Spanish and French. In many languages, including Arabic, adjectives typically follow nouns, whereas in English they usually precede them, resulting in many Arabic-speaking ELLs saying things like "She is a woman smart." Haitian Creole verbs do not change to indicate either tense or person, which might lead to a Creole-speaking ELL overusing a single present-tense form like "The bus leave at 2:25." As a final example, Russian speakers use the present tense to convey ongoing actions that in English require the present progressive—thus, rather than saying, "I am reading right now," a Russian-speaking ELL might say "I read right now."

Jim Cummins' Common Underlying Proficiency Hypothesis

The **common underlying proficiency** (CUP) hypothesis states that a bilingual or emerging bilingual individual will draw on a **common pool** of cognitive and linguistic abilities to speak either language. Thus, his or her abilities and knowledge in L1 are available for and will facilitate L2 learning. Cummins' idea is often called the **dual iceberg model** because he used this image to illustrate his idea that two apparently distinct peaks of visible ice (L1 and L2) are actually connected below the surface in a vast, single iceberg (the CUP).

The CUP stands in contrast to the **separate underlying proficiency (SUP)**, which theorizes that each language a person uses is processed and stored separately in the brain, and thus there is no positive transfer between the two. Proponents of SUP often argue that ELLs should be enrolled in full English immersion programs because their use and development of L1 will only distract from and slow their English acquisition. The preponderance of the evidence, however, supports CUP, as it has frequently been demonstrated that the frequent use of L1 by students in bilingual programs does not slow their acquisition of English.

Rebecca Oxford's Strategy Inventory for Language Learning

Oxford developed a six-category classification of strategies students employ when learning a language:

- **Mnemonic strategies**—techniques used to remember and retrieve information. Acronyms, formulaic expressions, and forming connections with prior knowledge all count as mnemonic strategies.

- **Cognitive strategies**—strategies, such as analyzing or drawing conclusions, that allow students to manipulate the target language.
- **Compensatory strategies**—strategies used when students lack vocabulary in L2. Code-switching, or the insertion of L1 into L2 utterances, is an example.
- **Metacognitive strategies**—strategies used by students to improve their own learning habits. Self-monitoring is one example; planning is another.
- **Affective strategies**—strategies students use to control their own emotions. Both appeals for assistance and requests for clarification might be examples of affective strategies, as students seek reassurance or reinforcement of what they already know.
- **Social strategies**—strategies students use to employ language in social settings. Role-playing is one example. Requests for clarification could be another, as students often ask for clarification as a way of continuing a conversation.

The strategy inventory for language learning (**SILL**) examination, developed by Rebecca Oxford, is designed to identify the learning strategies used by foreign language students. The first version was developed for English speakers learning foreign languages, and a second version (v7.0) was created for students learning English as a foreign language. The SILL examination is used both for research purposes and to give individual learners insight into their own learning profiles.

Oxford's model is perhaps the most influential of several that have emerged from a research focus on language learning strategies. The latter concept grew out of an earlier (1970s) focus on the characteristics of a good language learner. This line of research aims at identifying the strategies used by successful language learners and promoting their widespread use. The cognitive academic language learning approach is another popular model based on the idea of language learning strategies. Oxford, in turn, updated her thinking with the **strategic self-regulation model (S^{2}R) of language learning**.

CALLA and CALP

The **cognitive academic language learning approach (CALLA)**, developed in the 1980s by Anna Chamot and J. Michael O'Malley, is designed to help ELLs with limited English proficiency transition to mainstream content classrooms, usually in secondary school. CALLA emphasizes **cognitive and metacognitive approaches** to learning by explicitly teaching learning strategies and encouraging students to both plan and evaluate their undertakings in order to refine their use of these skills. Chamot and O'Malley developed a taxonomy of learning strategies based on three broad categories: metacognitive strategies, cognitive strategies, and social/affective strategies.

Cognitive academic language proficiency (CALP) shares with CALLA a focus on helping ELLs who are likely already proficient in social English (basic interpersonal communication skills, or BICS, in Jim Cummins' terms) gain proficiency in academic English, in what is often a daunting environment of an English-only mainstream classroom.

Promoting Language Acquisition and Literacy

The Matthew Effect

The Matthew effect was named after the biblical verse that spurred the saying "the rich get richer and the poor get poorer." It describes the well-verified educational observation that students who **learn to read** well and early experience wide and growing educational advantages over their peers who do not—even when other factors such as cognitive abilities are accounted for. Children who read slowly or poorly not only fail to understand other, content-area subject matter, but they are more likely to become discouraged and expend less effort. Critically, research shows that, in the aggregate, students do not overcome early reading lags later in their schooling; rather, the deficits and their consequences magnify over time. This research underscores the importance of **early phonetic instruction** and **interventions for students at risk**.

Balanced Literacy

Balanced literacy in its most basic form means combining **phonics instruction** with **whole language approaches**—those in which students are taught in the context of actual reading and writing exercises. Balanced literacy emerged in the 1990s as a corrective to instruction methods that relied too heavily on either phonics or whole language instruction.

Balanced literacy also refers to a more specific curriculum model that combines word work (phonics and vocabulary instruction) with a reading process and a writing process. In the balanced literacy reading process, teachers first **read aloud** to the students; then conduct **shared reading**, during which teacher and students read together; and finally provide **one-on-one help** to individuals or small groups reading on their own (these are typically called reading workshops.) The writing process is similar: at first, the teacher writes in a specific genre, articulating his or her reading to the class; then the teacher and students engage in interactive writing; and finally, the students write in small-group or individual writing workshops.

> **Review Video: Types of Vocabulary Learning (Broad and Specific)**
> Visit mometrix.com/academy and enter code: 258753

Language-Rich Classroom

A language-rich classroom is one in which students are continuously exposed to the language in many different forms. The concept includes ways in which the **classroom** is constructed. For example, teachers may build word walls (in which relevant spelling words, commonly-used words, or target vocabulary words are displayed), display student writing or other examples of written work in multiple genres, or label objects with various names or descriptive terms. The concept also refers to **student access to reading material**, such as ensuring that students have access to the school library and that the classroom itself is stocked with level-appropriate books. The concept also includes **teaching activities**, including classroom reading in all of its forms (shared, guided, etc.), and questions and activities that call upon students to read outside of the classroom and report on how they have done so.

Schema

A schema is the **background knowledge** someone has about a certain topic. The knowledge might be information, associations, remembered life experiences, or even emotional responses. Research has demonstrated that background knowledge is essential to reading comprehension, as written texts invariably rely on implied meanings and a reader's background knowledge. Only the simplest reading passages rely entirely on stated meaning.

Teachers can help **activate** student background knowledge by posing questions that help students relate the text to what they already know or that prompt them to involve their own experiences in their understandings of the text. Activating student background knowledge is important not only to enhance comprehension, it also raises student confidence by demonstrating that they have relevant experience and the tools to understand what they read, and it builds student enthusiasm for reading by connecting what they read to their broader lives.

Comprehensive Reading Program

The US National Reading Panel issued an influential report in 2000 calling for literacy teachers to create a **balanced reading curriculum**, incorporating a range of activities and reading skills: phonemic awareness, phonics (relating sounds to their written representations), fluency, vocabulary development, and comprehension. The panel built on the core insight that students with advanced phonics knowledge were not necessarily skilled readers. Reading well is a multi-faceted skill that requires attention to context and the ways in which successful communications are structured.

A well-balanced reading program incorporates a **range of reading activities** to help students build literacy, from phonics activities to shared and guided reading, cloze activities, and teacher prompts that require students to draw connections between texts or search for implied meanings.

Purposeful Activities vs. Decontextualized Language

Meaningful and purposeful literacy activities are ones that engage the student in something beyond the text. For example, a text might engage the student with subject matter taught in a content classroom. Or the text might appeal to something of particular interest to a student, like a hobby or an aspect of their background or experience. A text might direct the student to accomplish something, as when they follow instructions or create a project based on a written description, or to negotiate something, as when they follow up a reading passage with a small-group or peer-to-peer discussion.

Decontextualized language is language that addresses a subject that is unfamiliar to a student, and which offers few context clues that a student can use to aid comprehension. Reading and understanding decontextualized language is important for academic language fluency, but it is less appropriate for early learners. On the other hand, at appropriate levels of development, students should be challenged by inquiries that invite generalizations and abstractions rather than engage only with concrete and immediate things.

The Language Experience Approach

The key feature of the language experience approach to literacy development is the creation of a **class-specific text** based on a **shared student experience** (a field trip, for example). Typically, the teacher writes the first draft of the text, using student sentences and contributions, which can then be read for practice. The class revisits the text over time, adding new vocabulary, new syntax, and expanding the text to relate to new educational experiences. The text serves as a basis for both reading and writing instruction.

Proponents of this method of literacy development point to the strong association between student lives and the classroom text of which they are, in essence, authors. The approach is not widely used, however, in part because of the near-universality of statewide or region-wide curricula planning, which leaves little room for a text that evolves in undefined directions.

Motivation to Read

A strong correlation exists between frequent reading, skilled reading, and academic success, and yet reading in the traditional sense—as a sustained engagement with a printed text—has declined significantly in the student population. Teachers can encourage student reading by strengthening their **intrinsic motivation**. One way to do this is to make sure that the books they read are relevant to student interests, to contemporary events, and to their different cultures. A second way is to engage in pre-reading activities that activate their background knowledge. A third is to allow students an element of ownership in the reading process, such as allowing them to choose which book to read, or when to read, or how they will be assessed on their reading. Choosing **level-appropriate books** is critical. Students forced to read books that are either too hard or too easy quickly lose interest. Students should be allowed and encouraged to discuss what they read with their peers. Not only does conversation aid comprehension, but it can also foster the sense that reading is worthwhile. Finally, teachers should make sure students are exposed to **reading role models**, whether they are parents, celebrities, or the teacher him or herself.

Kenneth Goodman

Goodman's 1967 research discounted the idea that students read by systematically processing and compiling sequential information. Rather, he argued, reading is a "psycholinguistic guessing game" in which students take rapid **surveys** of the written text and use it to make **predictions** on the basis of their background knowledge and assumptions of what is to come. Goodman argued that reading this way, with a constant interplay between thought and language, is actually more efficient and effective than reading with careful and systematic attention to the text. In his view, the better a student is at reading, the less of a text they actually need to read in order to understand it. Goodman argued that many of the typical errors of early readers are in fact the manifestations of logical guesses that get refined through reading experience.

Appropriate Reading Materials

Extensive research, as well as common sense, attests to the importance of quality, age-appropriate **reading material** for the success of a literacy program. While ESOL teachers often don't have a choice of which materials to use in their classes, whenever they do, they should select materials that:

- Stimulate student interest, in part by including content and themes that are part of student **background knowledge**.
- Provide the proper **conceptual load**, or the amount of new versus familiar structures and vocabulary.
- Furnish sufficient **contextual support** for the narrative.
- Do not contain any **culturally insensitive** references.
- Are an appropriate **length**.
- Represent a **diversity of genres**.
- Have a **clear textual layout** that enhances comprehension rather than impedes it.

Explicit vs. Implicit Instruction

Explicit instruction is when a teacher informs students of a specific lesson goal, provides an explanation of the important concepts, demonstrates their use, and then guides the students in practice. With **implicit instruction**, the teacher does not explicitly teach targeted concepts but instead relies on the students to learn them during the course of communication-based activities. In a rough sense, advocates of implicit instruction model language as something that is **acquired**, and advocates of explicit instruction see it as something that is **learned**. Modern research suggests that teachers need to use both strategies; however, a consensus has emerged that certain skills should be explicitly taught. In the reading domain, this includes the vocabulary and syntax of academic (as opposed to social) language and various comprehension strategies, such as how to infer meaning from a text or synthesize information from multiple texts. In the writing domain, the process of writing itself is thought to best be taught explicitly, proceeding from planning to drafting, evaluating, revising, and editing, with best practices for each. At earlier stages of literacy, phonics instruction is often approached explicitly, as well as those grammatical structures that are least transparent or held in common with the students' native languages.

Implicit vs. Explicit Strategies

Teachers should teach grammar both **implicitly** and **explicitly**, according to both the subject matter and student needs. In general, students whose L1 is grammatically very different from English will require more explicit instruction. Several aspects of English grammar are hard for even speakers of closely-related languages—for example, word order, prepositions, auxiliary verbs, and modal verbs—and thus should be taught explicitly.

The goal of language instruction is **effective communication**, and teachers who are tempted to explicitly correct a student error should first ask themselves whether the error prevented communication. There are many reasons not to explicitly correct a student's spoken errors. Doing so interrupts the conversational flow, possibly embarrasses the student or discourages them from speaking in the future, and may not even help—research shows that certain types of errors appear during the normal process of language development and then disappear without explicit correction. Teachers should be more liberal when correcting written work, both because the affective consequences are fewer and because students need more explicit instruction when learning academic language.

The Importance of Scaffolding

Scaffolding is a teacher's use of supports to help student understanding of concepts or mastery of skills. Well-chosen **literacy scaffolding techniques** allow students to engage with texts and writing projects just beyond their current proficiency levels, or in what Vygotsky referred to as their **zones of proximal development**.

Numerous scaffolding techniques exist to support both reading and writing instruction. For example, a teacher using the **directed listening and thinking activity (DLTA)** would pause a story frequently to ask students questions that led them to predict what might come next and then eventually prompt the students to formulate their own questions and predicted answers. **Shared reading** is a common scaffolding technique in which a teacher reads along with a class, modeling things like pronunciation and fluency. For writing, an example is an **interactive dialogue journal**, in which a teacher and student pass a journal back and forth, each writing in response to the others' comments and prompts. **Mapping**, in which students brainstorm about the words and concepts that relate to a central theme, is a useful scaffolding technique to use in the planning stages of a writing activity.

Gail Tompkins' Five-Level Scaffolding Model

In an influential 2011 textbook, *Literacy in the Early Grades*, Gail Tompkins outlined a **five-stage model of scaffolding** conceived for widespread use in the classroom. The stages are designed to be used either successively—as a teacher gradually reduces the amount of support provided as students become more independent—or selected for use based on a given task or classroom composition. In the **stage of greatest support**, a teacher models the skill or task. In the second, **shared stage**, the students contribute to the task, but the teacher still performs the act or records the product. In the third, **interactive stage**, the students and teacher share in both the conceptualizing and the creation of the product. In the fourth stage, **guided practice**, the students undertake the task, either alone or in groups, with the teacher providing assistance as needed. In the final stage, **independent work**, the students perform the entire activity without significant teacher assistance.

Integrating the Four Basic Language Skills

The main reason to teach reading, writing, speaking, and listening in conjunction is that they all **reinforce** each other. All contribute, in a unique way, to a student's overall language knowledge and ability. Further, there is a *pragmatic* reason to teach all four: in the wider world (beginning in content classrooms) the students will need to use all four skills, often simultaneously, in actual communication contexts.

The ESOL teacher who is tempted to privilege the teaching of oral skills over written skills should remember that second-language learning often follows a different **pattern** than first-language acquisition. With L1, oral competency almost invariably precedes written competency; however, the sequencing is far more variable with L2. In particular, students with strong L1 literacy may progress more rapidly in L2 reading than in L2 speaking, and their reading skills will support and stimulate their speaking progress.

Teachers should find ways to combine the skills in **mutually-reinforcing ways** when designing learning activities. For example, students could read a text, discuss it, and then write about it, explicitly incorporating ideas that they heard in conversations with their peers.

Appropriate Cultural Content

Research demonstrates that students learn to read and write more effectively when texts activate their **background knowledge**. ELLs are likely to have acquired a substantial portion of that knowledge in a different cultural context.

Using **culture-specific content** accelerates language learning in at least two ways. First, students tend to be more interested in texts that relate to their culture. Second, when students read a text for comprehension, they are essentially using what they *already* understand as a means to grasp what they *don't* understand. A text that incorporates familiar cultural references will provide them with more points of comprehension with which to leverage meaning from the unfamiliar text.

In selecting culturally-specific texts or calling upon students to speak about their culture, teachers should be aware that not all students are experts on their native cultures. Nor should a teacher assume that a student wants to speak about their native culture or even be identified by cultural origin.

Integrating English Language Learning

Perhaps the stereotypical image of English language instruction is that of a full-time, separate program that focuses on English proficiency, developing everyday vocabulary and scenarios to build social language skills. While this model of instruction exists, it is increasingly rare, due primarily to the recognition that students benefit most when **language and content** are taught at the same time. One reason is that if students are not taught content until they are proficient in English, they will be significantly behind their peers in content knowledge. Furthermore, content classrooms put language in context, allowing students to build mental networks of related terms and concepts. Content classrooms also give students a setting in which to *apply* the English they learn, making it much less likely they will forget it.

School districts and states differ in *how* they integrate English and content instruction for second-language learners. There are many different program models based on variations of **three fundamental approaches**: having ESOL-trained teachers incorporate content knowledge into their curriculums, having content-trained teachers incorporate English language instruction into their curriculums, and having ESOL and content instructors work in tandem, either through co-teaching or via a pull-out or push-in model.

Coherence and Cohesion

Coherent Texts or Conversations

Discourse may be defined as a coherent sequence of written or spoken sentences. Linguists study the way in which competent language users connect individual sentences in order to create coherent wholes. Linguists may focus on small-scale (word- or phrase-based) connectors called **cohesive devices** or on broader, logical relations between sentences. For example, a sentence might **add information** to the broader text, perhaps through the use of a phrase like "In addition..." A sentence might illustrate the **effect** of a previous cause, using, for example, "Consequently..." Sentences might also **clarify** previous sentences (e.g., "That is to say..."), provide a **summary** (e.g., "In conclusion..."), establish a **logical or temporal order** (e.g., "First... second..."), furnish an **example** (e.g., "For example..."), or **qualify** or **contrast** a previous point (e.g., "However..."). Each of these ways of relating one sentence to another contributes to the overall **coherence** of a text or conversation.

Coherence vs. Cohesion

Coherence and cohesion are terms used in discourse analysis to describe written texts. A text is **cohesive** if its individual sentences are linked in ways that bring them together into a single whole. A text is **coherent** if its ideas, or content, belong together. Although it doesn't incorporate the entirety of the concepts, cohesion can be thought of as an achievement of grammar or rhetoric, whereas coherence demands that the text corresponds to logic or reality.

Linguists have identified five cohesive devices that establish links among sentences.

- **Reference** occurs when a word in one sentence refers to a word in another, such as a pronoun to its antecedent.
- **Conjunction** occurs when a sentence begins with a word or phrase, such as "however" or "alternatively," that ties it to the previous sentence.
- **Substitution** occurs when a specific word is replaced with a general word in a subsequent sentence—for example, first writing "I doubt he will study," and then "But if he does..."
- Writers may also intentionally leave out parts of a phrase previously used, a technique called **ellipses.**
- Finally, writers may employ lexical cohesion by replacing a word with an appropriate **descriptor**, as when "Edison" is replaced with "the inventor."

Connected Speech

"Connected speech" refers to the way in which the pronunciation of a word can be changed by the words around it. **Catenation** is the joining of the last consonant sound of one word with the beginning vowel sound of the next, as when "an apple" sounds like "a napple." **Elision** occurs when a sound is left out of a word—often a sound in a consonant cluster, as when "sandwich" is pronounced "sanwich." **Assimilation** is the blending of two sounds to create a new sound, as when "don't you" sounds like "doan chu" when spoken rapidly. **Intrusion** is the insertion of an unwritten sound into a phrase, as when "do it" is pronounced "dewit."

Connected speech presents obvious listening comprehension challenges for ELLs. In addition, ELLs who rely heavily on reading to learn English (as with grammar-translation methods still in use abroad) may not use any connected speech when speaking, and thus sound unnaturally formal or stilted.

Teaching Listening and Speaking

Verbal vs. Oral Communication

The term "verbal communication" is usually contrasted with "nonverbal communication," and in this sense, it means communication that occurs via words. **Verbal communication** can include all four **major language skills**: speaking, listening, reading, and writing. The term "**oral communication**" narrows this set of skills to two: speaking and listening.

One way to think about oral communication is to consider the various aspects of spoken language—beyond word choice—that convey meaning in conversation. These **prosodic aspects of language** include pitch, stress, rhythm, length, and loudness.

A second way to think about oral communication is to focus on the goals of a conversation and the different skills required to achieve those goals. For example, in some contexts, ELLs must be able to identify the main point of an utterance while setting aside details or irrelevant information; in other contexts, they may need to focus on the details. Similarly, the skills needed to recount an event or conversation when speaking to a peer are very different from those needed to give an oral presentation. ESOL teachers need to understand the range of necessary skills and provide instruction and practice in each.

Demonstrating Listening Comprehension

In the early stages of language learning, students may only be able to signal understanding by nodding, smiling, or performing whatever action is being requested. Their responses will be based heavily on **nonverbal signals** and references to **illustrations** or **realia**. Next, students will develop the capacity to signal comprehension by choosing one of a set of options ("Where did John go? Home or to the store?") before developing the capacity to formulate **simple answers without scaffolds**. In later stages, students will be able to provide **full-sentence answers** to comprehension questions and eventually to provide **multi-sentence summaries** that reveal their comprehension of literal and implied meaning, central and supporting arguments, and connections to other texts and real-world experiences.

Discourse Markers

A discourse marker is a word or phrase used to organize speech, manage the flow of a conversation, or convey an emotional attitude. **Discourse markers** are often inessential to the literal semantic meaning of a sentence but can be critical in conveying the **attitude** of the speaker. Examples include "well," "um," "you know," "right," and "maybe." Research shows that even proficient ELLs use fewer discourse markers than native speakers and that early ELLs misunderstand their pragmatic use. Discourse markers are heavily bound to context and are thus difficult to teach in any systematic way. However, ESOL teachers may illustrate some common forms, such as how the expression "Yeah, right" can signal either agreement or skepticism, depending on stress and tone.

Framing a Listening Comprehension Activity

Students who listen to audio or watch video files at their **zone of proximal development** are unlikely to be able to answer questions about multiple levels of meaning—at least not without repeated listening or viewing. Teachers can help **facilitate student listening comprehension** by identifying in advance what they are listening for: the main idea, details in support of an argument, or the attitude of one or more interlocutors toward a proposed idea. Teachers can also prime students to listen for implied meanings or idiomatic expressions by providing suggestive clues: for example, "The narrator in this video uses an interesting expression that means 'to lose something forever'—let's see if we can find out what it is." Teachers might divide the class into groups, have each group listen for a different element of comprehension, and then combine the elements in a subsequent discussion. Teachers should be aware that students may understand almost nothing that they hear—either because they panic and lose focus when they can't understand or because they translate L2 into L1 and miss the overall meaning.

Frontloading, Chunking, and Debriefing

Teachers frontload or pre-teach when they teach specific vocabulary, rhetorical devices, sentence structures, or content that students will encounter in a subsequent lesson. **Frontloading** or **pre-teaching** is particularly useful in preparing students for listening comprehension activities to ensure that students don't disengage when they encounter unfamiliar words or forms.

Chunking is the practice of dividing a lesson or text into mentally digestible parts, often by stopping and inviting students to ask questions, draw connections to prior knowledge, or make predictions about what is to come. Teachers often chunk a reading comprehension exercise to ensure that students understand one section of the text before moving on to the next.

Debriefing is a type of lesson summary or wrap-up, usually used to revisit a key point or reinforce a specific learning goal and to assess how well students mastered the lesson.

Initiating and Negotiating Conversations

Enabling students to hold successful conversations is one of the most important outcomes of any ELL program. Students who speak flawless English will nevertheless fail to achieve their communication objectives if they do not learn the patterns and conventions of conversational discourse. In order to become proficient in oral communication, students must learn how to **initiate a conversation** with greetings and formalities, using a **register** appropriate to the setting. Students must also learn how to **reinforce** their interlocutor's utterances, either through nonverbal cues (nodding, smiling) or appropriate and well-timed interjections. For social purposes, students should learn how to **alternate** conversation, ensuring that all parties are equal participants. Students should develop a repertoire of **active listening** techniques and learn to extend a conversation with open, closed, and clarifying questions. These skills are particularly important when students have a specific conversational objective, such as achieving a consensus or securing specific information. Finally, students must learn the conventions of **closing a conversation**.

Retelling, Restating, and Summarizing

Real-world communication relies heavily on one person summarizing an idea, event, or encounter for the benefit of others. ELLs need to learn how to deliver concise and accurate **summaries** for purposes of work and school and how to accurately **paraphrase** conversations and **telescope** narrative events during social interactions.

Learning how to use **reported speech**—such as reporting Joe's words "I am sick" as "Joe said that he was sick"—is a relatively advanced language skill. Even early ELLs, however, can practice retelling events and experiences, and more advanced students can practice narrating them in different registers, as when talking to a teacher rather than a peer. One common technique to practice this skill is to have students interview one another and then report their findings to the class. Another is to have the students summarize a story or video using a targeted number of sentences—with the target set to help the students approximate the amount of detail they should provide.

Purpose, Audience, and Subject Matter

In the context of language, the term "**register**" refers to the degree of formality of speech or to the way members of a group speak to one another. For example, a group of doctors may speak to one another in a medical register. Scholars often speak of three distinct registers: **informal** (which students might use in casual conversation among themselves), **neutral** (which might govern most student/teacher interactions), and **formal** (which students might use in a presentation or when speaking to an unfamiliar adult). In transitioning from informal to neutral or formal conversational registers, students will need to learn to use complete sentences rather than rely on contextual meaning, eliminate slang and excessive discourse markers, and avoid hyperbole and repetition.

English language learners also need to learn the basic conventions of the various **academic disciplines**. For example, it may be appropriate to use figurative language when writing or speaking about the arts but not when discussing math or logic. Language use also varies with purpose: the conventions that apply to speech intended to persuade are different from those that apply to exposition.

Review Video: Writing Purpose and Audience
Visit mometrix.com/academy and enter code: 146627

Teaching Reading and Writing

Decoding

Decoding, an essential early reading skill, is the practice of sounding out written words. In order to succeed at **decoding**, students need to understand the basics of **phonics**—how sounds correlate with letters—as well as how to blend sounds and segment words into **discrete sounds**. Successful decoding reveals what the word is but not what it means, either in isolation or in context. However, ELLs who decode a word may discover that they already know the word through speech. For this reason, decoding is often referred to as **word identification**.

Research suggests that phonics is best taught explicitly—teachers systematically teach letter/sound correspondence and advance through progressively more complex words by grouping words with shared sounds. Alternatively, phonics may be taught implicitly—teachers present whole words and then break them into sounds, inviting students to identify common, known sound patterns.

Print Awareness

Print awareness refers to a student's recognition that the written symbols on a page represent letters and words and correspond to spoken language. The term also refers to the awareness that English text is read from left to right and pages are turned from right to left. **Print awareness** is an essential skill which students must grasp before they can learn how to read, spell, or practice handwriting.

Teachers can develop print awareness in early ELLs by modeling how a book is read, using a finger to trace the progression of reading from left to right and then wrapping around to the next line, showing how pictures are associated with parts of a story, explaining the role of title and author, and discussing how a book represents a complete narrative.

Reading Fluency

Fluency in reading is the ability to read a text accurately, rapidly, and with feeling. The most important thing a teacher can do to promote fluency is to read aloud often, taking care to read with expression—modeling how words are not read one by one with equal spacing, but in groups with uneven pauses.

Students can practice reading a line of text after listening to the teacher read it or read the text in unison with the teacher—either one student at a time (**duet reading**) or the entire class (**choral reading**). Research suggests that **reading aloud** is more helpful to developing fluency than reading silently and that students can profit from reading the same passages repeatedly until they achieve fluency.

Fluency is highly correlated with **comprehension**. Jay Samuels developed the **automaticity theory** to explain this correlation. According to Samuels, students have limited mental attention, and the more reading functions—such as decoding—they can accomplish automatically the more attention they have to grasp the broader meanings of a text. In this view, fluency *is* automaticity.

Review Video: Fluency
Visit mometrix.com/academy and enter code: 531179

Pre-Reading, Reading, and Post-Reading

Research demonstrates that students who approach a text with a purpose comprehend it better than students who simply read it passively without any expectations or goals.

Teachers can promote reading comprehension in the **pre-reading phase** by explaining the **purpose** of the exercise and what the students will be doing with the text once they finish reading it. They can preview the format of the text so that students know what to expect as they read. They can solicit student background knowledge to build context and stimulate interest.

Teachers should encourage students to monitor their comprehension while they read with a variety of **self-questioning strategies**. For example, when reading a text with headings, students can stop at the end of a section and verify that they grasped the point anticipated by the heading. If they are reading a persuasive essay, they can stop periodically and ask themselves if they are convinced by the writer's argument and evidence.

Finally, students should **assess and summarize** once they have finished reading. If they find that they don't understand part of the narrative or the author's argument, they should return to the text to improve their comprehension.

A Text's Features, Structures, and Rhetorical Devices

An essential element of reading comprehension is the ability to predict how a text will be structured and how its author will present information or construct a narrative. Students who can successfully anticipate and identify these aspects of a text will have an advantage in overall comprehension because they can use what they already know to infer further meanings and evaluate the credibility of the author or the quality of his or her argument.

Students can be taught the general **features** of fiction, non-fiction, and academic texts. Given the nature of the text, certain **structures** can be expected. Fiction, for example, will likely contain a lot of dialogue composed of informal (social) language; academic texts, in contrast, will eschew dialogue and likely use only objective adjectives, such as those indicating size or number. Different types of texts incorporate different **rhetorical devices** as well: fiction may depend heavily on metaphor, while academic texts may rely on inductive and deductive arguments.

English Language Conventions

Modern approaches to writing treat the proper use of **English conventions** as one of several components of good writing, along with word choice, organization, voice, fluency, and message or content. Thus, while ESOL teachers may choose to teach some conventions explicitly, they must take care not to let a focus on grammar, punctuation, or error correction impede the overall writing process.

Process writing breaks the writing task into **five phases**: prewriting, drafting, revising, editing, and publishing. In this framework, students focus on the correct use of conventions in the editing phase (though the teacher or peers may point out errors in the revising phase), well after the creative and expansive portions of the task.

Main Genres of Academic Writing

- **Expository writing** is used to inform the reader by presenting information in an objective manner. It is written almost exclusively in the third person, uses complex sentences, and often utilizes the specialized vocabulary of an academic or technical field.
- **Descriptive writing** is used to portray an event, place, or person, usually with depth and detail. It may rely heavily on adjectives and adverbs to provide vivid descriptions of sensory images. Descriptive prose is common in fiction but may also be found in advertising and journalism.
- **Persuasive writing** is used to advance an argument or point of view. It often begins with the statement of a thesis, presentation of evidence, and a restatement of the thesis as a conclusion. The author may explicitly state his or her own opinions and likely will not pretend to be offering a balanced account of the subject.
- **Narrative writing** is used to tell a story, either fictional or factual. Narrations usually proceed in chronological order, often use literary devices (metaphors, etc.), and may make heavy use of description and dialogue.

Some typologies of academic writing consider poetry, letter, and journal writing to be separate genres.

Content-Area English Instruction

Integrating English Instruction into Content Areas

In addition to learning to use the English language proficiently, ELLs are required to learn the same **content knowledge** as native English speakers. Usually, this is done in an **integrated classroom**, including both native and non-native English speakers, and not always with a teacher who is trained specifically for teaching English. Many times, a school or district has a specialist present to support English language learners and their teachers in **modifying** or **developing curriculum** and instruction. To succeed in teaching ELLs in content areas, the teacher must determine which language skills are necessary to learn and perform well in the content objectives. For instance, when teaching a physics lesson on kinetics, the language features of prepositions and sequencing may be necessary to understand object placement and order of events, but students can still succeed if they make mistakes on plurals or struggle with their tense conjugations. In this content area, language-based corrective feedback may be counter-productive to the student learning the content knowledge. Focusing too much on unrelated language goals may take time away from the objectives at hand and may even artificially increase the students' cognitive load.

Specific Goals for Content-Area English Instruction

The primary goal when supporting ELLs in content areas is to make sure that the input they receive is **comprehensible**. The major factors of an ELL's ability to comprehend subject matter are **general academic English fluency** for the level and a foundation in the **content-specific vocabulary** and concepts involved. Specific strategies that content teachers may employ to ensure their instruction is effective for ELLs in their class are to **pre-test** to determine students' current knowledge levels, **pre-teach vocabulary** to ensure students are primed for the focal points of lessons, and to use frequent **comprehension checks** to ensure students are not lost. All students, not just ELLs, need a certain level of academic knowledge before being able to learn new and more complex ideas. Pre-tests can give a teacher a strong baseline for where to begin instruction if students do not demonstrate readiness in the foundational knowledge. If a comprehension check shows that students are not sure of the material, the teacher should try rewording with simpler, but still accurate, language or elaborating to clarify the point. Pre-teaching vocabulary is one of the most helpful ways of priming ELLs on new topics. Furthermore, cognates, or words that are shared between languages, are abundant in content areas and should be easy for the students to learn and retain with less effort.

Scaffolding Considerations for Content-Area Instruction

As with other types of English learning, employing a combination of instructional time and application time should help with retention of content knowledge. In instructional periods, the teacher should employ verbal scaffolding techniques, including prompting, questioning, and elaborating to ensure comprehension. Teaching should include **explicit teaching**, such as lecturing, but should also include modeling and opportunities for **practice and application** of ideas, especially discussion with classmates, as this helps with both expressive and receptive language skills. When using **modeling** to scaffold instruction, it is helpful to employ visuals and realia, or real-life objects, to help communicate ideas in a more concrete manner. In science, this may be a model or experiment. Mathematics instruction may benefit from using manipulatives or charts and graphs. In social science instruction, tables, timelines, and other types of visual representations of the information are helpful reinforcements of the concepts that may redirect the focus of the lesson to the visual and kinesthetic aspects of the materials, hopefully **reducing the language load** involved.

Discourse Complexity and Adaptation Techniques

It is important to note that different content areas may require distinct types and levels of scaffolding due to the language load involved in each subject. For instance, mathematics and science are inevitably going to have a lower **language load** than history or theatre instruction, but they do have a higher load of **specialized vocabulary** and processes. For instance, the names of laboratory equipment such as beakers, goggles, and microscopes are examples of specialized vocabulary that need to be understood to participate in activities safely. On the other hand, many history lessons may require reading passages that are several pages long to understand the narrative. The language may be less specialized, but the language load is certainly higher due to the volume of reading required. Depending on the circumstances, teachers may need to employ various types of adaptation techniques, including allowing time extensions on work, allowing the use of extra resources (e.g., a bilingual glossary or dictionary), or using excerpts from a reading instead of full-length passages.

Effective Resources for Language Learning

Selecting Materials and Resources

Teachers must take care that the **resources** they choose for the classroom are age-appropriate, culturally inclusive, language-accessible, affordable, varied, and easily accessible. One challenge ESOL teachers face is that resources that are language-appropriate for older ELLs may not be age-appropriate—that is, students may perceive them as childish or demeaning. When assigning **online language tasks**, teachers need to make sure students have time to complete the work in class rather than assume the students have access to technology or the Internet at home. Teachers should invite students to bring **realia and written texts** from their native cultures for discussion but shouldn't make the presentation of a home culture mandatory. Teachers should strive to provide resources in **different media** (audio, visual, performative guides, etc.) in order to appeal to different learning preferences and to provide reinforcement of learning through multiple media.

Authentic, Meaningful, and Purposeful Communicative Interactions

Meaningful and purposeful classroom activities are those that achieve a specific learning goal while engaging the students with a topic or a process that is interesting to them. The phrase "**communicative interactions**" points to the sociocultural aspect of language learning—students learn best when they are engaged in authentic communicative acts rather than simply listening to a lecture or practicing repetitive worksheet exercises.

In order to make lessons meaningful, teachers should use **authentic texts and realia**, examples and scenarios from the students' original cultures, and scenarios that reproduce scenes and activities that the students actually experience. Texts should include sympathetic characters facing familiar challenges.

In order to promote communicative interactions, teachers should stage activities that draw students into **conversations**, such as small-group discussions, problem-solving tasks, skits, or dialogue journals. In guiding the conversation, teachers should ask open-ended, exploratory questions that avoid right/wrong answers and invite elaboration. Students should assess and discuss what they read and should write in order to be read—whether it be a product like a classroom newsletter or a journal to be read by a classmate or a parent.

David Ausubel's Subsumption Theory

The educational psychologist David Ausubel's work underscored the importance of **context** for learning. In his view, students learn best when the new material relates to what they already know. He labeled this kind of learning **meaningful** and contrasted it with rote learning, in which students learn isolated information that they can only relate to other information in an arbitrary way. With meaningful learning, new information is **subsumed** under existing cognitive structures and knowledge. Ausubel suggested that the most important factor determining whether students will remember what they learn is not repetition but rather the **integration** of that knowledge in a system of meaning. Even information earned by means of an artificial mnemonic device will eventually be lost, Ausubel argued, unless it is used and, thus, anchored in a broader network of meaning.

Many of Ausubel's insights are now accepted as established principles, and his work is a useful reminder of the importance of activating students' prior knowledge, pre-teaching concepts, and in general providing students with a context for what is to be taught.

Use of Technology

The use of technology in the classroom—and indeed, to blur the line between the inside and outside of a classroom—is widespread, limited in most cases only by funding and teacher unfamiliarity with emerging platforms. The adoption of **technology** is leading to the growth of blended learning, in which online learning replaces a portion of the face-to-face instruction time. Technology plays a key role in many classroom differentiation strategies, as students using software can learn at their own pace and using different learning styles. Technologies that are of particular value in ESOL classrooms include **document cameras**, which can easily provide a visual accompaniment to a spoken lesson, and **online voice recorders**, which allow teachers and students to record specific lessons for targeted speaking practice. Any technology that gives quick access to pictures provides essential scaffolding for early ELLs. Anonymous chat and collaboration sites are particularly useful for ELLs who are not comfortable participating in class.

ESOL teachers need to be careful not to require technologies that their students cannot afford or to assume that students have internet connectivity at home.

Review Video: Benefits of Technology in the Classroom
Visit mometrix.com/academy and enter code: 536375

Computer Assisted Language Learning (CALL)

Computer assisted language learning (CALL) is the use of computer technology to learn languages. Discussions of CALL often distinguish between the use of computers as a tutor and their use as a tool for communicating with others. The most commonly used tutoring applications in ESOL classrooms include **pronunciation tutorials**, in which students listen to native English speakers and record their own speech; **reading tutorials**, in which electronic glossaries provide definitions and draw connections between related texts; and programs that provide outlines and graphic organizers to assist in the **writing process**.

The use of computers as a communication tool is often called **computer-mediated communication (CMC)**. CMC may either be synchronous (real-time interaction with a teacher or other students) or asynchronous (in which students post work for later review or augmentation by other users).

CALL is widely used to differentiate instruction and learning, as individual students can use CALL to learn different lessons at different rates. When used responsibly by self-motivated learners, CALL can provide unique opportunities for self-guided learning. As a communication tool, CALL expands the possibilities for distance learning and collaboration beyond the physical classroom. And finally, computer-based assessments can automate much of the grading and feedback functions of teaching.

Technology and Differentiated Instruction

The single greatest advantage of technology use in the classroom is the opportunities it provides for **differentiated instruction**. Using computer technology, a teacher can differentiate a lesson by content and degree of difficulty, by the amount or nature of scaffolding provided, by learner-style preference, and by a student's preferred method of demonstrating learning. If students have access to the learning technologies at home, they can listen to or read a lesson multiple times, gaining the critical advantages of time and repetition. The same technologies can be used to **differentiate assessments**. With the right technologies, students can listen to questions multiple times or access hyperlinks to contextual information.

School use of technology varies greatly, as does student access to technologies at home. Teachers must be mindful of these limitations and careful not to disadvantage students who lack access. While technology-based learning is great for differentiation and for autonomous learning, students who lack direction may waste their time or pursue inappropriate goals. Finally, even a well-equipped classroom may lack bandwidth or suffer technology failures—teachers have to be prepared with alternative lesson plans.

New Literacies of Online Research and Comprehension

The concept of new literacies of online research and comprehension (often simply called "new literacies") is based on the assertion that online reading and research require a different set of literacy skills than do traditional, paper-based reading, and research. According to this still-emerging body of research, success in traditional reading does not automatically translate to success in online reading. Further, students are likely to have significant advantages in online literacy over their teachers. And online literacy is **deictic**, or ever-changing, in ways that traditional literacy is not, making online literacy an ongoing, dynamic engagement.

Donald Leu has outlined **five functions** critical to online literacy. The first is **identifying the problem**. Students must initiate online research by accurately formulating a question or a search phrase—a skill seldom, if ever, needed in traditional reading. Second, students must know how to **locate information online**, skimming and choosing from search engine results. Third, students must be able to **evaluate sources for reliability and bias**. Fourth, they must be able to **synthesize information drawn from different sources**. (As the number of sources has grown, so has the likelihood that relevant information will be spread among multiple locations.) Finally, students may be called upon to **communicate their results in multiple new formats**, requiring a different range of rhetorical skills.

Corpus and Concordance

A corpus (plural: corpora) is a collection of texts gathered by linguists for purposes of **research**. Today, linguists use computers to search and analyze textual data for insights into language use. Corpora are used, for example, to compile dictionaries and to juxtapose prescriptive and descriptive grammars.

A **concordance** is a list of the ways in which a word is used in **context**. It can be very useful for an ESOL student trying to understand idiosyncratic constructions—for example, which prepositions go with which verbs—or to see how an unfamiliar word is actually used in discourse.

Simple search engines will return some of the information available from a concordance, but intermediate and advanced ESOL students may benefit from a **concordance program** that provides more information than a dictionary about actual usage. Concordances can also show which words are typically used in association with one another—a useful tool when building subject-matter vocabulary.

Variation in Language Application

Social Language vs. Academic Language

Social language is language used in everyday communication. **Academic language** is used in the classroom and workplace and on standardized assessments. Most students are exposed to social language earlier and more completely than they are exposed to academic language and become more proficient in social language as a consequence.

Social language often doesn't follow grammatical conventions—in casual settings, people often speak in phrases rather than complete sentences, use slang, repeat themselves, and use narrative strategies that favor expediency rather than economy or logic. In an academic setting, by contrast, people are expected to use full sentences linked by grammatical transitions. Academic language typically requires a specialized or higher-level vocabulary, and variety is expected instead of repetition.

It isn't uncommon for ESOL students to be fluent in social language while struggling to achieve even minimal competence in academic language. The students' perceived mastery of the more common social language may lessen their motivation to improve their academic language performance.

Use vs. Usage

The linguist Henry Widdowson drew a distinction between **language usage**—knowing how to construct words and sentences in accordance with formal rules—and **language use**—knowing how to use language in order to achieve an objective. Widdowson used these terms to draw a sharp distinction between **linguistic competence** and **communicative competence** and argued that the latter takes more time for second-language learners to achieve. Extending the same distinction, Widdowson argued that sentences have *significance* in isolation but *value* in the context of a communicative act. Widdowson's ideas influenced the **communicative approaches** to language learning, with their emphasis on authentic speech acts and the importance of pragmatic dimensions of communication.

Different Social Functions of Language

The primary purpose of language is to allow people to communicate with and understand one another. Linguists often distinguish between academic language and social language—the latter being the everyday language we use in informal settings—and classify various types of social language based on their function. For example, the linguist Geoffrey Leech identified five different functions of social language. First, language is **informational**: we use it to convey information, and in this form, we value its accuracy and relevance. Second, language may be **expressive**, as when we use it to convey feelings or attitudes. Third, language may be **directive**—we may use it to convey orders or exert influence. Fourth, language may be **aesthetic**, as when it is used creatively or artistically. Fifth, language may be **phatic**—that is, it may be used simply to sustain a social relationship, such as when we engage in small talk with a stranger.

Other linguists have classified social language in other ways—for example, many add a category of apologetic language. The importance of all this research is that it draws attention to the various functions of everyday language.

Various Functions of Language

Language has a number of functions. The most obvious is to **communicate facts, thoughts, or opinions** to others. Linguists describe this function as referential in that the language we use refers to something that exists in our minds. We also use language to **express emotions**—often involuntarily, as when we cry out in alarm. Language has a social function beyond the expression of thought—as when we engage in ritualistic pleasantries with a neighbor as a way of cementing a social bond. We use language to **record information** for future use, usually in written form. We also use language to **influence reality**—what the philosopher J. L. Austin called "perlocutionary acts," as when we christen a ship with the invocation "I hereby christen…" We also use language to **facilitate thought and memory**, as when we talk to ourselves to overcome a mental block. Finally, we use language to **express our personal or collective identity**, as when we join a cheer at a sports stadium.

Basic Interpersonal Communication Skills (BICS) and Cognitive Academic Language Proficiency (CALP)

The terms "BICS" and "CALP," coined by the educational psychologist Jim Cummins, correspond to the broader concepts of social and academic language. Social language, or **BICS**, is the language used in everyday life; while academic language, or **CALP**, is the language used in formal academic settings.

Cummins highlighted the importance of treating the two types of language as **separate systems**. An ESOL student will typically become proficient in BICS in as little as six months, while proficiency in CALP may take seven to 10 years. Furthermore, many English language learners never achieve full facility in CALP, whereas failure to acquire BICS is rare. Cummins warned educators not to make the mistake of assuming that a student proficient in BICS is also proficient in CALP—rather, it is natural for students to master the two competencies at different rates.

Different Academic Functions of Language

Academic language is the language used in the classroom, the workplace, and on formal assessments. ESOL students also need to become proficient in **academic language** in order to express, or demonstrate, their knowledge in various content areas of interest.

Whereas **social or everyday language** is used to convey information, express feelings, or simply to cement social bonds, **academic language** is used to achieve other functions. One classification suggests that academic language is used to describe, define, explain, compare, contrast, make predictions, and persuade.

Most ESOL students achieve proficiency in social language long before they achieve academic language proficiency. An ESOL student is likely to be immersed in social language early in his or her language experience but will need academic language to be expressly modeled, scaffolded, and reinforced through targeted practice.

Basil Bernstein's Theory of Language Codes

A language code is the way language is used by a particular social group, in part as an expression of social identity. In the 1970s, the linguist Basil Bernstein suggested that language could be described as consisting of either elaborated code or restricted code. Individuals use an **elaborated code** when they communicate with strangers or people who do not share a common experience. In these instances, they speak explicitly, at length, and with minimal colloquial or expressive language. When in the company of friends or members of a shared community, by contrast, people use a **restricted code**, which relies on implied meanings and references, thereby communicating a lot with few words. Only individuals with shared background knowledge and experiences can understand restricted code, whereas any listener can understand an elaborated utterance. Bernstein argued that restricted codes are used primarily in narrow, unchanging social contexts where shared values can be assumed, whereas elaborated codes are used for broader, unpredictable interactions. He also associated the use of restricted codes with the working class.

Communicative Competence

Communicative competence, a concept developed by the linguist Dell Hymes, refers to a language learner's ability to communicate effectively in various social settings. In order to succeed in communication, we need to know not only how to speak (or write) but what to say to whom and under which circumstances.

Later, Michael Canale and Merrill Swain identified four components of communicative competence. **Linguistic competence** refers to proficiency in grammar, vocabulary, and orthography. **Sociolinguistic competence** is the understanding of how to vary language use depending on the context or audience. **Discourse competence** is the knowledge of how to produce cohesive and coherent written or oral texts. **Strategic competence** is the ability to avoid or repair communication breakdowns—for example, by paraphrasing or using gestures to overcome the lack of useful vocabulary.

The concept of communicative competence focuses attention on the fact that there is more to communicative success than mastery of syntax or acquisition of vocabulary. Effective ESOL teachers implicitly or explicitly teach all of the component competencies.

Spoken vs. Written Language

Spoken and written language differ greatly in both form and purpose. The grammar of spoken language is generally less rigid, to the extent that many linguists believe that phrases are the fundamental units of speech, unlike the full sentences used in formal writing. **Spoken language** tends to include many repetitions, ellipses, and self-corrections and relies more heavily on slang and first-person pronouns than writing. Successful oral communication depends on paralanguage features—the nonverbal aspects of conversation, such as tone, gesture, and facial expression.

Written communication, by contrast, is more planned, uses more formal (and often complex) grammatical structures, avoids repetition, and relies on orderly presentation and evidence in order to be persuasive. Whereas speech is reciprocal—that is, it can be adapted to the reactions and emotions of the audience—writing is non-negotiable, as it is usually a non-synchronous medium, and thus must be crafted to be comprehensive. The differences between these types of communication, like many things, are not absolute; there are definite exceptions to the levels of formality, planning, and structure. Additionally, there are types of communication that blur the distinction between spoken and written language like prepared speeches and texting.

English-language learners have far more exposure to spoken English than to written English due to common social use of language. Written language learning tends to lean toward academic English and may be more challenging for English language learners than social English usage. ELLs tend to write in the same way in which they speak—that is, in phrases rather than sentences. Similarly, the argumentative forms typically used in writing, with ideas presented in a logical sequence or with a thesis followed by evidence or examples, are not the same as those used in typical speech and need to be expressly taught. Teachers should be aware that the English learning needs of their students will likely vary between their use of spoken and written language.

Variations in Languages and Dialects

Sociolinguistics, Dialect, and Sociolect

Sociolinguistics is the study of the factors that lead to variation in language use, such as region, gender, class, ethnicity, age, occupation, or bilingual status. A **dialect** is a variation in one or more features of a language, such as spelling, pronunciation, or word choice. **Sociolect** refers to language variations shared by members of the same social class.

Sociolinguists also study how our language use varies depending on the **situation**—people have a tendency to adopt the dialect of those they are speaking to, especially after lengthy exposure. People often adopt shared language as a means of showing solidarity with one another, as in numerous examples of working-class English. Many studies have shown, however, that people often adopt an **aspirational dialect**—in other words, they adopt the language patterns of a social or economic class they hope to join. Research has also suggested that women use higher-status language on average than men, perhaps to compensate for their perceived lower status in society.

Dialect vs. Language

A dialect is a variation in a spoken language that nevertheless is intelligible to the larger language community. (If the variation is so large as to prevent mutual intelligibility, it is considered to be a separate language.)

Dialects naturally arise when a language is spread across a wide area. Often gradients emerge such that all of the members of a dialect community can understand the neighboring dialects, but the differences between the communities farthest apart are so great as to impede communication. While the linguistic distinction between language and dialect is clear, the reality in use is complicated by political and cultural interests—Hindi and Urdu, for example, are treated as separate languages even though they are mutually intelligible, whereas Chinese is, in fact, a collection of mutually unintelligible dialects unified only by a written language and a national identity.

English language learners may bring varying dialects into the classroom, and teachers should be careful to appreciate legitimate variation rather than impose an arbitrary standard. Differences in dialect may also slow language comprehension and acquisition, though the overall effect is likely to be slight.

World English and World Englishes

The similar terms "World English" and "World Englishes" refer to different applications of the use of English internationally. **World English** describes English used as a means of communication across language barriers, especially those in business or other professional and educational fields. For instance, a Spanish-speaking individual might not be able to directly communicate with a Hindi-speaking individual, but due to the worldwide prevalence of English, they may be able to find a common path to communication by speaking in English instead of eithers' first language. The concept of communicating across language barriers using a third language as in this example is known as "**lingua franca,**" which means a common tongue.

World Englishes, on the other hand, refers to international variations of English as it is used and modified to suit the local populations. This is similar to the use of hybrid-languages, such as "Singlish" to denote a blend between English and the varied languages of Singapore (Mandarin, Malay, and Tamil) or "Spanglish," denoting a blend between English and Spanish. While World Englishes may have strong variance geographically, they remain distinct from hybridized languages. Scholars of World Englishes map its spread along the lines of colonial influence, through commercial and scientific hubs, among the world's educated and economic elite, and increasingly through the instruments of modern technology, such as the Internet or cell phone platforms.

Diglossia

Diglossia is the use of two different languages (or two forms of one language) by a single speech community. One form is usually distinguishable as a high form, which is taught in school, used in formal situations, is associated with prestige, and has a written form. The low form, by contrast, is acquired rather than taught, is used in informal settings, is often considered to signal low status, and often lacks a written form. Individuals who speak both forms typically engage in code-switching, alternating between the two languages to fit the context.

Classic diglossia describes the situation in which a community speaks two forms of a single language. Extended diglossia occurs when the community alternates between two separate languages depending on context.

Accentedness

Accentedness refers to how a language learner's pronunciation differs from that of a native speaker. **Accentedness** is a major factor in determining both the comprehensibility of speech, or how difficult it is to understand; and the intelligibility of speech, or whether it is, in fact, understood.

These definitions have led scholars to suggest that, given limited instructional time, English language teachers should prioritize improving the elements of accentedness that have the most effect on **comprehensibility and intelligibility**—in other words, not all irregular pronunciations are equal. Linguists have developed the concept of functional load to measure how important the proper pronunciation of a phoneme is for the production of intelligible speech. One pragmatic conclusion is that teachers should focus on correcting pronunciation errors that carry high functional loads and spend less or no time correcting those with low loads. Some educators argue that a student's accentedness should only be of concern if it affects intelligibility. Comprehensibility, while desirable, is not a priority when instruction time is limited.

Respecting an ELL's Home Language

Learning a second language can be an intimidating experience in any circumstance, but it is even more daunting for students who are adapting to life in a new country or attempting to gain social acceptance from their peers. ELLs often feel stressed and are wary of making errors, which can impede the learning process. Teachers should create a positive environment that recognizes student competence in their native language. Teachers should also ensure that all languages are treated equally and that one native language doesn't have priority over another. This is particularly important during group work, when cliques of like-language students might exclude others. Teachers should enforce rules about when students are allowed to speak in their native language. Teachers can also organize activities that invite translation of home languages or presentations by students of elements of their home cultures. Finally, teachers should attempt to involve parents in their students' lessons to create continuities between home and classroom experiences.

Cultural Concepts and Perspectives

External and Internal Culture

Culture is an integrated pattern of knowledge, belief, and behavior, held by a particular human group, that is learned and transmitted through generations. The term is broad, but culture can be thought of as consisting of what people (a) do, (b) believe or know, and (c) make and use.

Another way to think about culture is to differentiate between external and internal culture. **External culture** (often called material culture) refers to the objects and physical space people use to express their shared culture. Elements of external culture include architecture, clothing, food, technology, the arts, and language. **Internal culture** (often called non-material culture) refers to the shared patterns of thought and social behavior that exist as collective beliefs and customs. Elements of internal culture include values, family structures, social roles, beliefs and expectations, and worldview. External cultural markers are easier to recognize, but with the exception of language, the elements of internal culture have a greater influence on how students learn.

The Sapir-Whorf Hypothesis

The Sapir-Whorf hypothesis, which combines the work of the linguistic anthropologists Edward Sapir (1884–1939) and Benjamin Whorf (1897–1941), is the assertion that **language** has a strong, constraining influence on **thought**. Thus, they argued that speakers of different languages have different **worldviews**. In other words, language doesn't only reflect reality, but influences our perception of reality.

For example, research shows that a person is *more likely* to understand an idea or concept that they can name in their language with a single word, but that the lack of a word does not *prevent* conceptualization of an idea. The *strong form* of the Sapir-Whorf hypothesis is now commonly referred to as **linguistic determinism**, meaning that a person's language determines or sets hard limits a person's ability to think about concepts. Modern linguists largely reject linguistic determinism as the conceptualization of an idea is still possible through adoption of new terms, loan words, or through circumlocution. Language is also recognized as being in a constant state of adaptation to keep up with culture and technology, such as the adoption of new terms and the retirement of outdated phrases.

The Sapir-Whorf hypothesis is an example of a theory that posits that thought is dependent on language. The common-sense view holds the opposite: people have thoughts and put them into words when they wish to communicate. The consensus view is that both mental processes occur.

Hofstede's Cultural Dimensions Theory

Geete Hofstede's cultural dimensions theory is a useful tool for understanding cultural differences. In the late 1960s and early 1970s, Hofstede conducted a multinational survey of national values, and concluded that key differences could be explained along six dimensions.

- **Individualism versus collectivism** is whether people think primarily in terms of "I" or "we."
- **Uncertainty avoidance index** is the degree to which people are uncomfortable with uncertainty and ambiguity.
- **Power distance index** is the extent to which people expect hierarchy versus equality.
- **Long-term versus short-term orientation** includes a measure of whether people are pragmatic toward change or prefer to preserve cultural values.
- **Indulgence versus restraint** refers to whether a culture promotes leisure and self-gratification.
- **Masculinity versus femininity**, in Hofstede's theory, refers to masculinity as a preference for assertive behavior, achievement, and material success and to femininity as a preference for modesty, cooperation, and caring for others.

A teacher might use Hofstede's dimension of power distance index, for example, to understand a student's degree of comfort or formality in interacting with his or her teacher. Students with a sharp sense of hierarchy might be unlikely to speak to the teacher unless spoken to or offer an opinion different than the teacher's.

Individualist vs. Collectivist Cultures

The distinction between individualist and collectivist cultures is the element of Geete Hofstede's cultural dimensions theory that has had the most influence on educational psychology. **Individualistic cultures** are those that value individual achievement and development above those of group success or cohesion. Individualistic cultures (like mainstream American culture) value freedom and individual initiative and tend to ascribe success and failure to individual traits such as motivation or intelligence. Individualist cultures encourage students to stand out from the group, and students who do not are often viewed as mediocre and underachieving. **Collectivist cultures**, on the other hand, value group harmony and social acceptance, and may see standing out as a cause for concern or stress. In a collectivist culture, education is less the means to individual achievement and fulfillment and instead a means to social acceptance and fulfilling an expected role.

Teachers need to be aware of these differences in order to understand **student motivation** and also to understand the impact of classroom activities that emphasize **individual performance** or bestow **individual praise**. It may be particularly hard for teachers raised in an individualistic culture to understand that, for some students, public individual praise may be distinctly unwanted and a source of shame.

Speech Act

A speech act is an utterance aimed at achieving something (rather than describing something), such as requesting, promising, complaining, or apologizing. The form **speech acts** take in a given language and culture are often highly standardized and routinized. For example, a native English speaker will recognize the question "Do you have a dollar?" as a request, but it may appear as a simple and out-of-context question to a non-native speaker.

Speech acts perform a pragmatic function that cannot be understood by means of literal semantic analysis. The existence of language features such as speech acts makes it imperative that a language learner also develops **cultural competence** in order to become a full and effective member of the L2 culture.

Differentiating Between Authorized and Unauthorized Immigrants

Contrary to popular opinion, a majority of school-age ELLs were born in the United States. Approximately 75% have **legal status**. Of the 25% who do not, the majority entered the United States legally, usually with a nonimmigrant or visitor visa, and then failed to leave.

The centerpiece of US immigration policy is **family reunification**. The majority of immigrants qualify to come to the US by virtue of having a close family member who is a US citizen or permanent resident. **Refugees** from war, discrimination, or natural disasters are another significant class of immigrants. Fewer immigrants qualify by virtue of having high job skills in short supply or by investing money in job-creating businesses in the US. Finally, the United States administers a **diversity lottery program** through which a limited number of high school-educated people from underrepresented countries qualify to immigrate each year.

Since the 1982 Supreme Court case *Plyler v. Doe*, school districts cannot exclude students on the basis of **immigration status**. However, unauthorized immigrants are often afraid to enroll their students in school, or to engage with school officials, out of fear of being reported to immigration authorities.

Push and Pull Factors

Everett Lee coined the terms "push factors" and "pull factors" in a 1962 book in order to classify people's motives for **migrating** (moving from one area to another) or **immigrating** (migrating from one country to another). **Push factors** are the unattractive features of a home country that compel people to leave. The most common push factors are a lack of economic opportunities, war, natural disaster, and repression or discrimination. **Pull factors** are attractive features of the destination country. The most common pull factors are economic opportunity, the prospect of reuniting with family members, and social and political freedom.

Secondary Migration and Transnational Migration

Secondary migration is the entry of people into the US from a location other than their country of birth. There are two primary types of **secondary migrants** to the US: refugees who flee their home countries to neighboring countries and from there arrange legal entry into the US, and individuals who first immigrate to countries with more lenient immigration policies, such as Canada, and then stage economic or family-based immigration to the US. The term is also used to describe the movement of refugees within the US from their original point of resettlement to locations they find more attractive. ELLs who experience secondary migration are more likely to have experienced interrupted or uneven schooling, including potential instruction in a non-English foreign language.

The term "**transnational migration**" refers to the practice of immigrants to the US maintaining close ties to their country of origin. Common expressions of these ties include regular home visits (students may spend their summers in their countries of origin), sending money or remittances to family members abroad, or making plans to return to the home country for retirement or after achieving citizenship. Transnational migration is often seen as a challenge to assimilation, but ESOL teachers can cultivate students' ongoing ties to their home countries as an educational resource.

Generation 1.5

The term "generation 1.5" refers to individuals who immigrated to the United States in their late childhood or early teen years, and thus are neither first generation (adult immigrants) nor second generation (born in the US). They are likely to have substantial remaining ties to their home countries and, unlike younger siblings born in the US, may lack citizenship and thus be vulnerable to deportation. As late arrivals to the US school system, they may resist being labeled ELLs and thus avoid integration into standard ELL programs. While many will have a basic proficiency in social English, they may lag in the acquisition of **academic language**—a deficiency they might be unwilling to address if they are out of step with their peers who immigrated earlier in life or were born in the US. At the same time, as relatively mature ELLs, they are likely to have a very good grasp of the **social and pragmatic** aspects of communication, and to infer meaning readily from context.

Approaches to ESOL Instruction

Sheltered English Instruction (SEI)

In a **sheltered instruction program** (also called sheltered English instruction), intermediate English language learners are taught the full curriculum in English and are given appropriate support to further their content learning. SEI programs explicitly target **content knowledge** and only address English development indirectly by creating highly contextualized learning environments in which students can practice their English skills. Schools with large, homogenous ELL populations may have separate SEI content classes—sheltered 8th grade life science, for example—or a teacher may simply implement sheltering teaching techniques in a classroom of mixed native English speakers and ELLs.

SEI teachers deliver the same content as ordinary content instructors but attempt to communicate that content in ways that don't depend on **student English proficiency**. Thus, they often simplify, use demonstrations and realia, and allow students to use L1 resources to supplement their learning.

States and school districts use different variations of SEI. The most widely used include the Sheltered Instruction Observation Protocol (SIOP), the Specially Designed Academic Instruction in English (SDAIE) model, Guided Language Acquisition Design (GLAD), Quality Teaching for English Learners (QTEL), and the Cognitive Academic Language Learning Approach (CALLA).

Sheltered Instruction Observation Protocol (SIOP)

The Sheltered Instruction Observation Protocol (SIOP) was originally developed in the early 1990s as a 30-item **survey** to evaluate the effectiveness of a teacher's planning, implementation, and assessment of sheltered English instruction. The survey has been demonstrated to be valid and reliable and is still widely used to evaluate sheltered English programs, even those that do not follow SIOP as an **instructional model**.

The originators followed up on the success of SIOP as a survey tool by elaborating a full-scale approach to lesson planning and delivery, intended to give content instructors a systematic approach to teaching English language learners. SIOP divides the instructional process into **eight components**: lesson preparation, building background, comprehensible input, strategies, interaction, practice and application, lesson delivery, and review and assessment.

Content-Based Instruction

Content-based instruction (**CBI**) teaches language indirectly by teaching **content in the target language**. CBI is an **umbrella term** that subsumes all teaching methods—such as sheltered instruction—that teach language and content simultaneously. In general, proponents of CBI argue that students can best learn languages indirectly, by focusing on (and being motivated by) interesting subject matter content. Some CBI programs carefully structure the subject matter content so that it systematically treats sequential features of the target language, while others are more immersive in the sense that they rely more heavily on the student's ability to infer meaning from a context-rich learning environment.

Task Complexity

Peter Skehan developed the concept of **task complexity** in the late 1990s as a framework for understanding the complexity of learning tasks in an L2 classroom. Skehan identified three factors that contribute to the complexity of a task: its **code complexity**, which is determined by language factors such as vocabulary and sentence complexity; its **cognitive complexity**, which is determined by the nature of cognitive processing required of the students and whether they are accustomed to that type of cognitive processing; and the amount of **communicative stress** involved in the task. Examples of communicative stress include time constraints or uncomfortable group dynamics. According to the theory, effective teachers will scale the scaffolding they provide to match the complexity of the task evaluated within this framework.

Task-Based Language Teaching

Task-based language teaching (**TBLT**) promotes student language learning through the accomplishment of **real-world tasks**—for example, ordering a pizza or buying a phone. Proponents argue that instruction organized this way teaches both the formal aspects of successful communication (linguistic competence) and the social aspects of communication. In some contexts, TBLT can resemble English for special purposes, in which advanced students are taught the vocabulary and rhetorical patterns particular to a given occupation or medium.

While teachers implementing TBLT might pre-teach key vocabulary needed to perform a task, the method emphasizes students' use of their whole repertoire of language skills, including the negotiation of meaning in situations where their formal knowledge of English is inadequate. Critics suggest that completion of a task is a poor measure of language improvement—once students reach a certain baseline competence, they can navigate a broad range of performative tasks, but may not be motivated or receive the instructional assistance to improve.

Creating Background Knowledge

Teaching is most effective when it builds upon what a student already knows in order to introduce something new. Accordingly, teachers learn techniques for **activating student prior knowledge**, using techniques such as brainstorming on know-want to know-learned (KWL) charts. However, ELLs may have little or no knowledge to activate about certain topics (for example, US history). In these situations, teachers may need to create background knowledge before launching the core of a lesson.

In order to **create background knowledge**, teachers might use techniques such as anticipation guides, visuals, or parallels to the students' first culture or history. Teachers may also focus on key vocabulary by using techniques such as concept maps or word walls. If the new lesson depends on students drawing connections with a previous lesson, the teacher may need to make that connection explicit; while native English speakers may pick up on cues that suggest the connection, ELLs may not.

21st Century Learning

The 21st Century Learning Initiative, launched in 1995, attempted to identify the most important skills students need to learn in order to succeed in the 21st century. The initiative's organizers strove to update the 20th century model of education, which was based on the three Rs (reading, writing, arithmetic) and the objective of providing students with content knowledge. The transformative effect of the internet suggested that the next generation would succeed not by simply *knowing* things but by knowing *how to do* things. After multiple revisions, the organizers defined the key 21st century skills as the **four Cs**: communication, critical thinking, collaboration, and creativity. These skills have been increasingly incorporated into state standards.

Teachers may need to pay specific attention to ensure that ELLs engage in the four Cs. When ELLs collaborate with native English speakers, they often get left out or left behind. In sheltered instruction content classrooms, ELLs may lack the English proficiency to easily express the higher order concepts required for critical thinking and may require specific prompts or scaffolding to engage effectively in communicative activities.

Modeling Tasks for ELLs

ESOL teachers should not rely entirely on verbal instructions when staging a classroom task or activity. Even if ELLs understand enough to begin the activity, they may lack critical procedural understanding or the contextual understanding necessary to learn from the activity. In setting up such activities, teachers should **demonstrate** the key steps using both actions and words. When possible, verbal instructions should be supplemented with **visual displays**, such as flow charts, which divide the activity or process into identifiable stages. Teachers can also supplement verbal instructions with written summaries, ideally set out in brief, stepwise format. Finally, teachers might choose to **chunk** the instructions or stages in a task, pausing the students repeatedly to check their work and understanding before providing a demonstration of the next step.

Barriers to Academic Success for ELLs

Lois Meyer's Four Barriers

Meyer identified four **loads**—or challenges requiring effort to overcome—facing ELLs in the classroom. The first is **cognitive load**—the number of unfamiliar or unpracticed concepts presented in a lesson. The second is **culture load**—the untaught, assumed cultural references embedded in a lesson which may present impediments to an ELL. The third is **language load**—the degree to which the lesson language is unfamiliar and stretches a student beyond the range of comprehensible input. Meyer's fourth category is **learning load**—the extent to which the classroom learning activity is unfamiliar or stressful to the ELL. (For example, if the ELL is asked to debate an issue with a classmate but has no prior experience with debating and is uncomfortable with the interpersonal dynamic, the activity would present a high learning load.)

Meyer's work reminds ESOL teachers of the multiplicity of factors that need to be planned or controlled in order to create an optimal classroom learning environment.

Student's Linguistic Background

A student's **relative proficiency in their native language** (L1) is a factor in L2 language development. Students proficient in L1 already possess the perceptual ability to distinguish sounds, words, and syntactical patterns. They will likely also possess certain useful cognitive skills, such as the ability to compare, generalize, and predict. In addition, there may be specific similarities between L1 and L2 that allow for positive transfer.

The **common underlying proficiency model** is based on these ideas—that the various skills and concepts developed during L1 acquisition are available for subsequent learning. The model hypothesized that all language learning draws upon a common core of cognitive-linguistic knowledge rather than knowledge segregated in the brain by language. This model has largely been confirmed by subsequent research.

Age and L2 Acquisition

The **critical period hypothesis (CPH)** argues that, due to brain development, there is an optimal age for learning a language (roughly from age two to puberty) and that a person's ability to learn languages declines over time.

While the CPH strikes many as intuitively true, subsequent research has rendered the issue more complex. There is no doubt that children and adults learn languages differently. Adults have cognitive and experiential advantages and usually make more rapid progress in syntax and grammar than do children. Children tend to enjoy more exposure to the target language. In addition, they appear to have advantages in affect and motivation. For example, the fact that adults are conscious of the learning process and are aware of the difficulty of learning languages often reduces their motivation to learn. As implicit, intuitive learners, children are less likely to be discouraged by the difficulties of learning. Further, adults tend to be more self-conscious about making mistakes, a distinct disadvantage when learning a language.

A fair conclusion might be that, while adults have more disadvantages in learning languages, these can be overcome. The one exception appears to be accent: research does sustain the claim that children acquire a native accent more often than adults.

Disability Misdiagnoses

The **Individuals with Disabilities Education Act (IDEA)** of 1975 established the right of students with disabilities to receive appropriate education tailored to their individual needs. The legislation qualifies students for what is called **special education assistance** if they do not reach age-level benchmarks in several language and mathematical competencies, including oral expression, written expression, listening comprehension, reading comprehension, and reading skill. However, IDEA specifies that these deficiencies cannot arise from **environmental variables**, including limited English proficiency or cultural differences. As many researchers have pointed out, however, many of the characteristics ELLs manifest during the normal L2 learning process resemble those of native speakers with disabilities, leading to frequent misdiagnoses.

School districts in the United States are required to have a process in place to evaluate children with potential disabilities. Student assessments are made by a team of professionals. If the assessment team, in conjunction with the child's parents, determines that a child needs special education services, the team creates an **individualized education program (IEP)** that specifies, among other things, the program accommodations, testing modifications, and counseling the child will receive.

Individuals with Disabilities Education Act

The Individuals with Disabilities Education Act (IDEA) obligates schools to provide **special education and supportive services** to students with certain **disabilities**. The law covers 13 conditions. The most commonly encountered conditions include attention deficit hyperactivity disorder (ADHD), which is subsumed under:

- Other health impairment
- Specific learning disorders (including dyslexia, dysgraphia, dyscalculia, auditory processing disorder, and nonverbal learning disability)

The other categories covered by IDEA are:

- Autism
- Emotional conditions (such as anxiety and depression)
- Speech or language impairment (such as stuttering)
- Deafness
- Hearing impairments (other than deafness)
- Deaf-blindness
- Visual impairment
- Traumatic brain injury
- Orthopedic impairment
- Intellectual disability (such as Down syndrome)
- Multiple disabilities

Review Video: Medical Conditions in Education
Visit mometrix.com/academy and enter code: 531058

Learning Disability Characteristics

The responsibility to diagnose **learning disabilities** rests with trained professionals. However, ESOL teachers should have a basic understanding of how the manifestations of learning disabilities and **L2 learning complications** differ. The most important insight is that learning disabilities very rarely manifest in just one language, and so a teacher who witnesses the problematic performance in L2 can observe how that student interacts with colleagues in L1 or potentially ask his or her parents about L1 production at home. Another general indicator of a learning disability is a language deficit that doesn't improve over time or after targeted intervention. A third is a language deficit that comes and goes—in most instances of normal L2 acquisition, once a deficit is overcome, a student will make fewer and fewer repeated errors over time. Another sign of a potential learning disability is a domain-specific deficiency—if an L2 learner performs as expected in writing exercises, for example, but lags in speech production, a disability is likely.

Review Video: Understanding Learning Disability Needs of Students
Visit mometrix.com/academy and enter code: 662775

Instrumental or Integrative and Intrinsic or Extrinsic Motivation

According to Robert Gardner's original classification, students are **instrumentally motivated** if they are learning English to achieve a specific goal, such as acquiring a job or getting into college. By contrast, they possess **integrative motivation** if they have a positive view of their future L2 community and wish to fully join it. According to Gardner, integrative motivation is more reliable and durable.

Psychologists often distinguish between **extrinsic motivation**, which is a focus on rewards or punishments; and **intrinsic motivation**, which exists when an individual wants to do something for the sake of it without concern for reward and punishment. Research shows that intrinsic motivation is more reliable, as extrinsic motivation tends to be temporary and inflationary and often shifts a learner's focus from the lesson to the reward itself.

People differ in the nature, sources, and degrees of motivation, and so it is valid to speak of motivation as a trait. However, human motivation is also heavily context- and situation-dependent, and thus motivation is also a state that can and does change.

Benjamin Bloom and the Affective Domain

Benjamin Bloom differentiated between three learning domains—the **cognitive** (thinking), **sensory** (doing), and **affective** (feeling)—and developed a **taxonomy of concepts** for each domain. His taxonomy of cognitive learning skills and associated action verbs (explain, describe, evaluate, etc.) has been widely influential. His taxonomy of the affective domain is also of interest.

Bloom identified five **processes that lead to student growth** in affective response and understanding. The first process, in order from simple to complex, is **receiving**—a passive condition that is necessary for learning but which does not by itself add value. The second process is **responding**, in which a student is attentive to learning and responds with positive emotion. Bloom's third process is **valuing**, in which a student develops preferences and commitments. In the fourth process, **organization**, a student develops a value system, combining elements to create a logical relational framework. In the final, **characterizing** phase, the student internalizes what he or she has learned and acts in principled ways according to this knowledge.

Bloom's concept serves as a reminder that education concerns more than just cognitive development and that the experiences and valuations that students encounter early in life have a lasting impact on their affective outlook.

Zoltan Dornyei's L2 Motivational Self System

Zoltan Dornyei built on the broader theory of the ideal self in proposing that L2 students draw upon three different sources of motivation. The first is the **ideal L2 self**—the image the learner has of the person he or she would like to become through the process of language learning. The second source of motivation is the **ought-to L2 self**, which is an image driven by a sense of obligation, often one imposed by others' expectations. Finally, the **L2 learning experience** captures situational motivations, the types that arise daily in the classroom. Dornyei argues that teachers should find ways to appeal to a student's ideal L2 self in order to ensure persistent and consistent motivation.

Dornyei argues that teachers must attend to motivation in different ways. First, they must create the basic motivating conditions in the classroom. Second, they must generate initial, individualized motivation. Third, they must maintain and protect that motivation. And finally, because positive self-assessment is necessary for sustained motivation, teachers must encourage students to self-monitor.

Teacher Expectations Contribute to Success

Research has demonstrated the importance of **teacher expectations** in student performance. The core finding is that teacher expectations are, to a degree, **self-fulfilling**—high expectations lead to better results. Other prescriptions are also well established: teachers should not create differential expectations based on demographic factors, they should form groups composed of all levels of language proficiency rather than marginalize low performers, they should call on low-proficiency students as often as high-proficiency ones, and they should foster a culture in which errors are seen as a normal part of the learning process.

ESOL teachers should also use their knowledge of language development and communicative competence to shape their **error-correction strategies**. Certain types of errors are natural at a given stage of language learning and will likely disappear without explicit correction; teachers can thus afford to let these pass. As a general rule, corrections involving vocabulary are easier for students to learn than corrections of grammar. And finally, teachers should focus on correcting errors that impede communication. Experts agree that error correction is less important to student success than allowing abundant opportunities for language practice and authentic communication.

Self-Efficacy

Self-efficacy is the perception people have about their competence. **Self-esteem** is a broader concept—it refers to a person's overall sense of self-approval or self-disapproval.

Attribution theory, first applied to the academic domain by the psychologist Bernard Weiner, uses the concept of self-efficacy to analyze what students believe is the cause of their success or failure on an academic task. Research shows that students tend to attribute academic outcomes to one of four general causes: ability, effort, perceived difficulty, or luck. Students with low self-efficacy tend to attribute academic outcomes to causes outside of themselves (such as difficulty and luck) and are less likely to respond constructively to academic setbacks. Students with a high sense of self-efficacy, in contrast, tend to attribute outcomes to internal causes and are likely to respond to setbacks by working harder.

Educational psychologists studying the effects of **praise** on performance have demonstrated that students perform better, at least in the long run, if they are praised for their efforts or for a specific academic result rather than for their intrinsic ability. This finding reinforces the idea that students perform best when they focus on what they can control and when they believe they can influence the outcome.

Self-Esteem

Self-esteem is an attitude of approval or disapproval toward oneself. The psychologist Jonathon Brown has created a **typology of self-esteem** that is widely used in ESOL contexts. This typology differentiates between **general** or **global self-esteem**, which is a person's broad sense of self-worth; **situational self-esteem**, which is specific to a certain domain, such as athletics, social skills, or foreign language aptitude; and **task self-esteem**, which arises in the context of performing specific tasks or activities. Research suggests that, once formed by late childhood, global self-esteem changes little over a lifetime.

Self-esteem and academic success are linked in a chicken-or-egg type of cycle: high self-esteem is linked to better academic performance, and successful performance has been shown to be the most important factor in building situational self-esteem.

Learning a foreign language poses particular challenges to self-esteem. One reason is that students often feel the gap between what they can express in L2 and what they think or feel. In other words, they feel a large gap between their genuine self and the self they can communicate.

Anxiety

Anxiety is defined as an abnormal sense of apprehension, often accompanied by physiological signs of stress. As with many features of personality, anxiety can be thought of as both a trait, something which people experience in different degrees as a background feature of their personality, and as a state, in response to a particular event or experience.

Educational psychologists often differentiate between **three types of anxiety** experienced by the second-language learner: anxiety over one's ability to communicate in L2, anxiety that peers will view one's L2 communication negatively, and anxiety about evaluations and grades. Understanding the source of a student's anxiety will help the ESOL teacher mitigate the anxiety's harmful effects.

In general, anxiety is **debilitative**—that is, it is something that detracts or distracts a student from learning. Research has shown, however, that anxiety can also be useful or **facilitative to the learning task**. Anxiety may lead to greater focus, greater effort, or a sense of competitiveness that can drive a student to mastery.

Inhibition

Inhibition is defined as the inner impediment to free expression or action. It is usually viewed negatively and is often a defense mechanism erected by individuals with low self-esteem. It is important to note, however, that the absence of inhibition can be pathological, as in the case of many mental illnesses.

Inhibition is a critical concept in language learning because of the importance of **performance** to language learning. Scholars agree that one's willingness to communicate—to seek out opportunities to communicate in L2—is a key factor in L2 learning success. Successful language learning also requires a measure of risk-taking—the willingness to make mistakes, often public ones, in learning a language.

Given the importance of production for language learning, good ESOL teachers find ways to **reduce student inhibition**. Teachers should keep the classroom affective filter low; develop a classroom group identity conducive to risk-taking; allow inhibited students to proceed stepwise toward production, recognizing the necessity of a silent period; and ensure that inhibited students experience early success and ratification.

Language Ego

The psychologist Alexander Guiora asserted that individuals learning or using a second language experience widescale changes in their perceived identity, caused by what he referred to as the **language ego**. According to this theory, a person's original identity is closely tied to their L1 competency and mastery and is challenged or disrupted by an attempt to learn an L2. Guiora used this concept to explain why children acquire second languages more readily than adults—as their egos are less full-formed and less rigid, they suffer less from the feelings of incompetence or social embarrassment inevitable in the language learning process.

Subsequent theorists introduced the notion of **thick and thin language ego boundaries**, suggesting that students with thick boundaries feel fewer inhibitions in language learning and are more comfortable with the performance activities necessary for full linguistic competence.

Affective Filter

The concept of affective filter refers to the emotional response an ELL has to a language-learning environment. An ELL's emotional state can either hinder his or her learning (in which case he or she is described as having a **high affective filter**) or promote learning (a **low affective filter**). Factors that could contribute to a high affective filter include overcorrection of errors, fear of speech performance in front of peers, or test anxiety. Teachers can lower student affective filters by being cognizant of personality differences and language development differences, ensuring that peers are supportive, communicating that errors are expected and considered to be routine, and limiting the number and significance of summative tests.

Lack of Formal School Experience

Students who lack prior formal education are likely to need additional support in the context of an ESOL program. Students who have had their schooling interrupted by war or political upheaval (such as refugees) may suffer from trauma in addition to experiencing gaps in their education. Students who have never attended school are likely to completely lack **literacy skills**, putting them far behind their peers. They will also lack basic **learning and study skills**, which many students and teachers take for granted after a certain age. While students without educational experience are often highly motivated to attend school, they also have high drop-out rates, due in part to the demotivation they experience from lagging behind their age group in educational attainment. Even when such learners make dramatic progress, they often underestimate their achievement.

Acculturation Patterns

Acculturation is the adaptation of one person or group to the culture of another, often in the context of immigration. The term implies one-way adaptation of a minority group to the culture of a majority group. If the adaptation is complete and the minority comes to resemble the majority, it is termed "**assimilation**." If a minority community resists acculturation, we speak of **preservation** of their distinct culture. The term "**transculturation**" refers to the rare phenomenon of two equally dominant cultures mixing and each adopting elements of the other.

Linguist John Schumann's acculturation model argues that a person's **success in an L2** is directly related to his or her **acculturation into the L2 culture**. If a language learner joins the dominant-language culture, they will necessarily have more L2 language experiences, resulting in greater L2 competency. Schumann theorized that a number of factors could limit or even prevent an immigrant learner's acculturation, including his or her perceptions of the L2 language community, whether he or she lived in a cultural enclave or was geographically integrated, and whether the L1 and L2 languages were linguistically similar.

Elective Bilingualism vs. Circumstantial Bilingualism

The linguist Guadalupe Valdés draws a distinction between individuals who choose to study a second language (**elective bilingualism**), often for reasons of personal gain, and those who are forced to learn a second language (**circumstantial bilingualism**), as in the case of children immigrating to an L2 country.

Elective learners of a language, Valdés argued, usually learn the second language in an **artificial environment**, such as a classroom, rather than through immersion. Although they may eventually reach proficiency, their native language will usually remain dominant. Circumstantial learners, by contrast, do not learn a language because of an individual choice but as a result of **new circumstances** and in order to survive or succeed. They are likely to achieve greater mastery of L2 over time, and L1 and L2 are likely to assume complementary roles in their lives, with either dominant in a given situation.

The distinction between elective and circumstantial learners is likely to be most relevant in a class of **adult students**. Other conceptual categories may be more important when teaching children, such as their age when they immigrated or whether they will remain resident in the US or return to another country.

Family Expectations

One of the mainstays of education research is that students are more likely to succeed if their parents hold them to **high academic expectations**. These expectations may manifest themselves in parental reinforcement and encouragement, parental involvement in school meetings and functions, or parental engagement with their child's homework. All three of these areas are potentially problematic in the case of ELLs. Setting aside the issue that cultures value education differently, especially for girls, families that seek to preserve their home cultures may inadvertently or purposefully limit a child's motivation to master L2—research clearly shows that language proficiency is affected by the degree of acculturation. More importantly, parents of ESOL students may not involve themselves in school functions or even attend meetings with teachers, either because of different cultural understandings or because of their own limited English ability. Parents with limited English may not be able to help their children with their homework. And finally, research has revealed that a vicious cycle may develop in relationships in which a child's English proficiency far outstrips that of a parent—in these cases, the differential language abilities may lead to estrangement, conflict, and even withdrawal of parental support for language learning.

Political and Institutional Factors

The **educational policies** instituted at the federal, state, and local level influence the ways in which ESOL programs are structured and administered in schools. Within the bounds of those laws, however, schools vary in their **initiatives** and **institutional approaches** to their ESOL communities.

One way in which schools may differ is the degree to which their ESOL students are **integrated** into the broader student community. Schools that celebrate diversity and promote the integration of different language communities achieve better language outcomes. Similarly, schools that **recognize and showcase minority languages and cultures** achieve greater buy-in from ESOL students—if the value of their own cultures is recognized, they are more likely to embrace a new culture. Finally, school engagement with minority cultures should not stop with the students—successful schools also engage with the **community**, inviting parents and community organizations to participate in school activities and sponsor events that showcase minority cultures.

Impact of Poverty

The effects of poverty on student performance are numerous and well documented: low-income students often lag behind their peers in cognitive abilities, experience emotional deficits (and thus fail to exhibit a full and appropriate range of emotional reactions), and experience ongoing stress, which substantially reduces their ability to learn. English language learners are disproportionately poor—by some estimates, more than 50% of ELLs come from low-income families—and thus ESOL teachers need to understand how **poverty** influences learning and how to recognize students who may be at risk of failing academically or dropping out.

Many states or school districts have specific lists of **at-risk behaviors**, such as erratic attendance, behavioral issues, apathy, negative interaction with peers, and sudden changes in behavior. The at-risk concept is controversial because many believe it is applied wrongly to entire groups of students as a form of stereotyping rather than used constructively to identify students in need of additional support.

Role of Family Involvement for ELLs

Family Involvement and Student Success

Decades of research has demonstrated the strong correlation between **family involvement** and **student success**. ELLs are disproportionately at risk for academic failure and, thus, in need of support. Therefore, securing ELL parental involvement is particularly important and difficult to achieve, given language differences and cultural differences that may discourage parents from actively involving themselves in their children's education.

In order to overcome these obstacles, teachers should get to know each student's **cultural background** and **family circumstances** relevant to building a relationship between home and school. Teachers should introduce themselves to parents and guardians and invite them to group meetings and one-on-one conferences. Teachers should establish multiple means of communication (email, phone calls, office hours) and, where feasible, translate messages into frequent L1s. Parents should be encouraged to volunteer in the classroom or chaperone field trips. Teachers should establish certain periods when parents can visit and observe the classroom. ESOL teachers with relatively homogenous student populations might sponsor information sessions during which translators are available, either to discuss concerns specific to the ESOL classroom or to provide general school-related advice and information to interested parents.

Overcoming Parental Communication Challenges

While the **parents and guardians** of students are one of the most important audiences to target with school outreach and communication strategies, they are also one of the most difficult to reach because of multiple factors. Language barriers are the most obvious, but ELL parents and guardians may also come from cultures that discourage parental involvement in schooling. ELL families are also disproportionately low-income, and parents may work long hours or multiple jobs, preventing them from attending scheduled school events.

ESOL teachers should develop proactive and multipronged **outreach strategies** to overcome these obstacles. Teachers should distribute information through multiple channels, such as emails, blogs, and newsletters sent home with students. Teachers should strive to make their students' daily activities and responsibilities visible to parents in some way.

Teachers should signal their availability and strive to be approachable. They might perform home visits if allowed. Teachers should schedule regular (monthly) meetings as well as repeatedly invite parents to attend one-on-one conferences. Teachers may consider communicating with parents through student homework folders. In all of these engagements, teachers should provide translations and interpretations when possible and strive to use simple, clear language.

Professional Development for Teachers of ELLs

Content Instructors and ESOL Instructors

While content teachers in states with high numbers of ELLs are likely to receive **professional development courses** to help them understand how to work with ELLs, a minority of states mandate such training, even though a majority of content classrooms contain at least one ELL.

ESOL teachers are often called upon—either formally or informally—to **help their colleagues** effectively reach their ELLs. ESOL teachers might help by identifying an ELL's language proficiency level or go further to suggest appropriate teaching supports, reasonable expectations, and teaching methods. They might organize multi-teacher conferences to ensure that ELL students receive consistent instruction throughout the day. ESOL teachers might usefully join parent-teacher conferences to address language concerns. Finally, ESOL teachers might either recommend ESOL-oriented professional development activities to their colleagues or, in the absence of such activities, volunteer to lead periodic training seminars.

Furthering Professional Development

The best professional development provides a teacher with new ideas and the knowledge of how to implement them in the classroom. The simplest—and likely most effective—form of professional development is **networking** with other experienced ESOL teachers, either as a peer or as a mentee. **ESOL conferences** provide the best intersection of networking with learning about ESOL research. The latter can also be accessed through professional journals and the websites of informational clearinghouses such as the Center for Applied Linguistics or the Centre for Educational Research on Languages and Literacies. **Websites** such as Colorin Colorado and Brown University's Education Alliance can be invaluable, and ESOL teachers have established numerous useful blogs, online discussion groups, and Twitter feeds. Though they are potentially expensive in terms of both cost and time, **summer workshops** often offer more systematic training and a resume credential. Finally, committed career professionals should consider doing their own **research for publication**, particularly in an aspect of ESOL that they are passionate about.

TESOL, CAL, ACTFL, NCELA, and NABE

Teachers and prospective teachers of ESOL have a number of organizations they can turn to for information and professional development.

- **TESOL (Teachers of English to Speakers of Other Languages)**: the preeminent organization in the field, offering virtual seminars, online courses, certificate programs, and meetings and conventions dedicated to the field. www.TESOL.org
- **CAL (Center for Applied Linguistics)**: a nonprofit that conducts research into language and culture, develops assessment and curriculum material, and offers training and educational resources for teachers. www.CAL.org
- **ACTFL (American Council on the Teaching of Foreign Languages)**: a membership organization promoting language teaching, with particular expertise in language testing, including for teachers pursuing bilingual certifications. www.ACTFL.org
- **NCELA (National Clearinghouse for English Language Acquisition)**: a resource site run by the US Department of Education, providing data, research, and the English Learner Toolkit, which provides guidance to state and local educators on how to fulfill federal civil rights mandates in the area of English language acquisition. www.ncela.ed.gov
- **NABE (National Association for Bilingual Education)**: a nonprofit that advocates for educational equity and provides professional development and instructional resources for ESOL teachers. www.NABE.org

Supporting Vocabulary Development

Encouraging Vocabulary Acquisition Through Reading and Writing Activities

If a new text contains unfamiliar vocabulary words that are central to the meaning and/or may be difficult to decode, a teacher may **preview** the words with the group. After introducing the topic of the text, the teacher may flip to the words, show students their spellings, and ask students to share what the words may mean based on prior knowledge and picture clues. Exposure to these words before reading will build readers' confidence and help them recognize and decode the words faster, maintaining fluency. Knowing the meanings in advance will also assist with comprehension.

When reading aloud to students, teachers may pause at new vocabulary words and model how to use context clues, prior knowledge, and picture support to decode and comprehend the new words. Students can be encouraged to use these strategies when reading independently.

Readers need repeated exposure to vocabulary words to develop automatic recognition and comprehension. Teachers may display classroom charts containing vocabulary words and their meanings, possibly using picture clues for young readers.

Students can also be encouraged to incorporate vocabulary words in their own writing. Word walls or charts containing the words can assist students with spelling and remembering the meanings of the words.

Helping Readers Recognize and Explore the Meanings of Unknown Vocabulary Words

First, it is important for students to identify unknown vocabulary words when reading. Readers who are not monitoring their own comprehension may decode the words and continue reading, even if they do not understand their meanings. Teachers can model how to stop when they reach words they don't understand, even if they can decode them, and encourage students to do the same.

Next, readers need to determine which unknown words are central to the meanings of the text and worth exploring further. This is important because there may be many unknown words and, if readers stop extensively at each one, fluency and comprehension may be interrupted. Therefore, students can be encouraged to consider whether or not they can comprehend the sentences and overall meanings of the texts without devoting more energy to these particular unknown words.

If readers determine that the unknown words are central to the meaning of the text, they can be encouraged to use strategies such as using context clues, looking for known roots or affixes, or consulting dictionaries. Overall, readers should be encouraged to monitor their own reading and comprehension and determine when to apply known strategies.

Review Video: Acknowledging the Unknown When Reading
Visit mometrix.com/academy and enter code: 712339

Supporting Vocabulary Acquisition and Use Through Listening and Speaking

Young children begin their vocabulary development through listening well before they begin to read and write. Through listening to family members, caregivers, and others, children develop their meaning (oral) vocabularies. These are words that children understand when heard and eventually use in their own speech. These vocabularies can be developed by talking to the children frequently and for a variety of purposes, reading to them, exposing them to songs, rhymes, and poems, and many other language activities.

Children continue to build vocabulary through listening and speaking activities when they begin school. Teachers can read aloud to students often, varying the genres and purposes for listening. Engaging students in discussions about what was read aloud can give students a purpose for listening and opportunities to use text-related vocabulary in their own oral responses. Teachers can also incorporate key vocabulary words in class discussions.

Students should also have frequent opportunities to speak in the classroom. In addition to informal class discussions, students can present projects to classmates and explain their thinking during problem-solving. They should be encouraged to use content-specific vocabulary when appropriate.

Teaching Word Analysis Skills and Vocabulary to English Language Learners

Focusing on cognates is one way to help build word analysis skills and vocabulary for English language learners (ELLs). Cognates are words in different languages that share the same roots. For example, the English word *directions* and the Spanish word *direcciones* are cognates. ELLs can be encouraged to look for known parts of unfamiliar words. They can then use knowledge about the meanings in their native languages to determine the meanings of the English words. This strategy builds upon ELLs' prior knowledge. Explicitly teaching common roots and affixes can help ELLs quickly increase their vocabularies as well.

Scaffolding should also be provided when introducing ELLs to new words. This can be done using visuals that help demonstrate the meanings of the words. Real objects, pictures, and gestures can all be used. Graphic organizers can also be used to show how new words are related and how they connect to specific topics.

Teaching Word Analysis Skills to Struggling Readers

Struggling readers require consistent and explicit instruction, which often includes a combination of both whole-class instruction and targeted individual or small-group instruction daily. They also need frequent opportunities to manipulate words. Both building and breaking apart related words using letter tiles can help struggling readers develop understandings of patterns in the ways words are made.

Struggling readers can also benefit from explicit instruction on chunking words into component parts. Depending on the ages and prior knowledge of the students, this might include identifying syllable patterns, onsets and rimes, roots and affixes, or smaller sight words that are part of the larger words.

Struggling readers also need frequent opportunities to practice their word analysis skills using real texts. After explicit instruction on recognizing prefixes in words, for example, students can read texts that contain several prefixes. They can identify these words and their meanings. This will help them transfer their word analysis skills to realistic contexts. Scaffolding can be provided through anchor charts, graphic organizers, and teacher support during these independent reading experiences to provide reminders of known strategies.

Teaching Word Analysis Skills to Highly Proficient Readers

Proficient readers still have a need for differentiated reading instruction, even if they are meeting or exceeding grade-level expectations. They can benefit from developing the same word analysis skills as other readers, such as looking for known parts in unfamiliar vocabulary words, breaking words into components, and finding relationships between the meanings and spellings of different words. These strategies should be presented using materials and interactions that are both engaging and appropriately challenging for proficient readers. Use of texts that have some unfamiliar words will ensure that readers have opportunities to apply these strategies and continue to increase their vocabularies. Using assessments to determine reading levels or teaching readers to self-select appropriate texts can help ensure that the selected materials offer some challenges and learning opportunities for proficient readers.

Because proficient readers often devote less energy to decoding words than struggling readers, they are able to allocate more energy to reading comprehension, analysis, and reflection. Proficient readers can be asked to evaluate authors' word choices and discuss the effect that certain words have on the meaning or tone of the texts.

Assisting Readers with Comprehension Using Graphophonics, Syntax, and Semantics

Proficient readers understand how to use a variety of reading strategies and are able to apply them to different situations as needed. The types of text a student reads may differ greatly in terms of vocabulary, quality of context clues, picture support, and connections to the reader's prior knowledge. Therefore, the strategies that work to determine an unknown word in any one sentence or text may not work as well in another.

Decoding words using **graphophonic** clues is a strategy where readers consider the letter-sound relationships in the word. Another strategy is to consider **syntax**, or how the word sounds in the sentence and fits into the overall sentence structure. A third strategy is to consider **semantics**, or the meaning of the text, to guess the unknown word. To be correct, a guessed word should fit all three criteria. It should look right (graphophonics), sound right (syntax), and make sense (semantics).

When they come to unknown words, proficient readers try one strategy first and then cross-check their guesses using other strategies. If they realize they have made errors, they self-correct. Using a combination of these strategies helps ensure that readers make sense out of what they are reading.

Helping Beginning Readers Use Context Clues to Figure out Unknown Words

Like older readers, beginning readers also turn to context clues to figure out unknown words. The types of context clues available to beginning readers may differ, however, because the texts they read often contain simple sentence structures and picture support.

One strategy beginning readers can use is to look for picture clues. When a reader is stuck on an unfamiliar word, the teacher can guide the student to look to the picture for hints.

Another strategy is to ask the reader to skip the unknown word and read the rest of the sentence. After finishing the sentence, the teacher can ask the reader to fill in the blank with a word that makes sense. Context clues found in the rest of the sentence can often help the reader guess the missing word. If the reader guesses a word that makes sense but does not match the text, the teacher can guide the student to look for phonetic clues within the word, such as the first sound, and try again.

Texts for beginning readers sometimes contain other context clues, such as rhymes and repetitive vocabulary, that can be used to figure out unknown words.

> **Review Video: Reading Comprehension: Using Context Clues**
> Visit mometrix.com/academy and enter code: 613660

Helping Students Use Context Clues to Figure out the Meanings of Unknown Words

Teachers should explicitly introduce students to different types of context clues, including definition, antonym, synonym, and inference clues. Examples of sentences containing each type can be provided, and students can be asked to mark the clues, label each type, and explain the meanings of the unknown words. They can also be asked to find examples of each of these types of context clues in other texts. An anchor chart listing the different types of context clues and examples of each can also be posted in the classroom.

Students can also be given sets of words that are related in some way, such as pairs of synonyms or antonyms. They can be asked to write sentences that incorporate the word pairs, creating context clues for other readers. The students can then share their sentences with peers, asking them to identify the context clues and meanings of the unknown words.

Importance of Knowing Latin and Greek Roots

Many English words are formed from Latin and Greek **roots**. Therefore, recognizing these roots and knowing their meanings can help readers with both decoding and comprehending.

When readers automatically recognize Latin and Greek roots, they will be able to quickly decode the main parts of words that contain them. If they automatically recognize the affixes as well, they will be able to break words into parts and decode them effortlessly. This will allow the readers to maintain speed and fluency while reading.

The roots also hold most of the meaning in words and form the bases of entire word families. Knowing the meanings of these roots will help readers quickly determine the meanings of many newly encountered words, especially if they also know the meanings of any attached affixes. For example, if readers know that the Latin root *port* means to carry, they will have clues about the meanings of the words *transport, transportation*, *import*, and *export* as well.

Helping Readers Identify Latin and Greek Roots in Unfamiliar Words

When teaching readers about Latin and Greek roots in English words, one strategy is to help them see the relationships between words in the same word families. This can be done by creating charts or other visual representations of word families and their meanings. For example, a root and its meaning can be written in the middle of a web, and words containing the root and their meanings can be written in circles branching off from the root.

Another strategy is to create three sets of cards, including prefixes, suffixes, and roots. Students can experiment with combining the sets of cards to try to form real words. When real words are created, students can explain their meanings. Students can also be given words containing prefixes, roots, and suffixes. They can be asked to break the words into their components and identify the meanings of each part.

Additionally, students can be encouraged to locate words containing Latin and Greek roots in the texts they read independently. They can use their knowledge of the roots to define the words.

Approaches to Vocabulary Learning

- A **definitional approach** to vocabulary learning is the most traditional. Students are either provided definitions of words or look them up in a dictionary, and they are drilled until they commit the meanings to memory.
- A **structural approach** to vocabulary learning emphasizes the morphological features of words—the roots, prefixes, and suffixes. Once students learn the recurring morphemes in English, they can deduce the meaning of a word in isolation without relying on its context.
- A **contextual approach** to vocabulary learning provides the students with multiple examples of a word used in realistic contexts, allowing them to infer the meaning without resorting to a dictionary or an explicit definition.
- A **categorical approach** to vocabulary learning groups words into categories based on a semantic similarity. For example, a student might be given a list of words associated with driving a car, such as "steering wheel," "to brake," "to accelerate," and "gear shift."

- A **mnemonic approach** to vocabulary learning builds associations between target words and mental images so that hearing a target word evokes the image, facilitating recall of the word's meaning.

Review Video: Types of Vocabulary Learning (Broad and Specific)
Visit mometrix.com/academy and enter code: 258753

Role of Non-Contextual Strategies in Vocabulary Development

Non-contextual strategies are used when new vocabulary is learned without seeing or hearing the words in context. For example, teachers may give students lists of new vocabulary words they have not yet encountered in texts. The teachers may ask students to define the words, use them in sentences, and memorize them. Quizzes may then be given in which students must match the words to their definitions or provide examples of the terms.

There are times teachers may use non-contextual vocabulary strategies, such as when students are learning content-specific words that are not often found naturally in texts. When studying parts of speech, for example, teachers may have students memorize the definitions of *noun*, *verb*, and *adjective*. These words are important for students' understanding of sentence structure, yet students are not likely to encounter these words written in texts with contextual clues. However, it is recommended that teachers do use contextual strategies whenever possible.

Students can be taught to use tools such as dictionaries to define unknown words when contextual clues are not available. They can be prompted to draw pictures to explain word meanings or use graphic organizers to show the relationships among words.

Role of Contextual Strategies in Vocabulary Development

Contextual strategies are used to determine the meanings of unknown vocabulary words when they are encountered in context. The ability to use these strategies to quickly determine word meanings is important for both reading fluency and comprehension. Because words can have multiple meanings, readers also need to use contextual strategies to determine which meaning makes sense in a given sentence.

Teachers can explicitly teach students about the different types of contextual clues often found in sentences. They can encourage students to highlight the words and phrases that provide clues about meanings of the vocabulary words.

Contextual clues often include synonyms or antonyms for the unknown vocabulary words. Therefore, when introducing new words, teachers can assist students with creating lists of synonyms and antonyms. Teachers can also ask students to solve analogies or determine which word does not belong when given a group of related words. These activities will help students recognize synonyms and antonyms and understand relationships among words when they are encountered in context.

Criteria for Selecting Vocabulary Words for Instruction

Vocabulary words can be divided into three tiers. Teachers should consider these tiers when determining which words to focus on during instruction.

- **Tier one words** are common words used in everyday speech. They are typically learned by the early grades through normal conversation. Explicit instruction on the meanings of these words is seldom needed.
- **Tier two words** are found in both fiction and nonfiction texts and are common enough that readers will likely encounter them in multiple texts. Tier two words carry a lot of meaning and can negatively affect comprehension if they are not understood by readers. When deciding which tier two words to focus on, teachers should consider how the words affect the overall meanings of the texts and their morphologies. They should consider if students will be able to form connections between these words and other words, helping them understand unfamiliar words encountered in the future.
- **Tier three words** are mostly found in nonfiction texts and are domain-specific. These words are important for understanding the texts and their domains. Because students are unlikely to have encountered these words before, explicit instruction is needed. This often includes pre-teaching the words and analyzing them in context.

Chapter Quiz

Ready to see how well you retained what you just read? Scan the QR code to go directly to the chapter quiz interface for this study guide. If you're using a computer, simply visit the bonus page at **mometrix.com/bonus948/nystceeas** and click the Chapter Quizzes link.

Students with Disabilities and Other Special Learning Needs

Transform passive reading into active learning! After immersing yourself in this chapter, put your comprehension to the test by taking a quiz. The insights you gained will stay with you longer this way. Scan the QR code to go directly to the chapter quiz interface for this study guide. If you're using a computer, simply visit the bonus page at **mometrix.com/bonus948/nystceeas** and click the Chapter Quizzes link.

Types of Disabilities

Medical disabilities include problems related to diseases, illnesses, trauma, and genetic conditions. **Physical disabilities** include problems related to fine and gross motor skills and can include sensory input or sensory perception disorders. Medical and physical disabilities often manifest with other disabilities, such as **learning disabilities**. Medical disabilities that affect educational performance usually fall under the IDEA's "other health impairment" or "traumatic brain injury" categories. Students with physical disabilities, such as cerebral palsy, can be eligible for special education under the IDEA's "orthopedic impairment" category. However, for either medical or physical disabilities to qualify, they must **adversely affect educational performance**. For example, a student with cerebral palsy would not be eligible for special education or an IEP if the disability does not affect educational performance. The student would receive accommodations and modifications under a 504 plan.

Review Video: Medical Conditions in Education
Visit mometrix.com/academy and enter code: 531058

Low-Incidence Disabilities and High-Incidence Disabilities

Low-incidence disabilities account for up to 20% of all students' disabilities. Students with low-incidence disabilities have sometimes received assistance for their disabilities starting from an early age. **Low-incidence disabilities** include intellectual disabilities, multiple disabilities, hearing impairments, orthopedic impairments, other health impairments, visual impairments, certain autism spectrum conditions, deaf-blindness, traumatic brain injury, and significant developmental delays. **High-incidence disabilities** account for up to 80% of all students' disabilities. While students with high-incidence disabilities present with academic, social, communication, or behavioral problems they can often be held to the same standards as their regular education peers. Children with high-incidence disabilities may perform at the same capacities as their similar-aged peers but have deficits in reading, math, writing, handwriting, or maintaining attention. High-incidence disabilities include speech and language impairments, learning disabilities, attention deficit hyperactivity disorder, emotional disorders, mild intellectual disabilities, certain autism spectrum conditions, and cognitive delays.

Interventions for Students with Physical Disabilities

A physical disability refers to any disability that limits **gross mobility** and prevents **normal body movement**. For example, muscular dystrophy is a physical disability that weakens muscles over time. Students with physical disabilities require early interventions and should begin to receive them before grade school. When students with physical disabilities enter grade school, they may receive interventions and related services if they qualify for special education and receive **individualized education programs (IEPs)** or **504 plans**. When physical disabilities do not affect the students' academic success, they may be put on 504 plans to receive appropriate related services, accommodations, or modifications. When physical disabilities are present with other disabilities or the physical disabilities affect academic performance, students may be put on IEPs and receive appropriate related services, accommodations, and modifications. Teachers, intervention specialists, physiotherapists, occupational therapists, and speech language pathologists work as a team in implementing appropriate accommodations, modifications, and related services to assist students with physical disabilities.

Working with Students with Physical Disabilities

Students with physical disabilities should be included in **general education classrooms** with accommodations if their disabilities do not coexist with other disabilities, such as learning disabilities. IDEA states that students must be assigned to a classroom that conforms with the student's least restrictive environment, which generally means the general education classroom, unless appropriate accommodations cannot be made. If sufficient accommodations or modifications may are not able to be made within the general education, a student may be placed in a more specialized environment that provides for his or her particular needs. In any of these settings, it is essential for educators to practice **instructional strategies** that facilitate the learning processes and accommodate the needs of students with physical disabilities. Classrooms should be arranged so they can be **navigated** easily by everyone. This includes giving students using wheelchairs adequate aisle space and work space. **Partner work** is helpful for students with physical disabilities, who may struggle with handwriting or using keyboards. Partners can assist these students with skills like note-taking, which may be difficult for students with physical disabilities. Additionally, assignments can include **accommodations** or **modifications** to meet the specific needs of students with physical disabilities. For example, text-to-speech software can be provided for students who struggle with using regular keyboards.

Accommodations and Modifications

Students **with speech, language, visual,** or **hearing impairments** (including **deafness**) that adversely affect their educational performance receive **accommodations**, modifications, and related services specific to their disabilities. Students with these impairments may be educated alongside peers and provided with related services outside of the general education classroom. Accommodations, modifications, and related services are provided based on the severity of the disability.

An **orthopedic impairment (OI)** severely hinders mobility or motor activity. Accommodations, modifications, and related services in the classroom environment may be appropriate for students with OI. Students with **intellectual disabilities (ID)**, such as Down syndrome, often need supports in place for communication, self-care, and social skills. The educational implications of a **traumatic brain injury (TBI)** are unique to the individual and are therefore treated on a case-by-case basis. Students with **multiple disabilities (MD)** have needs that cannot be met in any one program. Sometimes their needs are so great that they must be educated in partial inclusion or self-contained settings.

Disability Categories in the Individuals with Disabilities Education Act (IDEA)

- **Specific Learning Disabilities (SLD)** is the umbrella term for children who struggle with issues in their abilities to read, write, speak, listen, reason, or do math.
- **Other Health Impairment (OHI)** is another umbrella term for a disability that limits a child's strength, energy, or alertness.

- **Autism Spectrum Disorder (ASD)** is a disability that mostly affects a child's social and communication skills, and sometimes behavior.
- **Emotional Disturbance (ED)** is a disability category for a number of mental disorders.
- **Speech or Language Impairment** covers children with language impairments.
- **Visual Impairment or Blindness** is a disability category for children with visual impairments that significantly impair their abilities to learn.
- **Deafness** is the category for students who cannot hear even with a hearing aid.
- **Hearing Impairment** describes hearing loss that is not a pervasive as deafness. This is distinguished from deafness categorically as the types of interventions needed are very different.
- **Deaf-Blindness** cover children diagnosed with both deafness and blindness.
- Those with **Orthopedic Impairments** have impairments to their bodies that interfere with the performance of daily living skills.
- An **Intellectual Disability** is the diagnosis for children with below-average intellectual abilities or intelligence quotients (IQ).
- **Traumatic Brain Injury (TBI)** covers children who have suffered from TBIs.
- **Multiple Disabilities** as a category means a child has more than one disability defined by IDEA and requires educational interventions that go beyond standard interventions for one category.

> **Review Video: Understanding Learning Disability Needs of Students**
> Visit mometrix.com/academy and enter code: 662775

Specific Learning Disability

Early Indications of a Specific Learning Disability

Early indications of SLDs can include medical history, problems with speech acquisition, problems with socialization, academic delays, and behavioral delays. Delays in certain milestones may indicate learning disabilities, but these delays may also be due to other causes. Premature birth, serious childhood illnesses, frequent ear infections, and sleep disorders are **medical factors** that can influence the development of learning disabilities. Children that develop SLDs may demonstrate early delays in **speech**. Late speech development, pronunciation problems, and stuttering may indicate SLDs, but they may also be issues that are unrelated to SLDs and can be addressed by individualized speech instruction. Students with SLDs may also have problems adjusting **socially** and may demonstrate social skills that are not age appropriate. Depending on when the children enter academic settings, they may demonstrate academic delays compared to similar-aged peers. These delays are usually determined using formal and informal assessments in educational settings. **Behaviors** such as hyperactivity or difficulty following directions may also indicate a child has an SLD. However, these indicators do not definitely mean that a child has a learning disability, and some of the indicators overlap with characteristics of other disabilities.

Instructional Strategies for Teaching Students with Specific Learning Disabilities

While there is no one strategy that works effectively with all students with specific learning disabilities, there are some strategies that tend to produce **positive outcomes** for these students. Direct instruction, learning strategy instruction, and a multi-sensory approach are three large-scale interventions that can be used to promote student learning. **Direct instruction** is teacher-driven instruction that targets specific skills; this is sometimes delivered in resource rooms. **Learning strategy instruction** is a method for teaching students with disabilities different tools and techniques useful for learning new content or skills. This includes techniques like chunking the content, sequencing tasks, and small group instruction. A **multi-sensory approach** ensures that students are receiving and interacting with new information and skills using more than one sense at a time. This approach is helpful for students with learning disabilities because it targets many different ways of learning.

Dyslexia and Dysgraphia Disorders

Students with dyslexia are eligible for special education under the specific learning disability category in the Individuals with Disabilities Education Act if their educational performance is significantly impacted by their disabilities. **Dyslexia** is a permanent condition that makes it difficult for people to read. This affects reading accuracy, fluency, and comprehension. Dyslexia also generalizes to difficulties in the content areas of writing, mathematics, and spelling. Children who have dyslexia often have difficulties with **phonemic awareness skills** and **decoding**. It is not a disability that affects vision or the way people see letters. Dyslexia may coexist with other conditions such as **dysgraphia**, which is a disorder that causes issues with written expression. With dysgraphia, children often struggle with holding pencils and writing letters accurately. It is difficult for students with dysgraphia to distinguish shapes, use correct letter spacing, read maps, copy text, understand spelling rules, and more.

Review Video: Phonics (Encoding and Decoding)
Visit mometrix.com/academy and enter code: 821361

Sensory Processing Disorders

A person with a deficit in the brain's ability to interpret sensory information has a sensory processing disorder (**SPD**). In people without SPD, their brain receptors can interpret sensory input and then they demonstrate appropriate reactions. In people with SPD, their sensory input is blocked from brain receptors, resulting in abnormal reactions. Previously known as a sensory integration disorder, SPD is not a disability specifically defined or eligible under the Individuals with Disabilities Education Act (IDEA). However, many students with disabilities defined by the IDEA, like autism, also experience some sort of sensory processing disorder. Students with SPD may display **oversensitive or under-sensitive responses** to their environments, stimuli, and senses. They may not understand physical boundaries, such as where their bodies are in space, and may bump into things and demonstrate clumsiness. These students may get upset easily, throw tantrums, demonstrate high anxiety, and not handle changes well.

Importance of Enforcing Word Recognition

Many students with specific learning disabilities demonstrate **deficits in their reading abilities**. This includes **word recognition abilities**. Teaching **word identification** is important for these students because developing age-appropriate word recognition skills is one of the essential building blocks for creating efficient readers. Children who do not develop adequate reading skills in elementary school are generally below average readers as they age in school. Most districts and teachers use **basal reading programs** that teach word recognition and phonics. Teachers often supplement basal reading programs with **instructional programs** that can be used at home and at school. These are especially useful for students with disabilities or students who are at risk and struggle with word recognition abilities. Elements of basal and supplementary reading programs include instruction for helping students make connections between letters and sounds, opportunities to become comfortable with reading, alphabetic knowledge, phonemic awareness, letter-sound correlations, word identification strategies, spelling, writing, and reading fluency.

Other Health Impairments

Qualifications to Be Eligible for Special Education Under the Category of OHI

The category of other health impairment (**OHI**) under the Individuals with Disabilities Education Act (IDEA) indicates that a child has **limited strength, vitality, or alertness**. This includes hyper-alertness or hypo-alertness to environmental stimuli. In order to be eligible for special education under this category according to the IDEA, the disability must **adversely affect educational performance**. It must also be due to **chronic or acute health problems**, such as attention deficit disorder (ADD), attention deficit hyperactivity disorder (ADHD), diabetes, epilepsy, heart conditions, hemophilia, lead poisoning, leukemia, nephritis, rheumatic fever, sickle cell anemia, or Tourette's syndrome. Since the OHI category encompasses a number of different disabilities, teachers and parents must rely on a student's individualized education program to ensure that individual academic needs are met and appropriate accommodations and modifications are provided.

Educational Implications for Students with ADHD or ADD

The Individuals with Disabilities Education Act (IDEA) does **not** recognize attention deficit hyperactivity disorder (ADHD) or attention deficit disorder (ADD) in any of its 13 major disability categories. Students may be diagnosed with ADHD or ADD by a physician, but this diagnosis is not enough to qualify them for **special education services**. When ADHD or ADD are present with an IDEA-recognized disability, the student qualifies for special education services under that disability. A student whose ability to learn is affected by ADHD or ADD can receive services with a 504 plan in place. **Section 504 of the Rehabilitation Act of 1973** requires that any child whose disability affects a major life activity receive appropriate **accommodations** and **modifications** in the learning environment. Parents who think a child's ADHD or ADD adversely affects educational functioning may request a formal evaluation to be performed by the school. If the child is found to qualify for special education services, they then receive services under the IDEA's **other health impairment** category.

ADHD and ADD

Children with **attention deficit hyperactivity disorder (ADHD)** may demonstrate hyperactivity, inattention, and impulsivity. However, they may demonstrate hyperactivity and inattention only or hyperactivity and impulsivity only. Children with **attention deficit disorder (ADD)** demonstrate inattention and impulsivity but not hyperactivity. Students with either ADHD or ADD may have difficulties with attention span, following instructions, and concentrating to the point that their educational performance is affected. Since ADD and ADHD symptoms are common among children, their presence does not necessarily indicate that a child has ADD or ADHD. ADD and ADHD are not caused by certain environmental factors, such as diet or watching too much television. Symptoms may be exacerbated by these factors, but the causes can be heredity, chemical imbalances, issues with brain functions, environmental toxins, or prenatal trauma, such as the mother smoking or drinking during pregnancy.

Autism Spectrum Disorder

Autism is a **spectrum disorder**, which means the characteristics associated with the disability vary depending on the student. However, there are common repetitive and patterned behaviors associated with communication and social interactions for this population of students. Students with autism may demonstrate delayed or different speech patterns, the inability to understand body language or facial expressions, and the inability to exhibit appropriate speech patterns, body language, or facial expressions. In a classroom environment, students with autism may demonstrate **repetitive behaviors** that are distracting, such as hand flapping or making vocalizations. Some students with autism demonstrate **preoccupation** with doing activities, tasks, or routines in certain ways. This preoccupation can lead to difficulties when the students are asked to make changes to activities, tasks, or routines. Furthermore, some students with autism prefer to **participate** in a limited range of activities and may get upset when asked to participate in activities outside of their self-perceived ranges. This preference for a limited range of activities may even translate into repetitive behaviors or obsessive and fanatic focus on particular topics. Extreme interest in one topic can lead to disruptions when students with autism are asked to speak or write about different topics.

Concurrent Autism Spectrum Disorder and Other Learning Disabilities

Misinformation about autism spectrum disorder (ASD) and its relation to other learning disabilities runs rampant within school communication and needs clarification to prevent harmful stereotyping of students. ASD, as a spectrum disorder, means that the way it presents varies widely and does not always affect students in the same ways. Autism spectrum disorder is frequently confused with intellectual disabilities (ID), which is when an individual has a low IQ; however, students with ASD can have IQs ranging from significantly delayed to above average or gifted. ASD is also distinctive in that it largely involves difficulties with social understanding and communication, as well as fixations on repetitive routines and behaviors. It is important for an educational professional to understand the difference between ASD and other types of disabilities that commonly co-occur or which have overlapping symptoms. For instance, students with learning disabilities and students with ASD may both have challenges with reading nonverbal cues, staying organized, and expressing themselves, but that does not mean that they have the same underlying conditions or needs. The professional educational community must be aware and cautious when describing various disabilities to prevent the spread of misinformation and harmful stereotyping.

Early Signs of a Child Having ASD

Early signs of **autism spectrum disorder (ASD)** include impairments or delays in social interactions and communication, repetitive behaviors, limited interests, and abnormal eating habits. Students with ASD typically do not interact in conversations in the same ways as similar-aged peers without ASD. They may demonstrate inability to engage in pretend play and may pretend they don't hear when being spoken to. Hand flapping, vocal sounds, or compulsive interactions with objects are repetitive behaviors sometimes demonstrated by students with ASD. They may only demonstrate interest in talking about one topic or interacting with one object. They may also demonstrate self-injurious behavior or sleep problems, in addition to having a limited diet of preferred foods. **Early intervention** is key for these students in order to address and improve functioning. These students may also benefit from **applied behavior analysis** to target specific behaviors and require speech and language therapy, occupational therapy, social skills instruction, or other services geared toward improving intellectual functioning.

Characteristics of Social Skill Delays in Students with ASD

Autism spectrum disorder (ASD) is a disability that can affect a student's social, communication, and behavioral abilities. **Social skill delays and deficits** are common for students with ASD. Social skill delays go hand in hand with **communication limitations** for students with ASD. This includes conversational focus on one or two narrow topics or ideas, making it difficult for them to hold two-way conversations about things that do not interest them. Some students with ASD engage in repetitive language or echolalia or rely on standard phrases to communicate with others. Their **speech and language skills** may be delayed compared to their similar-aged peers. This may also impact their abilities to engage in effective conversations. The **nonverbal skills** of students with ASD may also be misinterpreted, such as avoiding eye contact while speaking or being spoken to.

EARLY COMMUNICATION AND SOCIAL SKILL DELAYS IN STUDENTS WITH ASD

Students with delays in communication development often need and receive some type of assistance or instruction with communication and social skills. Early intervention for these students is key, as communication difficulties may be a symptom **of autism spectrum disorder (ASD)**. For students with ASD, the need for communication and social skills instruction varies depending on the individual student. Key characteristics of **early communication difficulties** for a student with ASD include not responding to his or her name, not pointing at objects of interest, avoiding eye contact, not engaging in pretend play, delayed speech or language skills, or repeating words or phrases. Children with ASD may also exhibit overreaction or underreaction to environmental stimuli. Key characteristics of **early social skill difficulties** for a student with ASD may include preferring to play alone, trouble understanding personal feelings or the feelings of others, not sharing interests with others, and difficulty with personal space boundaries. Infants with ASD may not respond to their names and demonstrate reduced babbling and reduced interest in people. Toddlers with ASD may demonstrate decreased interest in social interactions, difficulty with pretend play, and a preference for playing alone.

SOCRATIC METHOD FOR STUDENTS WITH ASD

With the Socratic method of teaching, students are **guided** by their teachers in their own educational discovery learning processes. This involves students intrinsically seeking knowledge or answers to problems. This method can be helpful for facilitating and enhancing the **social and emotional abilities** of students with disabilities, particularly autism spectrum disorder (ASD). The Socratic method requires **dialogue** in order to successfully facilitate the teacher/student guided learning process. This is beneficial for students with ASD, who generally struggle with appropriate communication and social skills. This method emphasizes **information seeking and communication skills** by engaging students in class discussions, assignment sharing, and group work. Communication for information-seeking purposes is often a deficit of students with ASD. Sharing of ideas is a concept that develops naturally in guided learning and often requires flexibility in the thought process, another skill that students with ASD struggle with. These skills can be taught to and reinforced in students with and without disabilities in order to develop skills essential to lifelong learning processes.

FOSTERING THE COMMUNICATION DEVELOPMENT OF STUDENTS WITH ASD

Students with **autism spectrum disorder (ASD)** vary in their need for communication and social skill assistance and instruction. Some students with ASD may demonstrate slight to extreme delays in language; difficulty sustaining conversations; and the inability to understand body language, tone of voice, and facial expressions. Since ASD is a **spectrum disorder**, there typically is no single instructional strategy or technique that works for all students with the disorder. Some **evidence-based strategies** are effective for teaching appropriate communication skills to students with ASD. **Applied behavior analysis (ABA)** is an evidence-based strategy that involves providing an intervention and analyzing its effectiveness for a student with ASD. **Discrete trial training (DTT)** is a teaching strategy that is more structured than ABA. It focuses on teaching and reinforcing skills in smaller increments. **Pivotal response treatment (PRT)** is an ABA-derived approach that focuses more on meaningful reinforcement when generally positive behaviors occur. Where ABA targets very specific tasks, PRT targets behaviors categorically or more generally. Furthermore, instead of using an unrelated, supplemented reward system, such as giving candy for completing a task, the rewards used should be related to the desired behavior. For instance, suppose a targeted goal is to have the individual work on politely asking for things generally. The PRT-based reward involved might be something more related like giving the individual the toy or desired object as a reward for asking for it.

Emotional Disturbances

A diagnosis of an emotional disturbance (**ED**) can also be referred to as a **behavioral disorder** or **mental illness**. Causes of emotional disturbances are generally unclear. However, heredity, brain disorders, and diet are some factors that influence the development of emotional disturbances. The emotional disturbance category includes psychological disorders, such as anxiety disorders, bipolar disorder, eating disorders, and obsessive-compulsive disorder. Children who have emotional disturbances that affect their educational performance are eligible for **special education** under IDEA. Indicators of emotional disturbances include hyperactivity, aggression, withdrawal, immaturity, and academic difficulties. While many children demonstrate these indicators throughout their development, a strong indicator of an emotional disturbance is a **prolonged demonstration** of these behaviors.

Issues Students with Emotional Disturbances Experience in the Instructional Setting

Students with the diagnosis of emotional disturbance as defined by the IDEA require **emotional and behavioral support** in the classroom. Students with ED may also require **specialized academic instruction** in addition to behavioral and emotional support. The amount of support given varies according to the needs of individual students. These students also need **scaffolded instruction** in social skills, self-awareness, self-esteem, and self-control. Students with ED often exhibit behaviors that impede their learning or the learning of others. **Positive behavioral interventions and supports (PBIS)** is a preventative instructional strategy that focuses on promoting positive behaviors in students. With PBIS, teachers or other professionals make changes to students' environments in order to decrease problem behaviors. PBIS involves collecting information on a problem behavior, identifying positive interventions to support the student before behaviors escalate, and implementing supports to decrease targeted negative behaviors. Supports can be implemented schoolwide or in the classroom. However, for students with ED, **classroom supports** are more effective because they can be individualized.

Speech and Language Impairments

Speech and language impairments, sometimes referred to as **communication disorders**, are disabilities recognized by the Individuals with Disabilities Education Act. Students diagnosed with communication disorders are eligible for special education if they qualify for services. Early indicators of communication disorders include but are not limited to:

- Not smiling or interacting with others
- Lack of babbling or cooing in infants
- Lack of age-appropriate comprehension skills
- Speech that is not easily understood
- Issues with age-appropriate syntax development
- Issues with age-appropriate social skills
- Deficits in reading and writing skills
- Beginning or ending words with incorrect sounds
- Hearing loss
- Stuttering

These indicators may also be linked to other disabilities, such as hearing impairments or autism spectrum disorder. Although prolonged demonstration of these indicators may suggest communication disorders, some children demonstrate delays and then self-correct over time.

Facilitating Learning for Students with Speech or Language Impairments

In order to teach students with speech or language impairments, also referred to as **communication disorders**, teachers and other professionals can use the **strategies** listed below:

- Use visuals and concrete examples to help students with communication disorders take in new information. Link the visuals with spoken words or phrases.
- Use visuals or photographs to introduce or reinforce vocabulary.
- Use repetition of spoken words to introduce or reinforce vocabulary.
- Model conversational and social skills, which helps students with communication disorders become familiar with word pronunciation.
- Speak at a slower rate when necessary, especially when presenting new information.
- Consistently check for understanding.
- Be aware that communication issues may sometimes result in other issues, such as behavioral or social skill issues.
- Pair actions and motions with words to emphasize meaning, especially for students with receptive language disorders.

Receptive Language Disorders

Children with receptive language disorders often demonstrate appropriate expressive language skills and hear and read at age-appropriate levels. However, they may seem like they are not paying attention or engaging in activities, or they may appear to have difficulties following or understanding directions. They may refrain from asking questions or interrupt frequently during activities, especially during read-aloud activities. It may appear as if they are not listening, but children with receptive language disorders have difficulty perceiving **meaning** from what they hear. Children with this disorder may consistently leave tasks incomplete unless the tasks are broken down into smaller steps. This is due to issues with processing directions, especially **verbal directions**. Children with receptive language disorders may not respond appropriately or at all to questions from peers or adults. Answers to comprehension questions, especially when texts are read aloud, may be off topic or incorrect. Children with receptive language disorders have trouble gathering and connecting meaning to what they hear. A receptive language disorder is not exclusively a learning disability. However, children who have receptive disorders may have learning disabilities.

Expressive Language Disabilities

Expressive language is the ability to express wants and needs. Children with disabilities related to **expressive language disabilities** may have trouble conversing with peers and adults and have trouble with self-expression. Answers to questions may be vague or repetitive. They may not demonstrate age-appropriate social skills with peers and adults. Children with expressive language disabilities have a limited vocabulary range and rely on familiar vocabulary words in their expressive language. They can be very quiet and seclude themselves from classroom activities because of difficulties expressing their thoughts and feelings. They may not be able to accurately express what they understand because children with expressive language difficulties have trouble speaking in sentences. Expressive language disabilities indicate issues with **language processing centers** in the brain. Children with these disabilities can sometimes understand language but have trouble **expressing** it. Children with traumatic brain injuries, dyslexia, autism, or learning disabilities demonstrate issues with expressive language.

Implications of Literacy Development for Children with Disabilities

Children may not always meet the **literacy stage milestones** during the specified ages. However, this does not always indicate a disability. Children who fall significantly behind in their literacy development, continually struggle with skill acquisition, or do not consistently retain skill instruction are more likely to be identified as having **disabilities**. Furthermore, children with **speech and language disorders** are more likely to experience problems learning to read and write. These issues are typically apparent before children enter grade school but can also become evident during their early grade school years. **Early warning signs** include uninterest in shared book reading, inability to recognize or remember names of letters, difficulty understanding directions, and persistent baby talk.

Effects of Deficits in Language Development on the Learning Processes

Without interventions, children with deficits in language development will likely have issues with overall academic success. **Academic success** is inextricably linked with good language development. Good **language development skills** include the ability to understand spoken and written words, as well as literacy skills. When a core knowledge of language is developed in young children, it can be built upon as the children grow and develop during their grade school years. Reading and writing are language-based skills. **Phonological awareness** is an essential skill and key building block for language development. Phonological awareness is a term that refers to students' awareness of sounds, syllables, and words. Students that develop strong phonological skills typically develop good literacy skills. Students with deficits in reading, writing, or math may have difficulties with phonological awareness and miss some building blocks essential for academic success. These deficits generalize to core subject areas as students are required to demonstrate grade-level appropriate skills.

Visual Impairment or Blindness

Visual impairments range from low vision to blindness. The Individuals with Disabilities Education Act defines a **visual impairment** as an impairment in vision that is great enough to affect a child's educational performance. **Blindness** is defined as a visual acuity of 20/200 or less in the dominant eye. Some people diagnosed with blindness still have minimal sight. Early indicators of a visual impairment or blindness in children include:

- Holding things close to the eyes or face
- Experiencing fatigue after looking at things closely
- Having misaligned eyes
- Squinting
- Tilting the head or covering one eye to see things up close or far away
- Demonstrating clumsiness
- Appearing to see better during the day

Students with visual impairments benefit the most from early interventions, especially when the impairments are present with other disabilities. Appropriate interventions vary based on students' needs and whether or not they have other disabilities. Modifications, such as magnified text, Braille, auditory support, and text-tracking software, can help level the learning plane for these students.

Deafness, Hearing Impairment, and Deaf-Blindness

Deafness, hearing impairment, and deaf-blindness are each considered their own categories under IDEA, as the types and levels of intervention vary widely between them. **Deafness** is defined as a complete or nearly-complete loss of hearing, to the degree that a hearing aid cannot help. Deaf students often need specialized interventions to help with safety and with communication, such as through communication aids, assistive devices, and sign language. **Hearing impairments** consist of all qualifying degrees of hearing loss that are not severe enough to qualify as deafness. Interventions may include communication aids and training, as well as hearing aids. **Deaf-**

blindness is restricted to students who are both deaf and blind concurrently. Deaf-blind students usually require considerable help with communication and daily living skills.

Effect of Hearing Loss on Language Development

Hearing language is part of learning language. Children with **hearing loss** miss out on sounds associated with language, and this can affect their listening, speaking, reading, social skills, and overall school success. Hearing loss can sometimes lead to delayed speech and language, learning disabilities in school, insecurities, and issues with socialization and making friends. Children with hearing loss may:

- Have trouble learning abstract vocabulary like *since* and *before*
- Omit article words in sentences like *a* and *an*
- Fall behind in core components of learning and development without early interventions
- Have difficulty speaking in and understanding sentences
- Speak in shorter sentences
- Have difficulty including word endings like *-ing* and *-s*
- Have issues speaking clearly because they cannot accurately hear sounds
- Omit quiet sounds like *p, sh,* or *f*
- Be unable to hear what their own voices sound like

Children with hearing loss are more likely to fall behind in school due to their hearing deficits. They can easily fall behind without support from interventions, teachers, and their families. Early **hearing testing** is essential to ensure that interventions, such as sign language, can be introduced to promote school and life success for children with hearing loss.

Orthopedic Impairment

Qualifications to Receive Special Education for Orthopedic Impairment

Students who qualify to receive special education under the Individuals with Disabilities Education Act orthopedic impairment (**OI**) category have an orthopedic impairment that adversely affects educational performance. This includes children with congenital anomalies, impairments caused by disease, or impairments from other causes, such as cerebral palsy or amputations. An orthopedic impairment alone does not qualify a student for special education and an IEP. Once a student's educational performance is proven to be affected by the orthopedic impairment, the student becomes eligible for special education and placed on an IEP. The **IEP** determines the student's least restrictive environment, individualized goals for academic skills or adaptive behavior, and any appropriate accommodations or modifications. Students with orthopedic impairments whose educational performance is not affected may receive accommodations and modifications on **504 plans**, if appropriate. Strategies for instruction should be determined and implemented on a case-by-case basis, as the orthopedic impairment category covers a broad range of disabilities.

Intellectual Disabilities

Determining If a Child May Have an Intellectual Disability

Intellectual disability is primarily diagnosed when a child under 18 years old scores lower than 70 on an IQ test. Individuals may also be diagnosed with intellectual disabilities when they have an IQ under 75 with a concurrent disability that also impairs their functional skills, such as spastic quadriplegia which severely impairs movement. Students diagnosed with intellectual disabilities (**ID**) demonstrate deficits in academic skills, abstract thinking, problem solving, language development, new skill acquisition, and retaining information. Students with intellectual disabilities often do not adequately meet developmental or social milestones. They demonstrate **deficits in functioning** with one or more basic living skills. Students with intellectual disabilities struggle conceptually and may have difficulties with time and money concepts, short-term memory, time management, pre-academic skills, planning, and strategizing. Students with ID demonstrate poor social judgment and decision-making skills because they have trouble understanding social cues and rules. They may grasp concrete social concepts before abstract ones and significantly later than their similar-aged, regular education peers. These students also tend to struggle with self-care skills, household tasks, and completing tasks that may be easy for similar-aged peers.

Determining Severity of Intellectual Disabilities

There are four levels of intellectual disabilities: mild, moderate, severe, and profound. Specific factors are used to determine whether a disability is mild, moderate, severe, or profound. Intellectual levels are measured using cognitive- and research-based assessments. An **intellectual disability (ID)** is defined as significant cognitive deficits to intellectual functioning, such as reasoning, problem solving, abstract thinking, and comprehension. A **mild intellectual disability** is the most common type of intellectual disability. People with mild to moderate ID can generally participate in independent living activities and learn practical life skills and adaptive behaviors. People diagnosed with **severe intellectual disabilities** demonstrate major developmental delays. They struggle with simple routines and self-care skills. Additionally, they often understand speech but have trouble with expressive communication. People with **profound ID** cannot live independently, and they depend heavily on care from other people and resources. They are likely to have concurrent congenital disorders that affect their intellectual functioning.

Educational Implications for Students with Intellectual Disabilities

According to the Individuals with Disabilities Education Act, students who are eligible for special education under the category of **intellectual disability** have significantly lower intellectual abilities, along with adaptive behavior deficits. Previously, intellectual disability was referred to as "mental retardation" in the IDEA. In 2010, President Obama signed **Rosa's Law**, which changed the term to "intellectual disability." The definition of the disability category remained unchanged. Educational implications of a diagnosis of an intellectual disability differ depending on students' needs as determined by their individualized education programs (IEPs). Students with intellectual disabilities often display **limitations to mental functioning** in areas like communication, self-care, and social skills (adaptive behavior). In many cases, these skills must be addressed in the educational environments in addition to any academic skill deficits. Learning adaptive behaviors and academic skills takes longer for students with intellectual disabilities. Their special education placements depend upon what environments are least restrictive. This depends on the individual student and is determined in the IEP.

Promoting a Positive Educational Performance for Students with Intellectual Disabilities

Students with intellectual disabilities often present with skill levels that are far below those of similar-aged peers. Because of deficits in academic, behavioral, and social skills, these students require **specialized instruction**, which varies depending on the needs of each individual student. An effective strategy for promoting a positive educational performance is to collect observations and data on the academic, behavioral, and social skill levels of the individual student. Teachers usually work with professionals in related services, like speech language pathologists, to address needs and implement educational interventions that work for this population of students. These students can benefit from **communication interventions** focused on interactions they may have with adults and peers. Students may benefit from augmentative and alternative communication (AAC) devices, visual activity schedules and other visual supports, and computer-based instruction when learning communication and social skills. Students with ID may also require **behavioral interventions** to teach appropriate behaviors or decrease negative behaviors. They may also benefit from increased **peer interactions** through structured social groups in order to promote appropriate communication skills.

Multiple Disabilities

Components of the Multiple Disability Eligibility Category According to the IDEA

The multiple disabilities category according to the IDEA applies to students who have two or more disabilities occurring simultaneously. The multiple disability category does not include deaf-blindness, which has its own category under the IDEA. Students with **multiple disabilities** present with such **severe educational needs** that they cannot be accommodated in special education settings that address only one disability. Placement in special education programs is determined by students' **least restrictive environments** as defined in their **individualized education programs**. Students with multiple disabilities often present with communication deficits, mobility challenges, and deficits in adaptive behavior and need one-on-one instruction or assistance when performing daily activities.

Intervention Strategies for the Instruction of Students with Multiple Disabilities

Working with students with multiple disabilities can be challenging. However, strategies used in other special education settings can be implemented to promote the success of students with multiple disabilities. Effective strategies include the following:

- Setting **long-term goals**, which may last for a few years depending on how long students are in the same classrooms
- Working **collaboratively** with team members, like paraprofessionals and related services professionals, to ensure that they carry out students' educational objectives consistently
- Developing and maintaining **group goals** that the adults and students in the classrooms can strive to achieve together
- Working with students and paraprofessionals and consulting paraprofessionals frequently for **feedback**
- Demonstrating **patience** when waiting for students to respond or complete tasks
- Learning about how students **communicate**, which may involve gestures, a Picture Exchange Communication System, or other methods
- Driving instruction and education goals based on how students **learn best**
- Considering how students will **respond** when designing lessons, including accounting for response time during instruction

Developmental Screening

Types of Developmental Assessments

Developmental assessments measure the development of infants, toddlers, and preschoolers. These **norm-referenced tests** measure fine and gross motor skills; communication and language; and social, cognitive, and self-help milestones that young children should achieve at certain ages. When a child is suspected of having a **developmental delay**, a developmental assessment is useful in identifying the child's strengths and weaknesses. These assessments map out the **progress** of a child compared to the progress of similar-aged children. Developmental assessments are also useful in identifying if the delay is significant or can be overcome with time. These assessments can be used to determine what **educational placement** is most appropriate for a child with a developmental delay. Developmental assessments are administered via observations and questionnaires. Parents, legal guardians, caregivers, and instructors who are most familiar with the child provide the most insight on developmental strengths and weaknesses.

Screening Tests for Identifying Students Who Need Special Education

When determining if a child needs special education, **screening tests** are the first step. The Individuals with Disabilities Education Act (IDEA) offers guidance for schools to implement screening tests. Districts and schools often have school-wide processes in place for screening students for **special education**. Screening tests can also be used to identify students who are falling behind in class. The advantage of screening tests is that they are easily administered. They require few materials and little time and planning in order to administer. Additionally, they can be used to quickly assess students' strengths and weaknesses, they do not have to be administered one on one, and they can be used class wide. Screening tests can be as simple as paper-and-pencil quizzes assessing what students know. They are used for measuring visual acuity, auditory skills, physical health, development, basic academic skills, behavioral problems, risk of behavioral problems, language skills, and verbal and nonverbal intelligence.

Individual Intelligence Tests vs. Individual Academic Achievement Tests

Intelligence tests measure a student's capacity for abstract thinking, mental reasoning, judgment, and decision-making. These **norm-referenced tests** help determine a student's **overall intelligence**, which correlates with **potential academic performance**. Intelligence tests can be used to determine if a student's deficits are due to intellectual disabilities or related to specific learning disabilities or emotional disorders. They can also measure verbal skills, motor performance, and visual reasoning. Intelligence tests are also known as **intelligence quotient tests (IQ tests)**. IQ tests should be administered by trained professionals to ensure the tests are administered accurately. Unlike intelligence tests, individual academic achievement tests measure a student's strengths and weaknesses in individual skills. They are also norm referenced and used to determine if a student needs **special education services**. Results from individual academic tests help determine areas of concern or possible deficits for an individual student. Unlike intelligence tests, individual academic tests can be administered by teachers.

Adaptive Behavior Scale Assessments

Adaptive behavior scales are useful for diagnosing a student with an **intellectual disability** that affects the development or progression of adaptive behavior. They are used in preschools and for determining eligibility for **special education** in grade schools. They are also used in planning the **curriculum** for students with intellectual disabilities. Adaptive behavior scales are standardized but not always norm referenced because of difficulties comparing expectations for some adaptive and maladaptive skills exhibited by similar-aged peers. In terms of curriculum planning, these assessments can determine the type and quantity of assistance a student may need. Adaptive behavior scale assessments identify a student's level of **independence**. Adaptive behavior scales can be used to determine **skill abilities** associated with daily living, community functioning, social skills, communication, motor functions, and basic academic skills. Teachers and other professionals can administer adaptive behavior scales to students with intellectual disabilities to determine starting points for improving their adaptive behavior deficits.

Curriculum-Based Measurement of Student Academic Progress

Curriculum-based measurement (**CBM**) is a way for teachers to track how students are **progressing** in mathematics, language arts, social studies, science, and other skills. It is also useful for communicating progress to parents or legal guardians. CBM results can determine whether or not current **instructional strategies** are effective for particular students. In the same respect, CBM can determine if students are meeting the **standards** laid out in their IEP goals. If CBM results shows that instructional strategies are not effective or goals are not being met, teachers should change instructional strategies. CBM can be revisited to determine whether or not the newly implemented strategies are effective. Progress can sometimes be charted to present a visual for how a student is progressing in a particular content area or with a specific skill.

Woodcock-Johnson Achievement Tests

High-Incidence Disabilities

Woodcock-Johnson achievement tests can be used as diagnostic tools for identifying children with **high-incidence disabilities**. The Woodcock-Johnson Tests of Achievement and the Woodcock-Johnson Tests of Cognitive Abilities are comprehensively useful for assessing children's:

- Intellectual abilities
- Cognitive abilities
- Aptitude
- Oral language
- Academic achievements

These norm-referenced tests are valuable in understanding children's strengths and weaknesses and how they compare to cohorts of normally progressing, similar-aged peers. For example, **Woodcock-Johnson achievement tests (WJ tests)** are useful in identifying children with language disorders because children with language disorders typically score lower on the listening comprehension and fluid reasoning test sections. The WJ tests are useful diagnostic tools for identifying children with attention deficit hyperactivity disorder (ADHD) as well. While children with ADHD may perform similarly to children with learning disabilities, their key deficits are in the cognitive efficiency, processing speed, academic fluency, short-term memory, and long-term retrieval test sections.

Prenatal, Perinatal, and Neonatal Disabilities

Prenatal, perinatal, and neonatal risk factors can be genetic or environmental. These risk factors put infants at risk for developing **intellectual disabilities** that affect their day-to-day lives. An intellectual disability (**ID**) is a disability that significantly limits a child's overall cognitive abilities. **Prenatal** risk factors include genetic syndromes (e.g., Down syndrome), brain malformation, maternal diseases, and environmental influences. Drugs, alcohol, or poison exposure can all affect an unborn child. **Perinatal** (during delivery) risk factors include labor and delivery trauma or anoxia at birth. **Neonatal** (post-birth) risk factors include hypoxic ischemic brain injury, traumatic brain injury, infections, seizure disorders, and toxic metabolic syndromes. Early screening and applicable assessments are tools used to identify young children with intellectual disabilities and can assist with providing special education services under the Individuals with Disabilities Education Act. These tools can also help assess the severity of deficits and the need for special services, such as occupational therapy.

Learning Disabilities in Reading and Mathematics

The Woodcock-Johnson achievement tests (WJ tests) include a test of **achievement** and a test of **cognitive abilities**. Together, these assessments are useful in the diagnostic process of identifying a student with a **disability**. Additionally, they are helpful for identifying specific **deficits** in a student's reading or math skills. WJ tests are norm-referenced and compare the results of a child's performance to that of a cohort of children of similar age and average intellectual abilities. These assessments provide information about **reading disorders**, such as dyslexia, because they measure phonological awareness, rapid automatized naming, processing speed, and working memory. WJ tests report on a child's cognitive functioning in these test areas. These assessments also provide useful information for students with learning deficits in **mathematics**. Performance on the math calculation skills and math reasoning test sections provides information on specific deficits in general comprehension, fluid reasoning, and processing speed. Deficits in these areas are correlated to learning disabilities in mathematics.

The Weschler Intelligence Scale

The Weschler Intelligence Scale is an assessment that measures the cognitive abilities of children and adults. The **Weschler Intelligence Scale for Children (WISC)** measures a child's **verbal intelligence** (including comprehension and vocabulary) and **performance intelligence** (including reasoning and picture completion). The WISC is an intelligence quotient test that is useful for helping diagnose a student with a **cognitive disability**. A score below 100 indicates below-average intelligence. WISC results are useful tools for evaluating a student with a disability. Tests results can be used to measure and report on a student's general intelligence and provide insight into the student's cognitive abilities in order to determine an appropriate educational pathway. Results can be reported in a student's evaluation team report and individualized education program (IEP) in order to justify special education services or have a starting point for IEP goals. WISC results are especially important in an evaluation team report, and are generally completed at least once every three years, because they contribute to describing the **overall performance profile** of a student with a disability.

Kaufman Assessment Battery for Children

The Kaufman Assessment Battery for Children (**K-ABC**) is a unique standardized test because it is used to evaluate preschoolers, minority groups, and children with learning disabilities. The K-ABC can be used to assess children ages 2–18 and is meant to be used with children who are nonverbal, bilingual, or English speaking. However, it is especially useful in assessing the abilities of students who are **nonverbal**. The K-ABC can be used to help determine students' educational placements and assist with their educational planning. This assessment has four components that measure students' abilities, which are described below:

- The **sequential processing scale** assesses short-term memory and problem-solving skills when putting things in sequential order.
- The **simultaneous processing scale** assesses problem-solving skills for completing multiple processes simultaneously, such as identifying objects and reproducing design shapes using manipulatives.
- The **achievement component** measures expressive vocabulary, mathematics skills, and reading and decoding skills.
- The **mental processing component** assesses the abilities a student demonstrates on the sequential and simultaneous processing scales.

The K-ABC is also unique because it includes a **nonverbal scale** that can be administered to children with hearing or speech impairments and children who do not speak English.

Vineland Adaptive Behavior Scales

The Vineland Adaptive Behavior Scales (**VABS**) assesses the personal and social skills of children and adults. **Adaptive behavior** refers to the skills needed for day-to-day activities and independent living. Children with disabilities sometimes have deficits in adaptive behavior, and the VABS is useful for planning their **educational pathways**. It is an especially useful tool for developing **transition plans and goals** for students of appropriate ages on IEPs. The VABS is a process that involves people who know the students best, like parents and teachers. The teacher version and parent version of this assessment can be delivered via interview or survey. The parent version focuses on a student's adaptive behavior at home, while the teacher version focuses on adaptive behavior in the school setting. Version III of the VABS assesses four **domains**: communication, activities of daily living, social relationships, and motor skills. A student's parents or caregivers fill out a form pertaining to home life and a teacher fills out a form pertaining to school settings. The comprehensive score from both the teacher and parent version are used to report abilities in the four domains.

Types of Cognitive Assessments

Cognitive tests assess the **cognitive functioning abilities** of children and adults. They are useful tools for diagnosing or identifying children with disabilities who are eligible for **special education services** under the Individuals with Disabilities Education Act. Examples of cognitive tests used in diagnosing or identifying children with disabilities include aptitude tests and intelligence quotient (IQ) tests. There are also cognitive assessments that measure verbal reasoning, numerical reasoning, abstract reasoning, spatial ability, verbal ability, and more. Children's cognitive abilities are related to how quickly they **process** information. Assessment results can be good measurements of how quickly children may learn new information or tasks. Cognitive assessments provide specific information about children's cognitive functioning by providing measurements of their intelligence, attention, concentration, processing speed, language and communication, visual-spatial abilities, and short- and long-term memory capabilities. Results can also be used on a child's evaluation team report or to develop goals for an IEP.

Advantages and Disadvantages of Curriculum-Based Assessments

Curriculum-based assessments (**CBAs**) determine if students are making adequate progress through the curriculum. They can be administered by a teacher, special educator, or school psychologist. CBAs have advantages over norm-referenced assessments, like developmental assessments, because they are not used to compare performance between students. Other types of assessments measure a student's cumulative abilities across multiple skills instead of assessing individual skills. CBAs measure student progress in more **individualized** ways. They are especially useful for measuring IEP goal progress. Since CBAs are **teacher-created assessments**, they provide opportunities to assess students informally and formally on IEP goals. For example, a teacher may verbally quiz a student on ten addition problems to determine if the student is making progress on math IEP goals. CBAs are also used in the "response to intervention" process to identify students with special needs by measuring the effectiveness of interventions provided to them.

Culture and Language Differences in Special Education

Role of Cultural Competence in Schools and Special Education

Cultural competence, the awareness and appreciation of cultural differences, helps avoid **cultural and linguistic bias**. Schools that demonstrate **cultural competence** have an appreciation of families and their unique backgrounds. Cultural competence is important because it assists with incorporating knowledge and appreciation of other cultures into daily practices and teaching. This helps increase the quality and effectiveness of how students with unique cultural and linguistic backgrounds are provided with services. It also helps produce better outcomes for these students. In special education, being culturally competent means being aware of cultural and linguistic differences, especially when considering children for the identification process. Adapting to the **diversity and cultural contexts** of the surrounding communities allows teachers to better understand flags for referrals. Teachers that continually assess their awareness of the cultures and diversity of the communities where they teach demonstrate cultural competence. In order for schools and teachers to be described as culturally competent, they should have a process for recognizing diversity.

Cultural and Linguistic Differences vs. Learning Difficulties

Many schools are enriched with cultural diversity. It is important for special educators to identify if a suspected learning disability may instead be a **cultural or linguistic difference**. Teachers and schools must increase awareness of cultural and linguistic differences in order to avoid overidentification of certain populations as having learning difficulties. Some ways a child's behavior may represent cultural or linguistic differences are demonstrated in the **interactions** between teachers and students. In some cultures, children are asked to make eye contact to ensure they are listening, whereas in other cultures, children are taught to look down or away when being spoken to by an adult. Certain facial expressions and behaviors may be interpreted differently by students because of their cultural backgrounds. Additionally, teaching methods that are comfortable and effective for some students may be ineffective for others due to differing cultural backgrounds. Cultural values and characteristics may vary between teachers and students and contribute to the students' school performance. It is important for teachers to be **self-aware** and constantly **assess** whether ineffective teaching methods are due to learning difficulties or cultural and linguistic diversity.

Strategies for Teaching ELLs and Students with Disabilities

English language learners (ELLs) are often at risk of being unnecessarily referred for special education services. This is frequently a result of **inadequate planning** for the needs of English language learners rather than skill deficits. To ensure that the needs of ELLs are met and discrimination is avoided, educators can implement strategies for **targeting their learning processes**. Strategies similar to those utilized in inclusive special education settings, such as using visuals to supplement instruction, are helpful. This type of nonlinguistic representation helps convey meaning to ELLs. Working in groups with peers helps students with disabilities and ELLs demonstrate communication and social skills while working toward common goals. Allowing students to write and speak in their first languages until they feel comfortable speaking in English is a scaffolding strategy that can also be implemented. Sentence frames that demonstrate familiar sentence formats help all students to practice speaking and writing in structured, formal ways.

> **Review Video: ESL/ESOL/Second Language Learning**
> Visit mometrix.com/academy and enter code: 795047

Teaching Appropriate Communication Skills to ELLs with Disabilities

Students with disabilities who are also English language learners (ELLs) have the additional challenge of **language barriers** affecting their access to learning. These barriers, combined with the disabilities, can make instruction for these students challenging. For ELL students with disabilities, it is important for teachers to rely on **appropriate instructional strategies** in order to determine what is affecting the students' access to information. Strategies for teaching ELLs are similar to those for teaching nonverbal students. Pairing **visuals** with words helps students make concrete connections between the written words and the pictures. Consistently seeing the words paired with the visuals increases the likelihood of the students beginning to interpret word meanings. Using sign language or other gestures is another way teachers can facilitate word meaning. When used consistently, students make connections between the visual word meanings and the written words. Teachers can also provide opportunities for ELLs to access language by having all students in the classroom communicate in a **consistent manner**. The goal of this instructional strategy is for peers to model appropriate verbal communication as it applies to different classroom situations.

Individualized Education Programs

Developing and Writing Measurable IEP Goals

According to the Individuals with Disabilities Education Act (IDEA), students eligible for special education receive **individualized education program** (IEP) goals, which must contain specific **components**. Components of a **measurable IEP goal** include condition, performance, criteria, assessment, and standard. Measurable goals also include how skill mastery will be **assessed**, such as through observations or work samples. In the provided example below, the criteria is clearly measurable, as Jacob will either succeed or fail at multiple trials, and the ratio of successes to numbers of attempts should be recorded and dated throughout the IEP year to show his progress. Goals should also be **standards-based** whenever possible and may be required.

For example, an IEP goal may state, "By the end of this IEP, Jacob will use appropriate skills to communicate his needs in 4/5 trials."

- **Condition** refers to when, where, and how the disability will be addressed. "By the end of this IEP" is the condition of the goal.
- **Performance** is what the student is expected to accomplish during the condition of the goal. In this case, that is "Jacob will use appropriate skills to communicate his needs."
- The last part of the goal stating "in 4/5 trials" is the **criteria** that outlines how well the goal will be performed.

Role of Local Education Agency Representatives in IEP Meetings

A local education agency (**LEA**) representative is a member of the IEP team who is trained in special education curriculum, general education curriculum, and community resources. In many cases, a school building leader or principal may fulfil the role of LEA representative. An LEA rep must be a licensed professional who knows the student and is familiar with the IEP process. The role of LEA representatives in IEP meetings is to make sure the information presented is compliant with the IDEA standards. LEA representatives are also responsible for ensuring that the school district is **compliant** with procedural components of IDEA and that eligible students are receiving free and appropriate public educations (FAPEs). This role is necessary on the IEP team because whereas the whole IEP team should have the students' best interests in mind, they may not understand the doctrines of IDEA law and be able to consider compliance. As a result, they must act as the primary advocate for effective implementation of the IEP.

Involvement of Students with IEPs in the Transition Process in High School

Most states require **transition statements** to be made when students reach age 14 during the IEP year. Federal law requires students 16 years of age or older to have transition statements; post-secondary goals for independent living, employment, and education; and summaries of performance that include the results of the most recent transition assessments. Per federal law, students of transition age must be invited to their **IEP meetings**. It is important for students on IEPs to **participate** in the transition process because it helps them figure out what they want to do after they graduate from high school. Participation in the process gets them thinking about living independently, post-secondary education options, and employment options. Students usually have opportunities to participate in formal and informal assessments like interest inventories that help them define their interests. Transition goals for independent living, employment, and education should be based on the results of these assessments and any other interests the students have expressed. The students participate in the **implementation** of the transition goals by completing activities associated with their indicated interests.

Student Support Teams

A **student support team (SST)** is a team made up of parents and educational professionals who work to support students in the general education classroom who are struggling with academics, disciplines, health problems, or any other anticipated or actual problem that does not qualify the student for special education or supports from an IEP. In this support team model, a group of educators works to identify and provide early intervention services for any student exhibiting academic or behavioral problems. The purpose of this kind of SST is to offer different supports, such as monitoring student progress, developing intervention plans, and referring students for intervention services. While the primary goal of this kind of SST is to provide support for students **struggling with school**, it can also shift focus to supporting students at risk of **dropping out of school**. Another primary objective of an SST is to identify students who are likely to have disabilities or who may need 504 plans to succeed in school and to recommend them for referrals so they are not left without necessary supports.

Amendments to an Individualized Education Program

A student's individualized education program (**IEP**) is in effect for one year. Academic goals, objectives, benchmarks, transition goals, and any accommodations and modifications are to be in place for the student for the duration of the IEP. An **amendment** to the IEP can be made when a change is needed before the year is over. An amendment is an agreement between the student, parents or legal guardians, and the IEP team. IEP meetings for amendments can be requested at any time. IEP amendments can be requested if a student is not making adequate progress toward the goals, if the goals become inappropriate in some way for the student, or when the student has met all IEP goals and requires new ones. If new information about the student becomes available, the IEP can be amended. Students, parents, and other team members may also request amendment meetings if they think that other accommodations and modifications are needed or should be removed.

How the Needs of Students with IEPs Are Met in the School Environment

IEPs communicate what **services** are to be provided for children with disabilities in the school setting, the children's **present levels of performance (PLOPs)**, and how their disabilities affect **academic performance**. IEPs also specify **annual goals** appropriate to the students' specific needs and any accommodations or modifications that need to be provided. Schools and teachers working with students with disabilities have the responsibility to implement these IEP components when working with the students. Additionally, schools and teachers working with students with disabilities must ensure that the students' individualized annual goals are met within a year of the students' IEP effective dates. It is up to the IEP teams to determine what classroom settings would most benefit the students while also appropriately meeting their IEP goals with the fewest barriers. Special educators must determine how data is collected, and then obtain and record data on how the students are meeting their IEP goals. Special educators are responsible for providing intervention services based on the data results. They must also ensure that any accommodations or modifications listed on the IEPs are implemented in both general education and self-contained classrooms.

Accommodation vs. Modification in IEPs

Formal accommodations, adaptations, and modifications for a student with a disability are listed on the individualized education program. **Accommodations** change *how* a student learns the material, while an **adaptation** or **modification** changes *what* a student is taught or expected to learn.

- **Accommodations** are changes to the instruction or assessment that do *not* alter the curricular requirements. For instance, a student with accommodations may be allowed to answer a test orally instead of writing the answers or might be given pre-structured notes to help organize thoughts during instruction. These types of changes do not fundamentally change the information taught or the requirements for passing.
- **Adaptations** or **Modifications** are changes to the instruction or assessment that fundamentally change the curricular requirements, but which enable a student with a disability to participate. Examples of adaptations include substitution of activities for related materials, exemption from answering particular types of questions on assessments, and removing or reducing time limits when taking tests.

For state standardized tests, accommodations like extra time and frequent breaks can be provided. Students that need modifications to state tests may complete alternate assessments that may not cover the same material as the standard exams.

Review Video: Adapting and Modifying Lessons or Activities
Visit mometrix.com/academy and enter code: 834946

Determining the Placement of a Student with a Disability

With every student, the ideal goal is placement in the **general education classroom** as much as possible while still meeting the student's educational needs and ensuring a successful educational experience. The IDEA does not require that students be placed in the regular education classroom, but it does require that students be placed in their **least restrictive environment (LRE)** as defined by the student's IEP team. Ultimately, the IEP team determines what **environment** best suits the student based on the student's specific needs. The IEP team is responsible for determining what educational environment would provide the student with the maximum appropriate educational benefit. While justification for removing a student from the regular education classroom is common and appropriate, as occurs when a student is placed in a resource room, the IEP team must explain the reasoning in the student's IEP. **Justification** must specifically state why the student cannot be educated with accommodations and services in the regular education classroom during any part of the school day. Justification for removal cannot be the perceived instructional limitations of the regular education teacher or concerns over extra instructional time needed to educate a student with a disability.

Creating a SMART Annual Goal in an IEP

A good IEP goal describes how far the student is expected to **progress** toward the goal by the next IEP. Since IEPs should be revised once a year, a good annual IEP goal should describe what the student is capable of doing in a one-year timeframe. Creating **SMART** IEP goals can help the student determine realistic expectations of what can be achieved in a year. SMART IEP goals are specific, measurable, attainable, relevant, and time-bound. Goals are **specific** when they list the targeted result in the skill or subject area. Goals should also be specific to the student's needs. Goals that are **measurable** state the way a student's progress will be measured. Measurable goals list how accurately a student should meet the goal. **Attainable** goals are realistic for the student to achieve in one year. **Relevant** goals outline what a student needs to do to accomplish the goal. For example, a SMART goal may state, "During the school week, Robert will use his device to communicate greetings 80% of the time in 4/5 trials." **Time-bound** goals include a timeframe for the student to achieve the goal. They also list when and how often progress will be measured.

Role of an Initial Evaluation Assessment in Qualifying a Student for Special Education

When a student is determined to need special education, it means the student has a disability or disabilities adversely affecting educational performance. It may also mean the student's needs cannot be addressed in the general education classroom with or without accommodations and that **specially designed instruction (SDI)** is required. An **initial evaluation** of the student is required for special education eligibility. The evaluation is comprehensive and includes existing data collected on the student and additional assessments needed to determine eligibility. Individual school districts decide what assessments should be completed for the student's initial evaluation. Each district is responsible for and should provide assessments that measure functional, developmental, and academic information. The student's parents or legal guardians are responsible for providing outside information relevant to the student's education, such as medical needs assessed outside of the school district by qualified providers.

Purpose of an IEP

The purpose of an individualized education program (IEP) is to guide the learning of a student with a **disability** in the educational environment. An IEP is a written statement for a student eligible for **special education**. An initial IEP is **implemented** once the child has been evaluated and determined to be in need of special education. After the initial IEP, **IEP meetings** are conducted annually (or more) in order to update the plan to meet the needs of the student. IEPs are created, reviewed, and revised according to individual state and federal laws. These plans include the amount of time the student will spend in the special education classroom based on the level of need. They also include any related services the student might need (such as speech-language therapy) as well as academic and behavioral goals for the year. As the student learns and changes, performance levels and goals change as well. A student's present levels of performance are included and updated yearly, as are the academic and behavioral goals.

Members of an Individualized Education Program Team

IEPs are updated **annually** following the initial IEP. IEP team members meet at least once a year to discuss a student's progress and make changes to the IEP. The required members of a student's IEP team include the student's parents or legal guardians, one of the student's general education teachers, the special education teacher, a school representative, an individual who can interpret the instructional implications of evaluation results, and if appropriate, the student. Anyone else who has knowledge or expertise about the student may also attend. **Parents and legal guardians** contribute unique expertise about the student, typically having the benefit of knowing the child well. **General education teachers** can speak to how the student is performing in the general education classroom. The **special education teacher** can report on progress made toward academic and behavioral goals and present levels of performance. A **school representative** must be qualified to provide or supervise specially designed instruction, be knowledgeable of the general education curriculum, and be knowledgeable about school resources. The **individual who can interpret evaluation results** can be an existing team member or someone else who is qualified to report on evaluation results. **Advocates**, such as counselors or therapists who see the student outside the school day, can also attend the meeting to speak on the student's behalf.

Legal Rights of Parents or Legal Guardians

IEP meetings occur annually for each student. However, it is a **parent or legal guardian's right** to request a meeting at any point during the school year. The student's school is responsible for identifying and evaluating the child; developing, reviewing, or revising the IEP; and determining what placement setting best suits the needs of the student. It is within the parent or legal guardian's rights to have **input** in all processes related to the student. Under the Individuals with Disabilities Education Act (IDEA), parents have the right to participate in IEP meetings, have an independent evaluation in addition to the one the school provides, give or deny consent for the IEP, contest a school's decision, and obtain private education paid for by the public school. In specific circumstances, if the student is determined to need services that the public school cannot provide, the public school district may need to pay for the student's tuition at a private school where the student's needs can be met.

Collaborative Consultation between Educational Professionals

Collaborative consultation refers to the special educator or other professional providing advice to the general education teacher about a student on an IEP. Special educators and other IEP team members, such as school psychologists and related service professionals, serve as the **experts** and have knowledge about how individual students learn and behave. This is especially important when students with IEPs are included in the general education classroom. Special educators and general education teachers must work collaboratively to ensure that students are reaching their potential in the general education setting. Examples of **collaborative consultation** include the special educator serving as a consultant to the general education teacher by providing advice on a student's IEP, accommodations, modifications, and IEP goal tracking. Another way the special educator or other professional can assist the general educator is by providing skill and strategy instruction to students on IEPs outside the general education classroom. The idea behind this method is for students to generalize these skills and strategies to the general education classroom.

Public School Responsibilities to Parents and Legal Guardians of Students on IEPs

The school must invite the parents or legal guardians to any **IEP meetings** and provide advance notice of the meetings. Each meeting notice is required to include the purpose of the meeting, its time and location, and who will attend. The location of the meeting is likely the student's school, but legally it must be held at a mutually agreed-upon place and time. If the parent or legal guardian cannot attend the IEP meeting, the school must ensure participation in another way, such as video or telephone conference. The meeting can be conducted without the parent or legal guardian if the school district cannot get the parent or legal guardian to attend. A parent or legal guardian can request a meeting, and the school can refuse or deny the request. If denied, the school must provide a **prior written notice** explaining their refusal. A prior written notice is a document outlining important school district decisions about a student on an IEP.

Modifications, Accommodations, and Adaptations

Accommodations and Modifications

Accommodations and Modifications are different types of educational supports put in place to help a student participate effectively in school. An **accommodation** changes *how* a student is taught or assessed by providing more time or other supports that remove barriers to the material. Students who receive accommodations are taught and assessed to the same standards as students without accommodations. A **modification** changes *what* is taught or assessed by changing or omitting parts of the materials. Students with modifications may receive fewer problems to solve or be given lower-rigor versions of the materials as other students.

Modifications

Modifications are changes to *what* students are taught or expected to learn. Students with disabilities can receive modifications as determined by their specific needs and as written out in their Individualized Education Programs.

- **Curriculum modifications** allow students to learn material that is different from what their general education peers learn. For example, students with classroom modifications may receive assignments with fewer math problems or with reading samples appropriate for their reading levels. Students with curriculum modifications may receive different grading tiers than their peers. The ways teachers grade their assignments may be different from how the teachers grade their peers' assignments. Students may also be excused from particular projects or given project guidelines that are different and better suited to their individual needs.
- **Assignment modifications** include completing fewer or different homework problems than peers, writing shorter papers, answering fewer questions on classwork and tests, and creating alternate projects or assignments.

Environmental Modifications

Students with disabilities may need environmental modifications in order to be successful in their classrooms, homes, and communities. **Environmental modifications** are adaptations that allow people with disabilities to maneuver through their environments with as little resistance as possible. They allow for more **independent living experiences**, especially for those with limited mobility. Environmental modifications ensure the health, safety, and welfare of the people who need them. Examples of environmental modifications in the home, community, or school include ramps, hydraulic lifts, widened doorways and hallways, automatic doors, handrails, and grab bars. Roll-in showers, water faucet controls, worktable or work surface adaptations, and cabinet and shelving adaptations are also environmental modifications that can be provided if necessary. Other adaptations include heating and cooling adaptations and electrical adaptations to accommodate devices or equipment. Environmental modifications in the home are typically provided by qualified agencies or providers. The Americans with Disabilities Act ensures that environmental modifications are provided in the **community** to help avoid discrimination against people with disabilities.

Accommodations

Accommodations are flexible classroom tools because they can be used to provide **interventions** without time or location boundaries. They remove **barriers** to learning for students with disabilities, and they change how students learn. Accommodations do not change what students are learning or expected to know. Classroom accommodations may be outlined in students' IEPs and 504 plans or simply provided as needed by special educators or general educators. Accommodations are put into place to ensure that students with disabilities are accessing the learning process with the fewest barriers, putting them on the same levels as their peers without disabilities. **Presentation accommodations** include allowing students to listen to oral instructions, providing written lists of instructions, and allowing students to use readers to assist with comprehension. **Response accommodations** include allowing students to provide oral responses, capture responses via audio recording, and use spelling dictionaries or spell-checkers when writing. **Accommodations to setting** include special seating (wherever the students learn best), use of sensory tools, and special lighting.

Types of Accommodations

Timing, schedule, and organizational accommodations change the ways students with disabilities have access to classrooms with the fewest barriers to learning. Students who need these accommodations receive them as written statements in their Individualized Education Programs, 504 Plans, or as teachers see fit during classroom time.

- **Timing accommodations** allow students more time to complete tasks or tests and/or process instructions. They also allow students to access frequent breaks during assignments or tests.
- **Schedule accommodations** include taking tests in chunks over periods of time or several days, taking test sections in different orders, and/or taking tests during specific times of day.
- **Organizational skill accommodations** include assistance with time management, marking texts with highlighters, maintaining daily assignment or work schedules, and/or receiving study skills instruction.

When accommodations are written in a student's IEP, the student has access to them for state standardized tests. When and how accommodations are put into place is left to the discretion of the teacher unless specifically written in the student's IEP or 504 Plan.

Obtaining Accommodations

When parents or legal guardians of children with disabilities believe that **accommodations** may help their children, they can arrange to speak with teachers about informal supports. **Informal supports** are strategies teachers can put into place to assist students with their learning processes. These changes do not require paperwork and can be implemented during classroom instruction. Teachers can experiment with informal supports to determine what will be most helpful for removing the barriers to learning students might be experiencing. If it is determined that students need bigger changes to how they learn, **formal evaluations** can take place. Students who do not already have IEPs or 504 plans may be evaluated to collect data on their needs. For students with IEPs or 504 plans, accommodations can be included the next time these plans are updated. The IEPs or 504 plans can also be **amended** if the need for the accommodations is immediate, such as if they need to be put in place before standardized testing time. **Data** supporting the need for the accommodations must be provided and listed in the comprehensive initial evaluations and all versions of IEPs and 504 plans.

Parents and Legal Guardians Ensuring Accommodations Are Being Provided

Accommodations are changes to the ways children with disabilities learn, not changes to what the children are learning. While parents and legal guardians may only receive **formal updates** on how accommodations are being provided or helping the students during specified reporting times (unless students' IEPs or 504 plans specifically state otherwise), they can ask for **reports** on goal progress or accommodations for their students at any time. Parents and legal guardians can ensure that accommodations are successfully implemented by using the progress reports and asking the right questions. Parents and legal guardians can ensure that accommodations are being provided in a number of ways. They can **advocate** for their students by making sure the accommodations are being implemented on a regular basis. Parents and legal guardians also have the right to ask if their students are using the accommodations on a **regular basis**. If they are being used on a regular basis, parents and legal guardians can explore additional options that might help their students. Parents and legal guardians can work with special education teachers and the IEP teams to ensure that their students' accommodations are being received and are effective.

Informal Supports vs. Formal Accommodations

Informal supports are generally easier to implement in the classroom setting. They do not necessarily have to be implemented only for students with IEPs or students with disabilities. Students who have not been evaluated for special education services can receive **informal supports** to ensure classroom success. Teachers may use informal supports to help students who are struggling with the ways they are learning. They may demonstrate that the students are able to learn with the accommodations in place. Informal supports are often the first step to indicating that students are in need of **special education services**.

Formal accommodations are put in place when students become eligible for IEPs or 504 plans. Formal supports are written into the IEPs or 504 plans and then required by law to be provided. Examples of informal supports include frequent breaks, special seating, quiet areas for test taking or studying, teacher cues, and help with basic organizational skills. These informal supports may eventually turn into formal supports if students become eligible for special education services.

Reasonable Accommodations According to ADA

According to the Americans with Disabilities Act, a **reasonable accommodation** is a change to workplace conditions, equipment, or environment that allow an individual to effectively perform a job. Title I under ADA requires businesses with more than 15 employees to abide by certain regulations, ensuring that their needs are reasonably met. Any change to the work environment or the way a job is performed that gives a person with a disability access to **equal employment** is considered a reasonable accommodation. Reasonable accommodations fall into **three categories**: changes to a job application process, changes to the work environment or to the way a job is usually done, and changes that enable employee access to equal benefits and privileges that employees without disabilities receive. These effectively level the playing field for people with disabilities to receive the same benefits as their peers. It also allows for the fewest barriers to success in the workplace. Many communities have resources available to help people with disabilities find jobs. They also have resources that help employers make their workplaces accessible for people with disabilities.

Types of Assistive Technology

Assistive technology (AT) tools can be physical objects and devices or online resources that assist students with disabilities in their learning. The purpose of AT tools is to provide students with disabilities **equal access to the curriculum** by accommodating their individual needs to promote positive outcomes. **Personal listening devices (PLDs)**, sometimes called FM systems, are devices that clarify teachers' words. With a PLD, a teacher speaks into a small microphone and the words transmit clearly into a student's headphone or earpiece. **Sound field systems** amplify teachers' voices to eliminate sound issues in classroom environments. **Noise-cancelling headphones** are useful for students who need to work independently and limit distractions or behavioral triggers. **Audio recorders** allow students to record lectures or lessons and refer to the recordings later at their own pace. Some note-taking applications will transcribe audio into written words. Captioning is available to pair visual words with spoken words. **Text-to-speech (TTS) software** lets students see and hear words at the same time. TTS and audiobook technology can help students with fluency, decoding, and comprehension skills.

Voice Recognition Software

Voice recognition software and communication software can assist students who struggle with speaking or communicating. **Voice recognition software** allows people to speak commands into microphones to interact with the computer instead of using a keyboard. This feature helps create a **least restrictive environment** for a student with a disability because it removes the sometimes challenging aspect of using a keyboard while working on a computer. Voice recognition software allows users to carry out actions such as opening documents, saving documents, and moving the cursor. It also allows users to "write" sentences and paragraphs by speaking into the microphones in word processing programs. In order for voice recognition software to be effective, the user must learn to dictate words distinctly into a microphone. This ensures that the correct word is heard and dictated by the voice-to-text software. Some programs collect information and familiarize themselves with people's particular voice qualities. Over time, the systems adapt to people's voices and become more efficient.

Effectively Instructing Students Using Assistive Technology

Assistive technology (**AT**) refers to tools that are effective for teaching students with learning disabilities, as they address a number of potential special needs. The purpose of AT is to level the playing field for students with **learning disabilities**, particularly when they are participating in general education classrooms. AT can address learning difficulties in math, listening, organization, memory, reading, and writing. **AT for listening** can assist students who have difficulties processing language. For example, a personal listening device can help a student hear a teacher's voice more clearly. **AT for organization and memory** can help students with self-management tasks, such as keeping assignment calendars or retrieving information using hand-held devices. **AT for reading** often includes text-to-speech devices that assist with students' reading fluency, decoding, comprehension, and other skill deficits. **AT for writing** assists students who struggle with handwriting or writing development. Some AT writing devices help with actual handwriting, while others assist with spelling, punctuation, grammar, word usage, or text organization.

Augmentative and Alternative Communication Systems

Students with communication disorders may require the use of augmentative or alternative communication systems. Communication systems are used to help the students effectively demonstrate **expressive and receptive language** and engage in **social skills**. Teaching appropriate communication skills is a collaborative effort between the students' caretakers, teachers, and other professionals. Typically, **speech services** are written into students' IEPs and the services are delivered by **speech language pathologists (SLPs)**. Depending on the requirements in the IEPs, the SLPs may work one on one with students or work with the teachers to incorporate speech and language skills throughout students' school days. In order for communication systems to work for nonverbal students, measures must be taken to ensure that the particular systems are appropriate for what the students need. It is important for the caretakers, teachers, other professionals, and even classmates to model using the devices so the students can learn how to "talk" appropriately. Students must also have constant access to the systems and receive consistent opportunities to communicate with the systems at home and at school.

Use of Visual Representation Systems with Students with Autism

Assistive technology (AT) helps increase learning opportunities for students with autism by eliminating barriers to learning. AT can help improve students' expressive communication skills, attention skills, motivation skills, academic skills, and more. **Visual representation systems** in the form of objects, photographs, drawings, or written words provide concrete representations of words for students with autism. Visual representations, such as simple pictures paired with words, can be used to create visual schedules for students with autism. Photographs can be used to help students learn vocabulary words and the names of people and places. Written words should be paired with the visual representations in order to create links between the concrete objects and the actual words. The goal is for students to eventually recognize the words without the pictures. Visual representation systems can also help facilitate easier transitions between activities or places, which can be difficult for students with autism.

Communication Systems

Students who are nonverbal may have access to **communication systems** implemented by trained professionals. Teachers, caretakers, and other professionals work with the students to use the communication systems effectively. The goal of a communication system is to teach a nonverbal student how to "talk" and engage in **age-appropriate social skills**. In order for nonverbal students to learn appropriate social interactions, they must spend time learning communication skills, just as they learn academic content. Communication skills can be taught in isolation or as part of students' daily activities. Giving nonverbal students opportunities to foster communication skills in **familiar environments** makes it easier for them to learn appropriate social interactions. Teachers, caregivers, and other professionals must demonstrate how to use communication systems to engage in conversations, make requests, and answer questions. Most importantly, nonverbal students must be instructed to **access** their "words" (communication systems) at all times throughout the school and home environments.

Accessibility Components of a Picture Exchange Communication System

A Picture Exchange Communication System (**PECS**) is a communication system for people with little or no **communicative abilities**. This system is a way for the students to access their environments using **picture symbols** to communicate meaning, wants, and needs. For example, a child may point to a picture symbol to request a book. A PECS is a way for students with communication disorders to develop their **verbal communication** without actually speaking. It reduces frustration and problem behaviors by providing students with an avenue to express what they want to say. It is commonly used for students with autism spectrum disorder in the form of augmentative communication devices. It can also be used for students with other impairments whose communicative abilities are affected. PECS focuses on **functional communication skills** and can be practiced in home, school, and community environments.

Supporting Nonverbal Students

Nonverbal students have extra challenges in addition to learning content. These students may need extra instruction in academic areas as well as specialized instruction in the area of communication skills. Students with **nonverbal disabilities** may also need social skills instruction, struggle with abstract concepts, and dislike changes to their routines. Teachers can **facilitate learning** for nonverbal students by making changes to their classroom environments, by teaching strategies for comprehending concepts, and by providing materials to accommodate their needs. Teachers can also provide accommodations or modifications to classwork and tests to make the content accessible to nonverbal students. Using visuals to represent actions, words, or concepts is a helpful instructional strategy for teaching nonverbal students, especially when teaching new material. Additionally, teachers can assist nonverbal students by taking measures to prevent undesirable behaviors from occurring.

Teaching Strategies and Accommodations for Students with Working Memory Deficits

Working memory is critical for remembering letters and numbers, listening to short instructions, reading and understanding content, completing homework independently, and understanding social cues. When **working memory skills** are absent or slow to develop, learning may be difficult. This may get worse for children over time. As they fail to develop or retain working memory capabilities, their overall **cognitive abilities** begin to suffer. Working memory deficits vary among people with disabilities, but accommodations can make up for missing or underdeveloped skills. Educators can implement **strategies** like reducing the children's workload; being aware of when children might be reaching memory overload; and providing visual cues, positive feedback, testing alternatives, and extra time. **Accommodations** in an IEP for a student with working memory deficits might include frequent breaks, small group instruction, and extended time for tests and assignments.

Social and Functional Living Skills

Targeting and Implementing Social Skills Instruction

Developing good social skills is essential for lifelong success, and people with disabilities often struggle with these skills. Addressing social skill behavior is most effective when specific **social skill needs** are identified, and **social skills instruction** is implemented as a collaborative effort between parents and teachers.

Evaluating **developmental milestones** is helpful in targeting social skills that need to be addressed and taught. If a child with a disability is not demonstrating a milestone, such as back and forth communication, the skill can be evaluated to determine if it should be taught. However, meeting milestones is not a reliable way to measure a student's social skill ability, as some children naturally progress more slowly. **Social skill deficits** may be acquisition deficits, performance deficits, or fluency deficits. A student with an **acquisition deficit** demonstrates an absence of a skill or behavior. A student with a **performance deficit** does not implement a social skill consistently. A student with a **fluency deficit** needs assistance with demonstrating a social skill effectively or fluently. Once a student's social skill need is identified, teachers, parents, and other professionals can collaborate to address it by establishing a routine or a behavior contract or implementing applied behavior analysis.

Using Instructional Methods to Address Independent Living Skills

When applicable, goals for independent living skills are included in the **transition section** of students' IEPs. However, **independent living skills education** should begin well before students reach high school, regardless of whether these skills are addressed in their IEP goals. **Functional skills instruction** is necessary to teach students skills needed to gain independence. Instructional methods used to address independent living skills for students with disabilities include making life skills instruction part of the daily curriculum. An appropriate **task analysis** can be used to determine what skills need to be taught. **Functional academic skills**, especially in the areas of math and language arts, should also be included in the curriculum. Telling time, balancing a checkbook, and recognizing signs and symbols are just some examples of basic skills that students can generalize outside of the classroom environment. The goal of **community-based instruction** is to help students develop skills needed to succeed in the community, such as skills needed when riding a bus or shopping. This type of instruction may be harder to implement than basic social skills training, which should be part of the daily curriculum.

Purposes and Benefits of Social Skills Groups

Social skills groups are useful for helping students with social skill deficits learn and practice appropriate skills with their peers. Social skills groups are primarily composed of similarly aged peers with and without disabilities. An adult leads these groups and teaches students skills needed for making friends, succeeding in school and life, and sometimes obtaining and maintaining a job. Other professionals, such as school psychologists or speech language pathologists, may also lead social skills groups. Social skills groups work by facilitating **conversation** and focusing on **skill deficits**. These groups can help students learn to read facial cues, appropriately greet others, begin conversations, respond appropriately, maintain conversations, engage in turn-taking, and request help when needed.

Evidence-Based Methods for Promoting Self-Determination

Students with disabilities often need to be taught **self-determination** and **self-advocacy** skills. These skills may not come easily to students with specific disorders, like ASD. Self-determination involves a comprehensive understanding of one's own **strengths and limitations**. Self-determined people are **goal-oriented** and intrinsically motivated to **improve themselves**. Teachers can facilitate the development of these skills in a number of ways, starting in early elementary school. In early elementary school, teachers can promote self-determination by teaching choice-making skills and providing clear consequences for choices. Teachers can also promote problem-solving and self-management skills, like having students evaluate their own work. At the middle school and junior high school level, students can be taught to evaluate and analyze their choices. They can also learn academic and personal goal-setting skills and decision-making skills. At the high school level, teachers can promote decision-making skills, involvement in educational planning (e.g., students attending their IEP meetings), and strategies like self-instruction, self-monitoring, and self-evaluation. Throughout the education process, teachers should establish and maintain high standards for learning, focus on students' strengths, and create positive learning environments that promote choice and problem-solving skills.

Teaching Self-Awareness Skills

Students engage in private self-awareness and public self-awareness. Some students with disabilities have the additional challenge of needing instruction in **self-awareness skills**. Special educators and other professionals can facilitate the instruction of self-awareness skills by teaching students to be **aware** of their thoughts, feelings, and actions; to recognize that other people have needs and feelings; and to recognize how their behaviors **affect other people**. Students can be taught self-awareness by identifying their own strengths and weaknesses and learning to self-monitor errors in assignments. They can also be taught to identify what materials or steps are needed to complete tasks and to advocate for accommodations or strategies that work for them. Special educators or other professionals should frequently talk with students about their performance and encourage them to discuss their mistakes without criticism.

Importance of Learning Self-Advocacy Skills

Self-advocacy is an important skill to learn for people entering adulthood. For students with disabilities, **self-advocacy skills** are especially important for success in **post-secondary environments**. Teaching and learning self-advocacy skills should begin when students enter grade school and be reinforced in the upper grade levels. Students with disabilities who have the potential to enter post-secondary education or employment fields need to learn self-advocacy skills in order to **communicate** how their disabilities may affect their education or job performance and their need for supports and possible accommodations. Students with disabilities who graduate or age out of their IEPs do not receive the **educational supports** they received at the grade school level. It is essential for students to advocate for themselves in the absence of teachers or caregivers advocating for them, especially when students independently enter post-secondary employment, training, or educational environments. Many colleges, universities, communities, and workplaces offer services to students with disabilities, but it is up to the students to advocate for themselves and seek them out.

Teaching Functional Living Skills

Also known as life skills, functional living skills are skills that students need to live independently. Ideally, students leave high school having gained functional skills. For students with special needs, **functional living skills instruction** may be needed to gain independent living skills. Students with developmental or cognitive disabilities sometimes need to acquire basic living skills, such as self-feeding or toileting. **Applied behavior analysis** is a process by which these skills can be identified, modeled, and taught. Students must also learn functional math and language arts skills, such as managing money and reading bus schedules. Students may also participate in **community-based instruction** to learn skills while completing independent living tasks in the community. These skills include grocery shopping, reading restaurant menus, and riding public transportation. **Social skills instruction** is also important for these students, as learning appropriate social interactions is necessary to function with community members.

Adaptive Behavior Skills Instruction

Adaptive behavior skills refer to age-appropriate behaviors that people need to live independently and function in daily life. **Adaptive behavior skills** include self-care, following rules, managing money, making friends, and more. For students with disabilities, especially severely limiting disabilities, adaptive behavior skills may need to be included in daily instruction. Adaptive behavior skills can be separated into conceptual skills, social skills, and practical life skills. **Conceptual skills** include academic concepts, such as reading, math, money, time, and communication skills. **Social skills** instruction focuses on teaching students to get along with others, communicate appropriately, and maintain appropriate behavior inside and outside the school environment. **Practical life skills** are skills needed to perform the daily living tasks, such as bathing, eating, sitting and standing, and using the bathroom. Adaptive behavior assessments are useful in assessing what adaptive behavior skills need to be addressed for each student. These assessments are usually conducted using observations and questionnaires completed by parents, teachers, or students.

Social Skill Deficits

Social skills generally develop alongside language development and emotional development, as they are a major component of communication and awareness. Social skills need to be taught to some students with disabilities, such as students with autism. **Social skills instruction** involves the teaching of basic communication skills, empathy and rapport skills, interpersonal skills, problem-solving skills, and accountability. These are skills that do not come naturally to students with social skill deficits.

- **Basic communication skills** include listening, following directions, and taking turns in conversations.
- **Emotional communication skills** include demonstrating empathy and building rapport with others.
- **Interpersonal skills** include sharing, joining activities, and participating in turn taking.
- **Problem-solving skills** include asking for help, apologizing to others, making decisions, and accepting consequences.
- **Accountability** includes following through on promises and accepting criticism appropriately.

Instructional Methods for Teaching Students with Social Skill Deficits

Students with social skill deficits may or may not require explicit social skills instruction. These deficits can be addressed in inclusive settings. **Social skills instruction** can be delivered to entire classes or individual students, depending on the needs of the students. Also, **one-on-one** or **small group social skills instruction** can be delivered by professionals like speech-language pathologists. In both settings, it is important to model appropriate manners, hold students responsible for their actions, and have clear and concise rules and consequences. This creates educational environments that are both predictable and safe. Social situations that produce undesired outcomes can be remediated by **role-playing** the situations and teaching students positive responses. **Social stories** are another way to foster social skills growth. Often, these social stories demonstrate appropriate responses to specific social situations. The goal is for the students to generalize learned concepts to their school and home environments.

Life Stage Transitions

Supporting Students Through Transitions

Transitioning to life after high school can be a difficult process, particularly for students with disabilities. It is important for teachers to facilitate and support these **transitions** before students exit their special education programs. **Structured learning environments** that include independent workstations and learning centers provide opportunities for independent learning to occur. **Independent workstations** give students chances to practice previously introduced concepts or perform previously introduced tasks. **Learning centers** provide small group settings where new skills can be taught. Students can also rotate through different learning centers that offer art lessons, focus on academic skills, or provide breaks or leisure activities. **Classroom layout** also plays an important role. Teachers should plan their classroom layouts based on individual student needs in order to create comfortable, predictable environments for students with disabilities. **Visual schedules** help students transition between centers by providing them with concrete schedule references.

Benefits of Vocational Education

Students with disabilities often participate in vocational education in order to gain **independent living skills**. Often, schools and communities offer services that provide vocational training for people with disabilities. These programs offer students **job-specific skills training** and opportunities to earn certifications, diplomas, or certificates. They often involve **hands-on learning experiences** focused on building skills specific to certain occupations. These programs are beneficial to students with disabilities who may struggle with grasping abstract concepts learned in typical classroom environments. Hands-on training in vocational programs can be a meaningful way for students with disabilities to both learn academic concepts and gain living skills needed to function in post-graduate life. Vocational education opportunities offer alternatives for students with disabilities who might otherwise drop out of high school. These programs also serve as a viable option for younger students to work towards, as most vocational education programs are offered to students in upper grade levels.

Vocational Skills Needed to Be Successful in Work Environments

Informal vocational training often begins before students even get to high school. Teachers include informal vocational training skills in their classrooms by teaching academic and communication skills. **Academic skills** can both spark and strengthen students' career interests and provide learning platforms to build upon. **Communication skills**, like giving and following instructions and processing information, generalize to work environments. **Social and interpersonal skills**, like problem-solving abilities and participating in phone conversations, are important for performance in workplaces. Students need to learn important **vocational and occupational skills** required by most jobs, such as interacting appropriately with coworkers and keeping track of worked hours. Students also need formal or informal training in completing resumes, cover letters, and tax forms. Training may also include interview practice and job search guidance.

Resources to Promote Successful Transitions to Life after High School

In some states, **statements of transition** should be included in individualized education programs at age 14 for students with disabilities. In most states, the Individuals with Disabilities Education Act mandates that transition plans be put in place for students with IEPs at age 16 and every year thereafter. Some schools and communities have programs and resources available to facilitate students' successful transitions to life after high school. Throughout the transition process, it is important that students and their caregivers participate in any decision-making processes. **Vocational education courses**, sometimes called career and technical education (CTE) courses, offer academic course alternatives. The courses usually specialize in specific trades or occupations. They can serve to spark or maintain students' interests in vocational fields. Some schools offer **post-secondary enrollment options (PSEO)**, where students can participate in college courses, earning both high school and college credits. **Career assessments**, including interest inventories and formal and informal vocational assessments, serve to gauge students' career interests. These can be worked into students' transitional goals in their IEPs and should be conducted frequently, as students' interests change.

Components of a Transition Plan

Transition plans are flexible, but formal plans that help a student identify his or her goals for after school and act as a roadmap to help the support team advocate for the student's future. They generally include post-secondary goals and expected transition services. The four goal areas are vocational training, post-secondary education, employment, and independent living. **Transition goals** must be results oriented and measurable. Goals can be general, but the transition activities need to be quantified to reflect what the student can complete in the IEP year. It is common for interests to change from year to year; therefore, goals and plans may change as well. **Transition services** are determined once the goals are established. Transition services include types of instruction the student will receive in school, related services, community experiences, career or college counseling, and help with adaptive behavior skills. Goals and transition services must be reviewed and updated each year. Academic goals in the IEP can also support transition goals. For example, math goals can focus on money management skills as part of a transition plan.

Factors That Influence Successful Transitions to Post-Secondary Life

Parents or legal guardians, teachers, school professionals, community members, and students themselves can all contribute to successful transitions to post-secondary life. Key **factors** that help students successfully transition include the following:

- Participation in standards-based education
- Work preparation and career-based learning experiences
- Leadership skills
- Access to and experience with community services, such as mental health and transportation services
- Family involvement and support

Standards-based education ensures that students receive consistent and clear expectations with a curriculum that is aligned to the universal design for learning standards. Exposure to work preparation and career-based learning experiences ensures that students receive opportunities to discover potential career interests or hobbies. Connections and experiences with community activities provide students with essential post-secondary independent living skills. Family involvement and support ensure that students have advocates for their needs and interests. Families can also help students connect with school and community-based supports that facilitate their career interests.

Instructional Design for Students with Disabilities

Developmentally Appropriate Curriculum

Choosing a developmentally appropriate curriculum is challenging for educators. Special educators have the additional challenge of finding a curriculum that meets the needs of the **individual students with disabilities**. The end result is not usually a one-size-fits-all curriculum because that goes against the intentions of IEPs designed to meet the needs of students with special needs. Instead, special educators often pick and choose curriculum components that best meet the needs of differing abilities in the classroom. When selecting an appropriate curriculum, special educators should consider the following:

- Standards and goals that are appropriate to the needs of the students
- Best practices that have been found effective for students
- Curricula that are engaging and challenging
- Instruction and activities that are multi-modal
- IEP goals
- Real-world experiences
- Different ways of learning that help teachers understand students' learning processes
- Collaboration with co-teachers to deliver appropriate instruction

In some special education settings, the curriculum is already chosen. In these settings, teachers can collaborate with co-teachers to find ways to provide instruction that meets standards and the individual needs of the students.

Components of a Differentiated Instruction

Differentiated instruction is different from individualized instruction. It targets the strengths of students and can work well in both special education and general education settings. **Differentiated instruction** is also useful for targeting the needs of students with **learning and attention deficits**. With differentiated instruction, teachers adjust their instructional processes to meet the needs of the individual students. Teaching strategies and classroom management skills are based largely on each particular class of students instead of on methods that may have been successful in the past. Teachers can differentiate content, classroom activities, student projects, and the learning environments. For example, students may be encouraged to choose topics of personal interest to focus on for projects. Students are held to the same standards but have many choices in terms of project topics. **Differentiated content** provides access to a variety of resources to encourage student choice over what and how they learn. **Differentiated learning environments** are flexible to meet the ever-changing needs of the students.

Effectiveness of Differentiated Instruction

Differentiated instruction is effective in general education settings, team-teaching settings, and special education settings because it targets the **strengths** of students. Differentiated instruction is used to target the different ways that students learn instead of taking a one-size-fits-all approach. Differentiated instruction is used in lieu of individualized instruction because it uses a variety of instructional approaches and allows students access to a variety of materials to help them access the curriculum. **Effective differentiated instruction** includes small group work, reciprocal learning, and continual assessment.

Small group work allows for the individual learning styles and needs of students to be addressed. In small groups, students receive instruction by rotating through groups. Group work should be used sparingly or be well-regulated to ensure that all of the students in the group is learning for themselves and contributing to group work sufficiently. Groups may be shuffled or have assigned roles within the group to ensure a good division of labor. In **reciprocal learning**, students play the role of the teacher, instructing the class by sharing what they know and asking content questions of their peers. Teachers who practice **continual assessment** can determine if their differentiated instructional methods are effective or if they need to be changed. Assessments can determine what needs to be changed in order for students to participate in effective classroom environments.

Different Educational Levels and Learning Styles

Learning styles of students differ, regardless of whether or not the students have disabilities. When addressing groups of students in inclusion settings, it is important for teachers to organize and implement teaching strategies that address learning at **different educational levels**. Students generally fall into one or more learning modes. Some are visual learners, some are auditory learners, some are kinesthetic or tactile learners, and some learn best using a combination of these approaches. Teachers can address students' educational levels by creating lessons that allow learning to take place visually, auditorily, and kinesthetically. **Visual learners** prefer information that has been visually organized, such as in graphic organizers or diagrams. **Auditory learners** prefer information presented in spoken words. Lessons that target auditory learners provide opportunities for students to engage in conversations and question material. **Kinesthetic learners** prefer a hands-on approach to learning. These learners prefer to try out new tasks and learn as they go. Lessons that include opportunities for these three types of learning to occur can successfully target different educational levels.

Multiple Modality Instruction and Activities

The purpose of multiple modality instruction is to engage students by offering different ways to learn the same material. **Multiple modality teaching** also addresses students' unique learning styles. Learning modalities are generally separated into four categories: **visual** (seeing), **auditory** (hearing), **kinesthetic** (moving), and **tactile** (touch) modalities. This way of teaching targets students who may have deficits in one or more modalities. It is also helpful for students who struggle in one or more of the learning categories. If a student struggles with understanding content that is presented visually, a lesson that includes auditory, kinesthetic, and tactile components may engage learning. Additionally, presenting lesson material and activities in a multi-modal approach helps improve student memory and retention by solidifying concepts through multiple means of engagement. This approach is also useful for students with **attention disorders** who may struggle in environments where one mode of teaching is used. The multiple modality approach ensures that activities, such as kinesthetic or tactile activities, keep more than one sense involved with the learning process.

Using Visual Supports to Facilitate Instruction and Self-Monitoring Strategies

Many students learn best when provided with instruction and activities that appeal to multiple senses. A **multi-modal approach** is especially important for students with developmental disabilities, who may need supports that match their individual ways of learning. **Visual supports** are concrete representations of information used to convey meaning. Teachers can use visual supports to help students with developmental disabilities understand what is being taught and communicated to them. Visual supports can help students with understanding classroom rules, making decisions, communicating with others, staying organized, and reducing frustrations. **Visual schedules** show students visual representations of their daily schedules. This assists with transitions between activities, which can sometimes be difficult for students with disabilities. Visuals can be used to help students share information about themselves or their school days with their peers and parents. Visual supports can also be used with checklists to help facilitate independence. For example, behavior checklists can be used to help students monitor their own behaviors.

Universal Design for Learning

Universal design for learning (UDL) is a flexible approach to learning that keeps students' individual needs in mind. Teachers that utilize **UDL** offer different ways for students to access material and engage in content. This approach is helpful for many students but particularly those with learning and attention issues. The **principles of UDL** all center on varying instruction and assessment to appeal to the needs of students who think in various ways.

Principles of the Universal Design for Learning	
Multiple means of *representation*	*Instructional content* should be demonstrated in various ways so that students may learn in a mode that is effective for them.
Multiple means of *expression*	*Assessment* should be administered in a variety of ways to adequately allow students to demonstrate their knowledge. This includes quizzes, homework, presentations, classwork, etc.
Multiple means of *engagement*	Instruction should include a variety of *motivational factors* that help to interest and challenge students in exciting ways.

Review Video: Universal Design for Learning
Visit mometrix.com/academy and enter code: 523916

Evaluating, Modifying, and Adapting the Classroom Setting Using the UDL

The **universal design for learning (UDL)** is a framework that encourages teachers to design their instruction and assessment in ways that allow for **multiple means** for the student to learn and express their knowledge. The UDL model is most successful when the teacher prepares a classroom setting that encourages the success of students with and without disabilities. Knowledge of the **characteristics** of students with different disabilities, as well as the unique **learning needs** of these students, enables the teacher to address these needs in the classroom setting. Setting clear short- and long-term goals for students is one way to meet the UDL standards. A traditional classroom may offer one assignment for all students to complete, but a UDL-compliant classroom may offer **different assignments** or **different ways** for students to complete assignments. UDL-compliant classrooms often offer **flexible workspaces** for students to complete their classwork and may offer quiet spaces for individual work or group tables for group work. UDL-compliant teachers recognize that students access information differently and provide different ways for students to gain **access** to the information, such as through audio text or physical models to work with. The universal design for learning assumes students learn in a variety of ways, even if those ways have not been clearly identified; it follows that all instruction and assessment can be improved by making it more varied and accessible.

Modifying Classroom Curriculum and Materials for UDL

In order for a **universal design for learning (UDL) model classroom** to be successful, the teacher must evaluate, modify, and adapt the **curriculum** and **materials** to best suit the needs of the individual students. UDL contrasts with a one-size-fits-all concept of curriculum planning, where lesson plans are developed and implemented strictly based on how teachers expect students to learn. Instead, a successful UDL model addresses the many **specific needs** of the students. These needs vary depending on the unique abilities each classroom of students presents. UDL-compliant teachers can evaluate the success of lessons by checking for comprehension throughout lessons instead of only upon lesson completion. Evaluation methods used informally can provide a lot of information about whether students are grasping the concepts. Teachers use the results of the evaluations to modify and adapt classroom instruction to meet the needs of the students. Other means for diversifying the materials include using multiple assignment completion options and use of varied means of accessing the materials, such as both written, digital, and audio forms of a text. These means of instruction can take place simultaneously. For instance, a UDL-compliant teacher may choose to pair audio output and text for all students during a reading assignment in order to target students with listening or comprehension difficulties.

Principles of the Universal Design for Learning Model

The UDL model contains three principles that aim to level the playing field for all learners. **Principle I** of the universal design for learning model primarily focuses on what **representation or version** of information is being taught. This principle aims to target an audience of diverse learners. By providing multiple ways for students to approach content, teachers can ensure that the unique needs of all learners in their classrooms are met. **Principle II** examines how people learn. This principle focuses on the concept that students learn best when provided with **multiple ways** to demonstrate what they have learned. In Principle II compliant classrooms, students are given more than one option for expressing themselves. **Principle III** focuses on providing multiple ways for students to engage in the learning process. Principle III compliant teachers provide options for keeping content **interesting and relevant** to all types of learners. Effective UDL-model classrooms provide multiple ways to present content, engage in learning, and express what was learned.

Specially Designed Instruction

Specially designed instruction (**SDI**) in special education refers to specialized teaching given to students in a co-taught inclusion classroom. While a teacher teaches the class, the special education teacher provides specialized instruction in parallel to a student to help clarify the information. This is distinctive from adaptation and modification, as the content and its medium do not change for SDI. While the general education class engages in instruction, a special education teacher provides SDI to meet the specific needs of learners who may not be successful learning in the same ways as their similar-aged peers. The main purpose of SDI is to provide a student with access to the general education setting without substantially changing the content as it is aligned with state standards.

Diagnostic Prescriptive Method

The diagnostic prescriptive approach to teaching is based on the fact that all students are unique learners. The **diagnostic prescriptive approach** examines factors that impede student learning and how to remedy specific issues. A successful approach begins with a **diagnosis** of what students are bringing to the classroom. This can be completed through careful observations and assessments. Once the skill deficits are clear, **prescriptive teaching** can be put into effect. In this process, teachers examine what will help students the most. It may be switching materials, changing to group settings, or recognizing the need for specialized interventions due to disabilities. In order to address multiple needs in the classroom, lesson plans should be **multi-modal**. Developing strategies in advance to address students' needs is also a highlight of this method. Another important part of this method is evaluating results to determine what was effective or ineffective for entire classes and individual students.

Guided Learning

Guided learning is practice or instruction completed by the teacher and students together. The goal of **guided learning** is to help students engage in the learning process in order to learn more about how they think and acquire new information. **Guided practice** occurs when the teacher and students complete practice activities together. The advantage of guided practice is that students can learn ways to approach concepts they have just learned. It allows students to understand and ask questions about lesson-related activities before working independently. Guided practice is useful in classrooms for students with and without disabilities because it helps teachers gauge how students learn and what instructional methods work best for them. Additionally, guided practice allows teachers to understand how students are learning the material. It also allows teachers to revisit concepts that are unclear or fine tune any missed lesson objectives.

How Cooperative Learning Works

Cooperative learning is an interpersonal group learning process where students learn concepts by working together in **small groups**. Cooperative learning involves collaboration among small groups to achieve common goals. With **formal cooperative learning**, an instructor oversees the learning of lesson material or completion of assignments for students in these small groups. With **informal cooperative learning**, the instructor supervises group activities by keeping students cognitively active but does not guide instruction or assignments. For example, a teacher might use a class period to show a movie but provide a list of questions for students to complete during the movie. In the special education classroom, cooperative learning is helpful when students need specific skills targeted or remediated. It is also helpful for separating students who are learning different content at different levels. For example, a cooperative learning activity may involve multiple groups of students with differing levels of mathematic abilities. Group work also promotes development of interpersonal skills as students interact with one another.

Intrinsic Motivation

Intrinsic motivation is a person's inner drive to engage in an activity or behavior. Students with special needs often struggle with intrinsic motivation as a skill. This requires special educators and other professionals to promote and teach intrinsic motivation to students. Teachers can **promote intrinsic motivation** by giving students opportunities to demonstrate **achievement**. This can be done by challenging students with intellectual risks and helping them focus on difficult classwork or tasks. Teachers can build upon students' strengths by providing daily opportunities in the classroom for students to demonstrate their **strengths** instead of focusing on their weaknesses. Offering choices throughout the day provides students with ownership of their decision-making and communicates that they have choices in the classroom environment. Teachers should allow students to **fail without criticism** and should promote self-reflection in order to build students' confidence. Teachers should promote self-management and organizational skills like instructing students on how to **break down tasks**.

Promoting Critical Thinking Skills

Critical thinking is a self-directed thinking process that helps people make logical, reasonable judgements. This is an especially challenging skill for students with **developmental disabilities**, who often demonstrate deficits in logical thinking and reasoning abilities. In order to teach these students **critical thinking skills**, the focus should be on encouraging critical thinking across **home and school environments** and providing opportunities for students to practice this type of thinking. Teachers and parents can encourage critical thinking by implementing teaching strategies focused on fostering **creativity** in students. Instead of providing outlines or templates for lesson concepts, students can use their prior knowledge to figure out the boundaries of the lessons independently and explore new concepts. Parents and teachers should not always be quick to jump in and help students who are struggling. Sometimes the best way to help is by facilitating ways for students to solve problems without doing things for them. Opportunities for brainstorming, classifying and categorizing information, comparing and contrasting information, and making connections between topics are teaching strategies that also facilitate critical thinking skills.

Career-Based Education

During their schooling years, students with disabilities have the additional challenge of determining possible **career options** for life after high school. Fortunately, instruction can be provided during the school day or within after-school programs that address career-based skills. Effective **career-based programs** for students with disabilities should work collaboratively with community and school resources. Students should receive information on career options, be exposed to a range of experiences, and learn how to self-advocate. Information regarding career options can be gathered via **career assessments** that explore students' possible career interests. Students should receive exposure to **post-secondary education** to determine if it is an option that aligns with their career interests. They should also learn about basic job requirements, such as what it means to earn a living wage and entry requirements for different types of jobs. Students should be given opportunities for job training, job shadowing, and community service. It is helpful to provide students with opportunities to learn and practice **work and occupational skills** that pertain to specific job interests. Students need to learn **self-advocacy skills**, such as communicating the implications of their disabilities to employers, in order to maintain success in post-secondary work environments.

Assessment for Students with Disabilities

Alternate Assessments

Students with and without disabilities are typically expected to take the same standardized tests, sometimes with accommodations and modifications. Some students with disabilities take **alternate assessments**, which are forms of the standardized tests that other students take. Students that participate in alternate assessments are unable to participate in state standardized tests even with accommodations. Less than 1% of students in public school districts participate in alternate assessments. They are mostly intended for students with **intellectual disabilities** or **severe cognitive delays**. Alternate assessments are based on **alternate achievement standards (AAS)**, which are modified versions of state achievement standards. Alternate assessments are a way for students' progress to be assessed with standards that are more appropriate for their skills. For example, a state standard for math may not be appropriate for a student with an intellectual disability. Instead, the student may have the alternate standard of demonstrating the ability to count money to make a purchase. Teachers, parents, and students work collaboratively to demonstrate that the achievement standards are met.

Role of Formal Assessments in the Education of a Student with Disabilities

Formal assessments measure how well a student has mastered learning material and are useful in detecting if a student is **falling behind** in general or at the end of a unit. Formal test results can be used to compare the performance of a student with disabilities against other students of similar demographics. **Developmental assessments** are norm-referenced tests that are designed to assess the development of young children. Developmental assessments are used to identify the strengths and weaknesses of a child suspected of having a disability. **Intelligence tests** are another type of norm-referenced test that can determine a student's potential to learn academic skills. Intelligence tests, sometimes called IQ tests, also indicate a student's specific level of intelligence. This is helpful in knowing if a student's learning problems are associated with sub-average intellectual abilities or other factors, such as an emotional disturbance. A student with an emotional disturbance or specific learning disability would have an average or above-average intelligence score, whereas a student with intellectual disabilities would have a sub-average score. **Curriculum-based assessments** are also helpful in determining where, specifically, a student needs the most help within a content area.

Interest Inventories

Interest inventories are tools for measuring people's interests or preferences in activities. They are useful for gathering information about a student's likes and dislikes. In special education, interest inventories are sometimes used to help develop the **transition portion** of an IEP. A student's interests as determined by an interest inventory can be used to drive the entire IEP. For an older student with a driving interest in mind, interest inventories can also be reflected in the annual IEP goals. Interest inventories can come in the form of observations, ability tests, or self-reported inventories. They can also work as age-appropriate **transition assessments** used in the transition statement section of the IEP. An advantage of interest inventories is that they help students get to know their own strengths and interests. They are also useful in guiding students with disabilities into thinking about post-secondary careers, education, or independent living.

Role of Informal Assessments in the Education of a Student with Disabilities

Informal assessments are a little more flexible for teachers, particularly in the ways they can be administered in the classroom. In special education, informal assessments play an important role in **adjusting instruction** to meet the specific needs of a student. Using informal assessment outcomes to drive instruction helps ensure that academic or behavioral student needs are met. Informal assessments are also helpful in adjusting instruction to meet **specific goals or objectives** on a student's IEP. Checklists, running records, observations, and work samples are all informal assessments from which data for IEP goals can be collected. **Checklists** can include behaviors or academic skills the student is meant to achieve. **Running records** help provide insight into student behavior over time by focusing on a sequence of events. **Work samples** are helpful in providing a concrete snapshot of a student's academic capabilities.

Special Education Settings

Least Restrictive Environment

The Individuals with Disabilities Education Act (IDEA) requires a free and appropriate public education (FAPE) to be provided in a student's **least restrictive environment (LRE)**. This means that a student with a disability who qualifies for special education should be educated in a free, appropriate, and public setting and be placed in an instructional setting that meets the LRE principle. The IDEA states that LRE means students with disabilities should participate in the general education classroom "to the maximum extent appropriate." **Mainstreaming** and **inclusion** are ways for students with disabilities to participate in general education classrooms while receiving appropriate accommodations, modifications, interventions, and related services. The amount of time students spend in an LRE suitable for their individual needs is stated in their Individualized Education Program (IEP). The accommodations, modifications, interventions, and related services the student should receive are also outlined in the IEP. Students who need special education services for more than 50% of the day may be placed in other instructional settings that meet their LRE needs, such as resource rooms or self-contained classrooms.

Continuum of Special Education Services

The IDEA mandates that school systems educate students with disabilities with students who do not have disabilities to the maximum extent that is appropriate. The IDEA also mandates that schools not take students out of regular education classes unless the classes are not benefiting the students. Supplementary aids and support services must be in place before students can be considered for removal. Schools must offer a **continuum of special education services** that range from restrictive to least restrictive. In a typical continuum of services, regular education classrooms offer the **least restrictive access** to students with disabilities. Next on the continuum are resource rooms, followed by special classes that target specific deficits. Special schools, homebound services, hospitals, and institutions are the most restrictive education environments. The number of students at each stage of the continuum decreases as restriction increases. Fewer students benefit more from being educated in hospitals or institutions than in resource rooms.

Inclusion Classroom Setting

The principle of **least restrictive environment (LRE)** is a right guaranteed under the Individuals with Disabilities Education Act (IDEA) to protect a student from unnecessary restriction or seclusion from the general population. IDEA does not expressly define an LRE for each specific disability, so it is the responsibility of the IEP team of professionals, including the student's parent or legal guardian, to determine the best **LRE setting** possible for an individual student. **Mainstreaming** or **inclusion** is the practice of keeping students with disabilities in the general education setting for the entire school day. The students may receive supports and services like aides, assistive technology, accommodations, and modifications that are appropriate for their individual needs. These supports and services are intended to help students with disabilities gain access to the general education curriculum with the fewest possible barriers. The principle of LRE also sits on a spectrum and allows for variable inclusion or separation throughout parts of the day depending on a student's particular needs. As this is a student right, any more restrictive setting must be **justified by necessity** in students' IEPs and cannot be determined by convenience or financial considerations of the school or staff.

Collaborative Teaching in an Inclusion Classroom

If determined by an individualized education program, a student with a disability may participate in an **inclusive setting**. In some classrooms, students participate in **co-taught settings**. In this **collaborative teaching environment**, the general educator and special educator work together to meet the goals of the students with disabilities in the regular education classroom. Students in this setting are all taught to the same educational standards. However, accommodations and modifications may be implemented for students with disabilities. In a successful collaborative teaching model, the special educator and general educator may cooperatively implement the accommodations and modifications for these students. A two-teacher setting also gives students more opportunities to receive individualized instruction, work in small groups, or receive one-on-one attention. Collaborative teaching in the co-taught setting can facilitate differentiated instruction, help teachers follow the universal design for learning framework, and provide individualized learning opportunities.

Implementing Modifications and Accommodations in an Inclusion Classroom

General educators can work with special educators to create an effective **co-teaching model**. In an effective co-teaching model, both general educators and special educators are guided by the **universal design for learning framework**. This helps ensure that the needs of the diverse group of learners are being met. Students' individualized education programs expressly document any required modifications, such as reduced work. In a co-teaching model, student modifications are communicated to the **general educator**. The **special educator** can work with the general educator to provide the modifications in an inclusive classroom setting. Students' IEPs also expressly document any required **accommodations**. These accommodations may or may not be used in an inclusive setting, depending on the relevancy of the accommodation. For example, the accommodation of using a calculator would be utilized in a math class but not a social studies class. In addition to expressly written accommodations, special educators and general educators can work together in an inclusive setting to provide appropriate accommodations during the learning process. These accommodations may be part of informal assessments used to adjust instruction.

Role of Paraeducators

Paraeducators, sometimes referred to as aides or paraprofessionals, are part of students' education teams. **Paraeducators** work under the supervision of special educators or principals and are key contributors to the learning process for certain students. Their primary role, especially if their positions are funded by the Individuals with Disabilities Education Act, is to provide **educational support** for students. The use of paraeducators is noted in students' IEPs. Paraeducators can facilitate the learning process for students by removing learning barriers, keeping track of goal progress, and organizing goal-tracking activities. Paraeducators cannot introduce new concepts or take over the role of teachers. Paraeducators cannot make changes to what students are learning unless specific modifications are listed in students' IEPs. They cannot provide accommodations unless the accommodations are appropriate for what is written in students' IEPs. Paraeducators may also be instructed by supervising teachers or principals to facilitate and monitor accommodations or modifications for students and reinforce learned concepts.

Self-Contained Classroom Setting

According to the Individuals with Disabilities Education Act, LRE standards require students to spend as much time as possible with their non-disabled peers in the **general education setting**. This means students should receive general education "to the maximum extent appropriate," and special classes, special schools, or removal from the general education classroom should only be considered when students' needs are greater than what can be provided by supplementary aids and services. A **self-contained classroom setting** can be a separate class within a school or a separate school for students with disabilities whose needs are greater than what can be offered in the general education classroom even with educational supports. These settings may provide specialized instruction and support for students with similar needs. Placement in self-contained classrooms must be justified in students' IEPs.

Partial Mainstream/Inclusion Classroom Setting

It is generally up to the individualized education program team of professionals and the parent or legal guardian to determine the LRE that best suits the needs of a student. In a partial mainstream/inclusion classroom setting, a student spends part of the day in the general education classroom and part of the day in a separate, special education classroom. This type of LRE is appropriate when a student's needs are greater than what can be provided in the general education classroom even with educational supports or services in place. For example, a student with severe deficits in mathematical skills may receive math instruction in a separate classroom or receive one-on-one or small group instruction. Placement in partial mainstream/inclusion classrooms must be justified in students' IEPs.

Specialized Education Settings

School districts sometimes offer specialized education settings for students with disabilities, such as **special preschools**. Preschools for children with disabilities typically focus on children aged 3–5 years. They are important resources for teaching early learning, communication, and social skills that are essential for children with disabilities. In **life skills settings**, students with disabilities can receive specialized instruction in academic, social, behavioral, and daily-living skills. **Social behavior skills settings** are sometimes called "applied behavior skills settings" or "behavior skills settings." In this setting, the primary focus is on social and decision-making skills. **Transition settings** are available for students making the transition from high school to life after high school. Students with IEPs can stay in high school until the age of 21 or 22, depending on the calendar month they turn 22. Transition settings assist students with work experiences, post-secondary education experiences, and independent living skills.

Behavioral Issues for Students with Disabilities

Behavioral Issues and Intervention Strategies

Behavior issues occur with students with and without disabilities. However, they may occur more frequently or to a higher degree for some students with disabilities. Behavior issues are often a **manifestation** of a child's disability. For example, students with attention-deficit/hyperactivity disorder may present with attention and focus issues and impulsivity. **Common behavior issues** include the following:

- Emotional outbursts
- Inattention and inability to focus
- Impulsivity
- Aggression
- Abusive language
- Oppositional defiance
- Lying or stealing
- Threatening adults or peers

Other behavior issues may include inappropriate sexual behavior, inability to control sexual behavior, self-harm, or self-harm attempts. Behavior issues can be **avoided** or **remediated** with classroom management skills like setting clear and consistent classroom goals, setting time limits, and providing visuals to assist with transitions or concepts. When a student is in an aggressive state, it is important for the teacher to remain calm, provide choices for the student, and restate the consequences of any aggressive outbursts.

Review Video: Student Behavior Management Approaches
Visit mometrix.com/academy and enter code: 843846

Review Video: Promoting Appropriate Behavior
Visit mometrix.com/academy and enter code: 321015

Managing Students with Emotional Disorders

Managing a classroom of students with emotional disorders can be challenging and unpredictable. Students with emotional disorders have Individualized Education Program (IEP) goals that focus on **controlling** or **monitoring** their daily behavior choices. However, this does not always mean they will engage in meeting these goals. It is important for educators to know how to **manage** issues that students with emotional disorders may bring to the classroom. When creating resources and lesson plans, an educator should do the following:

- Establish a **safety plan**, which includes knowing how to implement a **crisis prevention plan**.
- Maintain an environment that reduces **stimulation** and provides **visual cues** for expected behavior.
- Implement **intervention-based strategies** for managing student behavior.
- Collect and use **data** to identify triggers, track behaviors, and recognize strategies that produce positive outcomes.
- Practice open **communication** about classroom expectations to students, parents, and other teachers.

Special education teachers can be helpful in implementing these guidelines, especially when students with emotional disorders are in inclusive settings.

Supporting Students with Mental Health Issues

Students with disabilities may also have mental health issues. These students may not necessarily be diagnosed with emotional disturbances, as mental health issues can occur concurrently with other disabilities. Students' mental health symptoms may fluctuate on an hourly, daily, or weekly basis. Intervention techniques and supports must be determined by the individual needs of each student. General and special educators across all special education settings can **support** these students by learning how to **recognize mental health issues** in schools. Teachers can use observations and research-based strategies for identifying issues. Training in working with students who have certain mental health disorders may also be useful. Occasionally, training in crisis prevention plans is required of teachers working with students who may become aggressive due to their disorders.

Behavior Assessment and Intervention

Cognitive Behavioral Theory

The cognitive behavioral theory states that people form their own negative or positive concepts that affect their behaviors. The cognitive behavioral theory involves a **cognitive triad** of thoughts and behaviors. This triad refers to thoughts about the **self**, the **world and environment**, and the **future**. In times of stress, people's thoughts can become distressed or dysfunctional. Sometimes cognitive behavioral therapy, based on the cognitive behavioral theory model, is used to help people address and manage their thoughts. This process involves people examining their thoughts more closely in order to bring them back to more realistic, grounded ways of thinking. People's thoughts and perceptions can often affect their lives negatively and lead to unhealthy emotions and behaviors. **Cognitive behavioral therapy** helps people to adjust their thinking, learn ways to access healthy thoughts, and learn behaviors incompatible with unhealthy or unsafe behaviors.

Concept of Antecedents, Behavior, and Consequences as Stimuli Used in Behavior Analysis

Antecedents and consequences play a role in behavioral analysis, which is important for evaluating the behaviors of students. The purpose of behavior analysis is to gather information about a specific behavior demonstrated by a student. **Antecedents** are the actions or events that occur before the behavior occurs. It is important to recognize antecedents for behaviors to better understand under what circumstances the behavior is occurring. The **behavior** is the undesirable action that occurs as a result of the antecedent. **Consequences** are what happens immediately after the behavior occurs. These can be natural or enforced. A student might desire a certain consequence when engaging in the behavior. Understanding the relationships between antecedents, behavior, and consequences allows a professional to determine how to minimize or eliminate the behavior. In some circumstances, antecedents and consequences can be manipulated, changed, or removed in order to avoid reinforcing the undesired behavior.

Behavior Rating Scale Assessments

Behavior rating scales address the needs of students with emotional disorders who are referred to special education. Problems with behavior are often the reason a student has been referred for special education. These scales are used in determining a student's **eligibility** for special education, and in addressing **undesirable behaviors** demonstrated by students already in special education for reasons other than behavior problems. They are similar to adaptive behavior scales in that teachers or other professionals can administer the scales with little training as long as they are familiar with the students. Behavior rating scales help measure the frequency and intensity of the behaviors for a particular student often by assigning numbered ratings. They serve as a starting point for learning more about a student's behavior so that behavior interventions and management can take place. These scales are **norm-referenced**, so the outcomes of the behavior rating scales are compared to the behaviors of others.

Negative and Positive Reinforcement Related to Applied Behavior Analysis

Part of applied behavior analysis (ABA) is applying negative and positive reinforcement strategies, which are forms of conditioning strategies. In behavioral conditioning, the term **reinforcement** refers to trying to increase the frequency of a desired behavior, whereas the term **punishment** refers to trying to decrease the frequency of an undesired behavior. Similarly, when discussing behavioral conditioning methods, the word **positive** refers to the *addition* of a stimulus, whereas the word **negative** refers to the *removal* of a stimulus. These four terms tend to be confused, but are very specifically used to denote particular types of behavioral conditioning.

Positive reinforcement works by providing a desired **reward** for a desired behavior. For example, parents may give a child an allowance (the positive reinforcement) for doing chores (the behavior). In contrast, **negative reinforcement** removes an aversive stimulus to encourage a desired behavior. An example of this might be that a parent rewards a child's behavior by taking away some of his chores. Negative reinforcement is different from a punishment because the goal of punishment is to *discourage* an unwanted behavior while the goal of negative reinforcement is to *encourage* a desirable behavior. Although it is not commonly discussed, positive and negative stimuli may be used at the same in conditioning to effect a greater change.

Term:	Example:
Positive Reinforcement	A teacher *gives* the high-scorers on a test a sticker.
Negative Reinforcement	A teacher *takes away* an assignment if the class performs well on a test.
Positive Punishment	A police officer *gives* a driver a speeding ticket.
Negative Punishment	A parent grounds a student, *taking away* video games for two weeks.
Combination Reinforcement	A physical education teacher *replaces* a workout (negative) with a game (positive) because the class was well-behaved.
Combination Punishment	A student gets low grades and is required to complete extra school work (positive) and is not allowed to participate in sports for a week (negative).

Developing Positive Behavioral Interventions and Supports

Positive behavioral intervention and support (**PBIS**) plans can be implemented in classrooms or schoolwide to encourage specific, positive outcomes in groups of students with and without disabilities. A PBIS plan, such as an anti-bullying campaign, is put in place to encourage **good behavior** and **school safety** and to remove **environmental triggers** of undesirable behavior. The goal of a PBIS plan is for students to learn appropriate behavior just as they would learn an academic subject. Effective PBIS plans are based on research and analysis of data collected on targeted, large-scale behaviors. As with any behavioral plan, the success of PBIS plans is determined by monitoring student progress. PBIS plans should change if they do not work or if they stop working.

Developing a Functional Behavior Assessment

A functional behavior assessment (**FBA**) is a formal process used to examine student behavior. The goal of an FBA is to identify what is causing a specific behavior and evaluate how the behavior is affecting the student's educational performance. Once these factors are determined, the FBA is useful in implementing **interventions** for the behavior. When an FBA is developed, a student's behavior must be specifically defined; then the teacher or other professional devises a plan for collecting data on the behavior. These points of data are helpful in determining possible causes of the behavior, such as environmental triggers. The teacher or other professional can then implement the most appropriate plan for addressing the student's behavior. Often, this means implementing a **behavior intervention plan**, which includes introducing the student to actions or processes that are incompatible with the problem behavior. It is important to monitor the plan to ensure its effectiveness or remediate certain steps.

Review Video: Functional Behavior Assessments
Visit mometrix.com/academy and enter code: 783262

Developing Behavior Intervention Plans

A behavior intervention plan (BIP) is based on a **functional behavior assessment (FBA)**. The purpose of the BIP is to teach the student actions, behaviors, or processes that are incompatible with the problem behavior. The BIP may be included in an Individualized Education Program or 504 Plan, or components of the BIP may be written out as IEP goals. Once an FBA is conducted, a BIP is put in place that describes the target behavior, lists factors that trigger the behavior, and lists any interventions that help the student avoid the behavior. The interventions include problem-solving skills for the student to use instead of demonstrating the target behavior. If the interventions fail to target the problem behavior or are no longer effective for targeting the behavior, then the FBA must be revisited and a new BIP developed.

Positive Classroom Discipline Strategies

A core element of effective classroom management, positive classroom discipline is a means of holding students accountable for their actions and it starts with establishing clear and consistent **consequences** for poor choices. Students learn to predict consequences and self-correct their behaviors. It is helpful to give students **reminders** about behavior and rules instead of immediately resorting to consequences. **Pre-reminders** about expectations can be given before starting a lesson. **Nonverbal reminders** such as looks, touches, silence, or removal are possible ways to discourage students from engaging in poor choices. Removal as a consequence involves sending the student out of the classroom either to protect the other students from harm or to prevent a student from impeding the course of instruction. Removal laws vary between states and local districts, but removal is generally mandatory whenever a student is being violent. **Spoken reminders** can be used to further encourage self-management skills and should be used as precursors for reminding students about expectations instead of delivering immediate consequences.

Promoting Appropriate Behavior in Inclusive Learning Environments

Effective classrooms have good management strategies in place that promote good learning environments and minimize disruptions. Teachers with effective classroom management strategies demonstrate good leadership and organization skills. They also promote positive classroom experiences, establish clear expectations for behavior, and reinforce positive behaviors. In **inclusive learning environments**, it is important for teachers to keep all students on track with their learning. When it comes to students with disabilities, planning classroom management strategies presents different challenges. Effective teachers understand how students' special needs come into play with expected classroom behaviors. General and special educators can demonstrate effective classroom management strategies by figuring out what is causing students to act out or misbehave. They should collaborate with other professionals and students' parents to ensure the success of students with special needs in their classrooms. Lastly, effective classroom management includes setting goals for inclusive classrooms to achieve. Clear goals help establish good rapport with students with special needs because they know what is expected of them.

Crisis Prevention and Management

Crises and Crisis Prevention and Management Plans

Crises

A **crisis** is generally defined as a situation that is so emotionally impactful that an individual is not able to cope with the situation by normal means and is at risk of harming themselves or others. Crises can arise from either developmental changes that happen throughout life, such as going through puberty or graduating from school, or they can be situational and arise at any time. Examples of situational crises include sickness, losses, family deaths, and any other kind of unpredictable situation that comes up throughout life. Students with disabilities often have particular difficulty coping with stressful life situations and may need the help of a **crisis prevention plan** as a result. Crisis prevention and management goals generally focus on coping mechanisms and healthy anticipation of unavoidable situations to help the individual understand and safely navigate their way through a crisis.

Crisis Prevention Plans

Crisis prevention plans essentially serve to help with early identification of a crisis and to provide the necessary support to help the individual through a crisis to an effective resolution. These plans are often put together with the help of various members of an individual's support team, taking into account past behaviors, health, and other factors of his or her life. Some organizations, such as the Crisis Prevention Institute (CPI), specialize in crisis prevention and intervention training for professionals. Crisis prevention plans should take into account principles of least restrictive environment (LRE) to support individuals in their normal environments, while also removing or being aware of any known **behavioral triggers** that may be problematic. In the event that the individual in crisis becomes physically violent or harmful to themselves, stronger emergent response may be warranted. The ultimate goal is to keep the individual and others safe until his or her emotional state has been normalized. There is no specific duration of time for a crisis, but any intervention should be treated as short-term to prevent restricting the individual's rights through unnecessary intervention. It is important to provide the individual with clear structures and expectations to help understand direct consequences for undesired choices prior to entering a crisis. Crisis prevention plans should also provide clear processes that professionals and family members can use when students do enter a crisis in order to de-escalate the situations.

Review Video: Crisis Management and Prevention
Visit mometrix.com/academy and enter code: 351872

Special Education Models

Purpose of Special Education

Special education is specially designed instruction delivered to meet the individual needs of children with disabilities. Special education includes a free and appropriate education in the least restrictive environment. In the past, a special education model might consist of a self-contained classroom of students with special needs whose needs were addressed in that setting. Today, students who qualify for special education must receive instruction in **free and appropriate settings**. This means they receive special education services in settings that provide the **fewest barriers** to their learning. The most appropriate setting varies, depending on the student and the disability. The purpose of special education is to ensure that the unique needs of children with disabilities are addressed. In the public school setting, the Individuals with Disabilities Education Act mandates that students with disabilities receive free and appropriate public educations. The goal of special education is to create **fair environments** for students with special needs to learn. Ideally, the settings should enable students to learn to their fullest potential.

Co-Teaching Models

Co-teaching models are utilized in collaborative, inclusive teaching settings that include students with and without disabilities. General educators teach alongside special educators and hold all students to the same educational standards. In the **one teach/one support model**, one instructor teaches a lesson while the other instructor supports students who have questions or need assistance. A **parallel teaching model** involves a class being split into two groups, with one instructor teaching each group. The **alternative teaching model** may be appropriate in situations where it is necessary to instruct small groups of students. In this model, one instructor teaches a large group of students while the other provides instruction to a smaller group of students. In **station teaching**, students are split into small groups and work in several teaching centers while both instructors provide support. Teachers participating in **team teaching** collaboratively plan and implement lesson content, facilitate classroom discussions, and manage discipline. Successful co-teaching uses all of these models as appropriate to meet the needs of diverse groups of learners in the inclusive classroom setting.

Remedial Instruction vs. Special Education

Though the terms are sometimes used interchangeably, remedial instruction does not always equal special education. The difference between remedial instruction and special education has a lot to do with the intellectual levels of the students. In **remedial instruction**, a student has average or better-than-average intellectual abilities but may struggle with **skills** in one or more content areas. Remedial instruction provides one-on-one instruction to students who are falling behind. Remedial programs are often mainstreamed into general education classrooms to address the varying learning abilities of students. Remedial instruction can be delivered by general education teachers. **Special education** programs address the needs of students who may have lower intellectual abilities that require individualized instruction. Students in special education have **disabilities** specified by the Individuals with Disabilities Education Act and use individualized education programs. Unlike remedial instruction, special education requires qualified and credentialed special educators to decide how to best provide interventions in classroom settings for students with disabilities.

Remedial Instruction vs. Compensatory Approaches to Intervention

Compensatory interventions can be offered in the form of programs or services that help students with special needs or students who are at risk. The compensatory approach is different from remedial instruction because remedial instruction involves the breaking of concepts or tasks into smaller chunks and reteaching information. The **remedial approach** focuses on repetition and developing or reinforcing certain skills. The **compensatory approach** is implemented when a remedial approach is not working. It focuses on building upon students' strengths and working with or around their weaknesses. Tools such as audiobooks, text-to-speech software, speech recognition software, and other types of assistive technology are compensatory accommodations that help provide a free and appropriate education for students with disabilities who might otherwise continue to demonstrate skill deficits without these tools. Compensatory approaches and remedial instruction can and should be delivered at the same time to help ensure that students with disabilities are meeting their potential.

Chapter Quiz

Ready to see how well you retained what you just read? Scan the QR code to go directly to the chapter quiz interface for this study guide. If you're using a computer, simply visit the bonus page at **mometrix.com/bonus948/nystceeas** and click the Chapter Quizzes link.

Teacher Responsibilities

Transform passive reading into active learning! After immersing yourself in this chapter, put your comprehension to the test by taking a quiz. The insights you gained will stay with you longer this way. Scan the QR code to go directly to the chapter quiz interface for this study guide. If you're using a computer, simply visit the bonus page at **mometrix.com/bonus948/nystceeas** and click the Chapter Quizzes link.

Legal and Ethical Use of Resources

LEGAL AND ETHICAL REQUIREMENTS FOR USING RESOURCES AND TECHNOLOGIES

The legal and ethical requirements regarding the use of educational resources and technologies serves as an important frame of reference for teachers when selecting learning materials. Understanding these guidelines is beneficial in effectively determining which resources and technologies are **safe**, **secure**, **appropriate**, and **legal** for classroom use. This helps to protect the data and privacy of both teachers and students when interacting with instructional materials. In addition, this ensures that teachers and students are aware of what constitutes acceptable use of technology resources to protect their safety when engaging online. It is also important to be cognizant of legal and ethical standards in relation to the **reproduction** and **redistribution** of learning materials and technologies. Doing so ensures teachers understand how to properly adhere to copyright laws so as not to infringe upon the original creator's ability to profit from their work.

COPYRIGHT ACT

When selecting educational resources and technologies to implement in the classroom, it is important that teachers consider the guidelines of the **Copyright Act**. The Copyright Act protects creators by prohibiting the unauthorized use, reproduction, or redistribution of their original works. This extends to digital resources as well, including photographs, video clips, website articles, or online learning materials. While the **Fair Use Doctrine** permits teachers to utilize copyrighted materials for educational purposes, they must be mindful of its restrictions and take the proper precautions to avoid **copyright infringement**. When using copyrighted resources or technologies, teachers can obtain permission directly from the creator, purchase the materials or licenses for use themselves, or ask their school, district, or students to purchase them. In addition, when using, reproducing, or distributing lesson materials, teachers should always cite the appropriate source in order to give credit to the original creator.

FAIR USE DOCTRINE

Under the **Fair Use Doctrine**, teachers are permitted to utilize, reproduce, and redistribute copyrighted materials for educational purposes. However, this doctrine includes limitations that teachers must adhere to when selecting educational resources and technologies to implement in the classroom. The **purpose** of utilizing copyrighted materials must be strictly educational and intended to achieve specific objectives. Teachers must also consider the **nature** of all copyrighted resources and technologies to determine whether they meet the requirements of the Fair Use Doctrine. All copyrighted materials must be used for informational purposes, and typically should be limited to published, nonfiction works. The **amount** of copyrighted material that is reproduced or redistributed must be limited to small excerpts rather than the entire work, and teachers must appropriately cite the original source. In addition, teachers must consider the effect of their use of copyrighted resources and technologies on the future **potential market**. Use of copyrighted materials must not interfere with the creator's ability to profit from their work.

Data Security

Teachers, staff, and students engage with numerous digital resources for a variety of administrative and educational purposes. As such, protecting **data security** when interacting with these materials is increasingly important in establishing a safe, secure learning environment. When selecting educational technologies, such as student information systems (SIS) or digital learning tools, it is imperative that teachers ensure they are aligned with legal and ethical standards regarding data security. All resources must adhere to the requirements outlined by the **Family Educational Rights and Privacy Act (FERPA)** regarding the disclosure of students' sensitive or personally identifiable information. Teachers must also observe their **district and school's policies** regarding the implementation of educational technologies to ensure they are approved for use. In addition, many education technology companies collect students' data as they interact with digital resources with the intention of utilizing it to inform future educational decisions. It is therefore important that teachers consider the nature of the technology they are implementing to ensure that the data collected from students is used strictly for educational purposes. Taking measures to protect students' data when interacting with educational technology resources ensures their safety both within and outside of the classroom.

Privacy

Protecting students' privacy when interacting with educational resources and technologies is paramount to ensuring their safety both within and outside of the classroom. Prior to selecting learning materials, teachers must ensure that they follow all legal and ethical requirements regarding student privacy. This includes determining whether the resources and technologies in question follow the standards outlined by the **Family Educational Rights and Privacy Act (FERPA)** and the **Children's Online Privacy Protection Act (COPPA)**. In doing so, teachers ensure that students' sensitive and personally identifiable information, such as academic, behavioral, or medical records, are secure when interacting with instructional materials. This is necessary to protecting students from encountering potentially harmful situations or individuals that could compromise their privacy and cause long-term negative impacts.

Acceptable Use Policies

Acceptable use policies to govern the use of educational technologies are integral to ensuring a safe, secure learning environment. These documents give guidelines for **acceptable behavior** when interacting with digital resources under the school network, as well as outline **consequences** for violating the terms. Acceptable use policies also inform teachers, staff, students, and families of the measures in place to protect **data security** and **privacy** within the school, such as only allowing individuals with the proper credentials to access the network. Acceptable use policies are beneficial in discouraging users from engaging in inappropriate behavior by outlining standards for responsible use to ensure that sensitive information remains secure. This helps to prevent interaction with potentially harmful individuals or situations that could threaten the safety and privacy of students, teachers, staff, or families, as well as the security of the school network.

Legal and Ethical Obligations Surrounding Student Rights

Legal Requirements for Educators

Special Education Services

Establishing an inclusive, equitable learning environment for students with disabilities requires educators to adhere to strict legal guidelines regarding special education services. According to **IDEA (Individuals with Disabilities Education Act)**, educators must provide students with disabilities a **free and appropriate public education (FAPE)** in the **least restrictive environment (LRE)**. To do this effectively, educators are required to fully comply with students' **IEP (Individual Education Plan)** at all times. This includes providing students requiring special education services with the necessary supports, accommodations, and modifications according to their IEP throughout all stages of instruction. Educators must also document the academic and behavioral progress of these students in relation to the goals outlined in their IEP to report to the designated case manager. In addition, the specifics of students' special education services must be kept confidential in order to protect their privacy. Adhering to these legal requirements promotes equity in the classroom by ensuring that the unique needs of students with disabilities are met, thus allowing them to effectively participate and engage in learning.

Review Video: Medical Conditions in Education
Visit mometrix.com/academy and enter code: 531058

FERPA

Understanding and observing the legal requirements related to students' and families' rights is integral to maintaining their confidentiality and establishing a safe, secure learning environment. Educators are required to follow the guidelines of **FERPA (Family Educational Rights and Privacy Act)** regarding students' education records and personally identifiable information. According to FERPA, educators may not release students' education records or personally identifiable information except in authorized situations, such as when the student enrolls in another school, or the information is requested by a financial aid institution in which the student has applied. In all other instances, the educator must have written permission to disclose this information. FERPA also provides students' parents or legal guardians the right to access their child's education records and request that the education records be amended. While educators may not disclose personally identifiable information, they are permitted to release directory information regarding the student, including their name, phone number, or student identification number. However, educators must provide an appropriate amount of time to allow for the refusal of such disclosure. It is also important to note that the rights guaranteed under FERPA become applicable only to the student once they have turned 18 or begun postsecondary education.

Discipline Procedures and Student Code of Conduct

Adhering to legal requirements regarding student discipline procedures is necessary to ensure a safe, orderly, and unbiased learning environment. School districts are responsible for developing a **student code of conduct** to distribute among teachers, staff, students, and families. This document outlines expectations for student behavior, as well as specific consequences for varying degrees of infractions that may occur on school grounds. Educators must strictly adhere to the guidelines stated in the student code of conduct when enacting disciplinary measures. This includes ensuring that consequences for student misbehavior align with the nature of the action and do not interfere with the student's right to a free public education. Disciplinary actions must be free of bias, and must not endanger the student's physical, mental, or emotional health. In addition, the educator must document instances of student discipline, and keep these records confidential to protect the student's right to privacy. Extended suspensions and expulsions must be reserved for instances in which all other disciplinary measures have been exhausted. In such cases, the student is entitled to a hearing at the board of education, and teachers must provide adequate instructional materials for the time that the student is out of the classroom.

Guidelines for acceptable student behavior on school property are outlined in a student code of conduct. Providing students with this reference helps to ensure that the school functions in a safe, orderly, and productive manner so as to create and maintain an environment focused on learning. This document typically addresses a number of topics related to **daily school procedures**, including student dress code standards, acceptable use policies for the internet and digital devices, attendance, grading policies, and academic integrity. Student codes of conduct also address **potential behavioral issues**, such as acceptable conduct while riding school buses, the use of illegal substances on school property, and harmful or disruptive behavior, including bullying, harassment, or fighting. The expectations iterated in student codes of conduct are typically accompanied by an ascending matrix of classroom, administrative, and district-level **consequences** that coincide with the severity and frequency of student infractions.

Establishing an Equitable Learning Environment for All Students

An **equitable environment** is one in which students receive the individual support necessary to facilitate their success in learning. Establishing such an environment requires educators to adhere to several legal guidelines to ensure all students are provided with fair access to learning opportunities. Educators must be sure that all students are included in the educational program, and therefore, may not discriminate based upon students' race, religion, gender, background, disability, or any other differentiating characteristics. All students must be provided with equal access to learning materials, resources, technologies, and supports. In addition, educators must fully comply with all accommodations outlined in students' **IEPs**, **504 plans**, and **Behavior Intervention Plans (BIP)**, and implement all required supports to provide them with equitable access to learning.

Review Video: 504 Plans and IEPs
Visit mometrix.com/academy and enter code: 881103

Child Abuse

One of the primary responsibilities of an educator is to ensure the safety of all students. In order to do so, it is important that educators understand and follow all legal requirements related to child abuse. Within the classroom, educators are responsible for establishing a safe, secure learning environment. All interactions with students must be appropriate and refrain from harming students' **physical**, **mental**, or **emotional health**. Educators must also recognize the signs of potential **child abuse** or **neglect** among their students. If any abuse or neglect is suspected, educators are legally required to report it immediately to the proper agency according to their state and local laws, regardless of whether there is concrete evidence, as waiting to report it may place the student in continued danger. Reports of potential child abuse or neglect must be **confidential** so as to protect the students' privacy. Depending on the protocols established by individual school districts, educators may be required to notify their school's administration and resource officer of the report.

Significance of Understanding and Adhering to Legal Requirements

Understanding the legal requirements for educators ensures that teachers know what is expected of them to maintain professionalism and establish a safe, secure learning environment. This avoids misconception regarding the teacher's **roles** and **responsibilities** within the educational program so teachers understand how to adhere to legal guidelines properly. When teachers are aware of the legal requirements they must follow, they are more effectively able to implement the appropriate protocols for addressing specific education-related situations. This includes instances related to establishing an equitable learning environment, providing special education services, interacting appropriately with students, colleagues, and families, as well as protecting students' privacy. In addition, understanding the legal requirements for educators ensures that they are aware of their own professional rights and how to protect themselves in various education-related situations.

Ethical Guidelines

Confidentiality

Adhering to ethical guidelines in relation to confidentiality is an important part of demonstrating professionalism as well as protecting the privacy of students, their families, and others in the school building. Teachers are required to follow all standards outlined by **FERPA** regarding student and family privacy. This includes preserving the confidentiality of all **personally identifiable information** about students, such as grades, medical history, discipline records, or special education services, except in authorized situations. By following these guidelines, teachers ensure that they do not release any information that may compromise the safety of students or their families. In addition, when students and families feel their personal information is kept confidential, they are more likely to seek necessary supports from the educational program without the fear of being stigmatized. Similarly, teachers must follow ethical guidelines to protect the privacy of their colleagues. Any knowledge about a colleague's personal information must be kept confidential so as to establish positive, professional relationships founded on mutual trust. Doing so facilitates productive collaboration among colleagues to benefit student success in learning.

Interactions with Students and Others in the School Community

The daily interactions among students, teachers, staff, and administration largely determine the quality of the school environment. A positive, safe, and professional school community is one in which educators adhere to ethical guidelines regarding interactions with one another and students. Communication with colleagues must be respectful of one another's privacy and confidentiality. This includes avoiding gossiping situations and ensuring that all discussions about colleagues are factual, neutral, and professional in nature. In addition, interactions with members of the school community must **avoid discrimination** of any sort. Similarly, all interactions with students must be inclusive, accepting, and respectful of differences. In addition, educators must maintain proper **boundaries** when communicating with students. This includes avoiding communication outside of the school setting except in authorized situations and ensuring that all interactions maintain professionalism. Any interactions with students must avoid compromising their **physical or mental health**, **safety**, or **ability to learn**. By adhering to these ethical guidelines, educators can ensure that all communication with students and members of the school community contribute to establishing and maintaining a safe, appropriate, and professional learning environment.

Teacher's Role as an Advocate

Advocating for Students

The teacher's role as an advocate is invaluable in ensuring students receive the necessary support to facilitate their achievement. As teachers spend most of the school day with students, they are equipped with an understanding of how to best meet the unique needs within their classroom. Teachers will inevitably encounter situations in which advocacy for students is integral to providing equitable learning opportunities. Students with **physical**, **social**, **emotional**, or **learning disabilities** need teachers to advocate on their behalf to ensure special education services or accommodations are implemented. Teachers may also need to advocate for **underprivileged students** to ensure they have equitable access to the learning materials, resources, and technologies necessary for success. Additionally, students experiencing **bullying** may need teachers to ensure the appropriate measures are taken to resolve the issue and maintain a safe learning environment. Effective advocacy requires teachers to listen and communicate with students to determine their needs and seek the appropriate avenues for support. Teachers must also communicate with colleagues, administration, and families to collaborate in addressing students' needs. In some instances, teachers may need to contact the board of education or education advocacy organizations specific to students' needs to ensure they are provided with adequate support.

Advocating for the Educational Profession

Teachers offer valuable perspectives regarding ways to enhance the quality of the education profession. As such, it is important that teachers advocate for themselves in order to help ensure they have the **conditions**, **resources**, and **support systems** necessary to facilitate student success. This includes advocating for equitable allocation of funding, learning materials, technology resources, and professional development opportunities that would help teachers more effectively meet students' learning needs. Teachers can advocate for the profession in a variety of ways. **Communicating frequently** with students, families, and administration allows teachers to discuss their needs and ways to improve the education system. Attending **PTA meetings, public forums**, or **school board meetings** allows teachers to voice their concerns and offer potential solutions. Teachers can also contact **state legislators** to influence their decisions regarding education policies that would impact the quality of the profession. In addition, there are numerous **education advocacy organizations** that teachers can join to connect with one another and influence such decisions. Taking measures to advocate for the education profession is an important part of creating a positive, productive school climate focused on supporting student achievement.

Roles and Responsibilities within the Local Education System

Department Chairpersons

Department chairpersons are appointed to act as **leaders** within their subject area. These individuals are responsible for a variety of instructional and administrative duties to ensure the **efficacy** of their academic department in supporting the goals and mission of the school. This includes contributing to curriculum development, communicating instructional expectations from administration to their colleagues, and ensuring that daily instruction within the department aligns with campus and district academic standards. Department chairpersons also serve as **resources** for their team, including collaborating with them to design instructional activities and assessments, offering support, and facilitating positive communication with administration. When working with administration, department chairpersons discuss the progress of their department in meeting academic goals, collaborate to develop strategies for assisting faculty in supporting student learning, and ensure their colleagues have the support, materials, and resources necessary for effective instruction. In addition, department chairpersons are often responsible for coordinating department activities and programs that promote student achievement and contribute to creating a positive school community.

School Principal

The primary role of the **principal** is establishing and maintaining a **school culture** that supports students, teachers, staff, and families in the educational program. This role comprises a multifaceted array of responsibilities that extend to nearly every aspect of the school. The principal is responsible for supervising the **daily operations** of the school to ensure a safe, orderly environment in which teachers, staff, and students are working in alignment with the school's mission. To achieve this, the principal must communicate expectations for a positive, productive school community, ensure academic and behavioral policies are followed by staff and students, and assign staff members specific duties to facilitate an organized, efficient learning environment. In addition, it is important that the principal support staff, students, and families by engaging in frequent, open communication, addressing concerns, and providing resources necessary to promote growth and achievement. The principal is also responsible for ensuring that the school's educational program is effective in supporting teachers, staff, and students in the achievement of academic standards. This includes overseeing curriculum, monitoring instructional practices, measuring their school's performance in relation to district academic standards, as well as communicating the progress and needs of the school to the board of education.

Board of Trustees

Each school within a district is overseen by a **board of trustees** responsible for making decisions to ensure that the educational program supports students' learning needs for academic achievement. The board of trustees is comprised of a group of **elected individuals** that are typically members of the community in which they serve. As such, they have an understanding of the educational needs of the students within the community and can apply this knowledge to make effective decisions regarding the learning program. Members within a board of trustees are responsible for creating an educational program in alignment with students' needs, as well as setting goals and developing strategies that support students in achieving them. This includes determining a **budget plan, allocating resources**, and making **administrative decisions** that benefit the school. In addition, board members are responsible for analyzing assessment data to make informed decisions regarding strategies to best support individual schools within the district and ensuring that measures are being implemented to effectively meet students' learning needs.

Curriculum Coordinators

Curriculum coordinators are responsible for the **development** and **implementation** of curriculum that is aligned with campus and district academic goals. These individuals work closely with teachers and administrators to analyze student progress in relation to the educational program, primarily through **assessment scores**, to determine the overall effectiveness of the curriculum in supporting students' achievement. Analyzing student progress enables curriculum coordinators to identify strengths and areas for improvement within the curriculum to make adjustments that best meet students' learning needs as they work to achieve learning targets. Ensuring that curriculum aligns with academic standards and students' learning needs facilitates more effective teaching and learning. Doing so provides teachers with a clear understanding of how to adequately prepare students for success, thus allowing them to design focused instruction and implement necessary supports to promote the achievement of campus and district academic standards.

School Technology Coordinators

Incorporating technology into the classroom is highly valuable in diversifying instructional strategies to promote student learning and engagement. School **technology coordinators** facilitate this integration to enhance teaching and learning, as they are responsible for the **organization, maintenance**, and **allocation** of available technology resources within the school building. This includes ensuring that all technology is functional, updated, properly stored, and accessible to teachers. These individuals are also responsible for **staying current** on developing digital resources that could be implemented to improve the learning experience, as well as communicating with the board of education regarding **acquiring** technology resources for their school. Doing so ensures that teachers have the materials necessary to best support students' learning. In addition, technology coordinators **educate** teachers and staff on the uses of technology resources, as well as strategies to implement them in the classroom for more effective instruction.

Special Education Professionals

Special education professionals work with students of various disabilities, their teachers, and families to provide an equitable, inclusive environment that supports learning and development. These individuals are responsible for creating an educational plan that is tailored to support the unique needs of disabled students and ensuring that this plan is followed in all areas of the school. Special educators develop **individualized education programs** (IEPs) according to students' areas of need, develop academic and behavioral goals, as well as provide supports and modifications to accommodate students in achieving them. Special education professionals work with teachers to educate them on the proper implementation of individualized accommodations to ensure all students have the support necessary to successfully engage in learning. This includes collaborating with teachers to adapt and modify curriculum, instructional activities, and assessments to meet the individual needs of students with disabilities. In addition, special educators may work alongside classroom teachers in a team-teaching setting or provide individualized instruction as necessary. Students' academic and behavioral progress is monitored over time, and special educators communicate this information to families in order to collaborate in developing future goals and strategies to support achievement.

Roles and Responsibilities of Professionals Within the Education Program

The roles and responsibilities of various professionals within the educational program are described as follows:

- **Principal**—The principal is responsible for ensuring that the daily operations of the school function in a safe, orderly manner that aligns with the goals of the educational program. This includes delegating tasks to staff, enforcing academic and behavioral policies, ensuring instructional practices support student achievement, and communicating with students, staff, and families to establish a positive learning environment.
- **Vice Principal**—The vice principal's role is to assist the principal in supervising the daily operations of the school to create a safe, orderly, and productive learning environment. They are responsible for working with teachers, staff, students, and families to support them in the educational program. This includes enforcing academic and behavioral policies, addressing concerns, facilitating communication, and ensuring instructional practices support student achievement of campus and district academic goals.
- **Board of Trustees**—The board of trustees is responsible for developing an educational program that reflects the learning needs of students within the community. This includes developing educational goals, strategies to support students in achieving them, and ensuring that schools within the district are in alignment with the educational program. The board of trustees is also responsible for such administrative decisions as developing a budget plan and allocating resources to schools within the district according to students' needs.
- **Curriculum Coordinator**—Curriculum coordinators are responsible for developing a curriculum that aligns with campus and district academic goals, and ensuring it is implemented properly to support student achievement. This includes working with teachers and administrators to measure student progress within the curriculum and adjusting instructional strategies as necessary to support student success.

- **Assessment Coordinator**—Assessment coordinators schedule, disperse, and collect standardized assessments and testing materials within the school building. They are responsible for educating teachers on proper assessment protocols to ensure that all practices align with district policies, collaborating with them to develop strategies that support student achievement, and ensuring all students are provided with necessary accommodations according to individual need.
- **Technology Coordinator**—Technology coordinators facilitate the integration of digital resources into the curriculum. They are responsible for acquiring, organizing, maintaining, and allocating technology within the school. These individuals also work with teachers and staff to educate them on ways to utilize technology resources to enhance instruction.
- **Department Chair**—Department chairpersons act as leaders among the teachers within their content area. Their responsibilities include contributing to curriculum development, facilitating communication between administration and their colleagues, and ensuring instructional practices align with the educational program. They also collaborate with members of their team to develop instructional practices that best support student achievement of campus and district academic goals.
- **Teacher Assistant**—The teacher assistant's role is to support the classroom teacher in both instructional and non-instructional duties. This includes assisting with the preparation, organization, and cleanup of lesson materials, working with small groups of students, managing student behavior, and ensuring the classroom functions in a safe, orderly manner.
- **Paraprofessional**—Paraprofessionals are licensed within the field of education and are responsible for assisting the teacher with daily classroom operations. This includes working with individual or small groups of students to provide instructional support, assisting with the preparation of lesson plans and materials, managing student behavior, and completing administrative duties.
- **Speech-Language Pathologist**—Speech-Language pathologists are special education professionals that work with students that have varying degrees of language and communication difficulties. They are responsible for evaluating and diagnosing disabilities related to speech and language, as well as developing individualized treatment programs. Speech-language pathologists then work with these students to remedy language and communication disabilities, as well as collaborate with teachers, staff, and families regarding ways to support their progress.
- **ESL Specialist**—ESL (English as a second language) specialists work with students for whom English is not their native language. They are responsible for evaluating students' levels of English language proficiency across the domains of reading, writing, speaking, and listening, determining necessary linguistic supports, and working with teachers to develop strategies that support English language acquisition. ESL specialists also work with individual or small groups of students to monitor progress and develop English language proficiency skills.
- **Guidance Counselor**—The role of guidance counselors is to support students' social, emotional, academic, and behavioral needs. This includes providing counseling services, mediation, and for upper grade level students, advice regarding course selection and career choices. These individuals communicate with teachers, staff, and families to develop and implement plans to support students' personal growth and academic achievement.

- **School Nurse**—The school nurse is responsible for providing a range of healthcare to students and staff in the school building. This includes evaluating the physical, mental, and emotional health of students and staff, as well as delivering general first-aid treatments. School nurses are also responsible for organizing and dispersing prescribed medications to students in accordance with their healthcare plan and educating teachers and staff regarding best practices for ensuring students' health and safety. School nurses may work with special education professionals to assess students' needs in the development of an individualized education program.
- **Building Service Worker**—Building service workers are responsible for the general maintenance of the school building and outside campus. This includes ensuring that all areas, equipment, and furniture are clean, functional, and safe for student and staff use. These individuals are also responsible for transporting heavy equipment and furniture throughout the school building.
- **Secretary**—The school secretary is responsible for assisting the principal, vice principal, and other office personnel in daily administrative duties. This individual assumes a variety of responsibilities to ensure the efficient function of daily operations within the school. Their responsibilities include communicating with students, families, and other office visitors, directing phone calls to the appropriate location, handling financial matters, and coordinating the school calendar.
- **Library/Media Specialist**—Library and media specialists coordinate the organization, maintenance, and allocation of all library and media resources within the school building. They are responsible for educating students regarding the proper use of library and media resources to locate information, including how to navigate the internet safely and appropriately for educational purposes. Library and media specialists also direct students toward reading material aligned with their literacy skills and provide teachers with learning materials to incorporate into instruction.
- **Instructional Leadership Team (ILT)**—An instructional leadership team is comprised of individuals responsible for educating teachers regarding current and relevant instructional philosophies and practices to enhance student learning. These individuals collaborate with teachers to educate them regarding how to implement instructional strategies, activities, and assessments to effectively meet students' learning needs and support their achievement of campus and district academic goals.
- **School Resource Officer**—The role of the school resource officer is to maintain a safe, orderly environment for teachers, staff, and students. They are responsible for ensuring the physical security of the school, handling legal infractions within the school, and addressing conflicts among students. The school resource officer also works with administration and staff to develop emergency drill procedures.
- **Pupil Personnel Worker (PPW)**—Pupil personnel workers are responsible for addressing issues that hinder the academic achievement of at-risk students. These individuals communicate with teachers, administration, staff, and families to ensure these students are supported both within and outside of the school building. This includes addressing issues related to behavior, crisis intervention, attendance, and home lives. Pupil personnel workers direct families toward school and community support resources and collaborate with teachers to implement supports that facilitate success in learning.

Local, District, and State Educational Structure

Maintaining Accurate Student Records

Maintaining accurate **instructional** and **non-instructional** records is imperative for providing a comprehensive representation of students' academic and behavioral progress within the education program. Records pertaining to such matters as students' **academics**, **behavior**, **attendance**, **medical history**, and **special education services** must be well-organized and updated frequently in order to establish a safe, orderly environment that best supports their learning needs. Most school districts and campuses provide specific requirements regarding the procedures for maintaining accurate student records. This includes the frequency in which grades and attendance must be updated, as well as the processes for documenting behavioral progress and information related to goals outlined in students' IEPs, BIPs, and 504 plans. Educators must strictly adhere to these policies at all times in order to gain accurate insight regarding students' progress in relation to reaching academic and behavioral goals. This allows educators to make informed instructional decisions, seek the proper supports, and adjust their practices as necessary to meet students' learning needs. In addition, maintaining accurate records is also beneficial for communicating productively with students' families to develop and implement plans to support their achievement.

Procedures for Administering State and District Mandated Assessments

State and district mandated assessments measure students' progress in relation to reaching academic benchmarks. Properly administering these assessments requires the consistent adherence to strict procedures to ensure confidentiality, equity, and accuracy. Only authorized test **proctors** may administer these tests. These individuals are responsible for preparing the testing room and testing materials prior to the assessment. For digital exams, they must ensure all students have the proper credentials. Proctors must follow all testing instructions, including the procedures for administering test materials and reading directions aloud exactly as they are written. All students with IEPs must receive the proper **accommodations** for an equitable testing environment. Students must receive the same allotted time to complete the assessment unless IEP accommodations permit extra time. The testing environment must be free of any materials unrelated to the exam, and the proctor must observe students throughout the test to ensure they follow the correct procedures. After the test, proctors must collect and organize all answer sheets and booklets. For digital assessments, proctors must ensure students log off properly. Testing materials must be packaged according to the instructions and stored in a secure area until they are sent to the testing agency for scoring.

Importance of Adhering to Procedures

State and district mandated assessments are intended to measure students' progress in relation to achieving academic benchmarks, and the results are used for a variety of purposes. Assessment results influence decisions regarding the allocation of funding and resources among schools, changes to curriculum, and adjustments to the education program to more effectively meet students' learning needs. These results are also used to identify and address achievement gaps among various populations to increase equity. Therefore, the strict adherence to all required procedures for administering state and district mandated assessments is imperative to producing an **objective** and **accurate** representation of student achievement. Doing so ensures the same degree of **uniformity** in regard to testing conditions, operations, and materials across schools, as well as ensures all students are provided the necessary accommodations to ensure an **equitable** testing environment. Adhering to these procedures is also important in maintaining student **confidentiality** both during and after the assessment by preventing the sharing or reproduction of testing materials and ensuring students' completed exams are properly organized and stored in a secure area.

Seeking Information and Assistance

Understanding the State Education System Structure

State education systems are organized in a **tiered** structure, and each component is responsible for varying aspects of the education program. The **state department of education** is responsible for overseeing and establishing standards to regulate the operations of all school districts within the state. This includes allocating funds for individual districts, providing professional certifications, as well as developing comprehensive policies to govern curriculum, academic standards, and assessments at the district level. **School districts** are responsible for implementing the policies established by the state department of education. Each district is governed by a board of trustees elected by members of the community to oversee the operations of all public schools within the district. This includes hiring staff members, determining a budget plan for individual schools, and developing an education program aligned with state policies. **School campuses** within a district are tasked with maintaining the daily operations within the building. This includes addressing matters related to students, staff, and the community, as well as ensuring instructional practices are aligned with the educational program created by the district. Recognizing the roles of the varying components within the education system is beneficial in understanding the proper avenues to take when seeking information or assistance.

Understanding the Professional Roles of Individuals Within the School Campus

The school campus is comprised of a complex network of professional roles that work together to establish an efficient, orderly, and productive learning environment focused on student achievement. Each professional within the building is responsible for specific duties to maintain the daily operations of the school campus and meet students' learning needs. Understanding the nature and responsibilities of these varying roles, including how they work together in supporting the education program, is beneficial in effectively navigating the school campus when seeking information or assistance. This knowledge is important for determining which individual or department will be most helpful in addressing specific situations or providing support, as well as the proper procedures for doing so.

Available Resources at the Campus, Local, and State Level

Understanding the structure of the education system is beneficial in determining the proper avenues for seeking information and assistance related to specific situations at the campus, local, and state level. Professionals within the **school campus** serve as valuable support resources for a variety of matters, including those related to students, families, staff, and academics. For example, principals and administrators can provide information and assistance regarding the daily operations of the school building. Guidance counselors and other specialists are important resources for student and family matters, special education services, and support programs. Mentors, department chairs, and colleagues can provide support in relation to instructional practices. At the **district level**, members of the board of trustees can provide information and assistance regarding the education program, such as budget and resource allocation, assessments, curriculum development, and transportation. Additionally, varying departments within the local board of education are beneficial resources for information pertaining to human resource matters, professional development opportunities, and community support services. The **state department of education** is comprised of several factions that provide a variety of services, including information and assistance regarding professional certification, continuing education, updates to education policies, as well as grants and funding for schools.

Professional Development

Available Resources and Support Systems

Effective educators continuously seek professional development opportunities to refine their teaching practice. There are multiple resources and support systems that teachers can utilize to develop their professional knowledge and skills. Within the school building, mentors are available to offer ideas, advice, and support in developing teaching practices and strategies to implement in the classroom for effective teaching and learning. The school's **instructional leadership team** (ILT) is also a valuable resource for educating teachers regarding current instructional practices to enhance student engagement and learning. Teachers can continue their professional education by enrolling in university courses or participating in state-initiated programs to stay informed on relevant pedagogical theories and practices. Service centers are also available that offer workshops, training, and conferences on a variety of topics related to education to support teachers' professional development. In addition, numerous digital support resources are available that allow teachers to enroll in courses, participate in informational webinars, and collaborate with other educators in professional learning communities to build and enhance their teaching practice.

Example Opportunities That Can Enhance Teaching Practice

Professional development opportunities are available to address a variety of needs for refining one's practice and developing pedagogical knowledge. Professional development trainings can serve to educate teachers on how to utilize and incorporate current technologies into the classroom, as well as teach strategies for implementing relevant and engaging instructional techniques, materials, and resources into the classroom. These opportunities can also be beneficial in teaching educators how to demonstrate cultural competency and skills for productive collaboration with colleagues to enhance student learning. Teachers can also seek professional development opportunities to learn best practices for addressing a variety of student needs, such as intellectual, physical, social, or emotional disabilities, or linguistic needs of ELLs. Actively seeking and participating in professional development trainings helps to ensure teachers stay current on pedagogical theories that can serve as a framework for their instructional practice.

Effectively Utilizing Resources and Support Systems

The field of education is multifaceted and continuously evolving. As such, it is important that teachers of all experience levels engage in the vast array of **available resources** and **support systems** to develop and refine their professional skills. Doing so enhances students' learning, as teachers that actively seek professional development are more current on pedagogical theories and practices, as well as instructional strategies, resources, and technologies to incorporate in the classroom. This allows teachers to design and implement more effective instruction, as it provides them with an increased range of knowledge and tools to enhance student engagement and understanding. In addition, as students' individual needs are diverse, participating in resources and support systems allows teachers to educate themselves on how to properly accommodate them to enhance the learning experience. Utilizing resources and support systems also enables teachers to learn from and collaborate with other educators in professional learning communities to continuously develop new skills, ideas, and instructional methods that enhance student learning.

Teacher Appraisals

Characteristics, Goals, and Procedures

Teacher appraisals are a method of evaluation intended to provide the teacher with continuous feedback regarding their **performance** and areas in which they can improve their professional skills to enhance student learning. Feedback is provided periodically throughout the school year and derives from classroom **observations** typically conducted by the principal or grade-level administrator. Observations can either be **formally** scheduled and last the duration of a lesson, or can be in the form of shorter, informal **walk-through** evaluations. In both instances, the observer watches and collects information as the teacher delivers instruction, directs learning activities, and interacts with students. The teacher's performance is then measured against **criteria** across several domains pertaining to planning, preparing, and delivering instruction. This score is used to provide the teacher with detailed feedback in post-observation meetings regarding their strengths and specific areas in which they can improve their practice to more effectively meet students' learning needs. Feedback is used to support the teacher in developing specific **professional goals** and strategies for improving their teaching skills.

Benefits of Appraisal Results in Improving Professional Skills

The results of teacher appraisals are beneficial in providing educators with **specific feedback** regarding areas in which they can improve their professional skills. Effective teachers understand the value of continuously **refining their practice** to enhance student learning, and therefore, actively seek opportunities to do so. However, it may prove difficult for teachers to objectively assess their own efficacy in the classroom. Appraisal results communicate feedback from the outside perspective of the observer for a comprehensive evaluation of their performance, thus providing teachers with clarity regarding their strengths and areas for growth. This allows educators to effectively develop **professional goals** to improve their skills in targeted areas and **strategies** to achieve these goals successfully.

Working with Supervisors, Mentors, and Colleagues

Enhancing Professional Knowledge and Skills

When teachers collaborate with supervisors, mentors, and other colleagues, it facilitates a productive **professional learning community** that supports the continuous development of knowledge and skills related to education. Doing so provides teachers with the opportunity to work with educational professionals of varying backgrounds, experiences, and expertise. This exposes teachers to a wide range of **perspectives**, **approaches**, and **philosophies** that they can learn from to build and enhance their practice. In such a setting, teachers can interact with other professionals within the school community to share ideas, support one another, and collaborate productively in developing strategies to improve their efficacy in the classroom. Additionally, actively engaging with supervisors, mentors, and colleagues facilitates the open communication necessary for productive collaboration in effectively addressing issues to enhance the school community.

Addressing Issues and Building Professional Skills

Productive collaboration with supervisors, mentors, and colleagues is essential to addressing issues related to the educational program and continuously developing professional practices. There are multiple opportunities for such collaboration within the school community that accommodate varying purposes. By participating in **professional learning communities**, members of the educational program can collaborate and support one another in addressing concerns and building professional skills. In subject-area **department** or **team meetings**, educators can work together to share ideas, strategies, and resources related to their content area for more effective instruction. Working with supervisors and mentors in **post-observation conferences** provides teachers with valuable feedback regarding their strengths and areas for improvement. Such collaboration is beneficial in creating specific goals and strategies for professional growth. Additionally, engaging in collaborative **professional development opportunities**, including workshops, conferences, programs, and courses, is beneficial in allowing educators to build upon one another's experiences, backgrounds, and expertise to enhance professional practices.

Professional Development Resources

The various professional development resources available to teachers and staff are discussed below:

- **Mentors/Support Systems**: Mentors and other dedicated support resources within the school system are intended to provide teachers with guidance to enhance their professional knowledge, skills, and expertise. These individuals are typically highly experienced and work with teachers to develop effective instructional strategies, classroom management techniques, and learning materials to improve their teaching skills.
- **Conferences**: Education conferences are multifaceted events in which teachers can learn about current developments in their field to improve their professional knowledge, pedagogical skills, and technical expertise. Conference events are comprised of numerous professional development opportunities, including presentations on current pedagogical theories and practices, collaborative workshops, and training sessions regarding the implementation of new instructional strategies and technology resources. At these events, teachers can also network with one another to connect and share resources, ideas, and strategies that enhance their teaching practice.
- **Professional Associations**: Education associations provide teachers with access to numerous professional development opportunities for improving knowledge, pedagogical skills, and technical expertise. These associations can be related to general education or content specific, and offer information regarding education conferences, workshops, training opportunities, and courses to enhance teaching practices. Professional education associations also allow teachers the opportunity to network with one another to build professional knowledge by sharing ideas, resources, and strategies to implement in the classroom.
- **Online Resources**: Numerous online resources, including websites, blogs, webinar trainings, and discussion forums are available to support teachers in enhancing their professional knowledge, skills, and technical expertise on a variety of topics. Teachers can utilize these resources to learn current pedagogical theories and practices, instructional and classroom management strategies, as well as relevant technology resources to implement in the classroom for enhanced student learning. Online resources are also valuable for collaborating with other teachers in building professional knowledge and sharing ideas, learning materials, and resources that improve instructional practices.
- **Workshops**: Workshop training sessions provide teachers the opportunity to build professional knowledge, skills, and expertise by educating them on current instructional strategies, classroom management techniques, and digital resources in a hands-on setting. Workshops are typically dedicated to a specific pedagogical topic and allow teachers to collaborate with one another in learning how to implement it in their classroom.
- **Journals**: Education journals publish newly researched information regarding pedagogical theories and practices teachers can utilize to enhance their professional knowledge. These journals include scholarly articles and case studies regarding topics such as instructional strategies and practices, classroom management techniques, and the implementation of digital resources. Education journals allow teachers to stay current on pedagogical developments in order to continuously improve their teaching skills.

- **Coursework**: Engaging in coursework is beneficial in continuing formal professional education to enhance knowledge, pedagogical skills, and technical expertise. Doing so allows teachers to learn from other experienced educators regarding current educational theories, practices, instructional strategies, and technology resources. By participating in formal coursework, teachers can continuously build upon their teaching skills and stay current regarding developments in their field.

Reflection and Self-Assessment

Improving Teaching Performance and Achieving Professional Goals

Just as students are encouraged to reflect upon their academic performance, it is important that teachers **reflect** on and **self-assess** their own efficacy in the classroom. Doing so is integral for improving professional knowledge and skills to enhance student learning. Effective teachers continuously self-evaluate their performance to ensure they are providing engaging, relevant instruction that effectively meets students' learning needs for success. Frequently reflecting upon and assessing the effectiveness of their lesson plans, instructional strategies, assessments, and approaches to classroom management is beneficial in providing teachers with insight regarding their **professional strengths** as well as specific **areas for growth**. With this insight, teachers can identify the knowledge, skills, and strategies they need to improve upon to deliver more effective instruction. This ultimately allows teachers to set relevant professional goals to enhance their teaching practice and determine the steps they need to take in achieving them.

Methods

Continuous reflection and self-assessment through a variety of methods is beneficial in providing teachers with insight into the effectiveness of their teaching practice. **Reflecting on lessons** after they are finished allows teachers to self-assess their instruction by identifying specific elements that were successful, as well as components that can be improved in the future to enhance student learning. By eliciting **student feedback**, teachers can evaluate whether their instructional strategies, lesson activities, and assessments promote student engagement and understanding. Working with **mentors** and **colleagues** to discuss the effectiveness of lessons, instructional approaches, and classroom management techniques is also valuable in facilitating self-evaluation of teaching practices to seek areas for improvement. In addition, teachers are typically provided the opportunity to **respond to post-observation feedback** prior to attending an appraisal conference. This provides teachers with the opportunity to reflect on their overall performance and prepare to collaborate with the observer in developing professional goals.

Team Teaching and Professional Collaboration

Team Teaching

Team teaching refers to the collaboration of two or more teachers, paraprofessionals, instructional aides, or special education workers in planning and delivering instruction and assessments. There are **several structures** to this approach to accommodate varying teaching styles and student needs. One teacher may provide direct instruction while another engages in lesson activities or monitors student progress. Similarly, one teacher may instruct while another observes and collects information to improve future planning. Students may be grouped with teachers according to their needs to provide differentiation, or teachers may participate simultaneously and equally in all aspects of the learning process. The intention of this approach is to create a **student-centered environment** focused on enhancing and deepening the learning experience. Team teaching is beneficial in allowing increased **individualized instruction** that more effectively meets students' learning needs. Additionally, when multiple teachers are present, students have access to varying

ideas and **perspectives** that strengthen their understanding. Team teaching also benefits teachers, as it enables them to utilize one another's strengths for improved instruction. There are, however, limitations to this approach. Differences in **classroom management** styles, **teaching practices**, and **personalities**, when not addressed properly through respectful communication and flexibility, hinder the effectiveness of team teaching.

Vertical Teaming

Communication and collaboration among teachers of varying grade levels is integral to effective instruction that supports students' learning and development. Through **vertical teaming**, content specific teachers **across grade levels** have the opportunity to work together in discussing and planning curriculum, instruction, assessments, and strategies that prepare students for achievement. Teachers of lower grade levels are often unsure of what students in upper grade levels are learning. As a result, these teachers may be uncertain of the skills and abilities their students need to be adequately prepared for success as they transition through grade levels. Likewise, teachers of upper grade levels are often unsure of what students have learned in previous grades, thus hindering their ability to adequately plan instruction and implement necessary learning supports. Vertical teaming facilitates the communication necessary for teachers across grade levels to collaborate in **establishing expectations for preparedness** at each grade level and developing a common curriculum path. This enhances teaching and learning, in that teachers are more effectively able to plan instruction that is aligned with learning targets and prepare students with the necessary knowledge, tools, and supports for continued academic success.

Horizontal Teaming

Horizontal teaming refers to the collaboration of **same-grade level** teachers and staff that work with a common group of students. These teams may comprise teachers within a **single subject area** or **across disciplines** and may also include special education workers, grade-level administrators, paraprofessionals, and guidance counselors. Horizontal teaming is beneficial in facilitating the **coordinated planning** of curriculum, instruction, and assessments, as well as discussion regarding students' progress in the educational program. In addition, this method of teaming provides teachers and staff the opportunity to work together in developing educational goals, addressing areas of need, and implementing strategies to support students' success in learning. Horizontal teaming is also beneficial in encouraging teachers and staff to cooperate with one another in alignment with the goals and mission of the school to create a positive learning community focused on promoting student achievement.

Benefits of Mentors in Enhancing Professional Knowledge and Skills

Mentors within the school community are typically experienced teachers that are available to offer support, guidance, and expertise to new teachers. As these individuals typically have a great deal of experience as educators, they are highly valuable resources in increasing professional knowledge and improving teaching skills. Mentors can provide **strategies, tools**, and **advice** for planning and delivering instruction, classroom management, and meeting students' learning needs to promote achievement. This includes suggesting ideas and resources for lesson activities and assessments, as well as techniques for differentiating instruction, enhancing student engagement, and promoting positive behavior. In addition, mentors can offer insight on how to effectively **navigate the school community**, including how to interact appropriately with colleagues and superiors, complete administrative duties, and communicate effectively with students' families. Regularly working with mentors in the school building ensures that new teachers are supported in developing the knowledge and skills necessary to become effective educators.

Interaction with Professionals in the School Community

In order for an educational community to function effectively, professionals in the building must work together cohesively on a daily basis to support the school's mission and student learning. The nature of these interactions significantly determines the climate and culture of the school environment. Appropriate, professional interactions are important in facilitating the productive collaboration necessary to create a positive school community that promotes student success in learning. All interactions must therefore be **respectful**, **constructive**, and **sensitive** to the varying backgrounds, cultures, and beliefs among professionals in the school community. This includes using **appropriate language**, practicing **active listening**, and ensuring that discussions regarding colleagues, superiors, students, and other individuals in the building remain positive. When interacting in a team setting, it is important to maintain open dialogue and support one another's contributions to the educational program. All professionals in the school building must understand one another's roles and appreciate how these roles function together to support the educational program. Doing so ensures that collaboration is productive, purposeful, and aligned with enhancing students' learning experience.

Supportive and Cooperative Relationships with Professional Colleagues

Supports Learning and Achievement of Campus and District Goals

Effective collaboration among school staff and faculty members is reliant on establishing and maintaining supportive, cooperative professional relationships. Doing so facilitates a sense of **mutual respect** and **open communication** that allows colleagues to work together constructively in developing educational goals, plans to support students in achieving them, and strategies to address areas of need within the educational program. Mutual support and cooperation are also beneficial in fostering the **coordinated planning** of curriculum, learning activities, assessments, and accommodations to meet students' individual needs for academic achievement. Such professional relationships allow for more effective teaching and learning, as students are supported by a school community that works together cohesively to promote learning and the achievement of campus and district academic goals.

Strategies for Establishing and Maintaining Relationships

Building and maintaining professional relationships founded on mutual support and cooperation is integral in creating a positive, productive school community focused on student achievement. **Frequent communication** with colleagues in a variety of settings is an important factor in establishing and sustaining such professional relationships. Maintaining continuous and open communication allows professional colleagues in the school building to develop the respect for and understanding of one another necessary to establish a strong rapport. By participating together in **school activities**, **events**, and **programs**, teachers and staff members can build connections while contributing to enhancing the school community and climate. **Community building** strategies, such as participating in activities or games that require teamwork, are also valuable opportunities for developing supportive and cooperative professional relationships among colleagues. In addition, **collaborating** with one another in regard to curriculum, lesson planning, and promoting student achievement, contributes significantly to developing positive professional relationships. There are multiple avenues for such collaboration, including participating in professional learning communities (PLC's), department meetings, vertical or horizontal teaming, or engaging in team teaching. Doing so provides teachers and staff the opportunity to communicate and develop mutual goals that support the educational program and student learning.

Participating in the Local Educational Community

Impact of Volunteering on Positive Educational Community

Participating in school activities, events, and projects positively impacts the nature of the school community and culture. When teachers and staff members volunteer their time to contribute in such a way, it strengthens **connections** to the school community that foster positive attitudes toward it. By actively engaging in activities, events, and projects, teachers and staff have the opportunity to collaborate in making **positive contributions** to the school community. This facilitates the development of relationships among colleagues that enhance their ability to work cooperatively in creating a positive learning atmosphere that benefits students and the educational program. Students are more supported in such an environment, and therefore, develop positive attitudes toward learning and strong relationships with their teachers that enhance the overall school **climate**. In addition, as students are influenced by the behaviors, actions, and attitudes modeled by adults in the building, contributing positively to the school community encourages them to do the same.

Participation Opportunities

Participating in school activities, events, and projects is valuable in integrating oneself into the school community while making positive contributions. Such participation can occur through a variety of avenues, both within and outside of the school campus. Teachers can assist in school fundraisers, food and clothing drives, or field trips, as well as serve as tutors, lead school clubs or other extracurricular activities. By attending school sporting events, recitals, concerts, or plays, teachers can participate in the school community while supporting students. Events such as open-house and parent teacher nights, as well as public forum meetings, are also valuable opportunities to participate in the school community in a way that positively contributes to students' learning.

Enhancing the Educational Community

As teachers work closely with students, colleagues, and administration, their contributions to the school and district are integral in enhancing the school community. Teachers provide valuable insight regarding the needs of the educational program and ways to improve the school environment. As such, their participation in the school and district is beneficial in helping to ensure the needs of staff and students are adequately met to create a positive educational community. In addition, active participation in the school and district facilitates the collaboration necessary for establishing relationships among colleagues that contribute to a positive school culture and climate. Teachers can contribute to building such an educational community in a variety of ways. By participating in **school activities**, **events**, and **projects**, teachers can work cooperatively to create a positive learning atmosphere. Teachers can also attend **school meetings** and serve on focused **committees** to solve problems and influence decisions that improve the nature of the school environment. At the district level, teachers can communicate with members of the board of education and participate in **public forums** to express ideas, discuss concerns, and offer input regarding ways to enhance the educational community.

Chapter Quiz

Ready to see how well you retained what you just read? Scan the QR code to go directly to the chapter quiz interface for this study guide. If you're using a computer, simply visit the bonus page at **mometrix.com/bonus948/nystceeas** and click the Chapter Quizzes link.

School-Home Relationships

Transform passive reading into active learning! After immersing yourself in this chapter, put your comprehension to the test by taking a quiz. The insights you gained will stay with you longer this way. Scan the QR code to go directly to the chapter quiz interface for this study guide. If you're using a computer, simply visit the bonus page at **mometrix.com/bonus948/nystceeas** and click the Chapter Quizzes link.

Family Involvement and Collaboration

Effectively Working and Communicating with Families

Utilizing multiple means of communication when working with students' families ensures information is **accessible** to and **inclusive** of all involved family members. As students' home lives are dynamic, conveying information through several avenues allows families in various situations to participate in their child's education. This is invaluable in establishing and maintaining the positive relationships necessary between students' families and schools for effective teaching and learning. General classroom information, including concepts being taught, important dates, assignments, or suggestions for activities to do at home that reinforce learning in the classroom, can be communicated both digitally and in written form. Newsletters, calendars, or handouts can be both printed and included on a class website to ensure accessibility for all families. Updates regarding individual students can be communicated electronically, through writing, or in person. Email, digital communication apps, and the telephone allow for frequent communication to address students' progress, express concerns, or offer praise. Teachers and families can also communicate through handwritten notes, progress reports, or students' daily agendas. In-person communication, such as during a scheduled conference, is beneficial for discussing individual students' progress and goals related to the education program in depth, as well as ways to support their success in learning.

Building Positive Relationships That Enhance Overall Learning

Students are more supported and learn more effectively when the relationships between their teachers and families are founded on **mutual respect**, **understanding**, and **cooperation**. Establishing this positive rapport requires the teacher to work and communicate frequently with students' families. Doing so creates an inviting learning atmosphere in which family members feel welcomed and included as **equal contributors** to the educational program. This sentiment empowers and encourages family members to take an active role in their children's education, thus strengthening students' support system and enhancing the overall learning experience. In addition, family members that feel a strong connection to their children's school are more likely to model positive attitudes toward education and reinforce learning at home. When teachers and family members communicate frequently, they develop a mutual sense of trust for one another. This allows for **productive collaboration** and the exchange of valuable insight regarding how to best support students' learning needs both within and outside of the classroom.

Appropriate Collaboration and Communication with Families

To effectively collaborate and communicate with students' families, the teacher must carefully consider appropriate methods for doing so. Communication and collaboration must always be **positive**, **respectful,** and **inclusive** to all families to ensure they feel welcomed as equal participants in their children's education. As such, the teacher must be mindful and responsive to the fact that students come from a variety of backgrounds, family dynamics and living situations. This includes demonstrating **cultural competency** when interacting with families from different backgrounds, providing multiple and varied opportunities for family involvement, and communicating through a variety of means. Doing so ensures that families of varying situations have access to pertinent information and feel equally included in the educational program. The teacher must also be mindful of the nature and purpose of communication in order to ensure that sensitive details about individual students are shared only with appropriate family members. General classroom information, such as important dates, events, or assignments, may be shared publicly among the classroom community, whereas such matters as individual student progress or behavior records must be reserved for private communication with the appropriate family members.

Involvement of Families, Parents, Guardians, and Legal Caregivers

Strategies to Encourage Engagement

As students' family dynamics are diverse, it is important that the teacher implement a variety of methods to engage parents, guardians, and legal caregivers into the educational program. Doing so creates an inviting atmosphere in which family members of all situations feel encouraged to participate in their children's education. Efforts to engage families must always be **positive, inclusive**, and **accommodating** to a variety of needs, schedules, and situations. This includes ensuring that all opportunities for involvement are culturally sensitive, meaningful, and accepting of all families. Utilizing a variety of **communication methods**, such as weekly newsletters, calendars, phone calls, and electronic communication, ensures that opportunities to engage in the educational program are accessible to all families. Providing **multiple** and **varied** opportunities for involvement, such as family nights, field trips, award ceremonies, or inviting families to participate in classroom activities, further encourages family engagement in the educational program. This enables families in various situations to become involved in their children's education in the way that best suits their needs and abilities.

Forms of Active Involvement

Active involvement in the educational program can take a variety of forms both within and outside of the classroom to accommodate differences in families' schedules, dynamics, and abilities. Providing multiple avenues for involvement engages families of various situations to actively participate in their children's education. Within the classroom, family members can **volunteer** their time to assist as teacher's aides, tutors, or chaperones. In addition, if a family member is skilled in an area related to instruction, the teacher can ask them to come in to speak or teach a lesson. Inviting family members to **visit the classroom** or participate in special class activities allows them to actively engage in the learning process and gain insight into the educational program. Outside of daily classroom activities, family members can be encouraged to participate by attending **family nights, school social events, fundraisers**, or **parent-teacher association meetings**. Active involvement in the educational program can also occur at home. By frequently communicating with teachers, assisting with projects or homework, and emphasizing the importance of learning at home, family members can be informed and actively involved in their children's education.

Importance in Children's Education

As students spend a great deal of time between school and home, the degree to which their family is involved in the educational program significantly influences the quality of the learning experience. When teachers take measures to engage families in their children's education, they establish a welcoming tone that facilitates relationships founded on mutual respect, understanding, and acceptance. These positive relationships are necessary for encouraging and empowering families to actively participate in the learning process. Such involvement contributes to establishing a **positive learning community** in which teachers and families can collaborate productively to enhance students' learning. When students' families are actively involved in their education, it strengthens the **support system** in both influential areas of their lives, thus establishing a sense of security that allows them to confidently engage in learning. Families that participate in the educational program are more likely to emphasize its value at home by extending and reinforcing learning outside of the classroom. This is highly beneficial in promoting positive attitudes toward learning, academic achievement, and social and emotional development.

Influence on Student Learning and Development

The degree of family involvement in the educational program significantly influences the quality of students' learning and development. Learning is more effective when parents, guardians, or legal caregivers are actively engaged in their child's education, as this promotes positive relationships between students' school and home lives that strengthen their **support system** and encourage the extension of learning beyond the classroom. Families that participate in the educational program are likely to emphasize and model its importance at home, thus influencing students to adopt the same positive attitudes toward learning. This facilitates **academic achievement**, **decreased absences** from school, and **positive learning habits**. In addition, when families are actively involved in the educational process, they are more effectively able to support students with resources at home that reinforce concepts learned in the classroom to strengthen connections and understanding. Students develop healthy **social and emotional skills** as well when their families are actively involved in the educational program. This facilitates positive self-esteem and interpersonal skills that contribute to academic success and fewer behavioral issues in the classroom.

Benefits for Parents, Families, Guardians, and Legal Caregivers

Families, parents, guardians, and legal caregivers that are actively involved in the educational program gain greater **insight**, **understanding**, and **resources** that enable them to support their children's learning more effectively both within and outside of the classroom. Active engagement in the educational program fosters a positive rapport founded on mutual respect and support among family members, teachers, and school. This provides family members with a sense of **confidence** in the merits of the educational program while contributing to the sense that they are **equal participants** in the learning process. These family members are more informed regarding what is being taught in the classroom, as well as beneficial resources to reinforce learning at home. This leaves family members feeling more **empowered** and willing to reinforce their students' learning. In addition, participating in the learning process provides family members with a greater understanding of the characteristics and capabilities of their children's developmental level, thus equipping them with the knowledge to effectively support learning and growth.

Benefits for Effective Teaching

The involvement of families, parents, guardians, and legal caregivers in the educational program is highly beneficial for effective teaching. Family members that actively participate in the learning process are likely to develop a greater sense of **understanding** and **appreciation** of the teacher's role within it. Such involvement also facilitates positive and frequent communication with families that fosters relationships founded on mutual respect and increases the teacher's **morale**, and therefore effectiveness, in the classroom. Active engagement from family members also allows the teacher to gain a better understanding of how to support individual students' needs. Family members provide valuable insight regarding students' cultures, values, beliefs, educational goals, and learning needs to allow for more effective teaching. In addition, family members that are involved in their children's education are more likely to reinforce and extend learning at home, thus allowing for more effective teaching in the classroom.

Positive Rapport

A positive rapport between teachers and families enhances the quality of the learning experience. Establishing these positive relationships requires that teachers frequently take measures to engage families in the educational program in ways that are **meaningful**, **relevant**, and **responsive** to varying situations, backgrounds, and needs. In doing so, teachers communicate the sentiment that all families are welcomed, valued, and considered equal participants in the learning process. This serves to create an open, inviting learning atmosphere in which family involvement is encouraged, thus fostering the **participation** and **communication** necessary for developing a mutual positive rapport. Working to build positive relationships strengthens the connection between schools and families that facilitates productive **collaboration** to best support and enhance students' learning.

Interacting with Families of Various Backgrounds

Diversities That May Be Encountered

Appropriate interaction when working and communicating with students' families requires the teacher to recognize the wide range of diversities in characteristics, backgrounds, and needs that they will inevitably encounter. With **culturally diverse** families, the teacher will likely experience variances in language, values, traditions, and customs, including differences in beliefs regarding best practices for raising and educating children. **Socioeconomic** differences may influence the degree to which families have the ability and access to resources to support their children in learning. In some instances, socioeconomic differences may also impact the level of education that family members have attained and potentially the value they place on the importance of education. The teacher must also be mindful of the diversities that exist among **family dynamics**. Some families may have a single caregiver, whereas others may have many. Students may be only children, have several siblings, or come from a blended family. Differences in dynamics also include varying work schedules, lifestyle demands, and living situations that the teacher must consider when working and communicating with families. By acknowledging the diverse characteristics, backgrounds, and needs of students' families, the teacher can take measures to ensure appropriate and inclusive interactions that enhance the learning experience.

Appropriate and Productive Interactions

Recognizing the diverse nature of students' cultures, backgrounds, and experiences provides teachers with insight regarding how to interact with their families appropriately and productively. By self-educating to become **culturally competent** and building relationships with students, teachers develop an understanding of the unique characteristics, values, beliefs, and needs of each family. This enables teachers to tailor their communication with individual families in a way that is respectful, **culturally sensitive**, and responsive to their concerns and needs. Doing so ensures that all families feel welcomed and supported in the school environment, thus establishing positive relationships that encourage families to actively engage in the educational program and collaborate productively with teachers to enhance students' learning.

Possible Obstacles

As teachers work and interact with families of diverse backgrounds and experiences, they likely will encounter obstacles that must be addressed to facilitate effective communication. **Cultural differences** in values, beliefs, language, and nonverbal communication may cause misinterpretations between teachers and families that make it difficult to understand one another. It is, therefore, important that the teacher educate themselves regarding students' backgrounds to learn how to communicate in a culturally sensitive manner. When language barriers are present, learning common words and phrases in the language or utilizing an interpreter is beneficial in facilitating communication. Family members may have experienced **negative interactions** with teachers in the past that affect their willingness to engage in communication. Taking measures to establish an inviting, accepting atmosphere that promotes open communication is beneficial in encouraging these families to become involved. **Lifestyle differences**, including varying work schedules, living situations, and family dynamics, may make it difficult to establish effective communication. In addition, **accessibility issues**, including lack of access to transportation, technology devices, or the internet, may hinder family members' abilities to maintain frequent communication. To address these issues, teachers must utilize several communication methods that accommodate families' varying needs and situations.

Considerations to Ensure Beneficial Interactions

The ultimate goal when working and communicating with families is to benefit students' learning and development. When teachers and families develop a positive rapport between one another, it fosters productive collaboration to support the students' educational and developmental goals. Doing so requires that teachers ensure all interactions with students' families are appropriate, respectful, and considerate. This includes demonstrating awareness of varying **backgrounds, characteristics**, and **needs** of each family and interacting in a way that is responsive and accepting of differences. Teachers must practice **cultural competency** when communicating with families, including recognizing differences in perspectives, values, beliefs, and nonverbal communication. Teachers must also consider families' unique situations, including differing **work schedules**, **living arrangements**, and **family dynamics** to ensure that all interactions are considerate of their time, accommodating to their needs, and supportive of their role in the educational program. When interacting with families, it is important that teachers practice active listening and respond appropriately, meaningfully, and constructively. This communicates to families that their opinions, goals, and concerns related to the educational program are respected, thus encouraging them to actively participate in supporting their children's progress and development.

Regular Communication with Families

Students' Progress and Important Classroom Information

Frequent communication regarding individual student progress and important classroom information is essential to actively engaging family members as equal contributors to the educational program. Doing so creates an inviting atmosphere focused on open and productive dialogue to enhance students' learning and development. Regular communication with families through a variety of methods establishes a strong connection between students' school and home lives that supports their achievement. When families are consistently updated and informed regarding their children's progress in the educational program, they can more effectively collaborate with the teacher to **proactively** address concerns and **implement necessary supports** for successful learning. Frequently communicating important classroom information, including curriculum, assignments, events, and opportunities for involvement, ensures that families are always informed regarding their children's educational program and ways in which they can actively participate. This equips family members with the knowledge and resources necessary to effectively support and reinforce learning both in the classroom and at home.

Review Video: Collaborating with Families
Visit mometrix.com/academy and enter code: 679996

Positive Rapport That Enhances Teaching and Learning

Regularly interacting and working with students' families facilitates the **continuous** and **open** line of communication necessary to establishing and sustaining a positive rapport. Building such positive relationships is integral to quality teaching and learning, as frequent communication allows families and teachers to develop a sense of mutual respect, trust, and understanding over time. By frequently communicating with families, teachers create a welcoming, inclusive learning environment in which family members feel encouraged and empowered to contribute as **equal participants** in their child's educational program. This facilitates productive collaboration between teachers and families that supports and enhances students' learning. Developing a positive rapport with family members is also valuable in providing teachers with insight regarding strategies to best support and accommodate students' learning styles, needs, and individual differences. When teachers and families have a positive relationship with one another, students feel more supported in their learning both within and outside of the classroom, thus promoting positive attitudes toward learning and academic achievement.

Listening and Responding to Families' Concerns

Actively **listening** and **responding** to students' families when interacting with them is an important part of building positive relationships that enhance teaching and learning. By listening attentively to families' concerns, ideas, and information regarding their child and the educational program, teachers gain a greater awareness of their unique backgrounds, characteristics, and experiences. With this understanding in mind, teachers can ensure that they respond to family members in a **sensitive**, **accepting**, and **empathetic** manner to promote the development of a mutual positive rapport. Doing so conveys the sentiment that family members are valued and respected as equal participants in the educational program, thus encouraging them to engage in positive communication to support their children's learning. Families can provide valuable insight regarding their children's learning styles, needs, and behaviors. When teachers listen and respond constructively to this information, they foster positive relationships with families by validating and including them in the learning process. In addition, listening and responding appropriately to students' families indicates acknowledgement and appreciation for their participation in the educational program that contributes to building positive relationships and encourages continued communication.

Conferences

Building Positive Relationships Between Schools and Families

Frequently conducting conferences with parents, guardians, and legal caregivers facilitates the consistent **in-person communication** necessary for building positive relationships founded on mutual understanding and respect. The conference setting provides a space in which teachers, school staff, and families can discuss the educational program and the student's individual progress, as well as address concerns and collaborate in developing goals. By conducting conferences regularly, teachers, school staff, and families can maintain a continuous, **open dialogue** that provides insight regarding one another's perspectives, intentions, and roles in the educational program. This allows for increased understanding and appreciation for one another that contributes to building positive relationships. Families that attend conferences regularly feel more included in the educational program as equal contributors to their children's learning, thus encouraging them to establish positive strong connections with the school.

Support of Students' Success in Learning

Effective conferences between teachers and families are focused on open communication, productive collaboration, and strengthening the connection between students' home and school lives. When families and teachers work together in conferences to benefit the student, it strengthens their **support system** in both influential areas of their lives. This is beneficial in enhancing students' **academic achievement**, promoting **healthy development**, and encouraging **positive attitudes toward learning**. Conducting conferences frequently ensures that family members are consistently **informed** and **involved** as equal participants in their child's progress and the educational program. This equips families with the information, understanding, and resources to more effectively support their child's learning both within and outside of the classroom. In addition, effective conferences provide teachers with insight from families regarding students' learning needs, behaviors, and individual situations. With this knowledge in mind, teachers can work with families to develop a plan and implement strategies that best support students' learning and development.

Guidelines for Effectiveness

Family conferences are a valuable opportunity to discuss students' individual progress, collaborate to develop educational goals, and address concerns. To ensure conferences are productive, teachers must take measures to make families feel welcomed, respected, and included in the process. Conferences must be scheduled at a **convenient time** for all attending family members in order to accommodate varying needs and situations. It is also important that conferences take place in a comfortable, **inviting atmosphere**, as this establishes a positive tone and facilitates discussion. Teachers must arrive **on time** and **prepared** with specific information to discuss regarding the student, including positive remarks that highlight their strengths. This demonstrates that teachers know the student well and want them to succeed, thus making family members feel comfortable in discussing their child. Asking **open-ended questions**, encouraging families to talk, and practicing active listening is important in facilitating productive discussion, as well as ensuring families feel heard and respected in their concerns. **Direct criticism** of the student must always be avoided; rather, teachers should focus on discussing ways that student can apply their strengths to improve in other areas.

Family Support Resources that Enhance Family Involvement

Families that are supported through school, community, and interagency resources are equipped to effectively support their child's learning and development. Often, families may be hesitant to become actively involved in their children's education because they lack the skills and understanding of how to do so. These support systems are beneficial in providing family members with the **tools, knowledge**, and **resources** that prepare them to effectively participate in the educational program and extend learning outside of the classroom. Such resources are valuable in educating families on the characteristics, needs, and abilities of their children's developmental level, as well as strategies for developing and engaging in age-appropriate activities that support learning at home. This instills a sense of confidence within families regarding their ability to successfully support their children's learning that empowers and encourages them to become actively involved.

When families are supported through **school**, **community**, and **interagency** resources, they are able to more effectively become involved in the educational program. Numerous resources dedicated to educating families on ways they can support their children's learning are available to accommodate varying situations, needs, and abilities. Within the school, **teachers**, **guidance counselors**, and other **staff members** can provide valuable information regarding students' developmental characteristics, needs, and abilities, as well as ways families can become involved to enhance learning within and outside of the classroom. **Support groups** hosted by the school enable families to share experiences and discuss ways to become involved in the learning process. Community support resources are often tailored to address the specific needs of families within the community. These resources offer **family education services** such as classes, meetings, or programs designed to provide families with the training, strategies, and knowledge necessary to become actively involved in their children's education. Several **national family support agencies** are also available to educate families on ways to become involved in their children's learning. Such agencies often have multiple locations, as well as an array of digitally printed information, discussion forums, and training opportunities to enhance family involvement in learning.

Chapter Quiz

Ready to see how well you retained what you just read? Scan the QR code to go directly to the chapter quiz interface for this study guide. If you're using a computer, simply visit the bonus page at **mometrix.com/bonus948/nystceeas** and click the Chapter Quizzes link.

General Pedagogy

Transform passive reading into active learning! After immersing yourself in this chapter, put your comprehension to the test by taking a quiz. The insights you gained will stay with you longer this way. Scan the QR code to go directly to the chapter quiz interface for this study guide. If you're using a computer, simply visit the bonus page at **mometrix.com/bonus948/nystceeas** and click the Chapter Quizzes link.

Learning Environments in Early Childhood

Guidelines for Indoor and Outdoor Space Use

Indoor and outdoor early childhood learning environments should be safe, clean, and attractive. They should include at least 35 square feet indoors and 75 square feet outdoors of usable play space per child. Staff must have access to prepare spaces before children's arrival. Gyms or other larger indoor spaces can substitute if outdoor spaces are smaller. The youngest children should be given separate outdoor times/places. Outdoor scheduling should ensure enough room and prevent altercations/competition among different age groups. Teachers can assess if enough space exists by observing children's interactions and engagement in activities. Children's products and other visuals should be displayed at child's-eye level. Spaces should be arranged to allow individual, small-group, and large-group activity. Space organization should create clear pathways enabling children to move easily among activities without overly disturbing others, and should promote positive social interactions and behaviors; activities in each area should not distract children in other areas.

Arrangement of Learning Environments

Arranging Indoor Learning Environments According to Curricular Activities

EC experts indicate that rooms should be organized to enable various activities, but not necessarily to limit activities to certain areas. For example, mathematical and scientific preschool activities may occur in multiple parts of a classroom, though the room should still be laid out to facilitate their occurrence. Sufficient space for infants to crawl and toddlers to toddle is necessary, as are both hard and carpeted floors. Bolted-down/heavy, sturdy furniture is needed for infants and toddlers to use for pulling up, balancing, and cruising. Art and cooking activities should be positioned near sinks/water sources for cleanup. Designating separate areas for activities like block-building, book-reading, musical activities, and dramatic play facilitates engaging in each of these. To allow ongoing project work and other age-appropriate activities, school-aged children should have separate areas. Materials should be appropriate for each age group and varied. Books, recordings, art supplies, and equipment and materials for sensory stimulation, manipulation, construction, active play, and dramatic play, all arranged for easy, independent child access and rotated for variety, are needed.

Arranging Learning Environments to Children's Personal, Privacy, and Sensory Needs

In any early childhood learning environment, the indoor space should include easily identifiable places where children and adults can store their personal belongings. Since early childhood involves children in groups for long time periods, they should be given indoor and outdoor areas allowing solitude and privacy while still easily permitting adult supervision. Playhouses and tunnels can be used outdoors, while small interior rooms and partitions can be used indoors.

Environments should include softness in various forms like grass outdoors; carpet, pillows, and soft chairs indoors; adult laps to sit in and be cuddled; and soft play materials like clay, Play-Doh, finger paints, water, and sand. While noise is predictable, even desirable in early childhood environments, undue noise causing fatigue and stress should be controlled by noise-absorbing elements like rugs, carpets, drapes, acoustic ceilings, and other building materials. Outdoor play areas supplied by a school or community should be separated from roadways and other hazards by fencing and/or natural barriers. Awnings can substitute for shade, and inclines/ramps for hills, when these are not naturally available. Surfaces and equipment should be varied.

Overview of Human Developmental Theories

Issues of Human Development

Historically, there have been a number of arguments that theories of human development seek to address. These ideas generally lie on a spectrum, but are often essential concepts involved in developmental theories. For instance, the nature vs. nurture debate is a key concept involved in behaviorist camps of development, insisting that a substantial portion of a child's development may be attributed to his or her social environment.

- **Universality vs. context specificity**: Universality implies that all individuals will develop in the same way, no matter what culture they live in. Context specificity implies that development will be influenced by the culture in which the individual lives.
- **Assumptions about human nature** (3 doctrines: original sin, innate purity, and tabula rasa):
    - Original sin says that children are inherently bad and must be taught to be good.
    - Innate purity says that children are inherently good.
    - Tabula rasa says that children are born as "blank slates," without good or bad tendencies, and can be taught right vs. wrong.
- **Behavioral consistency**: Children either behave in the same manner no matter what the situation or setting, or they change their behavior depending on the setting and who is interacting with them.
- **Nature vs. nurture**: Nature is the genetic influences on development. Nurture is the environment and social influences on development.
- **Continuity vs. discontinuity**: Continuity states that development progresses at a steady rate and the effects of change are cumulative. Discontinuity states that development progresses in a stair-step fashion and the effects of early development have no bearing on later development.
- **Passivity vs. activity**: Passivity refers to development being influenced by outside forces. Activity refers to development influenced by the child himself and how he responds to external forces.
- **Critical vs. sensitive period**: The critical period is that window of time when the child will be able to acquire new skills and behaviors. The sensitive period refers to a flexible time period when a child will be receptive to learning new skills, even if it is later than the norm.

Theoretical Schools of Thought on Human Development

- **Behaviorist Theory** – This philosophy discusses development in terms of conditioning. As children interact with their environments, they learn what behaviors result in rewards or punishments and develop patterns of behaviors as a result. This school of thought lies heavily within the nurture side of the nature/nurture debate, arguing that children's personalities and behaviors are a product of their environments.

- **Constructivist Theory** – This philosophy describes the process of learning as one in which individuals build or construct their understanding from their prior knowledge and experiences in an environment. In constructivist thought, individuals can synthesize their old information to generate new ideas. This school of thought is similar to behaviorism in that the social environment plays a large role in learning. Constructivism, however, places greater emphasis on the individual's active role in the learning process, such as the ability to generate ideas about something an individual has not experienced directly.
- **Ecological Systems Theory** – This philosophy focuses on the social environments in and throughout a person's life. Ecological systems theorists attempt to account for all of the complexities of various aspects of a person's life, starting with close relationships, such as family and friends, and zooming out into broader social contexts, including interactions with school, communities, and media. Alongside these various social levels, ecological systems discuss the roles of ethnicity, geography, and socioeconomic status in development across a person's lifespan.
- **Maturationist Theory** – This philosophy largely focuses on the natural disposition of a child to learn. Maturationists lean heavily into the nature side of the nature/nurture argument and say that humans are predisposed to learning and development. As a result, maturationists propose that early development should only be passively supported.
- **Psychoanalytic Theory** – Psychoanalytic theorists generally argue that beneath the conscious interaction with the world, individuals have underlying, subconscious thoughts that affect their active emotions and behaviors. These subconscious thoughts are built from previous experiences, including developmental milestones and also past traumas. These subconscious thoughts, along with the conscious, interplay with one another to form a person's desires, personality, attitudes, and habits.

Freud's Psychosexual Developmental Theory

Sigmund Freud was a neurologist who founded the psychoanalytic school of thought. He described the distinction between the conscious and unconscious mind and the effects of the unconscious mind on personality and behavior. He also developed a concept of stages of development, in which an individual encounters various conflicts or crises, called psychosexual stages of development. The way in which an individual handles these crises were thought to shape the individual's personality over the course of life. This general formula heavily influenced other psychoanalytic theories.

Erikson's Psychosocial Developmental Theory

Eric Erikson's psychosocial development theory was an expansion and revision of Freud's psychosexual stages. Erikson describes eight stages in which an individual is presented with a crisis, such as an infant learning to trust or mistrust his or her parents to provide. The choice to trust or mistrust is not binary, but is on a spectrum. According to the theory, the individual's resolution of the crisis largely carries through the rest of his or her life. Handling each of the eight conflicts well theoretically leads to a healthy development of personality. The conflicts are spaced out throughout life, beginning at infancy and ending at death.

Kohlberg's Stages of Moral Development

Kohlberg's stages of moral development are heavily influenced by Erikson's stages. He describes three larger levels of moral development with substages. In the first level, the **preconventional level**, morality is fully externally controlled by authorities and is motivated by avoidance of punishment and pursuit of rewards. In the second level, the **conventional level**, the focus shifts to laws and social factors and the pursuit of being seen by others as good or nice. In the third and final level, the **postconventional** or **principled level**, the individual looks beyond laws and social obligations to more complex situational considerations. A person in this stage might consider that a law may not always be the best for individuals or society and a particular situation may warrant breaking the rule for the true good.

George Herbert Mead's Play and Game Stage Development Theory

George Herbert Mead was a sociologist and psychologist who described learning by stepping into **social roles**. According to his theory, children first interact with the world by imitating and playing by themselves, in which a child can experiment with concepts. Mead describes this development in terms of three stages characterized by increasing complexity of play. A child in the **preparatory stage** can **play** pretend and learn cooking concepts by pretending to cook. As a child develops socially, they learn to step in and out of increasingly abstract and complex **roles** and include more interaction. This is known as the **play stage**, including early interactive roles. For instance, children may play "cops and robbers," which are more symbolically significant roles as they are not natural roles for children to play in society. As social understanding develops, children enter the **game stage**, in which the child can understand their own role and the roles of others in a game. In this stage, children can participate in more complex activities with highly structured rules. An example of a complex game is baseball, in which each individual playing has a unique and complex role to play. These stages are thought to contribute to an individual's ability to understand complex social roles in adulthood.

Ivan Pavlov

Ivan Pavlov was a predecessor to the behaviorist school and is credited with being the first to observe the process of classical conditioning, also known as Pavlovian conditioning. Pavlov observed that dogs would begin salivating at the sound of a bell because they were conditioned to expect food when they heard a bell ring. According to classical conditioning, by introducing a neutral stimulus (such as a bell) to a naturally significant stimulus (such as the sight of food), the neutral stimulus will begin to create a conditioned response on its own.

John B. Watson

Watson is credited as the founder of behaviorism and worked to expand the knowledge base of conditioning. He is famous for his experiments, including highly unethical experiments such as the "Little Albert" experiment in which he used classical conditioning to cause an infant to fear animals that he was unfamiliar with. Watson proposed that psychology should focus only on observable behaviors.

B.F. Skinner

Skinner expanded on Watson's work in behaviorism. His primary contributions to behaviorism included studying the effect of **reinforcement** and **punishment** on particular behaviors. He noted that stimuli can be both additive or subtractive may be used to either increase or decrease behavior frequency and strengths.

Lev Vygotsky

Vygotsky's sociocultural theory describes development as a social process, in which individuals mediate knowledge through social interactions and can learn by interacting with and watching others. Vygotsky's ideas have been widely adopted in the field of education, most notably his theory of the "**zone of proximal development**." This theory describes three levels of an individual's ability to do tasks, including completely incapable of performing a task, capable with assistance, and independently capable. As an individual's experience grows, they should progress from less capable and independent to more capable and independent.

Review Video: Instructional Scaffolding
Visit mometrix.com/academy and enter code: 989759

Bandura's Social Learning Theory

Albert Bandura's social learning theory argues against some of the behaviorist thoughts that a person has to experience stimulus and response to learn behaviors, and instead posits that an individual can learn from other peoples' social interactions. Bandura would say that most learning takes place from observing and predicting social behavior, and not through direct experience. This becomes a more efficient system for learning because people are able to learn information more synthetically.

Bowlby's Attachment Theory

Bowlby's attachment theory describes the impact that early connections have on lifelong development. Working from an evolutionary framework, Bowlby described how infants are predisposed to be attached to their caregivers as this increases chance of survival. According to Bowlby's theory, infants are predisposed to stay close to known caregivers and use them as a frame of reference to help with learning what is socially acceptable and what is safe.

Piaget's Cognitive Development Theory

Piaget's theory of cognitive development describes how as individuals develop, their cognitive processes are able to become more complex and abstract. In the early stages, an infant may be able to recognize an item, such as a glass of water, on sight only. As that individual grows, they are able to think, compare, and eventually develop abstract thoughts about that concept. According to Piaget, this development takes place in all individuals in predictable stages.

Maslow's Hierarchy of Needs

Maslow defined human motivation in terms of needs and wants. His **hierarchy of needs** is classically portrayed as a pyramid sitting on its base divided into horizontal layers. He theorized that, as humans fulfill the needs of one layer, their motivation turns to the layer above. The layers consist of (from bottom to top):

- **Physiological**: The need for air, fluid, food, shelter, warmth, and sleep.
- **Safety**: A safe place to live, a steady job, a society with rules and laws, protection from harm, and insurance or savings for the future.
- **Love/Belonging**: A network consisting of a significant other, family, friends, co-workers, religion, and community.
- **Esteem or self-respect**: The knowledge that you are a person who is successful and worthy of esteem, attention, status, and admiration.

- **Self-actualization**: The acceptance of your life, choices, and situation in life and the empathetic acceptance of others, as well as the feeling of independence and the joy of being able to express yourself freely and competently.

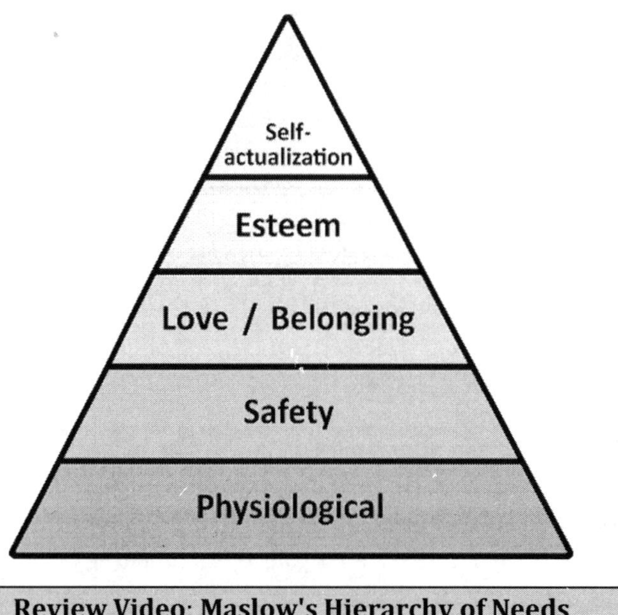

Review Video: Maslow's Hierarchy of Needs
Visit mometrix.com/academy and enter code: 461825

Cognitive Development

Piaget's Theory of Cognitive Development

Jean Piaget's theory of cognitive development consists of four stages that a child moves through throughout life. The four stages are the **sensorimotor stage** (birth-2 years), **preoperational stage** (2-7 years), **concrete operational stage** (7-11 years), and **formal operational stage** (12 years and beyond). Piaget believed that the way children think changes as they pass through these stages. In the **sensorimotor stage**, infants exist in the present moment and investigate their world for the first time through their five senses, reflexes, and actions. Key skills infants acquire during this stage include object permanence and self-recognition. In the **preoperational stage**, children learn to express ideas symbolically, including through language and pretend play. Markers of this stage include engaging in animism, egocentrism, and the inability to understand conservation (the knowledge that the quantity of something does not change when its appearance does). In the **concrete operational stage**, children develop logical thought and begin understanding conservation. The **formal operational stage** brings the ability to think abstractly and hypothetically. Piaget believed that children learn through experimenting and building upon knowledge from experiences. He asserted that educators should be highly qualified and trained to create experiences that support development in each of these stages.

Skills Typically Acquired at Each Stage of Cognitive Development

- **Sensorimotor:** As children in the sensorimotor stage gain an increasing awareness of their bodies and the world around them, a wide range of skills are acquired as they mature from infancy to toddlerhood. Early skills at this stage include sucking, tasting, smiling, basic vocalizations, and **gross motor skills** such as kicking and grasping. These skills increase in complexity over time and come to include abilities such as throwing and dropping objects, crawling, walking, and using simple words or phrases to communicate. As children near the end of this stage, they are typically able to exhibit such skills as stacking, basic problem solving, planning methods to achieve a task, and attempting to engage in daily routines such as dressing themselves or brushing their hair.
- **Preoperational:** This stage is marked by significant leaps in **cognition** and **gross motor skills**. Children in the preoperational stage are able to use increasingly complex language to communicate, and develop such skills as jumping, running, and climbing as they gain increasing control over their bodies. Preoperational children begin learning the basic categorization of alike objects, such as animals, flowers, or foods. This stage is also characterized by the development of pretend play and includes such skills as creating imaginary friends, role playing, and using toys or objects to symbolize something else, such as using a box as a pretend house.
- **Concrete Operational:** In this stage, children begin developing **logical reasoning** skills that allow them to perform increasingly complex tasks. Concrete operational children are able to distinguish subcategories, including types of animals, foods, or flowers, and can organize items in ascending or descending order based upon such characteristics as height, weight, or size. Children at this stage develop the understanding that altering the appearance of an object or substance does not change the amount of it. A classic example of this is the understanding that liquid transferred from one container to another retains its volume. This concept is known as **conservation**.
- **Formal Operational:** The formal operational stage is characterized by the development of **abstract** and **hypothetical** cognitive skills. Children at this stage are able to solve increasingly complex math equations, hypothesize and strategically devise a plan for engaging in science experiments, and develop creative solutions to problems. They are also able to theorize potential outcomes to hypothetical situations, as well as consider the nuances of differing values, beliefs, morals, and ethics.

Substages of the Sensorimotor Stage

Piaget's sensorimotor stage is divided into six substages. In each, infants develop new skills for representing and interacting with their world. In the first substage, infants interact **reflexively** and involuntarily to stimuli in the form of muscle jerking when startled, sucking, and gripping. Subsequent stages are circular, or repetitive, in nature, and are based on interactions with the self and, increasingly, the environment. **Primary circular reactions**, or intentionally repeated actions, comprise the second substage. Infants notice their actions and sounds and purposefully repeat them, but these actions do not extend past the infant's body. Interaction with the environment begins in the third substage as infants engage in **secondary circular reactions**. Here, infants learn that they can interact with and manipulate objects within their environment to create an effect, such as a sound from pressing a button. They then repeat the action and experience joy in this ability. In the fourth substage, secondary circular reactions become coordinated as infants begin planning movements and actions to create an effect. **Tertiary circular reactions** allow for exploration in the fifth substage, as infants start experimenting with cause and effect. In the sixth substage, infants begin engaging in **representational thought** and recall information from memory.

Examples of Primary, Secondary, and Tertiary Circular Reactions

The following are some common examples of primary, secondary, and tertiary circular reactions:

- **Primary:** Primary circular reactions are comprised of repeated **bodily** actions that the infant finds enjoyable. Such actions include thumb sucking, placing hands or feet in the mouth, kicking, and making basic vocalizations.
- **Secondary:** Secondary circular reactions refer to repeated enjoyable interactions between the infant and objects within their **environment** in order to elicit a specific response. Such actions include grasping objects, rattling toys, hitting buttons to hear specific sounds, banging two objects together, or reaching out to touch various items.
- **Tertiary:** Tertiary circular reactions are comprised of intentional and planned actions using objects within the environment to **achieve a particular outcome**. Examples include stacking blocks and knocking them down, taking toys out of a bin and putting them back, or engaging in a repeated behavior to gauge a caretaker's reaction each time.

Defining Characteristics of the Preoperational Stage of Development

The preoperational stage of development refers to the stage before a child can exercise operational thought and is associated with several defining characteristics including **pretend play**, **animism**, and **egocentrism**. As children learn to think and express themselves symbolically, they engage in pretend play as a means of organizing, understanding, and representing the world around them as they experience it. During this stage, children do not understand the difference between inanimate and animate objects, and thus demonstrate animism, or the attribution of lifelike qualities to inanimate objects. Egocentrism refers to the child's inability to understand the distinction between themselves and others, and consequentially, the inability to understand the thoughts, perspectives, and feelings of others. During the preoperational stage, the brain is not developed enough to understand **conservation**, which is the understanding that the quantity of something does not change just because its appearance changes. Thus, children in this stage exhibit **centration**, or the focusing on only one aspect of something at a time at. Additionally, children struggle with **classification** during this stage, as they are not cognitively developed enough to understand that an object can be classified in multiple ways.

Milestones Achieved During the Concrete Operational Stage of Development

The concrete operational stage marks the beginning of a child's ability to think logically about the concrete world. In this stage, children develop many of the skills they lacked in the preoperational phase. For example, egocentrism fades as children in this stage begin to develop empathy and understand others' perspectives. Additionally, they develop an understanding of conservation, or the idea that the quantity of something does not change with its appearance. Children in this stage begin to learn to classify objects in more than one way and can categorize them based on a variety of characteristics. This allows them to practice **seriation**, or the arranging of objects based on quantitative measures.

Development of Cognitive Abilities in the Formal Operational Stage

In the formal operational stage, children can think beyond the concrete world and in terms of abstract thoughts and hypothetical situations. They develop the ability to consider various outcomes of events and can think more creatively about solutions to problems than in previous stages. This advanced cognitive ability contributes to the development of personal identity. In considering abstract and hypothetical ideas, children begin to formulate opinions and develop personal stances on intangible concepts, thus establishing individual character. The formal operational stage continues to develop through adulthood as individuals gain knowledge and experience.

Lev Vygotsky's Theory of Cognitive Development

Lev Vygotsky's theory on cognitive development is heavily rooted in a **sociocultural** perspective. He argued that the most important factors for a child's cognitive development reside in the cultural context in which the child grows up and social interactions that they have with adults, mentors, and more advanced peers. He believed that children learn best from the people around them, as their social interactions, even basic ones such as smiling, waving, or facial expressions, foster the beginning of more complex cognitive development. He is well-known for his concept of the **Zone of Proximal Development (ZPD)**, which is the idea that as children mature, there are tasks they can perform when they receive help from a more advanced individual. He believed that children could move through the ZPD and complete increasingly complicated tasks when receiving assistance from more cognitively advanced mentors. According to Vygotsky, children develop the most when passing through the ZPD. Vygotsky's contributions are heavily embedded in modern education, and often take the form of teacher-led instruction and scaffolding to assist learners as they move through the ZPD.

Zone of Proximal Development

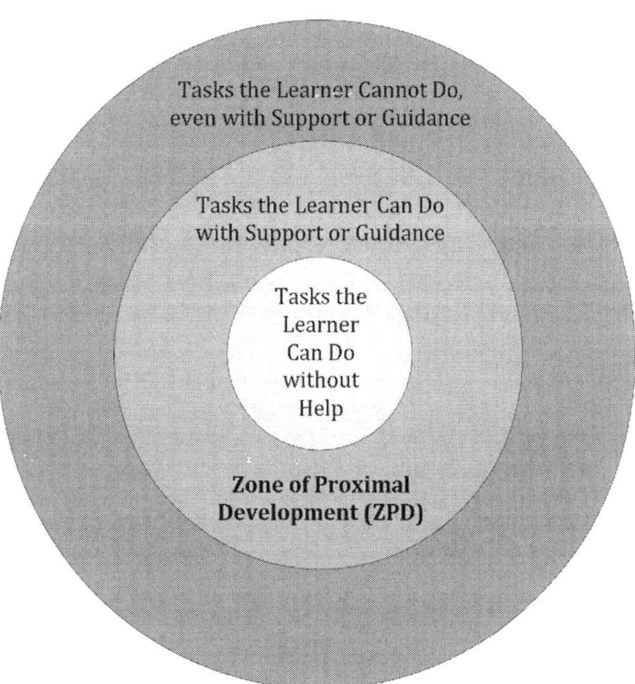

Review Video: Zone of Proximal Development (ZPD)
Visit mometrix.com/academy and enter code: 555594

Social and Emotional Development

Erik Erikson's Eight Stages of Psychosocial Development

Erik Erikson defined eight predetermined stages of psychosocial development from birth to late adulthood in which an individual encounters a crisis that must be resolved to successfully transition to the next stage. The first is **trust vs. mistrust** (0-18 months), where the infant learns that the world around them is safe and they can trust caregivers to tend to their basic needs. The next stage is **autonomy vs. shame** (18 months-3 years), where children learn to control their actions and establish independence. In the **initiative vs. guilt stage** (3-5 years), children acquire a sense of purpose and initiative through social interactions. Next, children enter the **industry vs. inferiority stage** (6-11 years), where they develop mastery and pride in completing a task. The next stage is **identity vs. role confusion** (12-18 years), in which children explore and develop characteristics that will comprise their identity and determine their role in society. The sixth stage is **intimacy vs. isolation** (19-40 years), where one forms relationships by sharing the identity developed in the previous stage with others. **Generativity vs. stagnation** (40-65 years) occurs in middle adulthood and focuses on contributing to society's next generation through finding one's life purpose. The last stage is **ego integrity vs. despair** (65 to death), in which one reflects on the productivity and success of their life.

EXPECTED BEHAVIORS AT EACH STAGE OF PSYCHOSOCIAL DEVELOPMENT

Stage	Examples of expected behaviors
Trust vs. mistrust	In this stage, the infant's primary goal is ensuring the fulfillment of their **basic needs**. Infants will cry or make other vocalizations to indicate to caregivers when they want something, such as to be fed or picked up. Separation anxiety from parents is also typical during this stage.
Autonomy vs. shame	Children in this stage begin attempting to perform daily tasks **independently**, such as making food, dressing themselves, bathing, or combing their hair. As children in this stage begin to realize they have a separate identity, they often begin attempting to assert themselves to parents and caregivers.
Initiative vs. guilt	Children at this stage often begin actively engaging and playing with other children. In play settings, these children will often assume **leadership roles** among a group of peers, create new games or activities, and devise their own rules for them. The initiative vs. guilt stage is also characterized by the development of feelings of sadness or guilt when making a mistake or hurting another's feelings.
Industry vs. inferiority	In this stage, children begin attempting to master concepts or skills with the intention of seeking **approval** and **acceptance** from others, particularly those older than themselves, in order to secure a feeling of competency. Children in this stage often become more involved in striving to succeed academically, extracurricular activities, and competitive sports.
Identity vs. role confusion	This stage is characterized by experimentation and uncertainty as young adolescents strive to establish an **independent identity**. Typical behaviors include interacting with new peer groups, trying new styles of dress, engaging in new activities, and considering new beliefs, values, and morals. As young adolescents in this stage are impressionable, they may potentially engage in risky or rebellious behavior as a result of peer pressure.
Intimacy vs. isolation	Individuals in this stage have typically established their identities and are ready to seek **long-term relationships**. This stage marks the development of a social network comprised of close friends and long-term romantic partners.
Generativity vs. stagnation	During this stage, individuals begin engaging in **productive** activities to benefit others and elicit personal fulfillment. Such activities include advancing in a career, parenting, or participating in community service projects.

Stage	Examples of expected behaviors
Integrity vs. despair	This stage occurs at the end of one's life and is characterized by **reflection** upon lifetime accomplishments and positive contributions to society. Doing so allows the individual to assess whether their life purpose was fulfilled and begin accepting death.

Incorporating Life Skills into Curriculum

In addition to academic achievement, the ultimate goal of education is to develop the whole child and provide a successful transition to independence and adulthood. Incorporating such valuable life skills as decision-making, goal setting, organization, self-direction, and workplace communication in early childhood through grade 12 curriculum is vital in ensuring students become productive contributors to society. Furthermore, the implementation of these life skills in early childhood is integral in allowing children to successfully progress in independence and maturity. The acquisition of such skills instills in students the self-motivation and ability to set goals, make decisions on how to effectively organize and manage time to complete them, and overcome obstacles. Additionally, teaching students to apply these skills promotes effective communication when working with others toward a goal. Through incorporating life skills into curriculum, teachers instill a growth mindset and foster self-empowered, confident lifelong learners with the necessary tools to navigate real-life situations and achieve success as they transition to adulthood. In the classroom, activities that promote leadership skills, cooperative learning, goal setting, self-monitoring, and social interaction foster an increasing sense of independence as children develop.

Effect of External Environmental Factors on Social and Emotional Development

Social and emotional development is heavily influenced by a child's home environment. Children learn social and emotional skills such as self-regulation, self-awareness, coping, and relationship building through modeling from parents and caregivers. A positive and supportive home environment is integral for proper social and emotional development. External factors, including lack of affection and attention, parental divorce, and homelessness, pose profound negative impacts on this development. In terms of social development, such external factors could lead to attachment or abandonment issues, as well as distrust. Furthermore, children exposed to negative environmental factors could struggle forging relationships, cooperating, and following societal rules. Emotionally, negative impacts on development cause aggression, poor self-regulation, insecurity, anxiety, isolation, and depression. Since developmental domains are interconnected, the impacts that external factors have on social and emotional development ultimately damage cognitive and physical development. Underdeveloped social skills impair cognitive development because the inability to properly interact with peers impedes the ability to learn from them. Additionally, inadequate emotional skills can inhibit concentration and understanding in school, thus inhibiting cognitive development. Physically, struggling to interact with others leads to impaired development of gross and fine motor skills as well as large muscle development that would be achieved through play.

Physical Development

Physical Changes Occurring in Early Childhood Through Adolescence

As children pass through stages of development from early childhood through middle childhood and adolescence, they experience significant physical changes. Children in early childhood experience rapid growth in height and weight as they transition away from physical characteristics of infancy. In this stage, children begin to gain independence as they develop and improve upon gross and fine motor skills. By early childhood, children develop the ability to walk, run, hop, and as they mature through this stage, learn to throw, catch, and climb. They learn to hold and manipulate small objects such as zippers and buttons, and can grasp writing utensils to create shapes, letters, and drawings with increasing accuracy. Physical growth varies for individual children in middle childhood as some children begin experiencing prepubescent bodily changes. Children in middle childhood experience further improvements and refinements of gross and fine motor skills and coordination. Significant physical and appearance changes occur in adolescence as children enter puberty. These changes often occur quickly, resulting in a period of awkwardness and lack of coordination as adolescents adjust to this rapid development.

Impact of External Factors on Physical Development

As children pass through physical development stages from early childhood to adolescence, it is important that environmental factors are supportive of proper growth and health. Physical development can be hindered by external factors, such as poor nutrition, lack of sleep, prenatal exposure to drugs, and abuse, as these can cause significant and long-lasting negative consequences. Exposure to such factors can lead to stunted physical growth, impaired brain development and function, poor bone and muscle development, and obesity. Furthermore, the negative impacts from such external factors ultimately impedes cognitive, social, and emotional development. Impaired brain development and function negatively affect cognitive development by impacting the ability to concentrate and grasp new concepts. In terms of emotional development, physical impairments due to external factors can cause a child to become depressed, withdrawn, aggressive, have low self-esteem, and unable to self-regulate. Improper physical growth and health impacts social development in that physical limitations could hinder a child's ability to properly interact with and play with others. Impacted brain development and function can limit a child's ability to understand social cues and norms.

Language Development

Stages of Language Development

The first stage of language development and acquisition, the **pre-linguistic stage**, occurs during an infant's first year of life. It is characterized by the development of gestures, making eye contact, and sounds like cooing and crying. The **holophrase** or **one-word sentence stage** develops in infants between 10 and 13 months of age. In this stage, young children use one-word sentences to communicate meaning in language. The **two-word sentence stage** typically develops by the time a child is 18 months old. Each two-word sentence usually contains a noun or a verb and a modifier, such as "big balloon" or "green grass." Children in this stage use their two-word sentences to communicate wants and needs. **Multiple-word sentences** form by the time a child is two to two and a half years old. In this stage, children begin forming sentences with subjects and predicates, such as "tree is tall" or "rope is long." Grammatical errors are present, but children in this stage begin demonstrating how to use words in appropriate context. Children ages two and a half to three years typically begin using more **complex grammatical structures**. They begin to include grammatical structures that were not present before, such as conjunctions and prepositions. By the age of five or six, children reach a stage of **adult-like language development**. They begin to use words in appropriate context and can move words around in sentences while maintaining appropriate sentence structure. Language development and acquisition has a wide range of what is considered normal development. Some children do not attempt to speak for up to two years and then may experience an explosion of language development at a later time. In these cases, children often emerge from their silent stage with equivalent language development to babies who were more expressive early on. A child who does not speak after two years, however, may be exhibiting signs of a developmental delay.

Oral Language Development

Oral language development begins well before students enter educational environments. It is learned first without formal instruction, with **environmental factors** being a heavy influence. Children tend to develop their own linguistic rules as a result of genetic disposition, their environments, and how their individual thinking processes develop. Oral language refers to both speaking and listening. Components of oral language development include phonology, syntax, semantics, morphology, and pragmatics. **Phonology** refers to the production and recognition of sounds. **Morphology** refers to how words are formed from smaller pieces, called morphemes. **Semantics** refers to meaning of words and phrases and has overlap with morphology and syntax, as morphemes and word order can both change the meaning of words. Semantic studies generally focus on learning and understanding vocabulary. **Syntax** refers to how words and morphemes are combined to make up meaningful phrases. In English, word order is the primary way that many components of grammar are communicated. Finally, **pragmatics** refers to the practical application of language based on various social situations. For instance, a college student is likely to use different vocabulary, complexity, and formality of language when speaking with a professor than when speaking with his or her peer group. Each of these five components of language are applied in oral language. Awareness and application of these components develops over time as students gain experience and education in language use. **Oral language development** can be nurtured by caregivers and teachers well before children enter educational environments. Caregivers and teachers can promote oral language development by providing environments full of language development opportunities. Additionally, teaching children how conversation works, encouraging interaction among children, and demonstrating good listening and speaking skills are good strategies for nurturing oral language development.

Review Video: Components of Oral Language Development
Visit mometrix.com/academy and enter code: 480589

Helping Students Develop Oral Language Abilities

Children pick up oral language skills in their home environments and build upon these skills as they grow. Early language development is influenced by a combination of genetic disposition, environment, and individual thinking processes. Children with **oral language acquisition difficulties** often experience difficulties in their **literacy skills**, so activities that promote good oral language skills also improve literacy skills. **Strategies** that help students develop oral language abilities include developing appropriate speaking and listening skills; providing instruction that emphasizes vocabulary development; providing students with opportunities to communicate wants, needs, ideas, and information; creating language learning environments; and promoting auditory memory. Developing appropriate speaking and listening skills includes teaching turn-taking, awareness of social norms, and basic rules for speaking and listening. Emphasizing **vocabulary development** is a strategy that familiarizes early learners with word meanings. Providing students with opportunities to **communicate** is beneficial for developing early social skills. Teachers can create **language learning environments** by promoting literacy in their classrooms with word walls, reading circles, or other strategies that introduce language skills to students. Promoting **auditory memory** means teaching students to listen to, process, and recall information.

> **Review Video: Types of Vocabulary Learning (Broad and Specific)**
> Visit mometrix.com/academy and enter code: 258753

Helping Students Monitor Errors in Oral Language

Oral language is the primary way people communicate and express their knowledge, ideas, and feelings. As oral language generally develops, their **speaking and listening skills** become more refined. This refinement of a person's language is called fluency, which can be broken down into the subdisciplines of language, reading, writing, speaking, and listening. **Speaking fluency** usually describes the components of rate, accuracy, and prosody. **Rate** describes how fast a person can speak and **prosody** describes the inflection and expressions that a person puts into their speech. **Accuracy** describes how often a person makes an error in language production. In early stages of language development, individuals generally do not have enough language knowledge to be able to monitor their own speech production for errors and require input from others to notice and correct their mistakes. As an individual becomes more proficient, they will be able to monitor their own language usage and make corrections to help improve their own fluency. In the classroom, the teacher needs to be an active component of language monitoring to help facilitate growth. Teachers can monitor **oral language errors** with progress-monitoring strategies. Teachers can also help students monitor their own **oral language development** as they progress through the reading curriculum. Students can monitor their oral language by listening to spoken words in their school and home environments, learning and practicing self-correction skills, and participating in reading comprehension and writing activities. Students can also monitor oral language errors by learning oral language rules for phonics, semantics, syntax, and pragmatics. These rules typically generalize to developing appropriate oral language skills.

Expressive and Receptive Language

Expressive language refers to the aspects of language that an individual produces, generally referring to writing and speaking. **Receptive language** refers to the aspects of language that an individual encounters or receives, and generally refers to reading and listening. Both expressive and receptive language are needed for communication from one person to another.

	Expressive	**Receptive**
Written	Writing	Reading
Oral	Speaking	Listening

Expressive Language Skills

Expressive language skills include the ability to use vocabulary, sentences, gestures, and writing. People with good **expressive language skills** can label objects in their environments, put words in sentences, use appropriate grammar, demonstrate comprehension verbally by retelling stories, and more. This type of language is important because it allows people to express feelings, wants and needs, thoughts and ideas, and individual points of view. Strong expressive language skills include pragmatic knowledge, such as using gestures and facial expressions or using appropriate vocabulary for the listener or reader and soft skills, such as checks for comprehension, use of analogies, and grouping of ideas to help with clarity. Well-expressed language should be relatively easy for someone else to comprehend.

Receptive Language Skills

Receptive language refers to a person's ability to perceive and understand language. Good receptive language skills involve gathering information from the environment and processing it into meaning. People with good **receptive language skills** perceive gestures, sounds and words, and written information well. Receptive language is important for developing appropriate communication skills. Instruction that targets receptive language skills can include tasks that require sustained attention and focus, recognizing emotions and gestures, and listening and reading comprehension. Games that challenge the players to communicate carefully, such as charades or catchphrase, can be a great way to target receptive language skills. As one student tries to accurately express an idea with words or gestures, the rest of the class must exercise their receptive language skills. Lastly, focusing on **social skills and play skills instruction** encourages opportunities for children to interact with their peers or adults. This fosters receptive language skills and targets deficits in these skills.

Stages of Literacy Development

The development of literacy in young children is separated into five stages. Names and ranges of these stages sometimes vary slightly, but the stage milestones are similar. Stage 1 is the **Emergent Reader stage**. In this stage, children ages 6 months to 6 years demonstrate skills like pretend reading, recognizing letters of the alphabet, retelling stories, and printing their names. Stage 2 is the **Novice/Early Reader stage** (ages 6–7 years). Children begin to understand the relationships between letters and sounds and written and spoken words, and they read texts containing high-frequency words. Children in this stage should develop orthographic conventions and semantic knowledge. In Stage 3, the **Decoding Reader stage**, children ages 7–9 develop decoding skills in order to read simple stories. They also demonstrate increased fluency. Stage 4 (ages 8–15 years) is called the **Fluent, Comprehending/Transitional Reader stage**. In this stage, fourth to eighth graders read to learn new ideas and information. In Stage 5, the **Expert/Fluent Reader stage**, children ages 16 years and older read more complex information. They also read expository and narrative texts with multiple viewpoints.

Review Video: Stages of Reading Development
Visit mometrix.com/academy and enter code: 121184

Relationship between Language Development and Early Literacy Skills

Language development and early literacy skills are interconnected. **Language concepts** begin and develop shortly after birth with infant/parent interactions, cooing, and then babbling. These are the earliest attempts at language acquisition for infants. Young children begin interacting with written and spoken words before they enter their grade school years. Before they enter formal classrooms, children begin to make **connections** between speaking and listening and reading and writing. Children with strong speaking and listening skills demonstrate strong literacy skills in early grade school. The development of **phonological awareness** is connected to early literacy skills. Children with good phonological awareness recognize that words are made up of different speech sounds. For example, children with appropriate phonological awareness can break words (e.g., "bat" into separate speech sounds, "b-a-t"). Examples of phonological awareness include rhyming (when the ending parts of words have the same or similar sounds) and alliteration (when words all have the same beginning sound). Success with phonological awareness (oral language) activities depends on adequate development of speech and language skills.

Promoting Literacy During the Early Stages of Literacy Development

Teachers and parents can implement strategies at different stages of literacy development in order to build **good reading skills** in children with and without disabilities. During the **Emergent Reader stage**, teachers and parents can introduce children to the conventions of reading with picture books. They can model turning the pages, reading from left to right, and other reading conventions. Book reading at this stage helps children begin to identify letters, letter sounds, and simple words. Repetitive reading of familiar texts also helps children begin to make predictions about what they are reading. During the **Novice/Early Reader** and **Decoding Reader stages**, parents and teachers can help children form the building blocks of decoding and fluency skills by reading for meaning and emphasizing letter-sound relationships, visual cues, and language patterns. In these stages, increasing familiarity with sight words is essential. In the **Fluent, Comprehending/Transitional Reader stage**, children should be encouraged to read book series, as the shared characters, settings, and plots help develop their comprehension skills. At this stage, a good reading rate (fluency) is an indicator of comprehension skills. **Expert/Fluent readers** can independently read multiple texts and comprehend their meanings. Teachers and parents can begin exposing children to a variety of fiction and non-fiction texts before this stage in order to promote good fluency skills.

Review Video: Phonics (Encoding and Decoding)
Visit mometrix.com/academy and enter code: 821361

Review Video: Fluency
Visit mometrix.com/academy and enter code: 531179

Managing Developmental Transitions

Developmental Changes Experienced in Early Adolescence

Early adolescence is a time of considerable development in all domains. Physically, children enter puberty, and must learn to deal with its emotional, social, and academic impacts. Consequently, children at this stage are impressionable, and begin developing habits that influence success as they transition to adulthood. Thus, early adolescents have specific developmental needs, and an accommodating approach to instruction is required. As the goal of education is providing the necessary skills to successfully transition into adulthood and increasing independence, it must be recognized that the shift from elementary to high school is drastic, and high school curriculum is not developmentally appropriate for early adolescence. The shift from elementary to high school is stressful and may negatively impact a child's attitude toward acquiring necessary life skills for success. Thus, middle-level education is integral in providing a developmentally responsive curriculum that eases this transition yet allows for increasing personal and academic independence. Middle-level education considers the physical developmental changes of early adolescents and fosters cognitive, social, and emotional growth through engaging instruction that encourages self-direction and responsibility, and positive social relationships. Middle-level curriculum instills skills such as organization, time management, and goal setting that promote success in high school and ultimately, adulthood.

Risks Faced by Students When Experiencing Challenges

As students in later childhood, adolescence, and young adulthood reconcile with rapid physical, cognitive, emotional, and social developments, they inevitably encounter challenges as they develop habits, beliefs, and relationships that will comprise their identity and future decisions. Such challenges as self-image, changing physical appearance, eating disorders, rebelliousness, identity formation, and educational and career decisions pose emotional, social, behavioral, and academic risks with long-term consequences if not addressed. Students may respond to challenges by engaging in risky behavior, or developing social and emotional issues such as depression, anxiety, or aggression. Such challenges may induce apathy toward academics and extracurricular activities and declining academic performance. These risks threaten the successful transition to adulthood and success throughout life in that they potentially hinder the educational and career choices that would lead to a successful future. Early intervention is imperative to provide supports for students facing challenges to try and prevent the consequences associated with them. Some supports include fostering and encouraging positive social relationships with peers and mentors, encouraging participation in extracurricular activities within the school and community, providing access to guidance counselors, and providing adequate health education to help students understand the challenges they are facing as they develop.

Indicators and Negative Impacts of Risky Behaviors in Students

The likelihood that students will engage in risky behaviors, such as drug and alcohol use, gang involvement, or other dangerous activities, increases as they approach adolescence. Such behaviors pose serious negative consequences on development and learning. Cognitively, risky behaviors harm brain function and development, and lead to trouble sleeping, focusing, and learning. Socially, these students may have trouble maintaining positive relationships and are more likely to associate with others engaging in the same behaviors. Emotionally, these behaviors could cause depression, anxiety, and low self-esteem. Physically, negative impacts include injury, illness, or long-term health consequences. Furthermore, risky behaviors are detrimental to learning. Students participating in these behaviors have trouble focusing, grasping new concepts, and become apathetic toward academics. It is important to recognize indicators of risky behavior to intervene as early as possible and prevent long-term negative consequences. Indicators include being withdrawn, poor grades, poor appearance, hygiene, sleeping and eating habits, and lack of interest in academics or extracurricular activities. Schools and communities must do their best to prevent students from engaging in risky behaviors through encouraging positive social relationships, participation in extracurricular activities, providing access to guidance counselors, and providing access to proper health education.

Roles of Peers, Acceptance, and Conformity During Adolescent Development

Adolescence is an insecure and impressionable time as students navigate rapid physical, emotional, social, and cognitive development. This stage introduces an increased sense of **independence** as adolescents begin developing the opinions, beliefs, values, and social relationships that will comprise their identity and establish the foundation for their future as they transition to adulthood. Social relationships are a vital part of identity formation during this stage, as adolescents engage with different peer groups, norms, and expectations, and seek acceptance in desired crowds. Adolescents will often conform their behavior to the social norms of a desired peer group for fear of rejection, and thus, the nature of the peer group has significant implications for teaching and learning. Involvement with unhealthy peer groups may lead to engaging in risky behaviors in seeking social acceptance, and a disinterest in learning and academic success. In contrast, association with healthy peer groups fosters the development of positive and supportive social relationships that encourage constructive behavior. Consequently, engaging in healthy peer groups increases the likelihood that the adolescent will be interested in academic involvement, achievement, and success.

Learning Goals and Objectives

Determining Instructional Goals and Objectives

Role of Assessment in Meeting Individual Student Learning Needs

Assessing students' prerequisite skills and knowledge is integral in gaining the understanding necessary to effectively determine instructional goals and objectives. This understanding provides the teacher with information about students' background knowledge, diverse experiences, and individual needs. With this information in mind, the teacher can establish goals and objectives based on state standards that are tailored to meet students' individual learning needs, and ensure that learning targets are relevant, challenging, and attainable. In assessing background knowledge, the teacher can develop high quality instruction that builds on students' prior experiences, thus fostering engagement in learning by allowing students to make personal connections in their learning. Additionally, assessing prerequisite skills and knowledge allows the teacher to identify gaps in learning, misunderstandings, or specific learning needs. This information allows the teacher to adjust and adapt instructional goals and objectives that align with students' abilities, learning styles, and knowledge, thus maximizing student learning potential by establishing student-centered instruction.

Assessment Strategies

Several assessment strategies can be utilized when determining student prerequisite knowledge and skills. Assessments may be either formal or informal and serve to provide valuable information to the teacher for effectively determining an instructional plan that is tailored to students' individual needs. Before introducing new content, the teacher can administer a formal diagnostic test that contains the new material to assess prior knowledge and skill level and can analyze the results to adjust goals and objectives as necessary. Additionally, knowledge and abilities can be evaluated by analyzing prior test scores or project portfolios to gauge student understanding of previously taught material. This allows the teacher to identify gaps in knowledge or make necessary clarifications to information. Some informal methods of assessment include conducting individual or whole-class formative assessments such as concept maps, polls, or observations to gain understanding of students' background knowledge on new material prior to teaching it. Teachers can also have students self-assess their prerequisite knowledge on new instruction through administering a test or questionnaire about content material. Often, when assessing prerequisite knowledge and skills, it is important that the teacher keep assessments anonymous to ensure they receive accurate and unbiased data on student understanding and ability.

Role of Standards in Determining Instructional Goals and Objectives

State standards for achievement provide a guideline and reference point for specific benchmarks of student academic progress based on grade level. Additionally, they serve to ensure that teachers and students are held to the same expectations for teaching and learning, thus focusing instructional goals and objectives. Teachers must have a solid understanding of state standards, as they are responsible for referring to them as an outline for planning instruction, lessons, learning outcomes, and assessments and ensuring that students achieve these learning targets. State standards provide a structure for teachers to effectively plan and adjust instructional goals and objectives based on individual student learning needs and ensure that all students have the necessary support to reach these academic standards. State standards are also the reference point for establishing the pace of instruction, monitoring student progress, and determining if learning goals have been met before progressing through the curriculum.

Appropriate Learning Goals and Objectives

Setting appropriate learning goals and objectives is an integral component of quality, effective instruction that communicates high expectations, is developmentally appropriate, and is tailored to students' individual learning needs. Specific learning targets allow the teacher to effectively determine the path of instruction based on students' skills and abilities in a manner that is challenging and attainable while supporting students in achieving state academic standards. Through focusing the method of instruction on specific targets, teachers can better determine which lesson materials, activities, and assessments will best support students' learning needs to achieve success in learning. Additionally, appropriate learning goals and objectives are necessary for student academic success because they communicate clear expectations and the purpose of learning. When students understand why they are learning a given concept and what they are expected to achieve, they are encouraged to be engaged and focused in learning. Clear learning goals and objectives are also important for monitoring student progress, as they allow teachers to concretely measure student achievement and provide specific, meaningful feedback that allows for student growth.

Elements of Appropriate Learning Goals and Objectives

When determining learning outcomes, the teacher must consider the elements of appropriate learning goals and objectives. Effective **learning goals** communicate long-term learning targets, such as at the end of a unit or chapter, whereas **objectives** should dictate what students are expected to learn at the end of a daily lesson or activity. Proper learning goals and objectives are derived from state academic standards and simultaneously reflect individual student learning needs. They are age and grade-level appropriate, challenging, and aimed toward higher order thinking while still attainable to students according to their developmental level and learning differences. Appropriate learning goals and objectives clearly and succinctly communicate measurable expectations and define a clear purpose for instruction to make learning relevant. Additionally, they consider students' current skills and abilities in order to set targets that build upon background knowledge and allow students to make personal connections in their learning.

Determining Effectiveness of Learning Goals and Objectives

Learning goals and objectives provide a necessary foundation for successful students. Proper learning targets clearly and succinctly communicate expectations, engagement, and achievement. The effectiveness of goals and objectives can be determined by their level of clarity, relevance, and significance desired outcomes to students, thus allowing for focused instruction and learning. Goals and objectives are most successful when they are relevant to both curriculum material and students' individual experiences, as this fosters engagement through allowing students to forge personal connections and apply new concepts to their own experiences. Moreover, appropriate goals and objectives convey significance to overall learning. When students understand why what they are learning is important, they are more likely to be engaged and focused on instruction, and ultimately, achieve success in learning.

Framing Learning Goals and Objectives to Promote Student Understanding

The language of learning objectives and goals must be **age-appropriate, clear**, and **succinct** for students to comprehend them. Learning goals must represent broader learning outcomes, whereas learning objectives outline the steps for doing so. This includes utilizing verbs that align with the level of understanding that teachers intend for their students to achieve. For example, when introducing a concept, learning objectives may include such verbs as *identify*, *match* or *define*. As students develop mastery, the language of objectives should incorporate **higher-order thinking** verbs, such as *analyze*, *interpret*, or *predict*. Learning objectives and goals should also be measurable in order to communicate to students exactly what they are expected to achieve by the end of the lesson or unit. For example, a learning objective written as, "students will be able to discuss the economic impact of World War II," provides students with a specific and tangible goal to work toward. Academic goals and objectives should include the **purpose** for learning, such as to prepare for an assessment, or complete part of a project, and should be connected to state or district standards.

Review Video: Learning Objectives
Visit mometrix.com/academy and enter code: 528458

Determining If Learning Goals and Objectives Are Responsive to Student Needs

In order for instruction and learning to be successful, goals and objectives must be responsive to student developmental levels and individual needs. Teachers must determine the responsiveness of learning targets by their age-appropriateness, consideration of students' skills and abilities, and reflection of their needs, interests, cultures, and backgrounds. Age-appropriate goals and objectives promote student achievement by providing realistic, yet rigorous expectations based on developmental level that facilitate academic success. Expectations must also match students' individual skill levels and abilities to design instruction and activities that are challenging, but not overwhelming, to ensure that students feel empowered in their learning. Responsive learning goals and objectives also consider students' individual needs and interests, thus allowing for instruction that is relevant and engaging. Additionally, learning targets should be sensitive to and incorporate elements of students' cultures and backgrounds. This fosters engagement and success in learning through allowing students to make personal connections between instruction and their own experiences.

Evaluating Appropriateness of Learning Goals and Objectives

When evaluating the appropriateness of learning goals and objectives, the teacher should first consider their relevance and specificity to the academic standard from which they are deriving learning targets, as well as how well they facilitate the design of effective instruction. Learning goals should express the desired outcomes of long-term learning, whereas objectives should measure daily achievement as students work toward the learning goal and the specified state standard. The teacher should evaluate whether the goals and objectives precisely communicate what the students are expected to achieve to effectively design instruction that supports students in achieving learning targets. Furthermore, they must ensure that learning targets are tailored to students' individual learning needs to design challenging and realistic instruction. Additionally, the teacher should consider the purpose of the learning goals and objectives to determine whether they communicate clear intentions for learning to students. The teacher must then decide which activities, instructional strategies, materials, and resources are most effective for supporting the achievement of learning targets and how they will design assessments to determine student achievement.

Role of Campus and District Goals in Student Academic Readiness

Aligning instructional learning goals and objectives with campus and district goals is imperative for student academic readiness. These standards indicate benchmarks of achievement that students are expected to reach at a given grade level and act as a framework for the design of goals and objectives that help facilitate this achievement. This allows for the focusing of instruction and learning, as well as providing a measurable framework for assessing student progress. Additionally, it ensures that all students are held to the same academic expectations and that all students are given the same opportunities for learning. Creating learning targets based upon campus and district goals ensures that students are successfully able to advance to the next grade level with the same academic preparedness relative to their peers.

Designing Goals and Objectives to Address Different Skills and Ability Levels

While learning targets must be aligned with state academic standards, they simultaneously must be tailored to address students' unique skills and abilities. By differentiating instructional goals and objectives, teachers ensure that the instructional strategies, activities, and materials that they implement are effectively varied to meet students' individual learning needs. Additionally, they ensure that instructional expectations challenge students based on their skill and ability while supporting all students in meeting academic benchmarks. The language of objectives and goals should be layered to include varying levels of rigor to accommodate students' differing abilities as they work toward achieving intended learning outcomes. Learning targets should include scaffolding in order to ensure students have necessary supports and allow opportunities for expansion or enrichment as necessary. They should include differentiation in skills students are expected to attain based on their background knowledge and ability, as well as variances in approaches to completing tasks and demonstrating understanding. In differentiating objectives and goals, teachers ensure that all students are challenged and supported as they work to achieve grade level academic standards.

Instructional Planning

Designing and Sequencing Lesson Plans and Units to Align with Instructional Goals

The effective sequencing of units and lesson plans is key to developing coherent, comprehensible instruction that aligns with instructional goals and fosters success in learning. The teacher must first determine the instructional goals that students will be expected to achieve based on state academic standards as a framework, as well as students' individual needs, knowledge, and abilities. The teacher must then logically arrange specific units of instruction aimed toward achieving the determined instructional goals. Each unit should build upon knowledge from the prior unit. Within each unit, the teacher must determine what students must achieve as they work toward instructional goals and determine objectives that facilitate success based on individual need and ability. Once objectives are defined, teachers must design lesson plans in a logical sequence that will facilitate students in reaching these objectives and increasingly build upon knowledge as students work toward achieving the learning goal. When planning lessons, teachers must decide which activities, procedures, and materials are necessary for successfully completing lesson objectives while ensuring that individual learning needs are met. The teacher must also decide what will be assessed at the end of each lesson and unit to determine student success in achieving instructional goals.

Creating Developmentally Appropriate Learning Experiences and Assessments

Multiple factors must be considered when designing developmentally appropriate learning experiences and assessments that effectively facilitate student growth and achievement. Teachers must consider the general cognitive, physical, social, and emotional developmental levels of students, as well as individual differences in background, skill, knowledge, and learning needs. With this understanding, teachers must then evaluate whether learning experiences are simultaneously appropriate to students' developmental levels and individual needs. This includes ensuring that learning activities and teaching strategies are varied in approach, tailored to students' interests and incorporate student choice in learning. Learning experiences must build upon students' background knowledge and experiences and provide challenging, yet attainable learning opportunities based on individual skills and abilities. Additionally, the teacher must consider whether learning experiences promote student participation and engagement as well as cooperative learning to ensure development across domains. Just as with learning experiences, the developmental appropriateness of assessments must also be evaluated. The teacher must consider whether assessments allow for choice in how students demonstrate their learning so as to address individual learning needs. Furthermore, it is important that teachers consider the purpose of each assessment regarding the feedback they are seeking and how it can help determine further instruction.

Role of Learning Theory in Instructional Process and Student Learning

Multiple learning theories exist to explain how people acquire knowledge, abilities, and skills. Each theory proposes its own approach for best practices in teaching and learning, and therefore, each is most effective and applicable based on the context of learning and individual student needs. Thus, learning theory has a significant role as the framework for the instructional process and facilitating student learning. The teacher must understand the principles of various learning philosophies as well as their students' unique learning needs to effectively design and implement instruction from the perspective of the most applicable theory. Learning theories serve as a context from which, upon identifying desired learning outcomes, teachers can make informed decisions about designing instruction, activities, and assessments that are most effective based on their students' learning styles, skills, and abilities. In developing an understanding of students' learning needs, teachers can determine which learning theory is appropriate in order to design the most effective instruction possible. This facilitates student learning in that it allows for the implementation of student-centered methodologies tailored to students' learning needs and preferences and enhances instruction through allowing the teacher to implement methods from the theory most relevant to students' needs.

The following are examples of some common learning theories that can be used as a framework in the instructional process:

- **Constructivism (Jean Piaget):** This theory proposes that students learn by interacting with the learning environment and connecting new information to their background knowledge to build understanding. This active process allows students to personalize their learning and construct their own perceptions of the world through the lens of their previous experiences.
- **Humanism (Abraham Maslow, Carl Rogers):** This theory proposes that learning should take a person-centered approach, with a focus on the individual's innate capacity for personal growth and self-actualization. It operates axiomatically from the principle that all humans have a natural desire to learn; therefore, a failure to learn is due to the learning situation or environment, rather than a person's inability to learn. Teachers should act as facilitators and strive to create a safe, accepting learning environment, celebrate students' differences, and praise academic and personal achievement.
- **Connectivism (George Siemens, Stephen Downes):** This theory proposes that learning occurs by making a series of connections across pieces of information, ideas, concepts, and perspectives. Connectivism is rooted in the notion that learning occurs externally, and technology resources facilitate connections, as learners have access to several outlets for acquiring and processing new information.

- **Experiential Learning (David Kolb):** This theory proposes that students learn and retain information best through physical exploration and interaction with the learning environment. In the classroom, teachers can facilitate this student-led approach by providing students with varying relevant experiences and opportunities for hands-on learning, such as projects or learning centers.
- **Multiple Intelligences (Howard Gardner):** Gardner's theory proposes there are several versions of intelligence, and as such, the process of learning differs among individuals. Some learners may have a stronger intelligence in one domain, but perhaps have difficulty in another, and therefore, learn best when instruction is presented through the lens of their dominant intelligence. Intelligences are categorized as logical-mathematical, verbal-linguistic, visual-spatial, bodily-kinesthetic, interpersonal, intrapersonal, musical, and naturalistic.

Connecting New Information and Ideas to Prior Knowledge

When students connect new information to prior knowledge, learning becomes relevant and engaging. Effective instruction encourages students to connect learning to background knowledge and experiences, which increases retainment, deepens understanding, and enhances the effectiveness of the overall learning experience. Fostering personal connections to learning is achieved through incorporating an array of strategies and technologies into instruction. Activities including KWL charts, anticipatory guides, graphic organizers, and brainstorming encourage students to consider what they know before learning new concepts, thus allowing them to build upon their prior knowledge and ability to make connections that strengthen learning. Cooperative learning strategies promote sharing and building prior knowledge with other students, thus increasing students' connections to new information. Numerous technologies exist to enhance the learning experience by fostering connections between prior knowledge and new information. Teachers can incorporate a wide range of apps and games across subject areas that build upon prior knowledge by providing activities with increasing levels of difficulty. Online polls, surveys, and word association websites allow students to demonstrate prior understanding of a topic to begin making connections. Self-reflection and closure opportunities at the end of instruction further strengthen learning by encouraging students to connect new material to prior knowledge and experiences.

Making Learning Meaningful and Relevant

Effective instruction occurs when learning is meaningful and relevant. When the purpose of learning is clear, students are engaged, motivated, and retain new information. Instruction must be student-centered, foster personal connections, and be applicable to real-life situations to create meaningful and relevant instruction. Teachers achieve this through an array of methods and technologies that are tailored to students' learning needs. Through forging positive relationships with students, teachers learn their unique interests, preferences, and experiences. Activities such as interest inventories, surveys, and community building develop a positive rapport between teachers and students. This allows teachers to make learning meaningful by creating learner-centered instruction that facilitates personal connections and builds upon prior knowledge. Field trips and community outreach programs are effective in enhancing relevancy through demonstrating the real-world applications of instruction. Additionally, technologies including virtual field trips and tours, videos, and documentaries, assist in increasing students' understanding the purpose of learning by illustrating the real-world applications of instruction. Self-assessments make learning meaningful and relevant through encouraging student ownership and responsibility over learning as students seek areas for improvement. Moreover, closure activities serve to demonstrate overall purpose for learning through encouraging students to connect learning to the lesson's objective and their prior knowledge.

Intradisciplinary and Interdisciplinary Instruction

Intradisciplinary and interdisciplinary instruction are both valuable strategies for teaching and learning. In **intradisciplinary** instruction, several elements of a single broad subject area are incorporated into the lesson. For example, in a science lesson, the teacher could incorporate elements of chemistry, biology, and physics into instruction. This method of instruction is beneficial in deepening students' understanding of the nuances of a particular subject area through demonstrating the various components that comprise the overarching discipline. **Interdisciplinary** instruction refers to the simultaneous integration of ideas, knowledge, and skills from several subject areas when approaching an idea, problem, or theme, and applying principles of one subject area to another. For example, in an interdisciplinary unit on food, the teacher could incorporate elements of math by teaching students to measure ingredients, language arts by teaching them to read or write a recipe, science through examining chemical reactions of the cooking process, and social studies through having students explore the impact of food agriculture on economy and society. Interdisciplinary instruction is beneficial in deepening students' understanding across subject areas and developing real-world critical thinking skills by encouraging them to make connections between disciplines and teaching them to consider an idea or problem from multiple perspectives.

Examples of Intradisciplinary Instruction

- **Language Arts:** A single language arts lesson can incorporate components of reading, writing, grammar, and listening skills. For example, a lesson on a particular poem can include a close reading of the poet's use of grammar, symbolism, imagery, and other literary techniques, as well as an audio recording of the poet reading aloud. At the end of the unit, students can be assigned to use what they learned to compose their own original poems.
- **Social Studies:** Social studies units can incorporate elements of history, anthropology, archaeology, sociology, psychology, or any other field that involves the study of humans, civilizations, cultures, and historical events. For example, a unit on the Aztec people may include an examination of their religious beliefs, customs, architecture, and agricultural practices.
- **Science:** Intradisciplinary units in science can include several branches within the field, such as chemistry, biology, physics, earth science, botany, or geology. For example, a unit on volcanoes may incorporate lessons on plate tectonics, the Earth's layers, chemicals released during a volcanic eruption, islands formed from cooled volcanic rock, as well as plants that grow best near volcanoes.
- **Mathematics:** An intradisciplinary math lesson may simultaneously include several branches within the field, such as arithmetic, algebra, or geometry. For example, in a geometry lesson on the Pythagorean theorem, students must utilize algebraic equations and arithmetic to determine the length of the sides of a right triangle.

Examples of Interdisciplinary Instruction

- **Language Arts:** A unit based in language arts may also incorporate several other disciplines, such as social studies, art, or music. For example, a unit on William Shakespeare's *Romeo and Juliet* may include a reading of the play and an analysis of the use of literary techniques within it, as well as a study of William Shakespeare's life and the society in which he lived to incorporate social studies. Students can also act out the play to incorporate the arts and participate in a rhythmic study on iambic pentameter to incorporate music.

- **Social Studies:** Units based in social studies can include lessons focused on multiple disciplines, including language arts, music, science, and math. For example, an interdisciplinary unit on Ancient Egypt may include a historical study of the culture, religion, architecture, and practices of the Ancient Egyptians while integrating other subject areas, such as a study of hieroglyphics to incorporate language arts and creating Egyptian masks to incorporate art. Students can also study the scientific advancements of the Ancient Egyptians, as well as incorporate math to study how the ancient pyramids were constructed.
- **Science:** Scientific units can also incorporate elements of art, math, social studies, and language arts in order to become interdisciplinary. For example, a unit on Punnett squares focuses on biology and genetics but can also include several other subject areas. Math can be incorporated by integrating lessons on probability, students can be assigned to research their genetics, create a family tree, and write a report on their findings to incorporate language arts and social studies. Art can also be incorporated by having students create portraits of the potential outcomes from Punnett squares.
- **Mathematics:** Interdisciplinary units in mathematics can also include lessons focused on such disciplines as art, social studies, science, and music. For example, a geometry unit on measuring triangles may also incorporate songs to memorize equations, lessons on the pyramids of Ancient Egypt to incorporate social studies, as well as an art project in which students use only triangles to create an original piece.

Incorporating Cooperative Learning Allowing Consideration from Multiple Viewpoints

In any classroom, teachers will encounter a wide range of diversities among students' backgrounds, cultures, interests, skills, and abilities. Thus, providing students with several opportunities for cooperative learning gives them access to others' perspectives and is highly valuable in teaching students to consider ideas from multiple viewpoints. As each student has different experiences and background knowledge, collaborative learning allows them to share their views on ideas with others. Additionally, in working together, students have the opportunity to work with others from different backgrounds that they may have otherwise never encountered and gain exposure to approaching ideas from multiple viewpoints. Cooperative learning opportunities allow students to understand and appreciate others' perspectives and teaches them that there are multiple approaches to problem solving and ideas.

Learning Experiences That Develop Real-World Life Skills

The ultimate goal of education is to develop the whole child and ensure that students develop into productive, contributing members of society once they leave the classroom. Therefore, it is imperative to provide learning experiences that will develop life skills that are applicable and beneficial in the real world. In an increasingly fast-paced global society, students must be prepared to enter the professional and societal world as confident, independent, responsible, and adaptive individuals. They must have the leadership skills necessary to compete in the professional arena. Students must be able to work cooperatively with others, respect and value multiple perspectives, and be effective problem solvers and critical thinkers in order to be successful outside of the classroom. Teachers must also aim to help students develop the skills necessary to become lifelong learners to ensure continuous growth and development as they enter society. Therefore, learning experiences that promote the development of real-world life skills in addition to academic skills are necessary in adequately preparing students for success.

Cross-Curricular Instruction for Exploring Content from Varied Perspectives

Cross-curricular instruction allows teachers to demonstrate that elements from one subject area can be applied to ideas or problem solving in another. Thus, this instructional strategy is highly valuable in developing students' abilities to explore content from varied perspectives. As this method incorporates several disciplines in approaching a topic, it deepens students' understanding that there are several perspectives that one can take when solving a problem, and that elements of one subject area are relevant in another. In addition, cross-curricular instruction prepares students for the real world through developing critical thinking skills and allowing them to make connections between disciplines, thus allowing them to understand how to successfully approach ideas from varied perspectives.

Benefits of Multicultural Learning Experiences

Multicultural learning experiences demonstrate to students the array of diversities that exist both inside and outside of the classroom. Just as each culture has its own values, norms, and traditions, each has its own perspectives and approaches to ideas and problem solving. Incorporating multicultural experiences in the classroom exposes students to cultures and groups that they may have otherwise never encountered and teaches them to respect and value perspectives outside of their own. As students learn other cultures' beliefs, customs, and attitudes, they develop the understanding that each culture solves problems and considers ideas from multiple viewpoints and that each approach is valuable. As students learn other perspectives, they can apply this knowledge, and ultimately build problem solving and critical thinking skills that will be beneficial in developing successful lifelong learning habits.

Incorporating Multiple Disciplines into a Thematic Unit

In **cross-curricular**, or **interdisciplinary** instruction, multiple disciplines are incorporated into a thematic unit in order to deepen students' understanding through fostering connections and demonstrating multiple perspectives and methods of problem solving. Effective interdisciplinary instruction requires careful planning to ensure that all activities are relevant to the overall lesson theme and effectively support students in achieving desired learning outcomes. The teacher must first select a thematic unit based on state academic standards and then determine desired learning outcomes. Then, the teacher must design lessons and activities for students to reach learning goals and objectives. When integrating multiple disciplines into a thematic unit, the teacher must seek out materials, resources, and activities from various subject areas that are applicable to the main topic and reinforce lesson objectives. The teacher can then integrate these elements into lesson planning to create multifaceted instruction. Additionally, the teacher can create activities that approach the overarching lesson theme from the perspective of different subject areas. The activities and materials should be coordinated and relate to one another in order to deepen students' understanding of the overall concept.

Effectively Allocating Time When Creating Lessons and Units

Effective time management is vital for successful teaching and learning. To ensure that all academic standards are covered within a school year, teachers must consider how to best allocate specific amounts of time for units and lessons that allow for review, enrichment, and reteaching. A unit plan for the school year is an effective strategy in allowing the teacher to visualize and plan the amount of content that must be covered. A unit plan can also be utilized on a smaller scale, as a framework for designing and allotting time for instructional goals, objectives, and lessons within each unit. By setting learning goals and daily objectives within individual units, the teacher can determine the amount of time available for completing each unit, thus ensuring more effective lesson planning by allowing the teacher to develop a daily schedule with dedicated time for teaching and learning.

When planning lessons, the teacher must consider how much instructional time is necessary to cover each topic and the time students will need to complete lesson activities. Additionally, teachers must ensure that they allow time at the end of each lesson for reteaching if students have misconceptions, as extra time can be utilized for enrichment if reteaching is unnecessary.

Opportunities for Reflection

Opportunities for reflection within lesson plans are beneficial in enhancing learning experiences through strengthening student understanding and influencing further instruction. When students are given the opportunity to reflect, they are able to connect their learning back to the original objective and better understand the overall purpose for learning, thus fostering engagement. Reflection deepens students' understanding by allowing them to connect new concepts to their own personal experiences, which ultimately helps in comprehension and retainment through making learning relevant. Reflecting on performance empowers students to become self-motivated lifelong learners by allowing them to analyze what they understood and did well, as well as encouraging them to identify areas for improvement. Teachers can utilize students' reflections to influence and drive further instruction. Students' reflections also allow teachers to identify areas in which students excelled, areas for improvement, and can aid them in tailoring future lesson plans to adapt to students' needs and interests.

Opportunities for Self-Assessment

Self-assessments within lessons are a valuable formative assessment strategy that enriches student learning and provides insight to the teacher. Providing students with the opportunity to monitor their progress and assess their learning supports them in developing a wide range of skills that are beneficial both inside and outside of the classroom. Self-assessments empower students in their learning by creating a sense of ownership and responsibility over their own learning, thus fostering self-motivation and engagement. They also serve to foster a sense of independence and objectivity within students to effectively review their own work and identify areas of improvement, which is a vital skill needed to becoming a lifelong learner. When students evaluate their own performance, the teacher is able to effectively assess student understanding, thus allowing them to identify areas of weakness or misconception for reteaching.

Opportunities for Closure Activities

Closure activities at the end of each lesson or topic are beneficial for both students and teachers. These short activities allow teachers to formatively assess student understanding of content covered within a lesson and identify areas of misconception for reteaching. Additionally, closure activities are valuable in measuring whether the intended lesson objective was achieved before moving to the next topic. For students, closures at the end of a lesson provide structure and organization to learning, as well as emphasize the purpose for instruction by allowing them to connect what they learned back to the original objective. Moreover, in having students restate what they have learned in a closure activity, learning is strengthened by giving students the opportunity to internalize new information. In demonstrating their understanding, they can better make personal connections between their own learning, background knowledge, and experiences.

Instructional Techniques

Implementing Multiple Instructional Techniques to Maximize Student Learning

Incorporating multiple instructional techniques into the classroom maximizes student learning by enhancing intellectual involvement and overall engagement. When instructional material is presented through a variety of means, it facilitates an **active learning** environment in which students' interest is captured and they are motivated to participate in learning. Varying teaching strategies stimulates engagement and fosters achievement by encouraging students to actively participate in their own learning and implement critical thinking skills to consider information more deeply. Students' understanding is strengthened when content is presented in different ways through various instructional techniques by providing them with multiple frames of reference for making connections and internalizing new concepts. In addition, utilizing multiple instructional techniques allows the teacher to effectively **differentiate instruction** to access multiple learning styles and address individual student needs to ensure understanding and enhance the overall learning process.

Instructional Strategies to Differentiate Instruction

Implementing a variety of strategies for differentiation helps to ensure that instruction appeals to students' varying learning styles and needs. By incorporating **multiple modalities** into direct instruction, such as visual representations, written directions, video or audio clips, songs, graphs, or mnemonic devices, teachers can differentiate the presentation of new concepts and information. Using strategies to differentiate instructional activities is also beneficial in diversifying the learning experience. By providing opportunities for **independent, collaborative**, and **hands-on** learning, teachers can ensure that learning is accessible and engaging to all students. In addition, learning activities should allow for a degree of flexibility in order to appeal to students' varying needs and preferences. Activities such as task cards, educational technology resources, and learning stations provide this **flexibility** and allow for a student-directed experience in which they can choose to learn in the way that best suits their needs. Similarly, assigning open-ended projects as summative assessments allows for a degree of **student-choice**, thus differentiating the method in which students demonstrate their understanding.

Varying the Teacher and Student Roles in the Instructional Process

Varying the roles of the teacher and students as an instructional technique is beneficial in creating an engaging, dynamic classroom environment that maximizes learning. When different roles are implemented, instruction is diversified, thus stimulating student interest and engagement. In addition, certain teacher and student roles are most applicable and effective in specific learning situations. When teachers acknowledge this and understand when to adopt and assign particular roles, they can effectively deliver instruction in a way that deepens student understanding and fosters success in learning. In presenting new content, directions, or modeling new skills for example, the roles of **lecturer** and student **observer** are effective. In hands-on learning situations, students can take on the role of **active participant** while the teacher acts as a **facilitator** to create a student-centered and engaging learning environment in which students are given ownership over their own learning. Such variation enhances intellectual involvement by promoting critical thinking and problem-solving skills through self-directed learning. Skillfully assigning different roles throughout the learning process also allows the teacher to effectively address students' individual learning needs and preferences to promote engagement and enhance the learning experience.

Fostering Intellectual Involvement and Engagement

Effective instruction includes a variety of strategies for fostering intellectual involvement and engagement to promote academic success. Presenting instruction using various approaches provides multiple avenues for learning new content, thus ensuring and strengthening student understanding to facilitate achievement. In addition, diversifying instructional strategies creates variety in the classroom that effectively stimulates students' interest and motivation to engage in learning. Such strategies as **cooperative learning**, **discussion**, and **self-directed opportunities** encourage active student participation that enhances intellectual involvement by allowing students to build on background knowledge, deepen understanding by exploring others' perspectives, and take ownership over their own learning. This ultimately increases student engagement and motivation for success in learning. Similarly, incorporating **inquiry**, **problem-solving**, and **project-based** strategies promote curiosity in learning, creativity, and the development of critical thinking skills that stimulate intellectual participation and engagement to create a productive learning environment. Implementing **digital resources** and media throughout instruction is integral in enhancing academic success by making learning relevant, interesting, and differentiated to accommodate various learning needs. At the end of a lesson or activity, allowing students the opportunity to reflect is a valuable strategy in increasing intellectual involvement, retainment, and academic success by facilitating personal connections with learning to build understanding.

Actively Engaging Students by Incorporating Discussion into Instruction

Classroom discussion is a valuable instructional technique in engaging students throughout the learning process. When the teacher skillfully poses higher-level questions in discussions, they establish an active learning environment in which students are encouraged and motivated to participate, thus enhancing overall engagement. Effective discussions prompt students to become **intellectually invested** in instruction by promoting the use of **critical** and **higher-order thinking** skills to consider information more deeply and devise creative solutions to problems. In addition, discussions stimulate engagement by providing students the opportunity to express their own thoughts and reasoning regarding a given topic to establish a sense of ownership over their learning. Furthermore, discussions foster a collaborative learning environment that actively engages students by prompting them to understand others' perspectives, consider alternative approaches, and build on one another's experiences to make deeper connections to learning.

Promoting Student Inquiry

The promotion of inquiry is a valuable instructional technique in enhancing student engagement and intellectual involvement. In an **inquiry-based** learning environment, students are encouraged to explore instructional material and devise their own conclusions or solutions to problems. This increases the effectiveness of the learning process by providing students with a sense of agency over their own learning. In addition, implementing this strategy fosters curiosity, self-motivation, and active participation, as it allows for hands-on, **student-led** learning that increases overall engagement. Incorporating inquiry into the classroom stimulates critical and higher-order thinking skills as students construct their own understanding by interacting with learning materials, analyzing their findings, and synthesizing their learning to create new conclusions, results, and responses. To effectively incorporate inquiry int the learning process, the teacher must provide several opportunities for self-directed and project-based learning, as well as student choice, to stimulate curiosity. Questions must be open-ended, and students must be encouraged to hypothesize, predict, and experiment in their learning. The teacher must be flexible in instruction to allow space and opportunity for exploration and allow time for reflection and extended learning opportunities to facilitate further inquiry.

Incorporating Problem-Solving into Instruction

Providing opportunities for creative problem solving within instruction effectively creates an engaging and successful learning experience. Students become more **intellectually involved** when encouraged to actively participate in learning and utilize **critical thinking skills** to test hypotheses, analyze results, and devise creative solutions to problems. This hands-on, **student-directed** approach promotes success in learning by allowing students to interact with learning materials as they seek answers to complex ideas and problems in an engaging environment. Problem-solving enables students to make deeper connections to their learning to enhance understanding, as this strategy prompts them to employ and develop background knowledge. In addition, problem-solving activities allow for collaborative learning in which students can actively engage with peers to build on one another's knowledge and experience, thus enhancing successful learning.

Relationship Between Intellectual Involvement, Active Student Engagement, and Success in Learning

A productive learning environment is comprised of intellectually involved students that are actively engaged in successful learning. A strong correlation exists between **intellectual involvement**, **active student engagement**, and **success in learning**, and each component is necessary for effective instruction. Effective instruction consists of challenging students based on their abilities and teaching them to think deeply about new ideas and concepts. This ultimately encourages students' intellectual involvement, as it prompts them to utilize their critical thinking skills to build on their background knowledge, consider alternative perspectives, and synthesize their learning to devise creative solutions. When students are intellectually involved in instruction, they become more personally invested and engaged, as learning becomes relevant, interesting, and challenging. Engaged students are active participants in their learning, thus enhancing their overall productivity and academic success.

Effectively Structuring Lessons

When developing instruction, it is imperative that the teacher is knowledgeable on how to effectively structure lessons to maximize student engagement and success. Each lesson must include a clear **objective** and explicitly state the process for achieving it. To initiate engagement, effective lessons begin with an **opening**, or "warm-up," activity to introduce a new topic, diagnose student understanding, and activate prior knowledge. Instruction of new material must be delivered through a variety of teaching strategies that are consciously tailored to students' individual learning needs to enhance participation and ensure comprehension. Direct instruction should be followed by **active learning** activities with clear directions and procedures to allow students to practice new concepts and skills. Throughout a successful lesson, the teacher checks frequently for understanding and comprehension by conducting a variety of **formative assessments** and adjusts instruction as necessary. Including **closure** activities is essential to successful learning, as it gives students the opportunity to reflect, process information, make connections, and demonstrate comprehension. In structuring lessons effectively according to students' learning needs, the teacher establishes a focused and engaging learning environment that promotes academic success.

Example of a Daily Lesson Plan Structure

Flexible Instructional Groupings

Flexible instructional groupings provide the teacher and students with a versatile, engaging environment for successful learning. Skillfully grouping students allows for productive, cooperative learning opportunities in which individual strengths are enhanced and necessary support is provided, thus enhancing motivation and engagement. When working in groups, students' understanding of instruction is strengthened, as they are able to learn and build upon one another's background knowledge, perspectives, and abilities. Instructional groups can include students of the **same** or **varied abilities** depending on the learning objective and task to increase productivity and provide scaffolding as necessary for support. This strategy is effective in enabling the teacher to

differentiate instruction and adjust groups as needed to accommodate varying learning styles, abilities, and interests to maximize engagement and success in learning.

Effective Pacing of Lessons and Importance of Flexibility to Students' Needs

Effective pacing is imperative to focused and engaging instruction. The teacher must be conscientious of the pace of their instruction and ensure that it is reflective of their student's learning needs and sustains their attention. Instruction that is delivered too quickly results in confusion and discouragement, whereas if instruction is too slow, students will lose interest and become disengaged. A well-paced lesson states clear learning goals and objectives while clearly outlining the means to achieve them to elicit student motivation. The teacher must consider the most **efficient** and **engaging** instructional strategies for presenting new material to establish a steady pace and maintain it by incorporating smooth **transitions** from one activity to the next. It is important that the teacher is conscious of the rate of instruction throughout all stages of learning while maintaining **flexibility** in pacing in order to be responsive to their students. As individual students have different learning needs and processing times, they may require a faster or slower rate of instruction to understand new concepts and remain engaged in learning. Frequent checks for understanding and reflection activities are essential strategies in determining if the pace of instruction must be adjusted to accommodate students' needs.

Connecting Content to Students' Prior Knowledge and Experiences

When the teacher implements effective instructional strategies for connecting content to students' prior knowledge and experiences, it enhances the relevancy of learning and fosters deeper connections that strengthen understanding. To achieve this, the teacher must educate themselves on students' backgrounds, experiences, communities, and interests to determine what is important and interesting to them. With this knowledge in mind, the teacher can successfully locate and implement **authentic materials** into instruction to enhance relevancy. Additionally, encouraging students to bring materials to class that reflect their backgrounds and including these materials in instruction makes learning relevant by allowing students to make **personal connections** to content. Instructional strategies such as brainstorming, KWL charts, prereading, and anticipation guides allow the teacher to determine what students know prior to learning a new concept, thus enabling them to connect content to students' background knowledge in a relevant way. Incorporating digital resources further enhances relevancy in learning in that the teacher can locate videos or audio clips that relate to instruction and reflect students' background experiences and interests. Using digital resources to introduce a new concept is a valuable strategy in developing students' **schema** on a topic to build prior knowledge and make learning meaningful by fostering connections.

Making Learning Relevant and Meaningful

For learning to be relevant and meaningful, it is essential that the teacher present content in a way that connects with students' **prior knowledge** and experiences. When students are able to apply new ideas and information to what they already know through effective instructional techniques, it facilitates strong **personal connections** that make learning relevant and meaningful. In addition, personal connections and **relevancy** are strengthened when the teacher consciously incorporates materials to reflect students' individual backgrounds and experiences in instruction. Linking content to students' background experiences enables them to relate instruction to real-world situations, thus establishing a sense of purpose for learning by making it applicable to their lives. Intentionally connecting content with students' prior knowledge and experiences enhances the effectiveness of the instructional process and fosters positive attitudes toward learning.

Enhancing Student Engagement and Success in Learning

Engaging instruction employs a variety of instructional strategies and materials to create a relevant, meaningful, and successful learning experience. Effective content establishes a clear and applicable purpose for instruction that increases student participation in the learning process. Presenting relevant and meaningful content enhances understanding and engagement by enabling students to create real-world, **personal connections** to learning based upon their own backgrounds and experiences. In addition, when instruction is tailored to reflect students' unique interests and preferences, content becomes more appealing and students' willingness to learn is enhanced. When students can perceive content through their own frames of reference with instructional materials that reflect their unique differences, they are able to effectively internalize and relate information to their lives, thus increasing engagement. Engaged learning ultimately facilitates academic success in that when students are motivated to learn, they demonstrate positive attitudes toward learning and are more likely to actively participate.

Adapting Instruction to Individual Needs

Evaluating Activities and Materials to Meet Individual Characteristics and Learning Needs

The careful selection of instructional activities and materials is integral to accommodating students' varying characteristics and needs to foster success in learning. When evaluating the appropriateness of activities and materials, several considerations must be made. The teacher must consider whether activities and materials align with state and district **academic standards**, as well as their quality and effectiveness in supporting students' unique differences as they achieve learning goals and objectives. All materials and activities must be **developmentally appropriate** across domains, yet adaptable to individual students' learning needs. In addition, they must be challenging, yet feasible for student achievement relative to students' grade level and abilities to promote engagement and the development of critical and **higher-order thinking** skills. The teacher must evaluate activities and materials for versatility to allow for student choice and differentiation in order to address varying characteristics and needs. The teacher must also ensure that activities and materials are accurate, **culturally sensitive**, and reflective of students' diversities to foster an inclusive learning environment that promotes engagement.

Instructional Resources and Technologies

The implementation of varied instructional resources and technologies is highly valuable in supporting student engagement and achievement. Effective use of resources and technologies requires the teacher to evaluate their appropriateness in addressing students' individual characteristics and learning needs for academic success. The teacher must be attuned to students' unique differences in order to seek high quality technologies and resources that address their students' needs to support and enhance the achievement of learning goals and objectives. Technologies and resources must be **accurate**, **comprehensible**, and easily **accessible** to students, as well as **relevant** to the curriculum and the development of particular skills. The teacher must also consider the grade-level and **developmental appropriateness** of technologies and resources, as well as their adaptability to allow for differentiation. Effective technologies and resources are interactive, engaging, and multifaceted to allow for varying levels of complexity based on students' abilities. This allows the teacher to provide appropriate challenges while diversifying instruction to appeal to varied characteristics and learning needs, thus fostering an engaging environment that supports success in learning for all students.

Adapting Activities and Materials to Meet Individual Characteristics and Needs

In effective instruction, activities and materials are adapted to accommodate students' individual characteristics and needs. The teacher must be attuned to students' unique differences and understand how to adjust activities and materials accordingly to facilitate academic success and growth. To achieve this, the teacher must incorporate a **variety** of activities and materials that appeal to all styles of learners. Activities and materials should provide **student choice** for engagement in learning and demonstration of understanding. By differentiating instruction, the teacher can effectively scaffold activities and materials to provide supports as necessary, as well as include extensions or alternate activities for enrichment. **Chunking** instruction, allowing extra time as necessary, and accompanying activities and materials with aids such as graphic organizers, visual representations, and anticipation guides further differentiates learning to accommodate students' learning characteristics and needs. Conducting **formative assessments** provides the teacher with valuable feedback regarding student understanding and engagement, thus allowing them to modify and adjust the complexity of activities and materials as necessary to adapt to varied characteristics and learning differences.

Instructional Resources and Technologies

When the teacher understands students' individual characteristics and needs, they can adapt instructional resources and technologies accordingly to maximize learning. To do so effectively, the teacher must incorporate a diverse array of **multifaceted** resources and technologies that support and enhance learning through a variety of methods. This ensures that varying learning needs are met, as students of all learning styles are provided with several avenues for building and strengthening understanding. Additionally, the teacher can adapt resources and technologies to accommodate individual students by **varying the complexity** to provide challenges, support, and opportunities for enrichment based on ability level. Supplementing technologies and resources with **scaffolds**, such as extra time, visual representations, or opportunities for collaborative learning, further enables the teacher to adapt to individual learning needs. When effectively implemented and adapted to students' characteristics and needs, instructional technologies and resources serve as valuable tools for differentiating curriculum to enhance the learning experience.

Flexible and Responsive Instructional Practices

Evaluation of Instruction

Evaluating the appropriateness of instructional materials, activities, resources, and technologies is integral to establishing a successful learning environment. Doing so provides students with high-quality and inclusive instruction by ensuring **clarity**, **accuracy**, **relevancy**, and **reflection** of student diversities. By determining whether these components of instruction meet varying characteristics and learning needs, the teacher can deliver **student-centered** instruction, that is challenging based on individual ability, to promote development and academic success. This process also allows the teacher to effectively **differentiate** instruction to provide necessary personalized support for success in achieving learning targets, as well as create engaging learning opportunities tailored to students' unique differences and interests. Effectively determining the appropriateness of activities, materials, resources, and technologies in meeting students' learning needs ultimately maximizes academic achievement and fosters positive attitudes toward learning that establish a foundation for future success.

Continuous Monitoring of Instructional Effectiveness

Successful instruction must be flexible and adaptable to meet students' dynamic learning needs. To achieve this, teachers must continuously monitor the effectiveness of their instruction to determine if their teaching strategies, activities, and communication are effective. Frequent evaluation of instructional effectiveness is necessary to ensure that students understand **foundational concepts** before moving on to more advanced concepts. **Adaptations** to instruction, communication, or assessment may be necessary to ensure students are able to comprehend and retain concepts before moving on to more advanced topics. **Remediation** of missed concepts is often much more challenging and less successful than checking for comprehension within context and providing more detailed instruction. This ultimately fosters long-term achievement, as the teacher can identify and address student needs as they arise and prevent compounding issues. Continuous monitoring enables the teacher to ensure that learning opportunities are engaging, relevant, and challenging based on students' ability levels, as it provides immediate feedback on the effectiveness of instruction, which allows the teacher to make necessary changes. This ultimately enhances instruction by establishing a student-centered learning environment that is tailored to individual needs, interests, and abilities.

Pre-Instructional, Peri-Instructional, and Post-Instructional Strategies

Instructional effectiveness must be monitored on a whole-class and individual level throughout all stages of teaching. Prior to instruction, administering **pre-tests** provides the teacher with insight regarding whole-class and individual understanding. This enables them to select effective and appropriate instructional strategies that can be differentiated to meet individual needs. Pre-tests allow the teacher to identify and clarify misunderstandings before instruction to ensure effectiveness. During instruction, **observation** of students' participation in instruction during independent and group activities enables the teacher to evaluate overall and individual understanding and engagement. Frequent checks for understanding and **formative assessments** throughout instruction provide feedback on whole-group and individual learning, as the teacher can assess understanding and participation to adapt teaching strategies or individualize instruction. Leading student discussions allows the teacher to identify areas of misunderstanding among the class or individuals that may need reteaching through a different approach. Closure and reflection activities after instruction are valuable in monitoring effectiveness, as they indicate both whole-class and individual comprehension and retainment of new concepts. Likewise, incorporating **summative assessments** and analyzing the results provides the teacher with information regarding the overall effectiveness of their teaching process, as well as students' individual strengths and weaknesses to consider for future instruction.

Applying Feedback to Make Necessary Changes to Instruction

Continuous monitoring of instruction indicates the instruction's effectiveness on a **whole-class** and **individual** level, as it provides the teacher with immediate insight on student understanding, progress, and areas for improvement. Monitoring instructional effectiveness enables the teacher to evaluate students' **pace** in achieving learning goals and adjust the rate of instruction as necessary. Additionally, it allows the teacher to identify whole-class and individual **misconceptions** that require correction to ensure students do not fall behind schedule in meeting academic benchmarks. If monitoring reveals misunderstanding among the whole class, the teacher must alter their overall instructional approach and teaching strategies to clarify and regain understanding. Individual misconceptions indicate the need to differentiate instruction, adjust groupings, and provide supports and remediation as necessary to ensure the student progresses at the same rate as the rest of the class. By identifying student strengths and weaknesses through consistent monitoring of instructional effectiveness, the teacher can effectively make instructional decisions that are attuned to whole-class and individual student needs to maximize learning.

Flexibility in Instruction

Situations Requiring Flexibility

The classroom environment is dynamic in nature. Teachers will inevitably encounter situations throughout instruction and assessment in which **flexibility** is integral to successful teaching and learning. As students have varying learning styles, needs, and interests, teachers may find that their instructional approaches are ineffective in maintaining engagement and may need to adjust strategies, activities, or assessments to better meet learning needs. Students may have difficulty grasping new material, which could result in a lack of engagement in instructional activities and, potentially, disruptive behavior. Teachers must consistently be attuned to students' level of comprehension and allow flexibility with their lesson plans to modify strategies, activities, or pacing as necessary to facilitate engagement and understanding before advancing in instruction. Students may also progress more quickly than others through instructional activities or assessments. **Scaffolding** activities to include opportunities for extension and enrichment allows for flexibility within instruction to ensure that all students are adequately challenged and engaged in learning. Throughout instruction and assessments, teachers may find valuable, unexpected learning opportunities. By remaining open and flexible to these instances, teachers can enhance the learning process by incorporating them into instruction to strengthen student understanding.

Enhancing the Overall Learning Experience

Flexibility is an integral component of effective instruction, as it enables the teacher to adequately address and accommodate students' individual needs and interests for maximized success in learning. When the teacher considers their lesson plan as a **framework** while allowing for flexibility, they demonstrate an awareness of their students' individual differences and the potential for deviation from original instruction. This enables them to more effectively modify instructional and assessment strategies, activities, and approaches to create a **responsive**, **student-centered** environment that enhances the overall learning experience and promotes achievement. When instructional activities and assessments are adaptable to accommodate students' needs and interests, learning becomes more personalized and relevant, thus strengthening understanding and increasing motivation to engage in active learning. A flexible approach to instruction and assessment also provides students with the ability to explore content of interest on a deeper level and potentially encounter unanticipated learning opportunities that foster personal connections and enhance learning. In addition, this approach allows for **versatility** in assessment, as flexibility enables the teacher to modify assessments by providing necessary support to meet students' individual needs and supports students' choice in demonstrating learning.

Poor Student Comprehension

Throughout instruction and assessments, students may have difficulty **comprehending** new or difficult material, despite being engaged in instruction. This may lead to confusion that can cause students to become discouraged and disengaged in learning, as well as have continued and compounded difficulty in grasping increasingly complex concepts. Difficulties with comprehension hinders academic success, as students that struggle face challenges in building the foundation of understanding necessary for advancing through curriculum. To ensure student comprehension throughout all stages of learning, the teacher must be aware of students' individual learning styles and needs and be able to respond flexibly to obstacles they may encounter. **Formative assessments** during instruction enable the teacher to evaluate the level of student comprehension and identify areas of need for flexible **adjustment** or additional support. This includes modifying **pacing** and allowing additional time for student processing to ensure understanding. In addition, the original lesson plan may require **chunking** into smaller, more manageable parts to allow students to internalize new concepts before moving on. The teacher may also need to respond flexibly to students' needs during instruction by **differentiating** teaching strategies, activities, groupings, or assessments to ensure that material is accessible and comprehensible to all students for enhanced success.

Unanticipated Learning Opportunities

Unanticipated learning opportunities, when embraced by the teacher, are often highly valuable in establishing a classroom environment that promotes student engagement, motivation, and success. These instances often divert from the original lesson plan, but when utilized effectively, serve to strengthen student understanding and foster **personal connections** for an enhanced learning experience. Facilitating such opportunities allows students to investigate topics of interest and relevancy to them on a deeper level, thus increasing active engagement and promoting **self-directed** learning. This ultimately supports students in forming connections and recognizing the real-world applications of their learning, which increases the likelihood that they will internalize and **retain** new information. Responding flexibly to unanticipated learning opportunities includes acknowledging students' questions and comments, as well as demonstrating an awareness of their individual differences and learning needs. This enables the teacher to maximize the effectiveness of these opportunities by facilitating student-led instruction that is attuned to their learning styles, interests, and preferences for enhanced engagement and achievement.

Conducting Ongoing Assessments and Making Adjustments

Conducting **ongoing assessments** throughout instruction provides the teacher with continuous feedback regarding student comprehension, engagement, and performance. When practiced consistently, the teacher is more attuned and responsive to students' individual learning needs. This enables them to effectively modify instructional strategies, activities, and assessments accordingly for a **student-centered** learning environment that provides the support necessary for enhanced engagement, comprehension, and achievement. It allows the teacher to identify and address areas of **misconception** and student need to ensure understanding prior to progressing through the curriculum. Feedback from ongoing evaluation of student performance indicates to the teacher areas of instruction in which adjustment is necessary to effectively support students in achieving learning goals. The teacher may need to adjust their pacing to ensure comprehension and engagement, as well as differentiate instruction based on feedback regarding individual progress to ensure all students are adequately challenged and supported based on their ability levels. Student groupings may need to be adjusted to scaffold instruction and facilitate increased comprehension. When the teacher effectively applies feedback from ongoing assessments of student engagement and performance, they can tailor instruction to accommodate their individual needs and interests to enhance success in learning.

Progressing Ahead of Schedule

Throughout instruction, the teacher will encounter instances in which individual students or the whole class progresses **faster than anticipated**. When this arises, the teacher must be prepared to respond flexibly to ensure that all students are engaged, on task, and challenged based on their ability level. Lesson plans should be **scaffolded** to include opportunities for enrichment and extended learning for students that finish before others. This includes incorporating such material as increasingly complex texts, practice activities, and project opportunities. The teacher can also establish a designated area in the classroom in which individuals or small groups that finish early can participate in **extended learning** or **review** activities that reinforce learning objectives. Such activities allow students to explore instructional topics on a deeper level for strengthened understanding and ensure they are engaging productively in meaningful activities that are relevant to instruction. When the whole class progresses faster than expected, the teacher can respond flexibly by incorporating **total participation** activities to reinforce instructional material. Such activities as review games, class discussions, and digital resources for extra practice ensure that the class remains engaged in instruction when they finish a lesson early.

Schedules, Routines, and Activities for Young Children

Ideal Schedule for Young Children

An ideal schedule for young children reflects their developmental characteristics and capabilities to maximize their learning. A **predictable** routine is necessary for young children to feel secure in their learning environment, and therefore, each day should follow a similar schedule while allowing room for **flexibility** if an activity takes longer than expected. Each day should begin with a clear routine, such as unpacking, a "warm-up" activity, and a class meeting to allow students to share thoughts, ask questions, and allow the teacher to discuss what will occur that day. This establishes a positive tone for the day while focusing the attention on learning. Similarly, the end of the day should have a specific routine, such as cleaning up materials and packing up for dismissal. Young children learn best by physically interacting with and exploring their environment. As such, each day should include large blocks of time for **active movement** throughout the day in the form of play, projects, and learning centers. Periods of **rest** must follow such activities, as this enables young children to process and internalize what they learned. **Direct instruction** should occur before active movement periods and last approximately 15-20 minutes to sustain engagement and attention on learning.

Example Daily Schedule for the Early Childhood Education Classroom	
8:00-8:30	Welcome, unpack, morning work
8:30-8:45	Circle time, review class calendar
8:45-9:30	Literacy/Language Arts
9:30-10:15	Learning Stations
10:15-11:00	Math
11:00-11:30	Music/Dance/Movement
11:30-12:15	Lunch
12:15-1:00	Recess/Unstructured play
1:00-1:20	Rest/Quiet time
1:20-2:00	Science
2:00-2:45	Creative Arts
2:45-3:15	Daily reflection, pack up, dismissal

Some examples of restful and active movement activities for young children are discussed below:

- **Restful:** Incorporating restful activities into the early childhood classroom are beneficial in helping young children process and retain new concepts and providing them the opportunity to unwind after active movement activities. Examples of such activities include nap time, class meditation, self-reflection activities, independent art projects, or self-selected reading time. Teachers can also read aloud to students or play an audiobook during these periods.

- **Active:** Providing young children with multiple opportunities for active movement throughout the day is beneficial in promoting the development of gross motor skills, connections to learning, and the ability to function in a group setting. Active movement opportunities should include whole-class, small group, and independent activities. Examples include class dances, songs, or games, nature walks, or total participation activities such as gallery walks or four corners. Physical education activities, such as jump rope, tag, sports, or using playground equipment are also beneficial. Young children should also be provided with ample time for both structured and unstructured play throughout the day.

Balancing Restful and Active Movement Activities

A schedule that balances **rest** and **active movement** is necessary for positive cognitive, physical, emotional, and social development in young children. Connecting learning to active movement strengthens students' understanding of new concepts, as it allows them to physically explore and interact with their environment, experiment with new ideas, and gain new experiences for healthy **cognitive development**. In addition, incorporating active movement encourages the use of **gross motor skills** and provides students with the space to physically express themselves in an appropriate setting, thus promoting physical and emotional development. Active movement also encourages the development of positive **interpersonal skills** as young children interact and explore with one another. Restful periods are equally as important to young children's development. Incorporating rest after a period of active movement further strengthens young children's connection to learning by providing them the opportunity to reflect, process, and internalize new information.

Providing Large Blocks of Time for Play, Projects, and Learning Centers

Providing young children with ample time for play, projects, and learning centers throughout the school day is integral to fostering their development across domains. Young children learn most effectively through active movement as they physically interact with their environment, and incorporating large blocks of time for such activities allows them to do so. Significant time dedicated to active play, projects, and learning centers on a variety of topics allows young children to explore and experiment with the world around them, test new ideas, draw conclusions, and acquire new knowledge. This supports healthy **physical** and **cognitive development**, as it provides young children the opportunity to engage in learning across subject areas while connecting it to active movement for strengthened understanding. In addition, allowing large blocks of time for these activities is necessary for **social** and **emotional development**, as it provides young children the space to interact with one another and develop important skills such as cooperation, sharing, conflict resolution, and emotional self-regulation. Dedicating large blocks of time to play, projects, and learning centers establishes a student-led, hands-on learning environment that is reflective of the developmental characteristics and needs of young children.

Developmental Characteristics of Young Children in Relation to Interactions with Others

Designing group activities that align with young children's ability to collaborate while supporting social development requires a realistic understanding of their capacity to do so. This entails understanding the **developmental characteristics** of young children at varying stages, including how the nature of their interactions with others evolves. Young children learn by exploring and interacting with their environment, so they need ample opportunities for play and active movement to do so. However, the teacher must recognize that the way young children play and collaborate develops over time. Young children typically exhibit little interest in actively playing with others until approximately age four. Until then, they progress through stages of solitary play, observing their peers, playing independently alongside others, and eventually, loosely interacting, perhaps with the same toys, while still primarily engaging in independent play. During these stages, it is important that the teacher foster **collaboration** by providing multiple opportunities for play as well as learning materials that encourage **cooperation** and **sharing**. The teacher must, however, maintain the understanding that these children have yet to develop the capacity to intentionally work with others. Once this ability is developed, the teacher can integrate coordinated group activities that encourage collaboration toward a common goal.

Considerations When Designing Group Activities for Young Children

For young children, thoughtfully designed group activities are integral in promoting development across domains. These opportunities facilitate social and emotional development by encouraging collaboration and positive communication, as well as physical and cognitive growth as children play, explore, and interact with others in the learning environment. It is therefore important that the teacher carefully consider the particulars of group activities when planning to ensure maximized learning and development. The teacher must consider the **developmental characteristics** of their students' age group, including their capacity to collaborate with others. This enables the teacher to plan group activities that align with students' abilities while promoting collaboration and development. All **learning materials** must be carefully selected to encourage collaboration, sharing, and the development of positive social skills at a developmentally appropriate level. The teacher must also consider **desired learning outcomes** and the nature of the learning taking place to determine whether group activities should be structured or unstructured. Unstructured play is valuable in allowing students to develop their social and emotional skills in a natural setting, whereas structured, teacher-led group activities allow for more focused learning. Desired outcomes also determine the size of groups for the activity to best promote collaboration and learning.

Group Activities that Reflect and Develop Young Children's Ability to Collaborate

Young children benefit from a variety of **whole-class** and **small-group** activities designed to reflect and develop their collaborative skills. When the teacher incorporates group activities to encourage cooperation, sharing, and positive interactions, young children gain important social and emotional skills necessary for development across domains. Whole-group activities such as **circle time** provide young children with the opportunity to interact with others, express ideas, and ask questions in a developmentally appropriate setting. This activity develops important collaborative skills, such as taking turns, active listening, and respectful communication. Other **whole-group activities**, such as reading aloud, group songs, dances, games, or class nature walks, are effective in teaching young children how to productively contribute to and function in a group setting. **Small-group activities** can be incorporated throughout all aspects of structured and unstructured learning to develop young children's collaborative skills. Learning centers, such as a science area, pretend play area, or building block center, provide materials that encourage collaboration while allowing students to interact with others according to their abilities in a student-led setting. Problem-solving activities, such as puzzles, games, age-appropriate science experiments, or scavenger hunts, are effective in teaching young children how to work together toward a common goal.

Organizing and Managing Group Activities to Promote Collaborative Skills and Individual Accountability

Well-planned group activities are beneficial in developing students' collaborative skills and sense of individual accountability. Such group activities are well-organized, effectively managed, and intentionally structured with a **clear goal** or problem that must be solved while allowing room for creativity to enhance the collaborative process. When designing these activities, the teacher must incorporate enough **significant components** to ensure all students within the group can productively contribute. If the assignment is too simple, students can easily complete it on their own, whereas a multifaceted activity instills a sense of interdependence within the group that fosters the development of collaborative skills. To promote individual accountability, **meaningful roles** and responsibilities should be assigned to each group member because when students feel others are relying on their contributions to complete a task, they develop a sense of ownership that motivates active participation. To further develop collaborative skills and individual accountability, students should be graded both as a **whole-group** and **individually**. This encourages group cooperation while ensuring that students' individual contributions are recognized. Including **self-assessments** at the end of group activities is beneficial in allowing students to reflect on the quality of their contributions to the group and ways they could improve their collaborative skills.

Thoughtful consideration of how to best organize and manage collaborative activities helps establish an environment that supports students in learning to work together productively and assume responsible roles within a group. When planning group activities, the teacher must consider the **desired learning outcomes** and the **nature of the task** to determine whether there are enough significant components that would benefit from collaboration. **Group size** must also be considered to most effectively foster collaboration and individual accountability when assuming responsible roles. Groups with too few students may be inadequate for addressing all the components of a complex task, whereas grouping too many students together limits productive collaboration and makes it difficult for each member to assume a significant, responsible role. The teacher must be selective regarding which students are grouped together to best facilitate productive collaboration. This includes determining which students will work well together, as well as grouping students that may need support with others that can provide scaffolding. It is also important to consider how **responsibilities** will be divided to ensure each member is given a significant role that allows them to contribute productively to the group, as well how their contributions will be monitored and **assessed**.

Communicating Effectively with Students

Clear and Accurate Communication

Significance

Successful teaching and learning is reliant on clear, accurate communication throughout all stages of the learning process. To create a positive and productive learning environment, it is vital that the teacher practice effective speaking, listening, reading, and writing skills to ensure focused instruction in which students understand expectations and desired learning outcomes. When communication is clear and accurate, learning becomes relevant and engaging, as students understand the purpose of instruction and are more successfully able to complete tasks and achieve learning targets. This ultimately enhances the overall learning experience in that it allows teachers to efficiently progress through the curriculum and challenge students with increasingly complex material as they master desired learning outcomes. In addition, effective communication is multifaceted and increases student comprehension and deepens their understanding of subject matter. When the teacher skillfully communicates instruction through a variety of methods, students of varying learning styles are better able to internalize new information according to their individual needs. By enhancing teaching and learning through clear and accurate communication, the teacher establishes positive attitudes toward learning among students that serve as a foundation for future academic success.

Appropriate Language for Varying Age Groups

Students' cognitive abilities develop as they mature, and therefore, the ability to focus, comprehend and process information differs among age groups. For successful teaching and learning, the teacher must be aware of these variances to clearly and accurately communicate in an age-appropriate manner that facilitates student understanding. The use of age-appropriate language throughout the teaching and learning process is vital in supporting students' attention and ability to focus, as well as challenging them according to their developmental levels to ensure prolonged engagement in instruction. Furthermore, age-appropriate language is necessary in promoting student understanding through making information accessible and relevant. When designing and communicating instruction, the teacher must consider students' cognitive and linguistic abilities, as well as their attention span relative to their age group to ensure a comprehensible, rigorous, and engaging learning environment. The teacher must also be sure to support verbal communication with eye contact, body language, and visuals appropriate to the specific age group to reinforce and deepen understanding.

Tailoring Communication to Students' Interests

Communicating instruction to reflect students' interests enhances the teaching and learning process by fostering an engaging, student-centered environment. Instruction that appeals to students by incorporating their interests strengthens comprehension and understanding through increasing relevancy by allowing for personal connections to learning. To accomplish this, the teacher must get to know individual students and work to build positive relationships to gain an understanding of their unique interests and preferences. With this understanding in mind, the teacher can provide learning experiences that reflect individual interests through examples, relevant activities, and encouraging active participation to allow students to express their own interests and connections when learning. In addition, the teacher must seek student feedback and evaluate their reactions when delivering instruction to determine whether it is reflective of their interests and adjust accordingly. When instruction is communicated according to students' interests and preferences, the teacher creates an inclusive and personalized learning experience that fosters positive attitudes toward learning and enhances academic achievement.

Using Language Appropriate to Students' Backgrounds

Understanding students' backgrounds and adjusting language accordingly is imperative for ensuring clear, accurate, and respectful communication that promotes success in learning. When communicating in the classroom, using language appropriate to students' individual backgrounds is essential in ensuring culturally **relevant**, **sensitive**, and **responsive** instruction. In addition, when teachers understand what is important to students based upon their background experiences, beliefs, and values, they can more effectively and accurately communicate instruction, as they can tailor their language in a manner that is responsive to students' needs and avoids misunderstanding. Such **culturally competent** communication promotes academic success by fostering an inclusive environment in which all students feel respected and are therefore motivated to learn. Moreover, using language that is appropriate to students' backgrounds enhances the teaching and learning process by making instruction engaging and relevant to students, as it enables personal connections to deepen understanding. When the language of instruction is easily accessible to students and reflective of their experiences, they can apply their learning to their own personal contexts. This ultimately fosters positive attitudes toward learning among students that promote academic success.

Instructional Strategies for Ensuring Clear and Accurate Communication

In effective instruction, the teacher frequently implements strategies to ensure and evaluate the clarity and accuracy of communication and adjusts accordingly to meet students' individual needs.

In order to provide instruction that is easily accessible to students, the teacher must incorporate a variety of **verbal** and **nonverbal** communication techniques to strengthen understanding. Verbal information must be accompanied by nonverbal means of communication, such as proper eye contact, body language, gestures, visuals, and written information. Additionally, the teacher can determine whether they are communicating clearly and accurately by asking students to repeat instructions and key information. Frequently monitoring student progress by conducting formative assessments throughout the learning process allows the teacher to determine student comprehension and adjust communication techniques as necessary to enhance clarity and accuracy. Moreover, allowing students opportunities to provide feedback on the learning process through discussions and reflection activities is an effective strategy in providing insight on the clarity and accuracy of communication. By implementing cooperative learning and small group activities, the teacher can further ensure clarity and accuracy of communication by allowing for more focused instruction that is tailored to students' individual learning needs.

Ensuring Student Understanding

Effectively Communicating Directions, Explanations, and Procedures

Successful learning requires the effective communication of directions, explanations, and procedures to ensure student understanding. When this information is clearly communicated, student confusion and misconception is avoided, allowing for smoother and more focused instruction. Effective and skillful communication eliminates distractions from instruction, thus allowing students to engage in learning confidently and successfully because they clearly understand the objectives, expectations, and methods for completing tasks. In addition, allocating specific time to provide specific directions, explanations, and procedures enhances student understanding by establishing consistency, order, and effective classroom management that enables students to focus on learning. This creates a safe, predictable, and ultimately, more engaging classroom environment that facilitates student understanding and success in learning.

Strategies for Adjusting Communication

In all stages of the teaching and learning process, the teacher must be flexible in instruction and implement strategies for adjusting communication to ensure student understanding. The teacher may have to adapt communication by adjusting their tone, pace, vocabulary, or method of communicating to meet students' individual learning needs. The teacher must get to know their students to understand their unique needs as well as what is interesting and relevant to them to tailor their communication accordingly. By building positive relationships and learning students' communication styles, the teacher can effectively deliver instruction that is easily understandable to students. Modeling good active listening skills, conducting formative assessments throughout instruction, and eliciting student feedback allows the teacher to evaluate student understanding and adjust their communication style as necessary. In addition, incorporating technology into instruction is a valuable strategy for adapting communication to meet students' needs and ensure understanding. By accompanying instruction with digital resources, the teacher can deliver information, directions, and explanations through a variety of methods to make communication accessible and comprehensible to students of varying learning styles.

Providing Examples When Communicating Directions, Explanations, and Procedures

When the teacher skillfully provides examples to support directions, explanations, and procedures, instruction is more effective because students' overall understanding is enhanced. In selecting appropriate, relevant examples, the teacher makes learning concrete and establishes a frame of reference for students to visualize the real-world application of the given information. Effective examples allow students to make personal connections to their learning by relating information to their own experiences, thus enhancing their understanding by making learning more engaging and meaningful. Additionally, as modeling is an influential instructional strategy, incorporating practical examples enhances student understanding by providing them with a model to reference, compare, and replicate. The use of effective examples in communicating directions, explanations, and procedures ultimately increases retainment of information, thus fostering success when students engage in learning.

Types of Examples

Accompanying directions, explanations, and procedures with a variety of examples is beneficial in strengthening student's connections for enhanced understanding. **Visual representations**, such as images, illustrations, diagrams, graphs, or charts, serve as valuable examples for student reference, as reminders, as well as to supplement instruction. Modeling is a highly effective instructional strategy, and **demonstrating** to students how to perform directions, routines, and procedures ensures that students are clear regarding what is expected of them. When communicating criteria for assignments, showing examples of **past student work** provides students with clarity regarding how they will be graded, as well as the characteristics of quality work. In addition, using real-life **scenarios** or **personal experiences** as examples is beneficial in making new information relevant, applicable, and as a result, easier for students to comprehend.

Simplifying Complex Ideas

To strengthen student understanding of content material, complex ideas often must be simplified. The teacher must take care with their communication and be aware of effective implementation of teaching strategies to provide comprehensible instruction. The language of instruction must be clear, succinct, free of distractions, and age-appropriate to ensure that new content is easily accessible to students. Complex ideas should be **chunked** into smaller parts when teaching to allow for focused instruction that avoids misconceptions and builds a solid foundation of understanding. This also enhances student understanding by allowing the teacher the opportunity to formatively assess comprehension throughout the learning process and adjust instructional strategies as necessary to simplify difficult content material. Accompanying instruction with visual aids such as graphic organizers, anchor charts, or infographics make complex topics easier to internalize by emphasizing key information. Likewise, incorporating media and other digital resources enhances student understanding by diversifying the instructional approach to make learning more accessible and reinforcing complex ideas.

Effective Communication Tools

In a productive learning environment, the teacher implements a variety of communication tools to ensure that students have a clear understanding of directions, explanations, and procedures. **Visual aids** throughout the classroom in the form of posters, anchor charts, and class bulletin boards serve to reinforce and remind students of pertinent information and expectations. Effective **transitions** communicate to students the process for moving from one activity or subject to the next. Allowing students opportunities for **reflection** provides the teacher with feedback on the clarity of directions, explanations, and procedures and enables them to adjust communication as necessary to enhance understanding. In addition, several digital communication tools are available to increase communication and understanding, including interactive apps that enable teachers to formatively assess clarity and apps to remind students and families of important information to reinforce understanding. Establishing communication with families by creating a classroom newsletter or website and requiring students to keep a daily agenda book are examples of valuable tools for ensuring understanding, as these allow students to be reminded of events, assignments, and expectations at home.

Verbal and Nonverbal Means of Communication

Directions, explanations, and procedures often must be communicated throughout instruction to enhance student understanding. In communicating this information through a variety of **verbal** and **nonverbal** methods, the teacher ensures that students are aware of every part of the instructional process, thus allowing for a focused and productive learning experience. When introducing a new lesson or activity, using effective speaking and listening skills, repeating explanations as necessary, and varying tone, pacing, and inflection to verbally communicate pertinent information and processes effectively establishes understanding. Verbally conducting formative assessments during instruction further supports student understanding by providing the teacher with feedback to adjust communication as needed for clarity. In addition, verbal instructions can be strengthened to increase student understanding by incorporating media such as videos and audio clips. Nonverbal communication is highly effective in reminding students of and reinforcing directions, explanations, and procedures. Gestures, facial expressions, body language, eye contact, and proximity are valuable tools for highlighting key information and reminding students of expectations and instructional steps. In addition, visual reminders around the classroom in the form of posters, charts, and presentation slides act as nonverbal reminders of processes and expectations to enhance understanding and allow for focused engagement in instruction.

Significance of Effective Communication Skills in Meeting Specified Goals

Effective communication skills are essential to successfully meeting learning goals across various contexts. When the teacher skillfully communicates desired outcomes in the instructional process and the steps to achieve them, students are able to meet learning goals because they have a focused understanding and purpose for learning. When communication is clear and free of distractions, students' engagement in instruction is enhanced, thus making it easier for them to achieve learning targets. In addition, using a variety of techniques to effectively communicate material across subject areas enhances understanding by providing multiple avenues for students to internalize, apply, and ultimately retain new information. Furthermore, when the teacher is conscientious of their communication, they become more attuned to students' individual learning needs and communication styles. This allows the teacher to effectively instill necessary supports and adjust communication to meet students' needs when meeting specified learning goals.

Significance of Effective Interpersonal Skills in Positive Learning Environment

Interpersonal relationships are a vital aspect of successful teaching and learning. When positive interpersonal skills are demonstrated and promoted, the teacher effectively establishes a supportive, inviting classroom environment in which students are empowered and motivated to learn. Strong interpersonal skills allow the teacher to build positive, respectful relationships with students, instilling in them a sense of confidence and engagement that fosters academic achievement. In understanding how to interact with students in a way that is relevant and meaningful to them, the teacher can enhance learning and achievement by tailoring instruction to students' unique interests and experiences. In addition, establishing a positive rapport with students enables the teacher to identify, address, and adapt instruction to students' individual learning needs, thus enhancing instruction to promote engagement and achievement.

Verbal and Nonverbal Communication

When developing and delivering instruction to meet specified goals across varying learning contexts, it is imperative that the teacher implement a variety of verbal and nonverbal communication techniques. **Verbal communication** methods, including repetition, providing explanations and examples, and changing the pace, tone, and inflection of speech are effective when introducing new, complex concepts and emphasizing key information to students. Incorporating videos and audio clips enhance verbal communication by providing an additional method for understanding when working to achieve learning goals. Incorporating clear **nonverbal communication** techniques is effective in reinforcing and reminding students of instructional targets and content. Body language, gestures, facial expressions, and eye contact highlight important information to support verbal communication and strengthen understanding when explaining new concepts or modeling new skills to students. In addition, visual aids such as posters, anchor charts, presentation slides, and images are tools for nonverbally restating procedures and concepts, as well as simplifying complex ideas to enable students to successfully reach specified learning goals.

Electronic Communication

In an increasingly digital world, electronic communication has become integral in enhancing teaching and learning to efficiently meet specified goals across learning contexts. Digital resources improve clarity by providing teachers with multiple means of communicating learning targets, delivering instruction, and providing feedback. Electronic communication makes learning more accessible and comprehensible, as teachers can utilize it to deliver information and instruction in a variety of ways, according to students' individual learning needs, to meet desired outcomes. Digital communication platforms, such as virtual classrooms and interactive apps, promote interaction and participation that increase student engagement in the learning process. In addition, such platforms increase the efficiency of meeting specified learning goals by allowing for immediate communication and feedback between teachers and students throughout all stages of instruction. Such platforms also allow the teacher to provide instructional materials that students can easily reference to increase understanding. Electronic tools such as email, class websites, and communication apps establish open communication between teachers, students, and families that is beneficial in meeting learning goals by allowing the teacher to easily provide pertinent information that can be reinforced at home.

Effective Feedback and Self-Assessment

Timely Feedback

Timely feedback improves the effectiveness of teaching and learning for enhanced student achievement. When the teacher consistently provides feedback on students' progress throughout all stages of instruction, it is more relevant, thus enabling students to effectively connect it to the context of their learning. Providing timely feedback also ensures that instructional content is at the forefront of students' minds, thus increasing the likelihood that students will effectively apply it for enhanced learning. Immediate feedback increases student motivation and allows for more focused instruction, as students are continuously aware of their strengths and areas for improvement. In addition, efficient feedback enables the teacher to quickly identify areas of misconception before advancing in instruction, thus ensuring student understanding before moving forward and avoiding the need for remediation. This allows the teacher to progress smoothly through instruction while ensuring comprehension to enhance student achievement.

Appropriate Language for Providing Feedback

The language of feedback influences its effectiveness in fostering student achievement. When providing students with feedback regarding their progress, the teacher must be mindful of their approach to ensure that it is properly received. It is important that the teacher consider students' **age** and **grade level** to tailor language accordingly and present feedback in a relevant and meaningful way. When the language of feedback is comprehensible to students, they are more effectively able to apply it to the context of their learning. The teacher's language must be

respectful, positive, and **encouraging** while constructively suggesting areas for improvement so as to support students' self-concept and positive attitudes toward learning. This includes framing feedback with remarks that identify and reinforce students' **strengths** while offering support and guidance to enhance development. Language must be **direct** and **specific** to ensure understanding and that necessary changes are made as students progress through instruction. The teacher must also be attuned to students' individual characteristics in order to address them with language that is responsive and considerate of their needs. When the appropriate language is applied in presenting feedback, it increases student motivation, engagement, and ability to make improvements that enhance their learning experience.

Effective Formats for Feedback

Successful instruction is reliant on continuous feedback through a variety of **formats** to ensure that the teacher's guidance is accurate, constructive, substantive, and specific. Varying formats for providing formative and summative feedback are applicable and effective in different stages of the learning process. **Formative feedback** is often informal and occurs throughout instruction to guide student learning. Some methods include oral feedback in the form of asking students open-ended questions and providing suggestions for improvement, written comments on assignments, and peer-to-peer feedback in which students can offer one another support to build understanding. **Summative feedback** is often formal and occurs at the end of a lesson or unit to evaluate students' progress in achieving learning goals. **Rubrics** are a versatile tool for providing summative feedback, as they vary in complexity and the criteria within them can be tailored to specific learning objectives. This format is valuable for communicating expectations and clearly demonstrating the characteristics of quality work. In utilizing rubrics to provide feedback, the teacher can outline specific areas for evaluation, assign point values, and explicitly specify areas of strength and skills that need improvement.

Substantive Feedback

When teachers provide **substantive feedback**, they ensure that students are given focused, useful, and relevant direction regarding their progress throughout the learning process. With such feedback, students receive **concrete information** regarding ways in which they can improve their performance in a given area that enables them to apply it to the context of their learning in a meaningful way. This ultimately strengthens students' connections between the teacher's substantive feedback and their work, thus enhancing understanding and success in learning. In addition, the nature of substantive feedback facilitates **personalized learning**, as it is tailored to address individual student progress and areas for improvement. This allows for student-centered instruction that enhances learning by addressing the needs of all students.

Constructive Feedback

Feedback on students' progress must always be **constructive** in nature to facilitate successful learning and development. Constructive feedback ensures students maintain a positive **self-concept** and attitude toward learning, which is integral to increasing self-motivation and engagement. When students are motivated and engaged, they are more likely to apply the teacher's suggestions to enhance their learning and understanding. When providing constructive feedback, it is important that the teacher consider the specific area in which the student needs improvement in order to provide effective guidance for enhancing comprehension and progress. In addition, the teacher must consider their approach to providing feedback to ensure that all suggestions are productive, encouraging, and helpful to the student. This includes presenting feedback through **positive** and **supportive language** that is free of negative connotations or inferences. The teacher should accompany feedback with comments that highlight students' **strengths** while offering **suggestions** and **guidance** on specific areas in which they can improve. Constructive feedback must include clear explanations on ways in which students can improve their performance, as well as establish how the teacher's suggestions will enhance their overall learning and growth.

Specific Feedback

Specific feedback provides students with clarity regarding how to effectively improve their progress as they work toward achieving learning targets. When the teacher consistently delivers specific feedback, students are clear on expectations, can identify areas for improvement within their performance, and make necessary changes. Students are more likely to effectively apply feedback that specifies areas for development as they progress toward learning goals. If feedback is too vague, students may either disregard it or make incorrect, uninformed changes that hinder understanding and progress. Providing detailed suggestions and guidance enhances student engagement and motivation, as it increases their focus on particular areas for improvement to allow for success in learning. In addition, highlighting students' strengths through specific feedback encourages them to apply their abilities to other areas of instruction, thus enhancing student productivity and success in achieving learning targets.

Promoting Use of Feedback

Students' ability to utilize feedback is a valuable tool in enhancing their own learning for increased achievement. To develop this skill among students, the teacher must emphasize the value of feedback, demonstrate its applications in specific learning situations, and explain how implementing it is beneficial in improving academic performance. This notion can be reinforced by effectively **modeling** how to receive and apply feedback to enhance student understanding of the process. Feedback must always be constructive and highlight students' strengths to help them identify specific areas for improvement. By **checking** students' understanding of feedback frequently, the teacher ensures they know how to productively apply it for enhanced learning. This includes encouraging students to **respond** to given feedback by contributing their thoughts and asking for clarification as necessary. In addition, students are more likely to internalize and effectively apply feedback that is **timely** and provided throughout instruction, rather than at the end, thus fostering their ability to utilize it in guiding their own learning. This allows students to establish personal connections between feedback and their learning that strengthen their understanding and promote their academic success.

Teaching Students to Use Self-Assessment

Developing students' **self-assessment** capabilities provides them with a sense of self-sufficiency for guiding and enhancing their own learning. To facilitate this, the teacher must establish a supportive **classroom environment** in which students feel comfortable and empowered to take risks and objectively evaluate their own progress as they seek areas for improvement. **Modeling** strategies for utilizing self-assessment to enhance learning and explaining its significance in supporting continued success are valuable strategies in enabling students to assess their own progress to guide and improve their learning. By guiding students with **open-ended questions** as they engage in learning, the teacher encourages students to assess their own progress and demonstrates how to implement effective questioning to seek areas for improvement within their own work. The teacher should include multiple outlets for self-assessment to facilitate the development of this skill, including **reflection** opportunities that enable students to evaluate their own understanding and guide their development as they engage in learning.

Significance of Self-Assessment in Facilitating Growth and Achievement

When students are able to objectively assess their own progress, they are equipped with the tools necessary to continuously seek areas for improvement that guide and enhance their learning. This empowers students with a sense of **ownership** and responsibility over their learning as they monitor their own performance to refine their skills for enhanced growth and achievement. Self-assessment and monitoring strengthen students' **personal connections** to their work, as they are able to relate their learning to their own prior knowledge and frames of reference. This ultimately makes learning more relevant, thus increasing motivation, productivity, and achievement. Students who regularly self-assess their work develop the independence necessary for engaging in **self-directed** learning, thus establishing a foundation for continued growth and success. In addition, continuously seeking areas for improvement allows students to develop a sense of confidence to take risks in their learning, as they understand how to overcome obstacles as they progress.

Development of Real-World Life Skills for Future Success

The ability to effectively apply feedback and self-assessment for enhanced learning prepares students with the life skills necessary for future success in academic and real-world situations. Developing this skill instills within students the notion that there is always room for improvement in their performance. In addition, it develops their understanding of the characteristics of quality overcoming learning obstacles and the **self-motivation** required to take initiative that is integral to success. Students that frequently employ feedback and self-assessment have a strong sense of **independence** for and enhancing their own learning. In addition, this skill provides students with the **self-awareness** necessary to recognize their strengths and weaknesses, thus making them more inclined to continuously seek areas for increased understanding and improvement for maximized achievement. Students' communication and cooperation skills are enhanced when they learn to properly use feedback and self-assessment, as it develops their ability to appreciate constructive criticism and internalize multiple perspectives as they work to improve their performance.

Self-Assessment that Encourages Evaluation of Learning and Continuous Improvement

Providing multiple strategies for self-assessment throughout instruction develops students' ability to monitor and evaluate their performance for continuous improvement. Self-assessment strategies can be formal or informal and can occur on an individual or whole-class basis. Teaching students how to set **SMART goals** (specific, measurable, attainable, relevant, time-bound) enables them to set learning goals, determine a path to achieve them, and reflect upon their performance to seek areas for improvement as they progress. Implementing strategies for students to indicate their level of comprehension is valuable in encouraging reflection on their own understanding and areas for improvement as they progress through the learning process. Such strategies include open-ended **questioning** to encourage reflection, color-coded **response cards** to signify understanding, or **whole-class activities** such as four corners. Graphic organizer activities such as **KWL charts** are beneficial in prompting students to consider prior knowledge and reflect on their progress after a lesson. This facilitates students in forming personal connections and determining areas in which they can extend and improve upon their learning. **Reflection** opportunities, such as exit tickets or learning logs, are also valuable for encouraging self-assessment, as they prompt students to consider areas in which they excelled, as well as potential room for improvement.

Characteristics of SMART Goals

S	**Specific**	The goal is clearly stated and narrowed down in scope. Details of the goal, including who, what, where, when, why, and how much, are explicitly outlined.
M	**Measurable**	The goal includes a quantifiable method of measuring progress toward achievement, such as reading twenty-five books in a year.
A	**Attainable**	The goal is challenging, yet realistic and within the realm of the individual's current abilities and skills.

Characteristics of SMART Goals

R	**Relevant**	The goal is meaningful to the individual and contributes toward personal improvement and the long-term goals.
T	**Time-Bound**	The goal sets a specific timeline for achievement. This helps the individual monitor progress and hold personal accountability.

Skilled Questioning to Support Learning

Higher-Level Questioning

Higher-level questioning that prompts students to **analyze**, **evaluate**, and **create** responses and solutions fosters effective student discussions by encouraging students to consider information beyond basic recollection. When students are asked to **explain**, **justify**, **predict**, and **provide examples**, they are encouraged to actively participate in learning, thus enhancing discussion. In addition, higher-level questioning increases the effectiveness of student discussion by promoting the use of higher-order and critical thinking skills to **consider alternatives**, **compare**, **contrast**, **discuss hypothetically**, and **develop** creative solutions to problems. Higher-level questioning encourages students to elaborate on their thinking and learning, thus allowing for productive discussions that strengthen the learning experience.

Impact of Student Discussions on Overall Learning Experience

Student discussion is a valuable instructional strategy for deepening and enhancing the overall learning experience. When students have the opportunity to discuss new concepts in their own words, it increases their ability to internalize and retain information. Effective student discussions prompt students to relate information to their own experiences and create personal connections that enhance learning by making it relevant and meaningful. Likewise, in listening to and interacting with their peers, students gain insight on differing perspectives and can build on one another's background knowledge to increase understanding. Incorporating effective discussions into instruction also produces an interesting and engaging learning environment by encouraging active student participation. When students are asked to inquire and consider information on a complex level, explain and elaborate on their reasoning, and think critically about situations, they are given an active role that serves to deepen and enhance the learning experience.

Impact of Skilled Questioning and Discussion

Exploration of Content and Learning

Skilled questioning and discussion are essential components in enhancing learning by establishing an engaging learning environment that promotes the exploration of content material beyond basic knowledge. By challenging students during discussions based upon their abilities through specific questioning, the teacher effectively prompts students to think critically about instructional content, devise new solutions to problems, and implement higher-order thinking skills that require further exploration of content material. Effective discussions encourage students to examine the nuances of subject matter and reflect upon others' perspectives to build upon their understanding. Furthermore, when students are provided with effective questions to promote interesting and engaging discussions, they become motivated to actively participate in their learning and explore instructional content on a deeper level.

Extending Students' Knowledge on Instructional Content

The implementation of skilled questioning when leading effective discussions is valuable in extending students' knowledge of instructional content. Skilled questioning activates higher-order thinking skills, as it prompts students to consider ideas and information on a more complex level.

When teachers skillfully craft questions on content material during discussions, they are able to extend students' knowledge on the instructional topic by creating specific, increasingly complex questions that build on students' capabilities. Effective questions during discussions also increase students' knowledge on content material by motivating them to seek further information and thoughtfully consider their answers to elaborate on and provide examples for their reasoning. Additionally, skilled questioning and discussions foster active participation in learning, giving students the opportunity to build and reflect upon other's knowledge and experiences. This ultimately increases their understanding of the instructional content by allowing them to integrate their frame of reference with others' perspectives.

Fostering Active Inquiry

An interesting and engaging environment is necessary in fostering active curiosity and inquiry for learning among students. Through skilled questioning and effective student discussions, the teacher creates an atmosphere in which students must actively engage and participate throughout the learning process, thus providing them with a sense of self-motivation for active inquiry. In addition, skilled questioning challenges students to utilize higher-order thinking skills that require them to inquire about a discussion topic beyond basic information and seek new information to thoughtfully consider and elaborate on their responses. In the discussion setting, students are also engaged and encouraged to ask each other questions to deepen understanding. Effective questioning and student discussions enhance learning and productivity by creating an engaging, **inquiry-based** environment that provides students with a sense of ownership over their learning as they seek new information.

Developing Higher-Order Thinking Skills

Skillful questioning when leading student discussions is an effective method of developing **higher-order thinking** skills to strengthen understanding and enhance the learning experience. In thoughtfully proposing questions that challenge students based on their abilities, the teacher establishes a foundation of knowledge to build upon with increasingly rigorous skilled questioning. When students are asked to apply their learning to **analyze**, **evaluate**, and **create**, higher-order thinking skills are developed in that students must think deeply and critically about ideas, information, and situations beyond the basic recall of information. Effective questioning in discussions prompts students to think more complexly and synthesize previously learned information to craft and support new ideas, responses, and solutions. Students are thus required to take more time to evaluate their responses carefully, consider alternatives and differing perspectives of their classmates, and create personal connections by applying their own experiences to their learning.

Increasing Problem-Solving Skills

Incorporating skilled questions into class discussions fosters the development of problem-solving skills by eliciting students' critical thinking abilities to devise creative solutions. By asking complex, open-ended questions that prompt students to **hypothesize**, **predict**, and **consider alternative** methods of solving a problem, the teacher creates an engaging learning environment that promotes curiosity, exploration, and inquiry. Such questioning effectively develops problem-solving skills by increasing student motivation for seeking new solutions and analyzing their results. Thoughtfully crafted questions encourage students to **synthesize** and **apply** their own experiences and previously learned information when devising a solution to a problem. In addition, in proposing skilled questions when leading discussions, the teacher fosters students' abilities to apply knowledge, understanding, and reasoning methods from one learning context to another, thus developing real-world problem-solving skills. Effective class discussions encourage students to collaborate to build upon one another's experiences and knowledge when seeking solutions, as well as demonstrate the validity of multiple approaches to situations to develop students' overall problem-solving abilities.

Promoting Positive, Supportive Interactions to Enhance the Learning Experience

In facilitating effective class discussions, the teacher must propose skillful questions that encourage positive and supportive interactions to ensure that all students feel respected when contributing. To achieve this, the teacher must lead discussions with open-ended questions that emphasize the validity of multiple responses and accompany students' responses with follow-up questions. Such skilled questioning fosters **prosocial** interactions by creating a safe and respectful learning environment that encourages students to collaborate, actively participate in discussion with one another, and appreciate varying perspectives. In addition, skillful questioning and effective discussions include appropriate wait time between questions and responses. This promotes supportive interactions by allowing students the opportunity to process their responses and by demonstrating the importance of active listening. In emphasizing this, students ultimately feel respected in their ideas and empowered to add to the discussion. When teachers effectively lead student discussions with thoughtfully crafted questions, they enhance the overall learning experience by creating a welcoming, respectful learning environment in which students feel confident to take risks and explore new ideas through discussion.

Significance of Appropriate Wait Time in Effective Student Discussions

Appropriate wait time is an integral component in leading effective student discussions. When students are given a few seconds after questioning to consider their responses, they are able to effectively process and synthesize information to formulate and elaborate on their ideas. Wait time during discussions leads to more thoughtful responses, as students are given time to consider their learning on a more complex level. In addition, providing time between questions and discussion allows students to process one another's responses to contribute more effectively to the conversation and enhance the overall learning experience.

Bloom's Taxonomy (1956)

Bloom's taxonomy is a framework for categorizing learning objectives with increasing levels of complexity to promote the development of higher-order thinking skills. Measures of ability are organized into **knowledge**, **comprehension**, and **application** as lower-level benchmarks, and **analysis**, **synthesis**, and **evaluation** as higher-level targets. Lower-level objectives are intended to build and evaluate student comprehension and ability to ultimately achieve higher-level targets intended to deepen understanding and develop higher-order thinking skills. Bloom's taxonomy is integral in engaging in skilled questioning. This model assists teachers in developing specific, increasingly-challenging questions, activities, and assessments that establish a foundation of knowledge and build upon it for the development of higher-order thinking skills. In addition, it provides an outline for identifying students' cognitive abilities and allows the teacher to effectively develop appropriate questions that build and enhance understanding to foster success in learning.

Bloom's Taxonomy

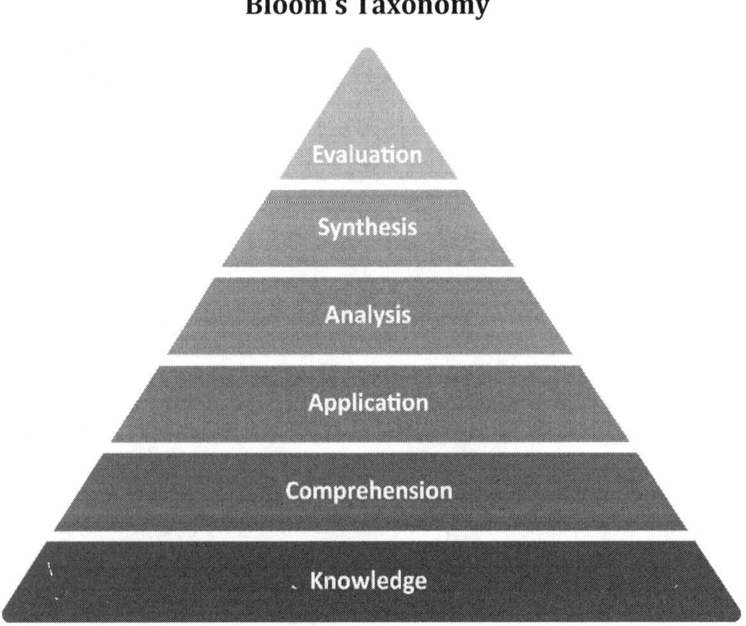

The Revised Bloom's Taxonomy (2001)

In 2001, a group of educators sought to update the original Bloom's taxonomy to better meet the needs of a 21st century audience. The revised version was not actually produced by Benjamin Bloom, who passed away in 1999, but was developed primarily by Anderson and Krathwohl. Many resources use the term "Bloom's Taxonomy" to refer to both, interchangeably. The major differences between the original and the revised versions of the taxonomy include a reordering of two of the tiers, as well as a modification of the names of the levels to be more action-oriented. Instead of using nouns, the revised version uses verbs that describe the types of tasks that are associated with each level of thinking. Teachers are encouraged to use task stem words associated with each level to help produce curriculum leading to higher-order thinking.

Assessment Methodology

Assessment Methods

Effective teaching requires multiple methods of assessment to evaluate student comprehension and instructional effectiveness. Assessments are typically categorized as diagnostic, formative, summative, and benchmark, and are applicable at varying stages of instruction. **Diagnostic** assessments are administered before instruction and indicate students' prior knowledge and areas of misunderstanding to determine the path of instruction. **Formative** assessments occur continuously to measure student engagement, comprehension, and instructional effectiveness. These assessments indicate instructional strategies that require adjustment to meet students' needs in facilitating successful learning, and include such strategies as checking for understanding, observations, total participation activities, and exit tickets. **Summative** assessments are given at the end of a lesson or unit to evaluate student progress in reaching learning targets and identify areas of misconception for reteaching. Such assessments can be given in the form of exams and quizzes, or project-based activities in which students demonstrate their learning through hands-on, personalized methods. Additionally, portfolios serve as valuable summative assessments in allowing students to demonstrate their progress over time and provide insight regarding individual achievement. **Benchmark** assessments occur less frequently and encompass large portions of curriculum. These assessments are intended to evaluate the progress of groups of students in achieving state and district academic standards.

Assessment Types

- **Diagnostic:** These assessments can either be formal or informal and are intended to provide teachers with information regarding students' level of understanding prior to beginning a unit of instruction. Examples include pretests, KWL charts, anticipation guides, and brainstorming activities. Digital resources, such as online polls, surveys, and quizzes are also valuable resources for gathering diagnostic feedback.
- **Formative:** These assessments occur throughout instruction to provide the teacher with feedback regarding student understanding. Examples include warm-up and closure activities, checking frequently for understanding, student reflection activities, and providing students with color-coded cards to indicate their level of understanding. Short quizzes and total participation activities, such as four corners, are also valuable formative assessments. Numerous digital resources, including polls, surveys, and review games, are also beneficial in providing teachers with formative feedback to indicate instructional effectiveness.
- **Summative:** Summative assessments are intended to indicate students' level of mastery and progress toward reaching academic learning standards. These assessments may take the form of written or digital exams and include multiple choice, short answer, or long answer questions. Examples also include projects, final essays, presentations, or portfolios to demonstrate student progress over time.
- **Benchmark:** Benchmark assessments measure students' progress in achieving academic standards. These assessments are typically standardized to ensure uniformity, objectivity, and accuracy. Benchmark assessments are typically given as a written multiple choice or short answer exam, or as a digital exam in which students answer questions on the computer.

Review Video: Formative and Summative Assessments
Visit mometrix.com/academy and enter code: 804991

Determining Appropriate Assessment Strategies

As varying assessment methods provide different information regarding student performance and achievement, the teacher must consider the most applicable and effective assessment strategy in each stage of instruction. This includes determining the **desired outcomes** of assessment, as well as the information the teacher intends to ascertain and how they will apply the results to further instruction. **Age** and **grade level** appropriateness must be considered when selecting which assessment strategies will enable students to successfully demonstrate their learning. Additionally, the teacher must be cognizant of students' individual differences and learning needs to determine which assessment model is most **accommodating** and reflective of their progress. It is also important that the teacher consider the practicality of assessment strategies, as well as methods they will use to implement the assessment for maximized feedback regarding individual and whole-class progress in achieving learning goals.

Assessments That Reflect Real-World Applications

Assessments that reflect **real-world applications** enhance relevancy and students' ability to establish personal connections to learning that deepen understanding. Implementing such assessments provides authenticity and enhances engagement by defining a clear and practical purpose for learning. These assessments often allow for hands-on opportunities for demonstrating learning and can be adjusted to accommodate students' varying learning styles and needs while measuring individual progress. However, assessments that focus on real-world applications can be subjective, thus making it difficult to extract concrete data and quantify student progress to guide future instructional decisions. In addition, teachers may have difficulty analyzing assessment results on a large scale and comparing student performance with other schools and districts, as individual assessments may vary.

Diagnostic Tests

Diagnostic tests are integral to planning and delivering effective instruction. These tests are typically administered prior to beginning a unit or lesson and provide valuable feedback for guiding and planning instruction. Diagnostic tests provide **preliminary information** regarding students' level of understanding and prior knowledge. This serves as a baseline for instructional planning that connects and builds upon students' background knowledge and experiences to enhance success in learning. Diagnostic tests allow the teacher to identify and clarify areas of student misconception prior to engaging in instruction to ensure continued comprehension and avoid the need for remediation. They indicate areas of student strength and need, as well as individual instructional aids that may need to be incorporated into lessons to support student achievement. In addition, these tests enable the teacher to determine which instructional strategies, activities, groupings, and materials will be most valuable in maximizing engagement and learning. Diagnostic tests can be **formal** or **informal**, and include such formats as pre-tests, pre-reading activities, surveys, vocabulary inventories, and graphic organizers such as KWL charts to assess student understanding prior to engaging in learning. Diagnostic tests are generally not graded as there is little expectation that all students in a class possess the same baseline of proficiency at the start of a unit.

Formative Assessments

Formative assessments are any assessments that take place in the **middle of a unit of instruction**. The goals of formative assessments are to help teachers understand where a student is in their progress toward **mastering** the current unit's content and to provide the students with **ongoing feedback** throughout the unit. The advantage of relying heavily on formative assessments in instruction is that it allows the teacher to continuously **check for comprehension** and adjust instruction as needed to ensure that the whole class is adequately prepared to proceed at the end of the unit. To understand formative assessments well, teachers need to understand that any interaction that can provide information about the student's comprehension is a type of formative assessment which can be used to inform future instruction.

Formative assessments are often a mixture of formal and informal assessments. **Formal formative assessments** often include classwork, homework, and quizzes. Examples of **informal formative assessments** include simple comprehension checks during instruction, class-wide discussions of the current topic, and exit slips, which are written questions posed by teachers at the end of class, which helps the teacher quickly review which students are struggling with the concepts.

Summative Assessments

Summative assessment refers to an evaluation at the end of a discrete unit of instruction, such as the end of a course, end of a unit, or end of a semester. Classic examples of summative assessments include end of course assessments, final exams, or even qualifying standardized tests such as the SAT or ACT. Most summative assessments are created to measure student mastery of particular **academic standards**. Whereas formative assessment generally informs current instruction, summative assessments are used to objectively demonstrate that each individual has achieved adequate mastery of the standards in question. If a student has not met the benchmark, they may need extra instruction or may need to repeat the course.

These assessments usually take the form of **tests** or formal portfolios with rubrics and clearly defined goals. Whatever form a summative takes, they are almost always high-stakes, heavily-weighted, and they should always be formally graded. These types of assessments often feature a narrower range of question types, such as multiple choice, short answer, and essay questions to help with systematic grading. Examples of summative assessments include state tests, end-of-unit or chapter tests, end-of-semester exams, and assessments that formally measure student mastery of topics against a established benchmarks.

Project-based assessments are beneficial in evaluating achievement, as they incorporate several elements of instruction and highlight real-world applications of learning. This allows students to demonstrate understanding through a hands-on, individualized approach that reinforces connections to learning and increases retainment. **Portfolios** of student work over time serve as a valuable method for assessing individual progress toward reaching learning targets. Summative assessments provide insight regarding overall instructional effectiveness and are necessary for guiding future instruction in subsequent years but are not usually used to modify current instruction.

Review Video: Assessment Reliability and Validity
Visit mometrix.com/academy and enter code: 424680

Benchmark Assessments

Benchmark assessments are intended to quantify, evaluate, and compare individual and groups of students' achievement of school-wide, district, and state **academic standards.** They are typically administered in specific intervals throughout the school year and encompass entire or large units of curriculum to determine student mastery and readiness for academic advancement. Benchmark assessments provide data that enable the teacher to determine students' progress toward reaching academic goals to guide current and continued instruction. This data can be utilized by the school and individual teachers to create learning goals and objectives aligned with academic standards, as well as plan instructional strategies, activities, and assessments to support students in achieving them. In addition, benchmark assessments provide feedback regarding understanding and the potential need for remediation to allow the teacher to instill necessary supports in future instruction that prepare students for success in achieving learning targets.

Alignment of Assessments with Instructional Goals and Objectives

To effectively monitor student progress, assessments must align with **instructional goals** and **objectives**. This allows the teacher to determine whether students are advancing at an appropriate pace to achieve state and district academic standards. When assessments are aligned with specific learning targets, the teacher ensures that students are learning relevant material to establish a foundation of knowledge necessary for growth and academic achievement. To achieve this, the teacher must determine which instructional goals and objectives their students must achieve and derive instruction, content, and activities from these specifications. Instruction must reflect and reinforce learning targets, and the teacher must select the most effective strategies for addressing students' needs as they work to achieve them. Assessments must be reflective of content instruction to ensure they are aligned with learning goals and objectives, as well as to enable the teacher to evaluate student progress in mastering them. The teacher must clearly communicate learning goals and objectives throughout all stages of instruction to provide students with clarity on expectations. This establishes a clear purpose and focus for learning that enhances relevancy and strengthens connections to support student achievement.

Clearly Communicating Assessment Criteria and Standards

Students must be clear on the purpose of learning throughout all stages of instruction to enhance understanding and facilitate success. When assessment **criteria** and **standards** are clearly communicated, the purpose of learning is established, and students are able to effectively connect instructional activities to learning goals and criteria for assessment. Communicating assessment criteria and standards provides students with clarity on tasks and learning goals they are expected to accomplish as they prepare themselves for assessment. This allows for more **focused instruction** and engagement in learning, as it enhances relevancy and student motivation. Utilizing appropriate forms of **rubrics** is an effective strategy in specifying assessment criteria and standards, as it informs students about learning goals they are working toward, the quality of work they are expected to achieve, and skills they must master to succeed on the assessment. Rubrics indicate to students exactly how they will be evaluated, thus supporting their understanding and focus as they engage in learning to promote academic success.

Rubrics for Communicating Standards

The following are varying styles of rubrics that can be used to communicate criteria and standards:

- **Analytic:** Analytic rubrics break down criteria for an assignment into several categories and provide an explanation of the varying levels of performance in each one. This style of rubric is beneficial for detailing the characteristics of quality work, as well as providing students with feedback regarding specific components of their performance. Analytic rubrics are most effective when used for summative assessments, such as long-term projects or essays.
- **Holistic:** Holistic rubrics evaluate the quality of the student's assignment as a whole, rather than scoring individual components. Students' score is determined based upon their performance across multiple performance indicators. This style of rubric is beneficial for providing a comprehensive evaluation but limits the amount of feedback that students receive regarding their performance in specific areas.
- **Single-Point:** Single point rubrics outline criteria for assignments into several categories. Rather than providing a numeric score to each category, however, the teacher provides written feedback regarding the students' strengths and ways in which they can improve their performance. This style of rubric is beneficial in providing student-centered feedback that focuses on their overall progress.
- **Checklist:** Checklists typically outline a set of criteria that is scored using a binary approach based upon completion of each component. This style increases the efficiency of grading assignments and is often easy for students to comprehend but does not provide detailed feedback. This method of grading should generally be reserved for shorter assignments.

Communicating High Academic Expectations in Assessments

The attitudes and behaviors exhibited by the teacher are highly influential on students' attitudes toward learning. Teachers demonstrate belief in students' abilities to be successful in learning when they communicate **high academic expectations**. This promotes students' **self-concept** and establishes a **growth mindset** to create confident, empowered learners that are motivated to achieve. High expectations for assessments and reaching academic standards communicates to students the quality of work that is expected of them and encourages them to overcome obstacles as they engage in learning. When communicating expectations for student achievement, it is important that the teacher is aware of students' individual learning needs to provide the necessary support that establishes equitable opportunities for success in meeting assessment criteria and standards. Setting high expectations through assessment criteria and standards while supporting students in their learning enhances overall achievement and establishes a foundation for continuous academic success.

Effective Communication and Impact on Student Learning

Communicating high academic expectations enhances students' self-concept and increases personal motivation for success in learning. To maximize student achievement, it is important that the teacher set high academic expectations that are **clearly** communicated through **age-appropriate** terms and consistently reinforced. Expectations must be reflected through learning goals and objectives, and **visible** at all times to ensure student awareness. The teacher must be **specific** in communicating what they want students to accomplish and clearly detail necessary steps for achievement while assuming the role of facilitator to guide learning and provide support. Providing constructive **feedback** throughout instruction is integral in reminding students of academic expectations and ensuring they are making adequate progress toward reaching learning goals. When high academic expectations are communicated and reinforced, students are empowered with a sense of confidence and self-responsibility for their own learning that promotes their desire to learn. This ultimately enhances achievement and equips them with the tools necessary for future academic success.

Analyzing and Interpreting Assessment Data

Teachers can utilize multiple techniques to effectively analyze and interpret assessment data. This typically involves creating charts and graphs outlining different data subsets. They can list each learning standard that was assessed, determine how many students overall demonstrated proficiency on the standard, and identify individual students who did not demonstrate proficiency on each standard. This information can be used to differentiate instruction. Additionally, they can track individual student performance and progress on each standard over time.

Teachers can take note of overall patterns and trends in assessment data. For example, they can determine if any subgroups of students did not meet expectations. They can consider whether the data confirms or challenges any existing beliefs, implications this may have on instructional planning and what, if any, conclusions can be drawn from this data.

Analyzing and interpreting assessment data may raise new questions for educators, so they can also determine if additional data collection is needed.

Using Assessment Data to Differentiate Instruction for Individual Learners

By analyzing and interpreting assessment data, teachers can determine if there are any specific learning standards that need to be retaught to their entire classes. This may be necessary if the data shows that all students struggled in these specific areas. Teachers may consider reteaching these standards using different methods if the initial methods were unsuccessful.

Teachers can also form groups of students who did not demonstrate proficiency on the same learning standards. Targeted instruction can be planned for these groups to help them make progress in these areas. Interventions can also be planned for individual students who did not show proficiency in certain areas. If interventions have already been in place and have not led to increased learning outcomes, the interventions may be redesigned. If interventions have been in place and assessment data now shows proficiency, the interventions may be discontinued.

If assessment data shows that certain students have met or exceeded expectations in certain areas, enrichment activities can be planned to challenge these students and meet their learning needs.

Aligning Assessments with Instructional Goals and Objectives

Assessments that are congruent to instructional goals and objectives provide a **clear purpose** for learning that enhances student understanding and motivation. When learning targets are reflected in assessments, instructional activities and materials become more **relevant**, as they are derived from these specifications. Such clarity in purpose allows for more focus and productivity as students engage in instruction and fosters connections that strengthen overall understanding for maximized success in learning. Aligning assessments with instructional goals and objectives ensures that students are learning material that is relevant to the curriculum and academic standards to ensure **preparedness** as they advance in their academic careers. In addition, it enables the teacher to evaluate and monitor student progress to determine whether they are progressing at an ideal pace for achieving academic standards. With this information, the teacher can effectively modify instruction as necessary to support students' needs in reaching desired learning outcomes.

Norm-Referenced Tests

On **norm-referenced tests**, students' performances are compared to the performances of sample groups of similar students. Norm-referenced tests identify students who score above and below the average. To ensure reliability, the tests must be given in a standardized manner to all students.

Norm-referenced tests usually cover a broad range of skills, such as the entire grade-level curriculum for a subject. They typically contain a few questions per skill. Whereas scores in component areas of the tests may be calculated, usually overall test scores are reported. Scores are often reported using percentile ranks, which indicate what percentage of test takers scored lower than the student being assessed. For example, a student's score in the 75th percentile means the student scored better than 75% of other test takers. Other times, scores may be reported using grade-level equivalency.

One advantage of norm-referenced tests is their objectivity. They also allow educators to compare large groups of students at once. This may be helpful for making decisions regarding class placements and groupings. A disadvantage of norm-referenced tests is that they only indicate how well students perform in comparison to one another. They do not indicate whether or not students have mastered certain skills.

Criterion-Referenced Tests

Criterion-referenced tests measure how well students perform on certain skills or standards. The goal of these tests is to indicate whether or not students have mastered certain skills and which skills require additional instruction. Scores are typically reported using the percentage of questions answered correctly or students' performance levels. Performance levels are outlined using terms such as below expectations, met expectations, and exceeded expectations.

One advantage of criterion-referenced tests is they provide teachers with useful information to guide instruction. They can identify which specific skills students have mastered and which skills need additional practice. Teachers can use this information to plan whole-class, small-group, and individualized instruction. Analyzing results of criterion-referenced tests over time can also help teachers track student progress on certain skills. A disadvantage of criterion-referenced tests is they do not allow educators to compare students' performances to samples of their peers.

Ways That Standardized Test Results Are Reported

- **Raw scores** are sometimes reported and indicate how many questions students answered correctly on a test. By themselves, they do not provide much useful information. They do not indicate how students performed in comparison to other students or to grade-level expectations.
- **Grade-level equivalents** are also sometimes reported. A grade-level equivalent score of 3.4 indicates that a student performed as well as an average third grader in the fourth month of school. It can indicate whether a student is performing above or below grade-level expectations, but it does not indicate that the student should be moved to a different grade level.
- **Standard scores** are used to compare students' performances on tests to standardized samples of their peers. Standard deviation refers to the amount that a set of scores differs from the mean score on a test.
- **Percentile ranks** are used on criterion-referenced tests to indicate what percentage of test takers scored lower than the student whose score is being reported.
- **Cutoff scores** refer to predetermined scores students must obtain in order to be considered proficient in certain areas. Scores below the cutoff level indicate improvement is needed and may result in interventions or instructional changes.

Formal and Informal Assessments

Assessments are any method a teacher uses to gather information about student comprehension of curriculum, including improvised questions for the class and highly-structured tests. **Formal assessments** are assessments that have **clearly defined standards and methodology**, and which are applied consistently to all students. Formal tests should be objective and the test itself should be scrutinized for validity and reliability since it tends to carry higher weight for the student. Summative assessments, such as end-of-unit tests, lend themselves to being formal tests because it is necessary that a teacher test the comprehension of all students in a consistent and thorough way.

Although formal assessments can provide useful data about student performance and progress, they can be costly and time-consuming to implement. Administering formal assessments often interrupts classroom instruction, and may cause testing anxiety.

Informal assessments are assessments that do not adhere to formal objectives and they do not have to be administered consistently to all students. As a result, they do not have to be scored or recorded as a grade and generally act as a **subjective measure** of class comprehension. Informal assessments can be as simple as asking a whole class to raise their hand if they are ready to proceed to the next step or asking a particular question of an individual student.

Informal assessments do not provide objective data for analysis, but they can be implemented quickly and inexpensively. Informal assessments can also be incorporated into regular classroom instruction and activities, making them more authentic and less stressful for students.

Using Various Assessments

The goal of **assessment** in education is to gather data that, when evaluated, can be used to further student learning and achievement. **Standardized tests** are helpful for placement purposes and to reflect student progress toward goals set by a school district or state. If a textbook is chosen to align with district learning standards, the textbook assessments can provide teachers with convenient, small-scale, regular checks of student knowledge against the target standard.

In order be effective, teachers must know where their students are in the learning process. Teachers use a multitude of **formal and informal assessment methods** to do this. Posing differentiated discussion questions is an example of an informal assessment method that allows teachers to gauge individual student progress rather than their standing in relation to a universal benchmark.

Effective teachers employ a variety of assessments, as different formats assess different skills, promote different learning experiences, and appeal to different learners. A portfolio is an example of an assessment that gauges student progress in multiple skills and through multiple media. Teachers can use authentic or performance-based assessments to stimulate student interest and provide visible connections between language-learning and the real world.

Assessment Reliability

Assessment reliability refers to how well an assessment is constructed and is made up of a variety of measures. An assessment is generally considered **reliable** if it yields similar results across multiple administrations of the assessment. A test should perform similarly with different test administrators, graders, and test-takers and perform consistently over multiple iterations. Factors that affect reliability include the day-to-day wellbeing of the student (students can sometimes underperform), the physical environment of the test, the way it is administered, and the subjectivity of the scorer (with written-response assessments).

Perhaps the most important threat to assessment reliability is the nature of the **exam questions** themselves. An assessment question is designed to test student knowledge of a certain construct. A question is reliable in this sense if students who understand the content answer the question correctly. Statisticians look for patterns in student marks, both within the single test and over multiple tests, as a way of measuring reliability. Teachers should watch out for circumstances in which a student or students answer correctly a series of questions about a given concept (demonstrating their understanding) but then answer a related question incorrectly. The latter question may be an unreliable indicator of concept knowledge.

Measures of Assessment Reliability

- **Test-retest reliability** refers to an assessment's consistency of results with the same test-taker over multiple retests. If one student shows inconsistent results over time, the test is not considered to have test-retest reliability.
- **Intertester reliability** refers to an assessment's consistency of results between multiple test-takers at the same level. Students at similar levels of proficiency should show similar results.
- **Interrater reliability** refers to an assessment's consistency of results between different administrators of the test. This plays an especially critical role in tests with interactive or subjective responses, such as Likert-scales, cloze tests, and short answer tests. Different raters of the same test need to have a consistent means of evaluating the test-takers' performance. Clear rubrics can help keep two or more raters consistent in scoring.
- **Intra-rater reliability** refers to an assessment's consistency of results with one rater over time. One test rater should be able to score different students objectively to rate subjective test formats fairly.
- **Parallel-forms reliability** refers to an assessment's consistency between multiple different forms. For instance, end-of-course assessments may have many distinctive test forms, with different questions or question orders. If the different forms of a test do not provide the same results, it is said to be lacking in parallel-forms reliability.

- **Internal consistency reliability** refers to the consistency of results of similar questions on a particular assessment. If there are two or more questions targeted at the same standard and at the same level, they should show the same results across each question.

Assessment Validity

Assessment validity is a measure of the relevancy that an assessment has to the skill or ability being evaluated, and the degree to which students' performance is representative of their mastery of the topic of assessment. In other words, a teacher should ask how well an assessment's results correlate to what it is looking to assess. Assessments should be evaluated for validity on both the **individual question** level and as a **test overall**. This can be especially helpful in refining tests for future classes. The overall validity of an assessment is determined by several types of validity measures.

An assessment is considered **valid** if it measures what it is intended to measure. One common error that can reduce the validity of a test (or a question on a test) occurs if the instructions are written at a reading level the students can't understand. In this case, it is not valid to take the student's failed answer as a true indication of his or her knowledge of the subject. Factors internal to the student might also affect exam validity: anxiety and a lack of self-esteem often lower assessments results, reducing their validity of a measure of student knowledge.

An assessment has content validity if it includes all the **relevant aspects** of the subject being tested—if it is comprehensive, in other words. An assessment has **predictive validity** if a score on the test is an accurate predictor of future success in the same domain. For example, SAT exams purport to have validity in predicting student success in a college. An assessment has construct validity if it accurately measures student knowledge of the subject being tested.

Measures of Assessment Validity

- **Face validity** refers to the initial impression of whether an assessment seems to be fit for the task. As this method is subjective to interpretation and unquantifiable, it should not be used singularly as a measurement of validity.
- **Construct validity** asks if an assessment actually assesses what it is intended to assess. Some topics are more straightforward, such as assessing if a student can perform two-digit multiplication. This can be directly tested, which gives the assessment a strong content validity. Other measures, such as a person's overall happiness, must be measured indirectly. If an assessment asserted that a person is generally happy if they smile frequently, it would be fair to question the construct validity of that assessment because smiling is unlikely to be a consistent measure of all peoples' general happiness.
- **Content validity** indicates whether the assessment is comprehensive of all aspects of the content being assessed. If a test leaves out an important topic, then the teacher will not have a full picture as a result of the assessment.
- **Criterion validity** refers to whether the results of an assessment can be used to **predict** a related value, known as **criterion**. An example of this is the hypothesis that IQ tests would predict a person's success later in life, but many critics believe that IQ tests are not valid predictors of success because intelligence is not the only predictor of success in life. IQ tests have shown validity toward predicting academic success, however. The measure of an assessment's criterion validity depends on how closely related the criterion is.

- **Discriminant validity** refers to how well an assessment tests only that which it is intended to test and successfully discriminates one piece of information from another. For instance, a student who is exceptional in mathematics should not be able to put that information into use on a science test and gain an unfair advantage. If they are able to score well due to their mathematics knowledge, the science test did not adequately discriminate science knowledge from mathematics knowledge.
- **Convergent validity** is related to discriminant validity, but takes into account that two measures may be distinct, but can be correlated. For instance, a personality test should distinguish self-esteem from extraversion so that they can be measured independently, but if an assessment has convergent validity, it should show a correlation between related measures.

PRACTICALITY

An assessment is **practical** if it uses an appropriate amount of human and budgetary resources. A practical exam doesn't take very long to design or score, nor does it take students very long to complete in relation to other learning objectives and priorities. Teachers often need to balance a desire to construct comprehensive or content-valid tests with a need for practicality: lengthy exams consume large amounts of instruction time and may return unreliable results if students become tired and lose focus.

ASSESSMENT BIAS

An assessment is considered biased if it disadvantages a certain group of students, such as students of a certain gender, race, cultural background, or socioeconomic class. A **content bias** exists when the subject matter of a question or assessment is familiar to one group and not another—for example, a reading comprehension passage which discusses an event in American history would be biased against students new to the country. An **attitudinal bias** exists when a teacher has a pre-conceived idea about the likely success of an assessment of a particular individual or group. A **method bias** arises when the format of an assessment is unfamiliar to a given group of students. **Language bias** occurs when an assessment utilizes idioms, collocations, or cultural references unfamiliar to a group of students. Finally, **translation bias** may arise when educators attempt to translate content-area assessments into a student's native language—rough or hurried translations often result in a loss of nuance important for accurate assessment.

AUTHENTIC ASSESSMENTS

An authentic assessment is an assessment designed to closely resemble something that a student does, or will do, in the real world. Thus, for example, students will never encounter a multiple-choice test requiring them to choose the right tense of a verb, but they will encounter context in which they have to write a narration of an event that has antecedents and consequents spread out in time—for example, their version of what caused a traffic accident. The latter is an example of a potential **authentic assessment**.

Well-designed authentic assessments require a student to exercise **advanced cognitive skills** (e.g., solving problems, integrating information, performing deductions), integrate **background knowledge**, and confront **ambiguity**. Research has demonstrated that mere language proficiency is not predictive of future language success—learning how to utilize knowledge in a complex context is an essential additional skill.

The terms "authentic" and "performance-based" assessments are often used interchangeably. However, a performance-based assessment doesn't necessarily have to be grounded in a possible authentic experience.

Performance-Based Assessments

A performance-based assessment is one in which students demonstrate their learning by performing a **task** rather than by answering questions in a traditional test format. Proponents of **performance-based assessments** argue that they lead students to use **high-level cognitive skills** as they focus on how to put their knowledge to use and plan a sequence of stages in an activity or presentation. They also allow students more opportunities to individualize their presentations or responses based on preferred learning styles. Research suggests that students welcome the chance to put their knowledge to use in real-world scenarios.

Advocates of performance-based assessments suggest that they avoid many of the problems of language or cultural bias present in traditional assessments, and thus they allow more accurate assessment of how well students learned the underlying concepts. In discussions regarding English as a second language, they argue that performance assessments come closer to replicating what should be the true goal of language learning—the effective use of language in real contexts—than do more traditional exams. Critics point out that performance assessments are difficult and time-consuming for teachers to construct and for students to perform. Finally, performative assessments are difficult to grade in the absence of a well-constructed and detailed rubric.

Technology-Based Assessments

Technology-based assessments provide teachers with multiple resources for evaluating student progress to guide instruction. They are applicable in most formal and informal instructional settings and can be utilized as formative and summative assessments. Technology-based assessments simplify and enhance the efficiency of determining comprehension and instructional effectiveness, as they quickly present the teacher with information regarding student progress. This data enables the teacher to make necessary adjustments to facilitate student learning and growth. Implementing this assessment format simplifies the process of aligning them to school and district academic standards. This establishes objectivity and uniformity for comparing results and progress among students, as well as ensures that all students are held to the same academic expectations. While technology-based assessments are beneficial, there are some shortcomings to consider. This format may not be entirely effective for all learning styles in demonstrating understanding, as individualization in technology-based assessment can be limited. These assessments may not illustrate individual students' growth over time, but rather their mastery of an academic standard, thus hindering the ability to evaluate overall achievement. As technology-based evaluation limits hands-on opportunities, the real-world application and relevancy of the assessment may be unapparent to students.

Advantages and Disadvantages of Technology-Based Assessments

Technology-based assessments can have many advantages. They can be given to large numbers of students at once, limited only by the amounts of technological equipment schools possess. Many types of technology-based assessments are instantly scored, and feedback is quickly provided. Students are sometimes able to view their results and feedback at the conclusion of their testing sessions. Data can be quickly compiled and reported in easy-to-understand formats. Technology-based assessments can also often track student progress over time.

Technology-based assessments can have some disadvantages as well. Glitches and system errors can interfere with the assessment process or score reporting. Students must also have the necessary prerequisite technological skills to take the assessments, or the results may not measure the content they are designed to measure. For example, if students take timed computer-based writing tests, they should have proficient typing skills. Otherwise, they may perform poorly on the tests despite strong writing abilities. Other prerequisite skills include knowing how to use a keyboard and mouse and understanding how to locate necessary information on the screen.

Portfolio Assessments

A **portfolio** is a collection of student work in multiple forms and media gathered over time. Teachers may assess the portfolio both for evidence of progress over time or in its end state as a demonstration of the achievement of certain proficiency levels.

One advantage of **portfolio assessments** is their breadth—unlike traditional assessments which focus on one or two language skills, portfolios may contain work in multiple forms—writing samples, pictures, and graphs designed for content courses, video and audio clips, student reflections, teacher observations, and student exams. A second advantage is that they allow a student to develop work in authentic contexts, including in other classrooms and at home.

In order for portfolios to function as an objective assessment tool, teachers should negotiate with students in advance of what genres of work will be included and outline a grading rubric that makes clear what will be assessed, such as linguistic proficiency, use of English in academic contexts, and demonstrated use of target cognitive skills.

Curriculum-Based Assessments

Curriculum-based assessments, also known as **curriculum-based measurements (CBM)**, are short, frequent assessments designed to measure student progress toward meeting curriculum **benchmarks**.

Teachers implement CBM by designing **probes**, or short assessments that target specific skills. For example, a teacher might design a spelling probe, administered weekly, that requires students to spell 10 unfamiliar but level-appropriate words. Teachers then track the data over time to measure student progress toward defined grade-level goals.

CBM has several clear advantages. If structured well, the probes have high reliability and validity. Furthermore, they provide clear and objective evidence of student progress—a welcome outcome for students and parents who often grapple with less-clear and subjective evidence. Used correctly, CBMs also motivate students and provide them with evidence of their own progress. However, while CBMs are helpful in identifying *areas* of student weaknesses, they do not identify the *causes* of those weaknesses or provide teachers with strategies for improving instruction.

Textbook Assessments

Textbook assessments are the assessments provided at the end of a chapter or unit in an approved textbook. **Textbook assessments** present several advantages for a teacher: they are already made; they are likely to be accurate representations of the chapter or unit materials; and, if the textbook has been prescribed or recommended by the state, it is likely to correspond closely to Common Core or other tested standards.

Textbook assessments can be limiting for students who lag in the comprehension of academic English, or whose preferred learning style is not verbal. While textbooks may come with DVDs or recommended audio links, ESOL teachers will likely need to supplement these assessment materials with some of their own findings. Finally, textbook assessments are unlikely to represent the range of assessment types used in the modern classroom, such as a portfolio or performance-based assessments.

Peer Assessment

A peer assessment is when students grade one another's work based on a teacher-provided framework. **Peer assessments** are promoted as a means of saving teacher time and building student metacognitive skills. They are typically used as **formative** rather than summative assessments, given concerns about the reliability of student scoring and the tensions that can result if student scores contribute to overall grades. Peer assessments are used most often to grade essay-type written work or presentations. Proponents point out that peer assessments require students to apply metacognition, builds cooperative work and interpersonal skills, and broadens the sense that the student is accountable to peers and not just the teacher. Even advocates of the practice agree that students need detailed rubrics in order to succeed. Critics often argue that low-performing students have little to offer high-performing students in terms of valuable feedback—and this disparity may be more pronounced in ESOL classrooms or special education environments than in mainstream ones. One way to overcome this weakness is for the teacher to lead the evaluation exercise, guiding the students through a point-by-point framework of evaluation.

The Learning Environment

Establishing a Positive, Productive Classroom Environment

Unique Characteristics and Needs of Students at Varying Developmental Levels

Students at each developmental level possess unique characteristics and needs that must be met in the classroom to ensure productivity and a positive classroom environment. For successful learning, the teacher must recognize the nuances of varying developmental levels to properly understand their students' abilities and design instruction accordingly. When the teacher is attuned to the distinct characteristics and needs of their students, they can align **curriculum**, **instructional strategies**, **activities**, and **assessments** in a way that is accessible and comprehensible to all students. This understanding enables the teacher to deliver instruction at a **pace** appropriate to students' developmental stage while ensuring they are challenged across domains based upon their ability for continuous whole-child development. In addition, knowledge of the general characteristics and needs of developmental stages enables the teacher to effectively identify and accommodate individual variances that occur within these stages for **student-centered** learning. When instruction is tailored to address the needs of varying developmental stages and individual differences, students feel supported in their learning. This ultimately fosters increased self-esteem, student engagement, and positive attitudes toward learning that contribute to an overall productive and successful classroom environment.

Addressing Developmental Characteristics and Needs of Younger Students

A positive and productive classroom environment for younger children requires the teacher to understand the intricacies of this developmental stage and implement strategies accordingly to promote success in learning. Younger students learn by **exploring** and **interacting** with the world around them and must be provided with multiple opportunities to do so. **Play** is integral to young students' development across domains. Therefore, both planned and free play should be incorporated throughout instruction. Play enables students to explore their environment and make connections that strengthen their learning while promoting the development of problem-solving and higher-order thinking skills. In addition, allowing frequent opportunities for play facilitates the acquisition of important social and emotional skills, such as cooperation, conflict resolution, and sharing. Likewise, incorporating frequent **movement** throughout lessons allows young students to explore their physical space and actively engage in learning for deeper understanding. Additionally, **cooperative learning** strategies encourage the development of necessary social and emotional skills and are important in teaching young children how to effectively work with others to solve a problem. When the teacher implements strategies appropriate to younger students' developmental levels, it enhances motivation, active engagement, and promotes positive attitudes toward learning for a productive classroom environment.

Collaborative Opportunities in Addressing Developmental Characteristics and Needs of Middle-Level Students

Middle-level students experience significant developmental changes as they approach adolescence and therefore, have unique characteristics and needs that must be met to ensure a positive and productive learning environment. **Collaborative opportunities** are beneficial in supporting the development of cognitive, social, and emotional skills of middle-level students and should be implemented frequently. This strategy enables these students to work productively with others and promotes the development of positive **interpersonal** and **communication** skills. This is especially important in middle-level education, as students at this developmental stage begin forming their identities, attitudes toward learning, and influential peer relationships. Middle-level students build **self-confidence** through collaborative learning, as it enables them to develop positive leadership skills. Additionally, collaborative opportunities expose students to the varying backgrounds and perspectives of their classmates, thus fostering appreciation for individual differences and contributing to a positive classroom climate. Collaborative learning is also beneficial for **cognitive development**, as it allows students to build upon one another's background knowledge for enhanced learning and encourages critical and higher-order thinking while working together to solve a problem. Providing middle-level students with collaborative opportunities increases overall engagement for a positive and productive classroom environment, as well as develops necessary skills for successful transition into adolescence.

Promoting Respect for the Community and People in It Among Older Students

As older students prepare for adulthood, it is important that they develop a respect for their community and the people in it. Implementing strategies to facilitate this is vital in equipping older students with **real-world skills** necessary to become productive contributors to society. By self-educating and modeling respect for the community and its people, the teacher can influence students to adopt the same sentiment. Establishing a positive community within the classroom through such activities as class meetings, discussions, and cultural activities promotes respect for others that extends to real-world situations. Strategies that demonstrate connection to the community strengthen students' overall respect and responsibility for it. This can be achieved by incorporating **authentic materials**, including news stories, art, music, and relevant speakers, to develop students' understanding and insight regarding the characteristics and needs of the community. Encouraging students to bring items from home to share fosters appreciation for their community by exposing them to the backgrounds and perspectives within it. **Community service** projects such as fundraisers, food drives, and service field trips further promote students' respect for their community while demonstrating the real-world applications of their learning. This ultimately makes learning meaningful and contributes to a positive, productive learning environment.

Positive Classroom Climate

Classroom climate refers to the overall atmosphere that the teacher establishes and is powerful in determining the nature of the learning experience. Students are most successful in their learning when the climate is positive, encouraging, and focused on creating a collaborative, supportive community. A positive classroom climate is **welcoming**, **inclusive**, and **respectful** of all individuals. Instruction is delivered in an engaging, comprehensible way in a structured, orderly, and safe environment. The atmosphere is **visually appealing** and stimulating, yet not overwhelming, and is physically arranged in a way that maximizes learning. **Collaboration** and **supportive interactions** are encouraged throughout the learning process to enhance engagement and develop positive social and emotional skills. Such an environment builds students' self-esteem and confidence by ensuring they feel safe and empowered to participate and work with others in the learning process. In addition, it encourages positive attitudes toward learning that are necessary for active student engagement and productivity. When the classroom climate is positive, students are more self-motivated, thus strengthening their learning and promoting academic achievement.

Collaboration and Supportive Interactions

Collaboration and **supportive interactions** are key components of a positive classroom climate and should be integrated throughout instruction to promote active engagement and success in learning for all students. To achieve this, the teacher must establish a classroom community focused on respect, inclusiveness, and open dialogue. This ensures students feel safe and empowered to express themselves and interact constructively. By teaching and **modeling** active listening skills, the teacher can demonstrate and influence respectful communication in the classroom. **Team-building activities**, including class meetings, games, and discussions, are valuable strategies for creating a community that encourages productive collaboration and supportive interactions. In addition, establishing **clear expectations** for positive communication and involving students in their creation instills a sense of personal responsibility to adhere to them when working with others. Once expectations are understood, students must be provided with multiple and varied **collaborative learning** opportunities to continuously practice developing positive interpersonal skills. As students participate in learning, the teacher must be sure to consistently praise cooperation and positive interactions to reinforce the standards of communication. When the teacher promotes collaboration and supportive interactions, they create a positive classroom climate that increases students' productivity and self-motivation to actively participate in learning for maximized achievement.

Respect for Diversity and Individual Differences

An emphasis on respect for **diversity** and **individual differences** in the classroom is necessary to establish a positive, productive learning atmosphere. Teaching and modeling this sentiment to students instills the notion that everyone has unique and valuable experiences, perspectives, and characteristics to contribute to the classroom community. Emphasizing respect for all individuals ensures students feel validated and secure in their own identities while teaching them to appreciate diversities among their classmates. Such an environment promotes collaboration and supportive interactions, as it is built on a foundation of welcoming, inclusiveness, and acceptance that empowers students to confidently interact with peers as they engage in learning. When students feel respected, it increases their self-esteem and positive self-concept. Students that feel confident in the classroom are more likely to develop positive attitudes toward learning. This ultimately fosters a positive classroom climate in which students are motivated to actively engage in instruction and achieve academic success.

Impact of Interactions on Classroom Climate

Teacher-Student Interactions

Interactions between teachers and their students play a significant role in determining overall classroom climate and the quality of the learning experience. The way in which the teacher interacts with students influences their **social**, **emotional**, and **cognitive development**, as well as sets the tone for how students interact with each other. This ultimately shapes students' **self-esteem** and contributes to their level of engagement, attitude toward learning, and academic achievement. Therefore, it is important that the teacher ensure all interactions with students on a whole-class and individual level are positive, unbiased, encouraging, and respectful of each individual. Working to build relationships with students demonstrates a genuine interest in their lives that contributes to a positive, productive classroom climate in which students feel welcomed, accepted, and empowered to actively engage in learning. Positive interactions between the teacher and students support a healthy sense of self-esteem as well as positive social and emotional skills that contribute to cognitive development. Students with greater self-esteem are more likely to develop positive attitudes toward learning that foster increased self-motivation to actively participate in learning, thus contributing to enhanced academic achievement.

Students' Interactions with One Another

The classroom climate is dependent on the nature of **students' interactions** with one another. These interactions largely determine the quality of student learning as well as development across domains. Positive communication facilitates the development of healthy **social** and emotional skills that serve to enhance cognitive development. Students with strong social and **emotional skills** are often more motivated to actively participate in learning and are more productive in collaborative situations, as they can build upon one another's knowledge. Therefore, the teacher must implement a variety of strategies to ensure interactions among students are positive, respectful, and supportive to establish a classroom climate focused on productive learning. **Community building** exercises establish a climate built on positive and supportive communication while demonstrating the benefits of productive cooperation in achieving a goal. Teaching and **modeling** positive communication skills sets the tone and expectations for how students will interact with one another. Students should be given **frequent opportunities** to interact both during and outside of instructional time to promote the development of necessary interpersonal skills for healthy social development. In addition, **strategic student groupings** during collaborative work and consistent monitoring help ensure maximized productivity and that the standards for communication are reinforced.

Communicating an Enthusiasm for Learning

Establishing Environments Promoting Positive Attitudes Toward Learning

The nature of the classroom environment is reliant on the **efforts**, **behaviors**, and **attitudes** of the teacher. The teacher is responsible for setting the tone of the classroom, which determines the overall climate and has significant impacts on the quality and effectiveness of the learning experience. The classroom environment influences students' engagement, positive communication, and attitudes toward learning, which contribute to their overall academic achievement. Successful teaching and learning require the teacher to intentionally take measures to establish a welcoming, accepting, and encouraging classroom environment that promotes excitement and positive attitudes toward learning. Teachers must model genuine respect for their students and enthusiasm for learning, as well as present instruction in a way that is engaging, comprehensible, and responsive to students' needs and interests. The physical classroom must be arranged in such a way that is visually appealing, safe, and facilitative of productive learning. It is also important that the teacher establish and consistently reinforce structured routines, procedures, and behavioral expectations to contribute to an overall positive climate and ensure students feel secure and willing to participate in learning. When the classroom environment is exciting, positive, and engaging, it encourages positive attitudes toward learning that increase motivation to succeed.

Influence on Students' Motivation, Productivity, and Academic Achievement

Modeling is perhaps one of the most powerful strategies in influencing students' attitudes, behaviors, and actions in the classroom. As students spend a great deal of time with their teachers, the level of enthusiasm for learning demonstrated by the teacher inevitably influences their own excitement in the classroom. Therefore, the teacher must conscientiously model enthusiasm for teaching and learning to positively influence students' internal motivation for productivity, learning, and achievement. Students are highly perceptive, and as such, if the teacher appears unmotivated in their practice or disinterested in the content, students will likely adopt the same sentiment and become disengaged or apathetic toward learning. The enthusiasm modeled by the teacher must be **authentic** to elicit the same genuine interest in learning from students. When the teacher demonstrates sincere excitement about the content they are teaching, it prompts curiosity for learning among students that enhances their motivation and attitudes toward learning. In addition, modeling enthusiasm for teaching and learning enhances the relationship between the teacher and students, thus contributing to a positive classroom climate that makes students excited to learn. When students have a positive attitude toward learning, they are more motivated to productively engage in learning and achieve academic success.

Methods and Impact on Classroom Climate and Student Engagement

Communicating sincere enthusiasm for teaching and learning is essential to establishing a positive, productive classroom climate focused on student engagement and achievement. Students' interest and excitement for learning are directly reflective of the sentiments exhibited by the teacher. As such, it is important that the teacher intentionally and consistently communicate excitement for their practice and content. To achieve this, the teacher must ensure that their **behaviors**, **actions**, **language**, **tone of voice**, and **interactions** with students are positive in nature. By working to build positive **interpersonal relationships** with students and demonstrating genuine interest in their lives, experiences, interests, and needs, the teacher can effectively communicate enthusiasm for their practice that motivates students to engage in learning. This is further reflected in the physical **classroom arrangement**. A classroom that is visually appealing, stimulating, and reflective of students' interests and achievements illustrates the teacher's enthusiasm and promotes a positive classroom climate in which students are excited and motivated to engage in learning.

Conveying High Expectations for All Students

Significance in Promoting Productivity, Active Engagement, and Success in Learning

Communicating **high academic** and **behavioral expectations** is necessary for establishing a classroom climate focused on productivity, active engagement, and achievement. Students are heavily influenced by the teacher's expectations for them, and therefore, when high learning standards are set, students will more likely strive to achieve them. High expectations increase the **relevancy** of learning by focusing instruction and providing a clear purpose that motivates students to participate. In addition, by conveying high expectations, the teacher demonstrates a **belief in their students' abilities** to overcome personal challenges and achieve success. This notion promotes a **growth mindset** among students, which is the belief that intelligence is not inherent, but rather, can be attained and consistently improved upon. This enhances students' self-esteem and confidence, which promotes positive attitudes toward learning that foster active engagement, productivity, and success. Communicating high expectations while providing necessary supports motivates students to challenge themselves academically and gives them a sense of self-responsibility over their learning that encourages them to work to their highest potential. This ultimately creates a positive classroom climate in which students feel supported and empowered to productively engage in learning and achieve success.

Strategies and Impact on Classroom Climate and Student Achievement

Communicating **high academic** and **behavioral expectations** is most effective when done so through a variety of means. This ensures that students are aware of the teacher's expectations of them and consistently reinforces high standards to establish a positive classroom climate focused on student motivation, productivity, and achievement. Expectations must always be **clear** and

visible in the classroom, and the teacher must frequently remind students by restating them throughout instruction. Establishing learning goals and objectives that are challenging, yet attainable based on students' abilities effectively communicates high expectations and the teacher's belief that students can achieve them. This is further iterated when students encounter challenges and rather than lowering expectations, the teacher maintains the same high standards while providing necessary supports for achievement. The teacher can also communicate high expectations by ensuring they provide students with timely, clear, and constructive **feedback** on their progress and ways in which they can improve to meet them. Frequent **communication with families** is beneficial in reinforcing academic and behavioral expectations at home to ensure student awareness and maximize their effectiveness in the classroom.

Literacy-Rich Environment

A **literacy-rich** classroom focuses on the development of all literacy components by immersing students in reading, writing, speaking, and listening skills across subject areas. While all students benefit from such an environment, it is especially important for **ELL students** and students with **developmental disabilities** in acquiring the literacy and language skills necessary for success. In a literacy-rich environment, the teacher provides multiple opportunities to engage in teacher-led and student-selected reading, writing, speaking, and listening activities in all areas of instruction. Students may be asked to solve word problems in math, write a report on a famous artist in art, or keep an observation log in science to encourage literacy development across content areas. Students are provided with multiple print and digital literacy materials on a variety of topics with varying levels of complexity to accommodate individual developmental levels while encouraging reading, vocabulary acquisition, and listening skills. Additionally, the teacher surrounds students with **print-rich** materials, including posters, word walls, labels, and bulletin boards on a variety of topics to further promote literacy development. A literacy-rich environment continuously promotes and emphasizes the importance of literacy skills in all areas of life that serve as a necessary foundation for academic and real-world success.

Review Video: Importance of Promoting Literacy in the Home
Visit mometrix.com/academy and enter code: 862347

Review Video: Characteristics of Literacy-Rich, Content-Area Classrooms
Visit mometrix.com/academy and enter code: 571455

Safe, Nurturing, and Inclusive Classroom Environment

A safe, nurturing, and inclusive classroom environment focuses on meeting students' emotional needs for healthy development in this domain. The overall climate in such an environment is welcoming and emphasizes **respect**, **acceptance**, and **positive communication** among the teacher and students. The classroom is brightly decorated and reflective of students' diversities, interests, and achievements to promote a sense of security and inclusivity that motivates active participation in learning. Instructional activities are also reflective of students' differences, learning styles, and interests, with necessary supports instilled to accommodate individual learning needs. This establishes an **equitable environment** that ensures all students feel respected, nurtured, and supported both academically and emotionally. Such an environment is **structured** and orderly with clear expectations, procedures, and routines to foster a sense of security as students engage in learning. Collaboration and supportive interactions among students are encouraged to create a positive, productive classroom community in which students feel confident to express themselves and participate in learning. A classroom environment that is safe, nurturing, and inclusive develops students' sense of self-concept that contributes to positive communication, relationships, and attitudes necessary for emotional development.

Developing Students' Emotional Intelligence

Emotional intelligence refers to the ability to recognize and regulate one's own emotions as well as identify and empathetically respond to the emotions of others. Developing this skill through a variety of strategies is integral to successful development across other domains. By **modeling** such skills as empathy and active listening, the teacher can influence students' abilities to identify and properly respond to their own and other's emotions. Teaching **coping strategies**, including journaling, breathing, or counting techniques, promotes students' self-regulation to manage emotions when faced with a conflict or challenge. Teaching emotional intelligence can also be integrated throughout instruction, such as prompting students to describe the feelings of a character in a book, or discuss emotions evoked from a painting. Students with strong emotional intelligence are likely to develop positive interpersonal relationships for healthy social development. This contributes to improved cognitive development in that when students collaborate productively, they build upon one another's knowledge. Emotionally intelligent students are also likely to have positive attitudes toward learning, as they have the capacity to self-regulate when faced with obstacles and properly engage in instruction for enhanced cognitive development.

Meeting and Respecting Students' Emotional Needs, Individual Rights, and Dignity

Successful learning and **whole-child** development are reliant on the degree to which students' emotional needs, individual rights, and dignity are met and respected in the classroom. This establishes the tone of the overall classroom climate that determines students' sense of safety, nurturing, and inclusion when interacting with others and engaging in learning. By taking measures to prioritize students' emotional needs and create a respectful, accepting classroom community, the teacher establishes a positive learning atmosphere that promotes cognitive, social, and emotional growth for whole-child development. When students feel emotionally supported and respected in their identities, they develop a healthy sense of self-esteem that positively influences their attitude toward learning and motivation to participate. This ultimately impacts **cognitive development**, as students that actively and confidently engage in learning are more likely to be academically successful. These students are also more effectively able to develop important interpersonal communication skills necessary for healthy **social development**, as students that feel secure and accepted are more likely to be supportive of others. By meeting students' emotional needs and respecting their individual rights and dignities, the teacher effectively prepares students with the skills necessary for academic and real-world success.

Classroom Routines and Procedures

Influence on Classroom Climate, Productivity, Student Behavior, and Learning

A well-managed classroom focused on productivity, positive behavior, and success in learning relies on the effectiveness and consistency of **routines** and **procedures** instilled for daily activities. By implementing these at the beginning of the school year and continuously reinforcing them throughout, the teacher establishes an orderly, efficient classroom that facilitates students' ability to productively engage in learning. Classroom management, and therefore, student behavior and productivity, is enhanced by structured routines and procedures, as students that are clear on expectations are more inclined to follow them. Such structure provides students with a sense of predictability and security in their environment that contributes to their willingness to participate in learning. Routines and procedures simplify daily tasks and allow for smooth transitions between activities. This minimizes opportunities for student distraction or disruption, thus promoting positive behavior, increasing instructional time, and enhancing students' ability to focus on learning in an orderly, productive classroom climate.

Review Video: Classroom Management - Rhythms of Teaching
Visit mometrix.com/academy and enter code: 809399

Considerations Regarding Age-Appropriateness to Ensure Effectiveness

Classroom procedures and routines must reflect the characteristics and capabilities of the students' **age group**. It is important that the teacher understand and apply their knowledge of students' **developmental levels** across domains when considering which routines and procedures to establish in their classroom. In doing so, the teacher ensures that expectations are age-appropriate, realistic, and effective in creating an orderly, productive environment. Procedures and routines must always be clear, succinct, and limited in number to avoid overwhelming students. However, in communicating them, the teacher must use comprehensible language relative to students' age-group. The nature of learning must be considered when determining age-appropriate routines and procedures. For young children, procedures for cleaning up toys after playtime is appropriate, whereas procedures for turning in homework and taking assessments applies to older students. The degree to which students are expected to perform routines and procedures independently must also be considered and reflective of their capabilities. Young children may need a great deal of assistance, whereas older students can perform certain tasks independently. Consequences for not following expectations must be appropriate to students' age group. Losing free play time may be appropriate for young children, whereas parent communication may be effective for older students.

Examples of Age-Appropriate Routines and Procedures

Young children: Young children can reasonably be expected to perform **basic daily routines** independently, although they likely will need frequent reminders. Daily procedures may include having young children hang up their coats, put away lunchboxes, and unpack their backpacks at the beginning of the day as they prepare to begin morning work. Similarly, young children can be expected to independently follow end-of-day procedures and routines, such as packing up their backpacks, cleaning up learning materials, and lining up at the door for dismissal. Young children should be able to follow simple behavioral procedures as well, such as keeping hands to themselves, responding to attention signals from the teacher, and cleaning up learning materials before transitioning between activities. Young children also benefit from being assigned classroom "jobs," such as line leader, paper collector, or teacher assistant, as these routines instill a sense of accountability and self-responsibility.

Middle-level: Middle-level students can be expected to follow a variety of routines and procedures with **increasing levels of independence**. These students can reasonably be expected to enter the classroom on time and prepared with necessary learning materials. In addition, middle-level students can be held responsible for independently turning in homework according to the procedures for doing so and beginning their morning work. Middle-level students should be able to follow procedures for accessing learning materials, transitioning to cooperative learning activities, cleaning up their own materials before moving to a new activity, and non-instructional tasks, such as sharpening pencils, using the restroom, or throwing away trash with minimal reminders from the teacher.

High school: Routines and procedures in the high school classroom should **reflect** students' level of **maturity and increasing capabilities for independence** as they approach adulthood. These students can reasonably be expected to independently come to class on time, prepared, and follow procedures for turning in homework and beginning morning work. In addition, high school students can be expected to follow procedures for direct instruction, cooperative learning activities, and independently transitioning between activities. High school students can be held to a greater degree of accountability regarding grading procedures, tardiness and attendance, and procedures for turning in late assignments.

Facilitating an Organized, Productive Environment that Maximizes Student Learning

Clear routines and procedures for daily classroom activities are necessary to create an organized, productive environment that maximizes student learning. In order to be effective, routines and procedures must be reflective of the teacher's **instructional** and **classroom management** style, explicitly stated, and consistently reinforced. This ensures expectations are relevant, realistic, and that students are continuously aware of them as they engage in learning. Procedures for entering and exiting the classroom, as well as how students will begin and end their day, establish a structured, **predictable** routine that enhances focus on instruction. Smooth **transition procedures** maintain order and enhance efficiency when moving between activities, as they eliminate idle time, minimize student distraction, and allow for increased time dedicated to productive teaching and learning. Such transition procedures include how and when to access and clean up materials, move from independent to collaborative group work, or move between learning stations. The teacher must also consider procedures for performing non-instructional activities, such as sharpening pencils or going to the restroom, as these further avoid disruptions to instructional time. Procedures and routines establish organization and efficiency in the classroom by simplifying tasks to allow for increased productive instructional time and enhanced student learning.

Procedures and routines are necessary for establishing a well-managed and productive classroom environment. While the specifics of routines may vary depending upon the teacher's classroom management style and students' learning needs, many common procedures and routines share similar guidelines.

- **Entering the classroom/morning routine:** A procedure for the beginning of class ensures that students enter the room in an orderly manner with a clear understanding of what is expected of them. This routine should include entering the room quietly, unpacking necessary items for class, turning in homework, and working on an opening activity while the teacher takes attendance.
- **Leaving the classroom/packing up routine:** A procedure for packing up and leaving the classroom at the end of class or the school day ensures that students have all of their necessary materials, leave the room clean and organized, and exit in an orderly manner. Such a routine may include cleaning up learning materials, putting away assignments or papers, straightening desks, throwing away trash, packing up backpacks, and lining up by the door prior to dismissal. Students may be assigned specific jobs for cleaning up and organizing the room.
- **Turning in work:** Procedures for turning in classwork and homework allow for smoother transitions between activities and limit interruptions to instruction. This should occur at a specific time during the class period and can include designating a "turn in" box in the classroom for students to hand in assignments, or having students pass their papers to the front in a specific order. A student may be designated to collect papers at the end of an activity as well.

- **Using the restroom:** Restroom procedures limit student distraction and interruptions to instruction. Restroom breaks should generally not occur during direct instruction, and students should be permitted to go one at a time to avoid misbehavior. Students should be given a restroom pass, sign out before leaving the room, and sign back in upon returning to ensure that the teacher is always aware of students' whereabouts. Specific hand signals in which students can silently request permission to use the restroom are beneficial in further minimizing disruptions.
- **Transitions between activities:** Procedures for transitions allow for an orderly learning environment in that they indicate to students when and how to move between activities in the classroom. These procedures should include an attention signal and a clear explanation of the steps for transitioning, such as cleaning up materials from the previous activity, and a signal to indicate when students are permitted to move. Students should be expected to transition between activities quickly, quietly, and without disruption.
- **Non-instructional tasks:** Procedures for non-instructional tasks limit interruptions to instructional time for more focused learning. Activities such as getting a tissue, sharpening pencils, and throwing away trash should occur during specific times when the teacher is not directly instructing and should be done quietly and without disruption.
- **Managing student behavior:** Clear procedures for misbehavior establish a predictable, orderly learning environment. These procedures should be explicit, consistent, and follow a logical sequence. They may include a verbal warning, seating change, loss of privileges, or communication with home.
- **Accessing and using materials, supplies, and technology:** Procedures for these activities are beneficial in limiting disruption, maintaining organization, and avoiding interruptions to instruction. Such procedures indicate when and how to access and use materials, supplies, and technology in a respectful and orderly manner. The teacher should clearly communicate expectations for access and use, as well as utilize a specific signal to indicate when students are permitted to move. These procedures should also include methods for proper cleanup at the end of the activity.
- **Finishing work early:** A procedure for finishing work early minimizes idle time and limits student disruption. Students that finish early may be permitted to work on other assignments or read quietly, or the teacher can dedicate an area of the room for extra practice and review activities for students to work on if they finish early. The teacher may also permit early finishers to assist other students in applicable learning situations.
- **Emergency drills:** Procedures for emergency drills ensure that students know how to complete them in a safe, orderly manner. When the drill begins, students should immediately stop what they are doing, leave all materials on their desks, and line up by the door in an organized fashion. Students should exit the room with the teacher and move quickly and quietly through the hallways to the designated drill location. For emergency drills that occur inside the classroom, students should move quickly and quietly to a previously designated location within the room and remain there until the drill is over.
- **Attention signal:** A dedicated signal to capture students' attention indicates that they need to stop what they are doing, focus, and listen quietly to the teacher for further information or instructions. This signal could be in the form of a hand signal, call and response, phrase, or sound and should be used consistently.

- **Direct instruction:** A procedure for direct instruction is beneficial in maintaining students' focus on learning. This should include steps for active listening, including sitting up straight, facing the teacher, maintaining eye contact, and refraining from distracting neighboring classmates. Students should have clear steps regarding how to ask questions, such as raising their hand or utilizing color-coded cards to indicate levels of understanding, and how to take notes, when applicable.
- **Independent work:** An independent work procedure limits distractions and promotes students' ability to focus. This should include communicating expectations for quiet time during this period, including refraining from talking to neighboring peers, working at and remaining in assigned seats, and engaging in the proper procedure if a student finishes early. If a student needs assistance, he or she can indicate it by raising a hand, or utilizing a dedicated signal to request help, such as color-coded cards.
- **Collaborative work:** A procedure for collaborative work indicates to students how to move from independent to group activities. This includes moving to a group setting without disruption, maintaining a normal volume, communicating respectfully, and cleaning up materials when finished before moving back to assigned seats in an orderly manner.

Non-Instructional Duties and Instructional Activities Maximizing Efficiency

Many non-instructional duties, such as taking attendance, grading papers, and facilitating communication, can be coordinated with instructional activities when effective **routines** and **procedures** are instilled to accomplish them. This enhances overall efficiency in the classroom, as time is not lost on completing administrative tasks, allowing more dedicated time to instruction for maximized student learning. Taking attendance, for example, can be incorporated into students' morning work routine, as they can mark their own presence as part of the procedure for entering the classroom and beginning the day. Grading and communication with colleagues or families can take place during independent work, assessments, or recreational time. The teacher can also observe, monitor, and assess students' progress as they engage in learning. Student **self-correction** in lieu of formal grading can be beneficial in allowing students to reflect on their performance, seek areas for improvement, and strengthen their understanding, while integrating grading as an instructional activity. In addition, a variety of **digital resources** are available that allow for immediate student feedback and communication with families throughout instruction. In utilizing such resources, the teacher can efficiently coordinate administrative duties with instructional activities to maximize time for student learning.

Effective Time Management

Practicing effective time management is beneficial in establishing an efficient, orderly classroom environment focused on productivity and maximizing student learning. By instilling specific **procedures** for managing daily routines such as transitioning, accessing materials and supplies, and using technology, the teacher can ensure that these tasks are completed in a timely manner while minimizing time lost on non-instructional activities and student distraction. This allows more time to be focused on instruction and student learning. To achieve this, procedures for such tasks must be **explicit** and consistently reinforced. Prior to transitioning between activities, accessing materials, or using technology, the teacher must provide a clear, detailed explanation of each step of the procedure, as well as expectations for how students will complete it. Modeling the procedure is beneficial in providing a visual example to ensure student understanding. In order to be effective, each procedure must include a specific **signal** to indicate when students can begin, and the teacher must consistently monitor to ensure students are completing the task correctly. When students have a clear understanding on how to accomplish daily activities, they can do so quickly, effectively, and without disruption. This increases overall efficiency in the classroom and maximizes time dedicated to student learning.

Using Technology to Perform Administrative Tasks

Technology resources are widely available to assist teachers in accomplishing a variety of administrative tasks, and therefore, are highly beneficial in establishing a **well-managed**, **organized**, and **productive** learning environment. Completing such tasks as taking attendance, maintaining gradebooks, or facilitating communication through technology allows the teacher to do so more **efficiently**. This allows for more time dedicated to productive teaching and learning, as well as smoother transitions between activities, as time is not lost on completing such duties. Increased efficiency in completing administrative duties is beneficial in sustaining students' attention, engagement, and productivity in learning, as it minimizes idle time that could lead to distraction or disruption. In addition, utilizing technology to perform administrative duties enhances overall organization, as all tasks performed digitally can be stored in a single area on the device used for easy access and recall of information. Through email, digital apps, or class websites, the teacher can efficiently communicate with colleagues and students' families to update them regarding important events, assignments, and individual progress. This creates a sense of connectedness between the teacher and community that contributes to a positive, productive classroom climate.

Volunteers and Paraprofessionals

Enhancing and Enriching Instruction

Paraprofessionals and **volunteers** are highly valuable in enhancing and enriching the overall learning experience, as their efforts contribute to an organized, positive, and productive classroom environment. These aides collaborate with the teacher throughout planning and instruction to implement best practices in meeting students' learning needs. Paraprofessionals and volunteers can lead small groups of students as they engage in instruction for a more focused, **student-centered** learning experience. They can also provide additional support to struggling students while the teacher engages in whole-class instruction. Specifically, paraprofessionals are typically licensed in the educational field and are qualified to provide **individual accommodations** to students with individual learning needs to create an inclusive learning environment. In addition, working with paraprofessionals and volunteers is beneficial in creating an efficient, organized classroom that enhances student learning, as they can assist with **non-instructional duties** that allow for smooth transitions during instruction, such as preparing learning materials, handing back papers, or grading assignments. **Classroom management** is also enhanced when paraprofessionals and volunteers are present, as they can assist in reinforcing expectations and monitoring behavior to ensure all students are positively and productively engaging in learning.

Monitoring Their Performance in the Classroom

Paraprofessionals and volunteers are invaluable resources for creating a positive, productive classroom environment. However, to ensure the contributions of these aides are consistently beneficial in meeting students' needs and maximizing learning, it is important to continuously monitor their performance in the classroom. Paraprofessionals and volunteers are typically interviewed by administration prior to entering the classroom to determine whether their qualifications are aligned with meeting students' needs to enhance instruction. The administration is also often responsible for monitoring their performance throughout the school year. Specifically, paraprofessionals are licensed in the field of education, and therefore, are often formally evaluated against specific **performance measurement tools**. **Observations** by administration can either be scheduled or conducted as an informal "walk-through" to assess how the paraprofessional or volunteer interacts with the teacher and students and their effectiveness in contributing to a productive learning environment. The teacher can also monitor the performance of volunteers and paraprofessionals in their classroom. By analyzing **students' progress** when working with these aides and eliciting **feedback** from students, the teacher can determine their effectiveness in enhancing the learning experience. Frequently communicating with paraprofessionals and volunteers provides valuable insight regarding whether they contribute to a positive classroom climate focused on student learning.

Classroom Organization

Physical Characteristics of a Safe and Productive Learning Environment

A classroom environment that is **safe** and facilitates **productivity** in learning is essential to fostering student motivation, engagement, and achievement. The physical space must be **clean, well-organized**, and **orderly**. All equipment, furniture, and materials must be in usable condition, well-maintained, and free of damage. This ensures that students are safe when engaging with the learning environment, as well as provides an appealing space that encourages participation. Furniture and equipment must be arranged in a way that facilitates safety and ease of movement as students transition between activities. Likewise, all furniture, materials, and equipment must be appropriate to the students' **age group** in terms of level of difficulty, height, and size to enable students to properly interact with them for productive learning. Students must have access to a **variety** of learning materials to promote interest and engagement for productive learning, including areas for individual and collaborative learning. The classroom should be decorated in such a way that is welcoming, stimulating without being overwhelming, and reflective of students' diversities and interests. When the physical environment is inviting, safe, and tailored to students' developmental levels, it creates a positive classroom climate in which students are motivated to productively engage in learning.

Significance of Effective Classroom Arrangement

A thoughtfully arranged classroom has significant and positive impacts on the nature of the learning atmosphere. Effective classroom arrangement creates an inviting learning environment in which students are motivated to engage in learning actively and productively. The manner in which the teacher organizes furniture, equipment, and learning materials influences students' **focus**, **access** to resources, and **behavior**, as well as the teacher's ability to effectively implement **classroom management** strategies. An organized, orderly classroom in which necessary resources are easily accessible enables students to properly focus on instruction, thus promoting active engagement and productivity in learning. This reinforces positive behavior, as students are less likely to be disruptive when their learning environment is free of unnecessary distractions. The classroom arrangement determines the flow and ease of movement and should be strategically planned to facilitate productive learning while enabling the teacher to easily monitor and assist all students for effective classroom management. Effective arrangement allows the teacher to control the level of student movement and prevent potential distractions while ensuring students can easily transition from one learning activity to the next to promote efficiency, active engagement, and productivity.

Establishing Safe, Productive, and Successful Learning Environments

Establishing a safe, productive, and successful learning environment requires the teacher to thoughtfully consider several factors when determining the most effective classroom arrangement for meeting desired learning outcomes and students' needs. Students' **age group, size**, and **developmental levels** influence which arrangement best facilitates safety and productivity in learning. For example, younger students learn through interaction with their environment and therefore need ample space for movement and play to support their development. A more structured arrangement that enables direct instruction while also facilitating hands-on, collaborative learning meets the needs of middle-level and older students. In addition, students' **individual needs** must be considered when determining classroom arrangement in order to ensure equitable access to instruction and learning materials. The teacher must also consider the **size** and **layout** of the classroom, including the location of learning resources such as the projector screen, computers, and chalkboard. With this in mind, teachers must determine the **style** of teaching and learning taking place, how they want students to move, what information must be visible, as well as which materials must be accessible to create a safe, productive learning environment that meets students' needs in achieving learning outcomes.

Considerations for Desk Arrangement

There are numerous possibilities for desk arrangements in the classroom, each with advantages and limitations that must be considered and addressed. **Desired learning outcomes**, as well as the style of teaching and learning, influence which arrangement is most effective. Arrangements that facilitate individual focus, limited distraction, and clear teacher-student visibility are suited to **direct instruction**. However, these arrangements often limit collaborative learning. To address this, the teacher can designate an area in the classroom for group work, utilize common areas such as the library, or move students' desks for collaborative activities. Variations of group arrangements facilitate **collaborative learning**, as students can easily face one another and work together. However, grouped seating may cause student distraction during individual work and limit teacher-student visibility. It is therefore important that the teacher establish clear expectations and frequently monitor students' progress to ensure they remain on task. The **classroom size** must be considered, as the space may not allow for certain desk arrangements and still facilitate ease of movement, visibility, and student learning. **Individual learning needs** must also be considered when determining seating arrangements. Some students require specific accommodations, such as preferential seating, an individual learning space for limited distractions, or a physical accommodation.

Various types of seating arrangements are described below:

- **Stadium Seating**—Desks in this classroom are situated in lines at a slight angle with the students facing directly toward the teacher. This seating method is useful for lectures and individual work, as the teacher can easily monitor whether each student is on task. This arrangement is generally unsuited for group work, as students are not able to easily face one another, and may limit the teacher's ease of movement between students to provide individual assistance.
- **Cluster Seating**—Desks in this classroom are arranged in groups of 3-5 throughout the classroom. This method is beneficial for supporting collaborative work and pairing students that need support with others that can provide scaffolding. However, this arrangement may be distracting during individual work and limit teacher-student visibility.
- **Rows and Columns**—Desks are individually spaced apart with the students facing directly toward the teacher and front of the room. This arrangement is useful for presentations, direct instruction, and individual work, as it limits distractions from other students. The teacher can easily see whether individual students are on task. However, this arrangement is not facilitative of group work, as students cannot easily face each other. This arrangement also limits the teacher's ability to move between students to provide assistance.

- **Horseshoe**—Desks in this classroom are arranged in a large "U" shape with students facing the teacher at the front of the room. This arrangement is useful for individual instruction, as it ensures teacher-student visibility and equal view of the chalkboard and projector screen during direct instruction. This method also facilitates whole-class discussions. However, this arrangement inhibits students' ability to work collaboratively in groups and, depending on classroom size, may limit ease of teacher and student movement.
- **Miniature Horseshoes**—Desks in this classroom are arranged in 2-5 miniature horseshoes with students facing the front of the room. This arrangement is beneficial for both individual and collaborative work, as the teacher can clearly monitor whether students are on task and can move between groups to provide individual assistance, while enabling students to easily face one another for group activities. However, this method may lend itself to student distraction during individual work, and the physical size of the classroom may limit the possibility for this arrangement.
- **Pairs**—Desks in this classroom are arranged two-by-two in rows with students facing the front of the classroom. This arrangement is useful for partner work and pairing students that need support with others that provide scaffolding, while limiting distractions during individual work. This method is not suitable for group work or whole-class activities, as students cannot easily face each other, and movement may be limited.
- **Combination**—This classroom incorporates a variety of desk arrangements, including individual seats, pairs, groups, and the "horseshoe" arrangements. This method is useful for accommodating varying learning styles and needs, as it can facilitate individual and collaborative work. However, this arrangement utilizes a great deal of space and may impede ease of movement and visibility for the teacher and students.
- **Flexible**—This classroom provides students with a variety of options for seating choices throughout the classroom, such as bean bag chairs, exercise balls, or floor seating. This option is beneficial for supporting students' individual learning needs, as they can choose to sit where they learn best. Flexible seating also supports collaborative learning and contributes to a welcoming, positive classroom climate. However, unstructured seating may lend itself to student distraction and limit student-teacher visibility during direct instruction.
- **Runway**—Desks in this classroom are arranged in rows on either side of the room with students facing the center, leaving the middle space clear for the teacher. This is useful for direct instruction, as students can easily see the teacher and class presentations, and the teacher can monitor whether each student is on task. This method also facilitates whole-class discussions. This arrangement is generally not suited for collaborative work, as students cannot easily face those seated near them, and it may limit the teacher's ability to provide individual assistance.
- **Conference**—All desks in this classroom are arranged in a large, two-by-two rectangle situated in the middle of the room with students facing one another. This arrangement is beneficial for collaborative work, whole-class activities, and class discussions, as students can easily face one another. The teacher can generally provide individual assistance and can easily monitor whether students are on task. However, the physical size of the classroom may not facilitate this arrangement. In addition, this method may lead to student distraction during individual work.

Classroom Seating Arrangements

Stadium Seating

Cluster Seating

Rows and Columns

Horseshoe

Miniature Horseshoes

Pairs

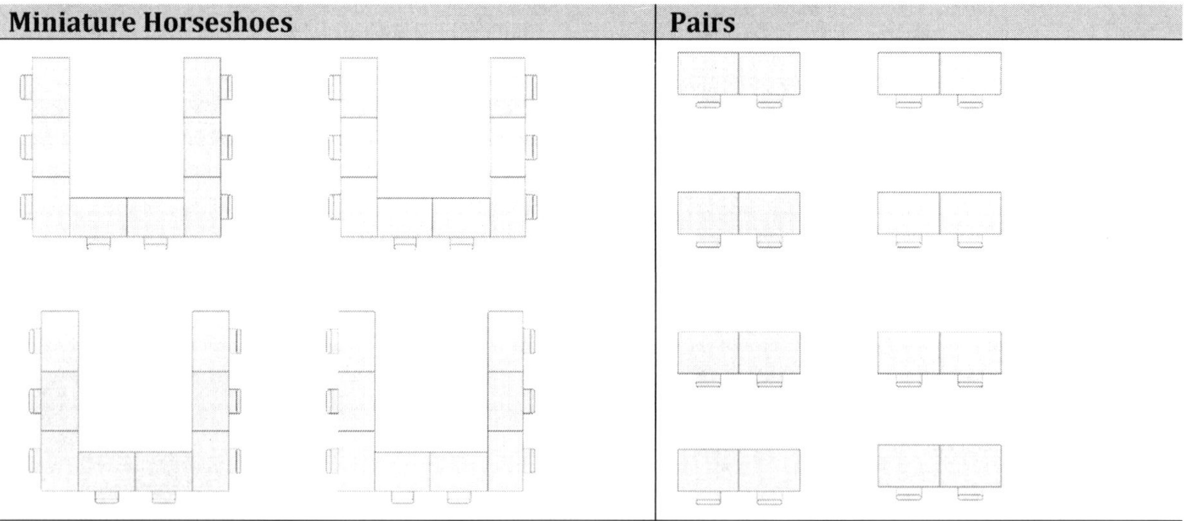

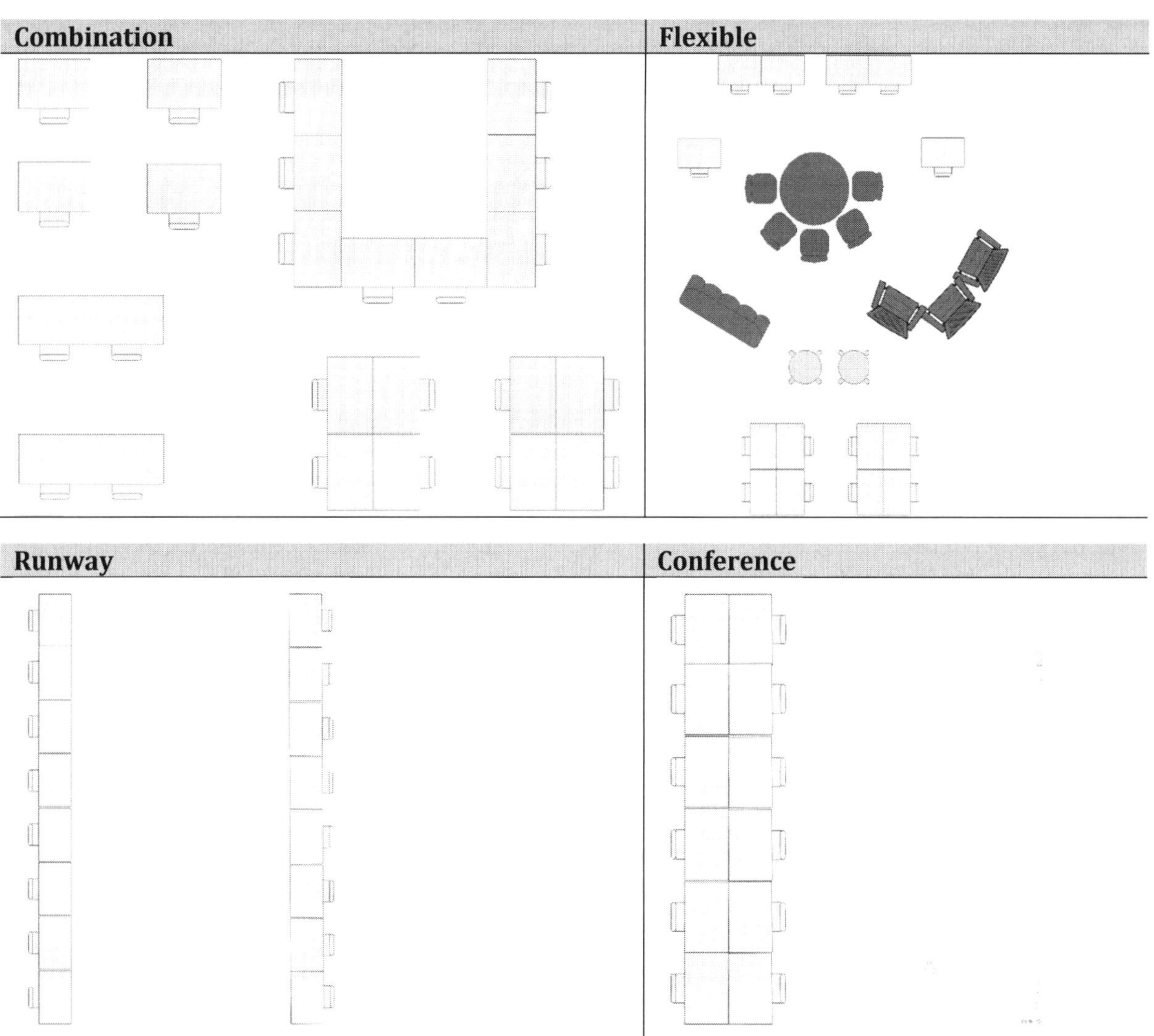

Classroom Organization Ensuring Accessibility and Facilitates Learning

Strategic classroom organization is necessary to ensure physical accessibility for all students and facilitating learning across instructional contexts. Students' **height, size**, and **special needs** must be considered and addressed when determining physical classroom arrangement. All furniture, equipment, and necessary materials must be equally accessible and facilitate ease of movement for all students as they participate in learning activities. Some students may require individualized **physical accommodations** to support their learning, such as preferential seating, special furniture arrangements to enable physical accessibility, or access to technology. By instilling these supports into the organization of the classroom, the teacher establishes an equitable environment that supports learning across instructional contexts. The classroom must be arranged to ensure all students have **visibility** and access to the teacher, as well as pertinent instructional information and resources, including the projector screen, chalk board, and computers. The physical environment must be aligned to and facilitative of the style of instruction taking place while supporting students' individual needs in achieving learning goals. When the teacher ensures that the classroom environment is physically accessible to all students, they empower students to engage in learning across instructional contexts successfully.

Behavior Management Theory

Managing and Monitoring Student Behavior

Behaviorism and Conditioning

The theoretical school of **behaviorism** was established by John B. Watson and further developed by Ivan Pavlov and B.F. Skinner. Behaviorism emphasizes the role of environmental and experiential learning in the behavior of animals and humans. Simply put, if a person experiences a desirable result from a particular behavior, that person is more likely to perform the behavior in pursuit of the result. Likewise, undesirable results cause a person to avoid performing an associated behavior. This process of **reinforcing** or rewarding good behaviors and **punishing** unwanted behaviors is known as conditioning. Behaviorists use the terms positive and negative to refer to the mode of conditioning. The term **positive** refers to an added stimulus, such as giving a child a treat as positive reinforcement or giving added homework as positive punishment. **Negative**, on the other hand refers to removing a stimulus, such as taking recess away as a negative punishment, or taking away extra classwork as negative reinforcement for students performing their homework independently. In the classroom, the teacher has the opportunity to help students learn to meet specific behavioral expectations. The tools of behaviorism may be carefully employed in the classrooms through positive and negative punishments and rewards. Classroom rules and expectations should be made clear as soon as possible and reinforced through verbal praise, prizes, or special privileges. Likewise, negative behaviors should be discouraged through verbal warnings, loss of privileges, and communication with the family or administrators when necessary.

Choice Theory

Choice theory, developed by **William Glasser**, states that behavior is chosen, either consciously or unconsciously, to meet the **five basic needs** of survival, love and belonging, power, freedom, and fun. Rather than implement positive and negative reinforcements to drive behavior, the teacher must aim to teach students self-responsibility for their actions. This includes encouraging students to reflect and consider the reasons for their actions and attempt to rectify any misbehavior. This method relies on the notion that if students understand how their desire to meet certain needs impacts their actions, they are more likely to engage in positive behavior. In the classroom, the teacher focuses on meeting students' **five basic needs** to encourage positive behavior by creating a classroom climate that emphasizes **communication, relationship building**, and **self-reflection**. This includes establishing positive relationships with students, holding class discussions, and teaching conflict resolution skills to create a safe, welcoming learning environment. Instructional activities are tailored to individual needs, and students have a great deal of choice in their own learning with the intention of promoting positive behavior by meeting their needs for power and freedom.

Assertive Discipline Theory

The **Assertive Discipline theory** was developed by **Lee** and **Marlene Canter**. This theory states that the teacher is in charge of **instruction**, **the classroom**, and **students' behavior**. The expectation is that the teacher establishes clear behavioral standards that protect their right to teach and students' right to learn without distraction or disruption. Negative consequences for unwanted behavior are instilled to deter students from deviating from behavioral expectations. This theory argues that if teachers are viewed as firm and consistent, students will have a greater respect for them and ultimately engage in positive behavior. In the classroom, the teacher is in control of **establishing** and **consistently reinforcing** standards for student behavior. This establishes a sense of predictability, as students are clear on what is expected of them as they engage in learning. Students are expected to comply with the teacher's expectations, and a system of **negative consequences** are in place to discourage unwanted behavior. Positive behavior is rewarded to further reinforce desired behavior. The teacher in this classroom believes that creating such an environment enhances students' ability to focus on learning without disruption.

Student-Directed Learning Theory

The **Student-Directed Learning theory**, or the idea of the **Democratic Classroom**, was founded by **Alfie Kohn** and emphasizes the importance of **student choice** and **classroom community** in influencing behavior. This includes having students contribute to the development of behavioral expectations, as this helps students understand their purpose while instilling a sense of ownership and accountability. Instructional activities are tailored to accommodate students' individual interests and natural curiosity while emphasizing cooperation to foster an engaging learning environment that promotes positive behavior. This theory focuses on eliciting students' intrinsic motivation to engage in positive behavior, rather than relying on positive and negative reinforcements. In the classroom, students primarily direct their own learning based upon their **natural curiosity** while the teacher acts as a **facilitator**. Students contribute to the development of behavioral expectations that are instilled to promote respect and focus on learning. **Active engagement**, **cooperation**, and **collaborative learning** are emphasized over direct instruction. Students may be engaging in differing activities simultaneously as the teacher moves around the classroom to monitor progress and assist as necessary.

Social Learning Theory and Behavior Management

The **Social Learning theory**, developed by **Albert Bandura**, asserts that one's **environment** and the **people** within it heavily influence behavior. As humans are social creatures, they learn a great deal by **observing** and **imitating** one another. This theory is also rooted in the importance of **self-efficacy** in achieving desired behavior, as students must be motivated and confident that they can effectively imitate what they observe. In the classroom, the teacher establishes behavioral expectations and focuses on **modeling** positive behaviors, attitudes, and interactions with the intention of encouraging students to do the same. The teacher recognizes and praises positive behavior from students to elicit the same behavior from others. The teacher also emphasizes a growth mindset in the classroom to promote students' sense of self-efficacy.

Behavior Standards and Expectations for Students at Developmental Levels

Behavioral standards that emphasize respect for oneself, others, and property are necessary in creating a safe, positive, and productive learning environment for students of all ages. However, as students at varying developmental levels differ in their capabilities across domains, behavioral expectations must be **realistic**, **applicable**, and reflect an **awareness** of these **differences** while encouraging growth. Young children, for example, are learning to interact with others and function in a group setting. Behavioral expectations must be attuned to this understanding while promoting the development of positive interpersonal skills. Young children also require ample opportunities for active movement and cannot reasonably be expected to sit still for long periods of time. Middle level students are at a unique transitional period in their development and often exhibit characteristics of both young children and adolescents. Behavioral standards for these students must recognize the significant social, emotional, cognitive, and physical changes occurring at this stage by emphasizing self-control, emotional regulation, and positive interactions. As older students prepare for adulthood, they can generally be expected to conduct themselves with a degree of maturity and responsibility in a variety of settings. Appropriate behavioral standards for these students emphasize self-responsibility, respectful interactions, and independently completing necessary tasks.

EFFECTIVE MANAGEMENT OF STUDENT BEHAVIOR

MANAGEMENT PROCEDURES AND SIGNIFICANCE IN POSITIVE, PRODUCTIVE, AND ORGANIZED LEARNING ENVIRONMENT

Promoting **appropriate behavior** and **ethical work habits** while taking specific measures to **manage student behavior** creates a safe, organized, and productive classroom. Such an environment is beneficial for students' motivation, engagement, and ability to focus on learning. This is achieved by communicating and consistently reinforcing **high**, yet **realistic behavioral expectations** for all students. This, when combined with **relationship building** strategies, establishes a positive rapport between the teacher and students that encourages appropriate behavior and ethical work habits. Students are more inclined to adhere to expectations for behavior and work habits when their relationship with the teacher is founded on mutual understanding and respect. In addition, students that feel they are a part of developing academic and behavioral expectations feel a greater sense of **ownership** and responsibility to follow them, and, therefore, it is beneficial to include students in this process. Encouraging students to **self-monitor** their behavior and utilize conflict resolution strategies furthers this sense of accountability, as it prompts students to positively manage their own actions and work habits. Misbehavior must be addressed appropriately and in a timely manner, and consequences must follow a logical sequence, such as a verbal warning, followed by loss of privileges or communication with family.

Review Video: Student Behavior Management Approaches
Visit mometrix.com/academy and enter code: 843846

Review Video: Promoting Appropriate Behavior
Visit mometrix.com/academy and enter code: 321015

STRATEGIES

Proactively implementing effective behavior management strategies is beneficial to establishing and maintaining a positive, productive learning environment. The **physical environment** should be arranged in such a way that facilitates ease of movement while limiting the amount of free space that could encourage student disruption. Planning for **smooth transitions** from one activity to the next further discourages behavioral disruptions. Desks should be arranged so that students can easily view the teacher, projector, chalkboard, or other information pertinent to learning. Expectations for behavior, procedures, and routines, including consequences, should be predictable, consistent, succinct, and visible at all times. Allowing students to participate in the development of classroom procedures and routines is valuable in providing students with a sense of personal accountability that increases the likelihood that they will follow them. Students also often respond well to incentives for modeling appropriate behavior, such as a **PBIS reward system**, verbal praise, or a positive phone call home. Nonverbal strategies are valuable in subtly managing student behavior throughout instruction, such as hand gestures, proximity, or eye contact. Misbehavior should be addressed discreetly and privately so as to avoid embarrassing the student or encouraging further disruption.

IMPORTANCE OF CONSISTENCY

Standards for behavior must be enforced consistently in order to establish a well-managed classroom in which students can focus on learning. This includes communicating **clear expectations**, holding all students equally accountable with specific **positive and negative consequences**, and **following through** on implementing them. In doing so, the teacher ensures that students are always aware of the behavior expected from them, and what will happen if they do not adhere to the standards. When students are clear regarding behavioral expectations and assured that they will be enforced, they are more inclined to demonstrate appropriate conduct. This creates a predictable, secure environment that promotes student motivation, engagement, and focused productivity in learning. Consistently enforcing behavior standards gives the teacher a sense of credibility among students, and therefore, students are more likely to respect and adhere to these expectations. In addition, holding all students to the same high behavioral standards contributes to a positive classroom climate in which all students feel they are treated fairly.

Materials and Resources

Materials and Resources That Enhance Student Learning and Engagement

Instructional Materials and Resources

The careful selection of instructional materials and resources for lesson plans is an integral component of enhancing student engagement and the overall learning experience. Lesson materials should be relevant to students' interests so as to facilitate personal connections to learning and ultimately, deepen understanding. In building positive relationships with students by educating themselves on students' backgrounds and interests, teachers can effectively locate and implement varied instructional materials and resources that are relevant to students and foster motivation for learning. Additionally, interactive materials, such as manipulatives or other hands-on learning resources, enhance learning and engagement through encouraging participation. Similarly, cooperative learning materials encourage student participation, and therefore, engagement, through fostering collaboration. Teachers can also enhance learning experiences through incorporating authentic materials that are relevant to instruction such as maps, brochures, historical documents, or similar materials that enhance student engagement and learning.

Technological Resources

Technology is integrated in nearly every aspect of life as a tool to enhance and assist in daily activities. This notion also applies in the classroom, as technological resources are an excellent method of increasing student engagement and interest, supporting students in their individual learning needs, and ultimately, enhancing learning. The use of computers, tablets, smartphones, and other technological resources serve to improve understanding of classroom instruction, foster relevancy and personal connections, and scaffold instruction to address diverse learning styles and needs. Additionally, teachers have myriad digital resources available in the form of interactive websites, videos clips, and apps that can be implemented to enrich lessons and increase development across all subject areas. Often, these resources accommodate students' individual learning needs through providing increasingly challenging activities based on individual skill level, and therefore, the teacher can utilize these resources to tailor instruction to address individual student needs. Technological resources can also add authenticity to learning experiences, making them more engaging and enhancing student learning. Virtual field trips or science experiments can provide real-world connections to instruction by recreating authentic learning experiences without students having to leave the classroom.

Community Resources

Community resources are beneficial in enriching instruction to foster engagement and enhance student learning. They provide students the opportunity to connect and apply what they learn in the classroom with the real world. This ultimately makes learning more authentic, as students are able to see the relevancy of what they are learning, and therefore, enhances learning by making it more engaging. Through field trips, teachers can incorporate community resources such as museums, art exhibits, science centers, and even local areas such as parks or historical sites into curriculum to accompany material learned in class. Additionally, if access to field trips is limited, teachers can take advantage of community outreach programs that bring learning experiences to classrooms. Reaching out to members of the community that are relevant to topics being covered in class, such as scientists or local historians, can be beneficial in allowing students to understand how what they are learning is applicable outside of the classroom. Locating and implementing community resources enhances student learning and engagement through making learning authentic, relevant, and applicable in the real world.

Developmentally Appropriate Materials and Resources

To create engaging and effective learning experiences, instructional materials and resources must be developmentally appropriate. Teachers must have a solid understanding of the general cognitive, physical, social, and emotional developmental levels of their students, as well as individual differences in skills and abilities to properly select developmentally appropriate materials. The age and developmental level appropriateness of instructional resources can be determined by considering the material's size, height, and level of difficulty for students. Whether materials accommodate individual differences in skill level, ability, or interest can be determined by their versatility. If a resource can be used in multiple ways, it will appeal to a variety of learning needs and interests and support development across domains. Developmentally appropriate materials are reflective and considerate of students' diversities. Teachers can determine this by using their knowledge of students' backgrounds to select materials that incorporate and are sensitive to their students' cultural differences to support development by fostering personal connections to learning.

Chapter Quiz

Ready to see how well you retained what you just read? Scan the QR code to go directly to the chapter quiz interface for this study guide. If you're using a computer, simply visit the bonus page at **mometrix.com/bonus948/nystceeas** and click the Chapter Quizzes link.

NYSTCE Practice Test #1

Want to take this practice test in an online interactive format?
Check out the bonus page, which includes interactive practice questions and much more: **mometrix.com/bonus948/nystceeas**

Diverse Student Populations

Refer to the following for questions 1 - 12:

Exhibit 1

Class Description

Mr. Morris has recently moved to a new city and begun teaching 8th-grade social studies. The school population is ethnically diverse, and Mr. Morris is unfamiliar with the backgrounds, customs, beliefs, and experiences of his students and their families. However, he is determined to build positive relationships and learn how to best meet the needs of his students and the community.

At the beginning of the school year, Mr. Morris reaches out to the administration regarding professional development opportunities that focus on methods for effectively teaching students of varying cultural backgrounds, and he self-educates regarding the priorities of his new community. He also attends the school's open-house night in order to meet his students' families and gain insight into their home lives and individual learning needs. In addition, Mr. Morris plans to involve himself in the school community by participating in such activities as PTA meetings and fundraisers and attending school sporting events. In the classroom, Mr. Morris focuses on creating a positive classroom community by conducting team-building exercises, icebreaker activities, and learning-style inventories to get to know his students. He creates a classroom newsletter and website to communicate important updates and intends to maintain frequent communication with families via conferences, phone calls, and emails.

Prior to beginning his first unit on the contributions and experiences of different immigrant groups throughout American history, Mr. Morris administers a diagnostic exam on the topic to assess his students' level of understanding. The results indicate a wide range of knowledge and abilities. Mr. Morris considers these results when planning lessons in an effort to proactively meet his students' needs by implementing the most effective instructional strategies and supports. He plans to deliver instruction through a variety of means, including presentations, class discussions, and hands-on activities, as well as opportunities for individual and small-group work in which struggling students are paired with others that can provide assistance. In addition, Mr. Morris carefully researches and seeks examples from the community that demonstrate positive contributions to today's society from varying immigrant groups. Throughout instruction, Mr. Morris conducts formative assessments to evaluate understanding and overall engagement in order to reflect upon and determine areas in which his instructional approaches may need adjustment to better support his students.

EXHIBIT 2

EXCERPT FROM MR. MORRIS'S LESSON PLAN

Topic: Immigration

Standard: Compare and contrast the experiences of different groups in the United States. Explain the contributions of specific groups to American society and culture (NYCCLS – 4.7a).

Essential Question:

- How have different immigrant groups contributed to shaping American society and culture throughout history?
- How do the experiences of early immigrants compare to those of recent immigrants?

Lesson Objectives:

- Students will be able to compare and contrast the experiences of early and recent immigrant groups in the United States.
- Students will be able to discuss ways in which early and recent immigrant groups have contributed to American society and culture.

Grouping: Students will be arranged in groups of three to five. The teacher will determine student groupings.

Lesson Component	Activity
Introduction	Students will be shown a political cartoon that refers to the United States as a melting pot. Students will be asked to discuss what they think that term means and how it applies to today's society. Students will then see a presentation on early immigrants to the United States, such as those from Ireland, Germany, and England, as well as recent immigrant groups from China, Vietnam, and Latin America. Throughout the presentation, the teacher will give examples of ways in which each group has influenced American society and culture, such as food, clothing, and music.
Individual Activity	Students will conduct independent online research regarding the contributions and experiences of a specific immigrant group that the teacher will assign. Some students will be assigned to research the same immigrant group for a later collaborative assignment.
Small-Group Activity	Students will work in groups of three to five with others that researched the same immigrant group. Working collaboratively, students will create a visual representation of their choosing (chart, comic strip, slideshow, skit, etc.) to depict their research findings. Members of each group will be assigned a specific role and present their visual representation to the class in a two- to three-minute presentation.
Whole-Group Activity	The teacher will lead a class discussion focused on comparing and contrasting the experiences and contributions of early versus recent immigrant groups in the United States. Throughout the discussion, the teacher will record key points on the chalkboard using a Venn diagram.
Extension/Enrichment	Gifted students will have the opportunity to extend their research on their assigned immigrant group by applying what they learned and imagining they are immigrating to the United States. These students will be asked to create a series of diary entries that detail their initial experiences based upon their research findings.

EXHIBIT 3

NOTES FROM MR. MORRIS'S FORMATIVE ASSESSMENTS

DIAGNOSTIC EXAM

The diagnostic exam results indicate that most students possess basic knowledge of recent immigrant groups, but very limited understanding of the experiences and contributions of early immigrants. Extra focus on early immigrant populations may need to be included in the introductory presentation. While most students demonstrated appropriate grade-level reading comprehension skills, many were unfamiliar with key vocabulary related to the unit, and a few students indicated below grade-level reading comprehension skills. These students will need extra supports in the form of visual aids, graphic organizers, and selective grouping during instructional activities. Three students performed extremely well on the assessment. Extra learning opportunities for enrichment will be beneficial for these students.

Introduction

The presentation included slides, images, video clips, and opportunities for students to answer open-ended questions. During the presentation, I moved around the room to assess students' level of attentiveness. Students appeared to be the most interested in viewing the images and video clips, and most were highly engaged in the open-ended questioning segment of the lesson. A few students in the back of the classroom, who indicated low reading comprehension skills on the diagnostic exam, appeared bored throughout the presentation. I used proximity and maintained eye contact to redirect their focus. Students were asked periodically throughout the presentation to indicate their level of understanding by giving a "thumbs-up" or "thumbs-down" sign. If the majority of students showed a "thumbs-down" sign, I reviewed previous presentation slides and provided extra examples. Overall, students seemed to respond well and were most enthusiastic about the real-world examples of contributions from immigrant groups in everyday life.

Individual Activity

Each student was given a color-coded card to indicate their level of understanding as they conducted independent research. One side of the cards was green, and the other was red. Students were instructed to flip their cards to the red side when they needed assistance or clarification. During the activity, I moved throughout the room and stopped to help students that flipped their card to the red side. This method seemed to work well for students that do not typically ask for help.

Small-Group Activity

Throughout the small-group activity, I moved between groups to listen to student discussions, ask questions, address misconceptions, and ensure all students were on task. Assigning specific roles to group members appears to have helped maintain group focus. Struggling students seemed to be more engaged and productive when paired with others that could provide assistance.

Exit Ticket

Students were instructed to write down three new things they learned, two questions they had for further exploration, and one way in which their culture has positively contributed to shaping American society and culture as preparation for a long-term project. Most students appeared to have a firm understanding of the key points of the lesson. A few students, however, seemed to have struggled with differentiating the experiences between specific immigrant populations. This will be reviewed in the next lesson for clarification. Questions for further exploration were primarily focused on reasons why different groups of people immigrated to the United States, which will be addressed in a future lesson.

1. Which of the following strategies best demonstrates Mr. Morris's efforts to get to know his students and promote a positive classroom community?

a. Delivering instruction through a variety of methods and allowing for student choice to engage all styles of learners
b. Planning a unit on the experiences and contributions of various immigrant groups to connect with students of varying cultures
c. Leading team-building exercises and icebreaker activities, establishing communication with families, and seeking professional development
d. Administering a diagnostic exam to evaluate students' prior knowledge before beginning the unit

2. Establishing and maintaining frequent communication with students' families through a variety of means is most likely to have which of the following effects?

a. Mr. Morris's efforts will reflect positively on his end-of-year evaluation by administration.
b. Families with varying work schedules, dynamics, and living situations will have access to important classroom information and will feel included in the learning process.
c. Students' families will gain access to daily updates regarding their child's grades.
d. Mr. Morris will gain a better understanding of the needs of the community in which he teaches.

3. Which of the following is an additional strategy Mr. Morris could have used to incorporate students' cultural backgrounds into the unit for a more authentic and engaging learning experience?

a. Encouraged students to share examples of their own culture's contributions to American society and culture in a class discussion
b. Included authentic historical documents that recount the experiences of individuals from specific immigrant groups
c. Instructed students to compare and contrast their own cultural experiences with those of an early immigrant group
d. Included images of famous individuals from early and recent immigrant groups

4. By incorporating opportunities for enrichment and extension, Mr. Morris does which of the following?

a. Prevents students that finish early from engaging in off-task or disruptive behavior
b. Strengthens students' understanding of diversity and its significance in shaping American society and culture
c. Provides gifted and talented students with extra work while they wait for their classmates to catch up
d. Acknowledges the learning needs of gifted and talented students by challenging them academically and intellectually

5. Keeping notes on students' responses to formative assessments is most beneficial for which of the following reasons?

a. Mr. Morris can reflect upon the effectiveness of his instructional strategies, interactions with students, and overall engagement to guide further instruction.
b. Mr. Morris can keep track of pacing when delivering instruction and transitioning between learning activities.
c. Mr. Morris can use this information to update families on their children's strengths and areas for improvement.
d. Mr. Morris can proactively implement strategies to prevent student distraction during instructional time.

6. Inquiring of the administration regarding professional development opportunities focused on teaching students from varying cultural backgrounds demonstrates which of the following?

a. The desire to gain insight into his students' values, beliefs, backgrounds, and experiences
b. The desire to develop cultural competence when delivering instruction and when communicating with students and their families to enhance the learning experience
c. The intention to incorporate students' diversity into the classroom and encourage the appreciation of cultural differences
d. The desire to refine his professional skills and pedagogical knowledge

7. Which of Mr. Morris's instructional strategies best demonstrates his incorporation of universal design principles?

a. Allowing opportunities for student choice, scaffolding instruction, implementing learning supports, delivering instruction through a variety of means, and selecting student groupings
b. Administering a diagnostic exam, conducting formative assessments, leading a class discussion, and incorporating opportunities for individual, small-group, and whole-class activities
c. Assigning an exit ticket, instructing students to consider additional questions for further exploration, and incorporating authentic examples of the contributions of specific immigrant groups
d. Instructing students to conduct independent research, selecting student groups, pairing students with others that could provide assistance, and applying the results of the diagnostic exam to lesson planning

8. Which of Mr. Morris's instructional strategies were likely most effective in enhancing the learning experience by incorporating authentic examples to promote appreciation for diverse groups of people?

a. Using a variety of methods to teach students about the experiences and contributions of various immigrant groups
b. Incorporating examples from the students' community that demonstrate how the contributions of immigrant groups influence everyday life
c. Arranging students in small groups to discuss the experiences and contributions of specific immigrant groups
d. Instructing students to conduct online research about the experiences and contributions of a specific immigrant group

9. Which of the following is an additional benefit to teacher-selected groupings when considering the culturally diverse nature of Mr. Morris's students?

a. Mr. Morris was able to effectively manage student behavior by ensuring disruptive students were not grouped together.
b. Mr. Morris was able to ensure students were assigned to research a diverse range of immigrant groups.
c. Mr. Morris was able to more effectively conduct formative assessments to evaluate student understanding.
d. Mr. Morris was able to assign culturally heterogenous groups to expose students to diverse perspectives.

10. By varying instructional strategies and incorporating learning supports, Mr. Morris does which of the following?

a. Ensures that students of varying abilities feel safe, accepted, and included in all parts of the learning process
b. Ensures that his lesson plan will last the duration of the class period to prevent idle time
c. Demonstrates cultural competence when planning lessons
d. Accommodates ELL students with varying levels of English language proficiency

11. Which of the following is the most likely reason that the students in the back of the classroom appeared disengaged in the lesson?

a. The presentation lacked authenticity and meaningful examples to make learning relevant.
b. Mr. Morris's teaching style did not match these students' learning styles.
c. The text within the presentation was too complex for their reading comprehension abilities and Mr. Morris did not provide sufficient scaffolding.
d. These students were situated in the back of the classroom and could not properly see the presentation.

12. After analyzing the information provided, write a response of approximately 150 to 200 words in which you:

- Describe an additional way that Mr. Morris could strengthen students' appreciation for diverse groups of people within his unit.
- Discuss one strategy Mr. Morris could implement in a future lesson to achieve this.
- Explain how doing so would strengthen students' understanding of the experiences and contributions of early and recent immigrants to the United States.

English Language Learners

Refer to the following for questions 13 - 24:

Exhibit 1

Class Description

Ms. Fisher is a fifth-grade teacher to a class of 28 students. The cultural demographic of her school is primarily Hispanic, and most of her students speak Spanish at home. While most of her students are bilingual and have grown up speaking both Spanish and English equally, assessment data indicates that twelve students meet the criteria to be considered English language learners (ELLs). Of these twelve students, four demonstrated advanced English language proficiency skills, six scored within the intermediate range, and two possess beginner-level English language proficiency skills. These two students have also demonstrated below grade-level literacy skills. Ms. Fisher has also learned that one of her beginner-level students has recently moved to the United States and has had minimal previous formal education.

Ms. Fisher does her best to support her ELL students in English language acquisition and proficiency. She works closely with the school ELL teacher to determine language skill goals for each student, and she provides regular updates regarding students' progress and upcoming units of instruction. Ms. Fisher's classroom is decorated with a variety of labels, word walls, lists, and anchor charts to promote vocabulary acquisition. She has also recently created a classroom library that includes multiple texts with varying levels of complexity to encourage literacy development.

Ms. Fisher incorporates as many linguistic supports as possible into her instruction, including visual representations, body language, gestures, and supplemental Spanish vocabulary words to help provide clarification.

Ms. Fisher is preparing to teach an English language arts lesson on identifying theme within a text. Prior to beginning instruction, she creates an anchor chart that includes the definition of theme, an explanation of strategies for locating supporting details, and vocabulary words that can be used to describe a theme. She plans to incorporate opportunities for whole-class and small-group activities for this lesson. Ms. Fisher also intends to keep a journal to reflect upon the effectiveness of her teaching strategies in supporting her ELL students' language and literacy development.

EXHIBIT 2

EXCERPT FROM MS. FISHER'S LESSON PLAN

Topic: Theme	
Standard: Determine a theme or central idea and explain how it is supported by key details; summarize a text (NYCCLS – 5R2).	
Essential Question: • How do I determine the theme of a text? • How do details in a text help support the overall theme?	
Lesson Objectives: Students will be able to identify theme by locating supporting details within the text.	
Grouping: Students will work together in self-selected groups of three to five for a portion of the lesson.	
Lesson Component	Activity
Introduction	Students will be shown a simple poem on the projector screen. The teacher will read it aloud and ask students to identify specific words or lines that evoke a feeling and will highlight the portions that students select. Students will then see a presentation that explains theme and how to determine theme from details within a text. After the presentation, the teacher will ask students to describe the theme of the poem based on the supporting evidence they found.
Individual Activity	Students will be assigned to read a text independently, identify the theme, and circle three supporting examples. The teacher will then lead a class discussion in which students share their findings. Three versions of the same text that vary in complexity will be provided to accommodate ELL students' varying abilities, and all students will receive an English and Spanish version of the text.
Small-Group Activity 1	Students will be assigned to complete a set of 10 task cards in which they read a short passage and identify the theme. Students will have the choice to work independently, in pairs, or in small groups of three to four students.
Small-Group Activity 2	Students will work in groups of three to five and will be assigned a particular theme. Students will work together in creating a product of their choosing (story, comic strip, poem, etc.) that demonstrates their assigned theme with three supporting details. Students will present their final product to the class.
Accommodations	• Key vocabulary words in the presentation will be in English and Spanish. • The poem reading and presentation will include visual representations. • English and Spanish versions of the text will be provided during the individual activity. • Extra time will be allotted as necessary for instructional activities. • English-Spanish dictionaries will be available. • Graphic organizers will be used during the second small-group activity.

Exhibit 3

Excerpt from Ms. Fisher's Reflection Journal

Day 1

Today, I introduced the concept of theme by reading students a poem, leading a discussion, and showing a presentation. Reading the poem aloud worked well for maintaining students' attention, and many were able to recall specific portions that evoked a feeling during the discussion. Embedding Spanish vocabulary words within the presentation seemed especially helpful to my intermediate ELL students. I noticed my beginner-level ELL students were quiet during the discussion portion, however, and eventually seemed to lose interest. These same students did not complete the individual activity.

Day 2

Today, students worked alone or collaboratively to complete a set of task cards to practice identifying the theme of a text. English-Spanish dictionaries were available for students to use when clarification was needed. The texts within the task card set varied in complexity, and while many students did well, my intermediate ELLs began to struggle with the more complicated texts. When I noticed this, I went over to them to explain unfamiliar vocabulary words. Most students seemed to enjoy the activity, but a few quickly became off task and had to be redirected.

Day 3

Students were asked to work in groups to create a product of their choosing that demonstrated an assigned theme. Students were allowed to choose their groups, and most decided to work with others whom they knew very well. Some students had to be redirected a few times, as they began to get off topic, but overall, most seemed to enjoy the chance to create their own product. Graphic organizers appeared to help all students organize their ideas. My intermediate ELL students asked a few questions for clarification and referred to their English-Spanish dictionaries several times. My beginner ELLs needed a great deal of assistance throughout the activity. I plan to ask the ELL teacher for some strategies to help these students in future collaborative assignments.

Day 4

Each student group was asked to present their work to the class and explain the overall theme of the product they created. In almost all presentations, native English speakers and advanced ELL students did most of the talking. My intermediate and especially my beginner-level ELL students were quiet and avoided eye contact with the rest of the class throughout their group's presentation.

13. Some of Ms. Fisher's students have grown up speaking both Spanish and English at home and are therefore fluent in both languages. This is an example of which of the following?

a. Coordinate bilingualism
b. Compound bilingualism
c. Late bilingualism
d. Sub-coordinate bilingualism

14. Which of the following additional strategies could Ms. Fisher have implemented in her lesson to provide her ELL students with linguistic support?

a. Requested a paraprofessional to provide individualized instruction
b. Presented the entire lesson in both English and Spanish
c. Assigned student groups strategically to ensure lower-level ELLs were paired with students of more advanced English language proficiency skills
d. Allowed students to present their work in English or Spanish according to their linguistic preference

15. Which of the following best explains why Ms. Fisher may share her lesson plans with the school ELL teacher?

a. To ensure that her lesson plans and accommodations are aligned with legal requirements pertaining to educating ELL students
b. To allow the school ELL teacher to review key vocabulary and concepts with ELL students prior to the beginning of the unit, provide clarification, and set language acquisition goals
c. To give the school ELL teacher important data regarding her ELL students' abilities and progress
d. To allow the school ELL teacher to prepare for individualized instruction for beginner-level students

16. Incorporating linguistic supports such as visual aids, graphic organizers, and modified texts to scaffold instruction demonstrates which of the following professional responsibilities in regard to teaching ELL students?

a. Adapting instruction as necessary to accommodate the linguistic needs of ELL students and ensure they are provided the support necessary to fully participate in learning
b. Giving ELL students easier instructional content to ensure their understanding
c. Implementing suggestions from the school ELL teacher to help these students reach language objectives
d. Providing ELL students with RTI services to help them catch up to their classmates academically

17. Which of the following best explains why Ms. Fisher's beginner-level ELL students demonstrated below grade-level literacy skills on their assessment?

a. Ms. Fisher's teaching style is incongruent with their learning preferences.
b. These students have limited or interrupted previous formal education.
c. Ms. Fisher did not provide them with adequate testing accommodations.
d. These students were experiencing testing anxiety.

18. Which of the following research-based strategies for promoting English language acquisition is evident in Ms. Fisher's classroom and instructional approach?

a. Differentiating instruction and allowing opportunities for student choice to accommodate varying learning styles
b. Providing individualized instruction and incorporating authentic materials
c. Applying knowledge of students' assessment data when planning instruction and learning activities
d. Creating a print- and literacy-rich environment, scaffolding instruction, and incorporating linguistic aids

19. Instructing students to create their own product to represent a theme is an example of which of the following beneficial strategies in teaching ELL students?

a. Authentic assessment
b. Differentiated instruction
c. Scaffolding instruction and providing linguistic aids
d. Teaching the whole child

20. Which of the following reasons most likely explains why some of Ms. Fisher's students were disengaged or off-task at various points throughout the lesson?

a. These students finished their work early and Ms. Fisher did not provide opportunities for enrichment or extension.
b. Ms. Fisher did not incorporate adequate modifications or scaffolds to the lesson activities.
c. Ms. Fisher is inconsistent with implementing behavior management strategies.
d. Students with limited English language proficiency skills had difficulty understanding the lesson and expectations during instructional activities.

21. Aside from providing clarification, which of the following is an additional benefit of including Spanish vocabulary words and translations throughout the lesson?

a. Ms. Fisher allowed ELL students to learn in the language in which they felt most comfortable.
b. Ms. Fisher demonstrated an awareness of the value of students' native language as an asset in learning a second language and its importance in promoting English literacy development.
c. Ms. Fisher practiced cultural competency and fostered personal connections to learning among her students.
d. Ms. Fisher provided her monolingual English-speaking students an opportunity to learn Spanish vocabulary.

22. Which of the following strategies should Ms. Fisher have implemented to further support her ELL students' English oral proficiency development?

a. Allowing these students to present their group work to the class in Spanish
b. Giving these students an alternative assignment that avoided speaking in front of the class
c. Letting students practice their presentations with the teacher or in a small-group setting prior to presenting in front of the class
d. Allowing these students to use note cards when presenting their work

23. Which of the following strategies could Ms. Fisher have implemented during the task card activity to accommodate varying linguistic abilities more effectively?

a. Created English and Spanish versions of the task cards
b. Provided an alternative assignment for lower- and intermediate-level ELL students
c. Created three separate versions of the task cards with varying levels of complexity
d. Allowed lower- and intermediate-level ELL students extra time to complete the assignment

24. After analyzing the information provided, write a response of approximately 150 to 200 words in which you:

- Identify one area in which Ms. Fisher could more effectively meet the needs of her ELL students to promote their English language skills and academic progress.
- Discuss some strategies she could implement to achieve this.
- Explain how implementing these strategies would promote ELL students' English language acquisition and academic achievement.

Students with Disabilities and Other Special Learning Needs

Refer to the following for questions 25 - 35:

Exhibit 1

Class Description

Ms. Patel is teaching a sixth-grade general education class of 25 students with varying abilities and learning needs. One student, Maya, has been diagnosed with ADHD and has an individualized education program (IEP). Ms. Patel works closely with Maya's special education teacher and is familiar with her accommodations, as well as academic and behavioral goals. Maya often has difficulty focusing on instruction, as she tends to fidget and speak out of turn and has trouble staying in her seat. She often rushes through her work, causing frequent errors. Maya is also behind the rest of her classmates in literacy development. She receives Tier 2 RTI services three times per week for 30 minutes each to help improve her reading comprehension skills and writing abilities.

Another student, Jordan, is able to see large objects and print, but is visually impaired. He often struggles to see words or images on the board, projector screen, or handouts. Jordan has a 504 plan that details the accommodations he needs to support him in learning effectively.

Ms. Patel has recently noticed that another student, Michael, tends to isolate himself from his classmates. He rarely interacts with others, avoids eye contact when spoken to, and appears frustrated when students near him are too loud. Michael loves to draw, and while he tries to make good grades, he often becomes distracted because he is focused on drawing in his sketchbook.

Ms. Patel is preparing to teach a lesson on the physical changes that occur when mixtures are combined or separated. As she plans her lesson and activities, Ms. Patel strives to implement the accommodations necessary to meet all of her students' learning needs. The school principal has scheduled a formal observation of this lesson.

Exhibit 2

Excerpt from Ms. Patel's Lesson Plan

Topic: Structures and properties of matter	
Standard: Plan and conduct an investigation to demonstrate that mixtures are a combination of substances (MS-PS1-8).	
Essential Question: What physical changes occur when mixtures are combined or separated?	
Lesson Objectives: Students will be able to investigate, identify, and explain the physical changes that occur when mixtures are combined or separated.	
Grouping: Students will work in teacher-assigned pairs for a portion of the lesson.	
Lesson Component	**Activity**
Introduction	Students will be shown a video clip from an educational science website that demonstrates what happens when various substances are combined or separated. The teacher will then conduct a physical demonstration by dissolving sugar in water. Students will be called upon to discuss their observations.
Individual Activity	Students will complete a worksheet in which they are given a list of relevant vocabulary words to look up and define using the glossary in their textbook. They will also be asked to use their textbooks to look up and list the steps of the scientific method.
Partner Activity 1	Students will work in pairs to conduct a scientific investigation in which they combine and separate a variety of mixtures. Students will devise a question and form a hypothesis prior to conducting the experiment. Each pair will then be provided the materials to filter sand from water, mix oil and water, and add food coloring to water. As students work, they will be asked to record their observations. Afterward, each student will analyze and discuss the results with their partner.
Partner Activity 2	Students will be asked to work with their partners to type up a conclusion in which they reflect upon the findings of their investigation.
Accommodations	• Preferential seating to limit distractions • Enlarged fonts for all printed activities • Photocopied and enlarged print for necessary textbook pages • Graphic organizers for second partner activity • Speech-to-text tool for second partner activity

Exhibit 3

Domain 1: Excerpt from Notes of Principal's Evaluation

1a. Demonstrating Knowledge of Content and Pedagogy

- Ms. Patel's lesson and instructional strategies demonstrate clear understanding of the content and are aligned with the developmental level of middle-school students.

1b. Demonstrating Knowledge of Students

- Ms. Patel asked students about their weekend at the beginning of class.
- Ms. Patel demonstrated knowledge of individual student needs. Accommodations were provided for individual students with disabilities, including enlarged print, graphic organizers, and allowing a visually impaired student to utilize a speech-to-text feature. A student with ADHD was seated at the front of the room close to Ms. Patel's desk.
- Instructional activities were aligned with middle-school developmental levels; the lesson included opportunities for collaboration and hands-on learning.

1E. Designing Coherent Instruction

- Ms. Patel's lesson was well structured. Her transitions were well prepared, and overall, students were aware of procedures for moving from one activity to the next. The student seated by herself took longer than her classmates to transition to the collaborative activity, as she stopped to talk with her friends, but after Ms. Patel redirected her, she moved to sit with her partner.
- The student seated by herself required frequent assistance and redirection throughout the lesson. She lost focus a few times during the individual activity and began engaging in social conversations during the collaborative portion. Ms. Patel helped this student and her partner significantly while they typed their conclusion essays.

Domain 2: Classroom Environment

2A. Creating an Environment of Respect and Rapport

- Ms. Patel interacts positively with all of her students, is very attentive, and demonstrates a genuine interest in their lives and academic achievement.
- Most students interacted well with each other. One student that was seated by himself in the back of the room seemed distant from his peers and unmotivated to participate in the collaborative activity. Ms. Patel went over to speak with him privately, and he ultimately moved to sit with his partner. However, he seemed uninterested in interacting with his classmate.

2D. Managing Student Behavior

- Classroom expectations and consequences are posted in the classroom and visible to students.
- Students that were on task throughout the lesson were given a ticket. Ms. Patel allows students to redeem these tickets periodically for various prizes.
- Most students were on task throughout the lesson. If students began to lose focus, Ms. Patel would give them a verbal warning and redirect their attention. The student seated at the front of the room had to be redirected at various points throughout the lesson. Ms. Patel eventually pulled her aside and spoke with her privately. Afterward, this student seemed to regain focus.

Domain 3: Instruction

3C. Engaging Students in Learning

- Ms. Patel demonstrates enthusiasm for the content and made genuine effort to engage students in learning.
- The student seated at the front of the room seemed to become frustrated while working with her partner to type their conclusion essay. She appeared to begin rushing through the assignment. Ms. Patel spent a great deal of time working with these students during this portion.
- The student that did not want to transition to the collaborative activity seemed to lose interest in the investigation after a few minutes and began drawing in his journal. Ms. Patel went over to him a couple of times to redirect his attention. He also seemed uninterested in working with his partner to write the conclusion essay.

3E. Demonstrating Flexibility and Responsiveness

- The student seated at the front of the room became fidgety during the video and demonstration and the individual activity. Ms. Patel gave her a stress ball to help her refocus her attention and help with fidgeting, and this seemed to help the student focus.

- Graphic organizers were provided for the second partner activity to allow students to organize and plan their ideas.
- Ms. Patel discreetly provided the visually impaired student with enlarged print for the individual activity.

25. Based on Ms. Patel's observations of Michael's behavior in class, she has the ethical responsibility to do which of the following?

a. Implement instructional strategies that are more engaging and aligned with Michael's learning style.
b. Consult the administration and refer him to the school special education department for further evaluation.
c. Schedule a conference with Michael's parents to discuss her concerns.
d. Consult other grade-level colleagues regarding strategies to more effectively support Michael in class.

26. The Family Educational Rights and Privacy Act (FERPA) mandates that Ms. Patel has the legal responsibility to enforce which of the following regulations regarding services for her students with disabilities?

a. Protect the confidentiality of these students both within and outside of the classroom, except in authorized situations.
b. Collaborate with the school special education teacher to ensure that her instruction provides these students with the appropriate accommodations.
c. Develop academic and behavioral goals for these students based upon their current skills and abilities.
d. Work with a team of special education professionals to develop an instructional plan that aligns with the needs of these students.

27. Which of the following best describes the intended benefit of providing Maya with RTI services for her literacy skills?

a. Maya will receive the accommodations detailed in her IEP necessary for facilitating fair access to education.
b. Maya will receive individualized instruction in an environment that helps increase her focus on learning.
c. Maya's standardized assessment scores will improve.
d. Maya will be provided additional support to improve her literacy skills outside of her special education services.

28. By integrating various accommodations and supports into her lesson, Ms. Patel does which of the following?

a. Provides her disabled students with easier assignments that are more tailored to their individual skill levels
b. Creates opportunities to observe her disabled students' academic progress as they engage in learning
c. Ensures that her lesson is fully prepared prior to the principal's observation
d. Demonstrates understanding of how to modify instruction to meet the individual needs of students with disabilities to give them equitable access to learning in the least restrictive environment

29. Based on the information provided about Maya, she is most likely to have difficulty during which portion of the lesson?

a. Productively collaborating with her classmates to conduct the scientific investigation
b. Writing the conclusion essay at the end of the lesson
c. Maintaining focus during Ms. Patel's demonstration of combining sugar and water
d. Effectively transitioning between instructional activities

30. Rewarding on-task students with tickets that they could redeem for prizes is an example of which strategy?

a. Positive Behavioral Interventions and Supports (PBIS)
b. Differentiated instruction
c. Appealing to students' internal motivation
d. Student-led learning

31. Based upon the information provided about Michael, he will likely need the most support during which portion of the lesson?

a. Transitioning between activities
b. Collaborating with his classmates during the investigation
c. Writing the conclusion essay
d. Locating vocabulary definitions in the textbook

32. By providing Jordan with enlarged print and speech-to-text technology, Ms. Patel does which of the following?

a. Adapts instruction to appeal to Jordan's learning style
b. Provides differentiated instruction to accommodate learners of varying abilities
c. Demonstrates knowledge of how to select appropriate materials, technology, and equipment to meet individualized needs of students with disabilities
d. Contributes to establishing a productive classroom environment

33. Which of the following was the most likely reason that Ms. Patel selected student pairs for the collaborative activity?

a. To maximize student productivity
b. To manage student behavior
c. To increase students' efficiency in transitioning between direct instruction and the scientific investigation
d. To strategically pair students in need of support with others in order to provide scaffolding

34. Which of the following is an additional accommodation that Ms. Patel could have implemented to further support Jordan's individual learning needs?

a. Extra time for processing
b. Preferential seating at the front of the room
c. Fewer distractions
d. Opportunities for breaks as necessary

35. After analyzing the information provided, write a response of approximately 150 to 200 words in which you:

- Identify an additional strategy that Ms. Patel could have implemented in her lesson to make it more engaging and accessible to students of varying abilities.
- Provide two specific examples of where she could have incorporated this strategy in her lesson.
- Explain why implementing this strategy would have increased engagement and helped meet the needs of individual students, particularly those with disabilities.

Teacher Responsibilities

36. A ninth-grade student has been involved in a physical fight with a classmate. Due to multiple previous behavioral infractions, the school has determined that a long-term suspension is an appropriate punishment for this student. According to federal law, this student is entitled to which of the following prior to being suspended?

a. The right to have his discipline records sealed to prevent future academic institutions from viewing them
b. Notice of a scheduled hearing at the school board in which the student can defend him or herself as part of due process
c. The option to have his discipline records amended
d. The right to request that personally identifiable information does not appear on his discipline records

37. Ms. Vo is preparing her eighth-grade class to take an end-of-year state assessment in English language arts. One of her students has been diagnosed with dyslexia and has an IEP that specifies accommodations. According to IDEA, the school is legally required to provide the student with which of the following?

a. Accommodations aligned with the student's IEP specifications to provide an equitable testing environment
b. An alternate location for testing in order to minimize distractions to the student
c. The opportunity to retake the assessment if the student's scores demonstrate below grade-level achievement
d. A modified version of the assessment with shorter reading passages and writing assignments

38. A fourth-grade teacher has noticed that one of her students is especially withdrawn lately and often seems anxious. This morning, the student came to class and had what appeared to be bruises on her arm. Based on this information, the teacher has the professional and legal responsibility to do which of the following?

a. Keep observing the student throughout the week to collect evidence
b. Call the students' parents to report the strange behavior and bruises
c. Pull the student aside after class and ask if they are being abused
d. Report her suspicions to the appropriate agency immediately

39. One of Mr. Green's fifth-grade students consistently has trouble focusing while in class. This student is often out of her seat, talks out of turn, and rarely finishes assignments. Despite Mr. Green's multiple efforts to redirect the student, her grades are suffering. He believes this student needs additional support in order to be successful in class. Which of the following describes the way Mr. Green could best advocate for this student?

a. Discuss this student's behavior with colleagues to develop more engaging instructional strategies to sustain her focus.
b. Communicate with this student's family to discuss disciplinary measures.
c. Schedule a meeting with the school administration and special education department to discuss his concerns.
d. Give this student shorter assignments to help her focus on completing her work.

40. One of Ms. Douglas's students has a failing grade after failing to turn in several assignments. The student's parents are angry that their child is failing in class and have requested a conference with Ms. Douglas, as they do not believe that their child has missed any assignments. Which of the following best describes the most appropriate way for Ms. Douglas to interact with these parents?

a. Promise to amend the student's grade with the agreement that the student will be more diligent in the future.
b. Refer the parents to the school administration to address their concerns.
c. Suggest that the parents contact the school special education department to discuss the need for an IEP.
d. Arrive promptly to the conference, listen and respond respectfully to the parents' concerns, and provide documentation from her gradebook that indicates the students' missing assignments.

School-Home Responsibilities

41. Which of the following best describes the effect of initiating and maintaining effective communication with students' families on student development and achievement?

a. Students' families will have access to weekly progress reports regarding their children's grades.
b. Students' families will feel welcomed and encouraged to participate in their children's education program.
c. The teacher will be able to establish a more culturally responsive learning environment.
d. Students' attendance rates will improve, fostering greater academic achievement.

42. Which of the following describes best practices for providing all families with access to communication regarding important classroom updates, information, and student progress?

a. Emailing students' families on an as-needed basis to inform them of their child's declining grades
b. Sending weekly notes home with students to communicate important updates
c. Communicating frequently through a variety of means, including newsletters, class websites, phone calls, emails, and handwritten notes
d. Leaving feedback in students' daily agenda books regarding their weekly progress in class

43. Which of the following strategies would likely be most effective in inviting students' families to share information regarding their children in order to enhance the learning experience?

a. Hosting an open-house night in which students' families are encouraged to attend and learn about the education program
b. Providing weekly updates regarding important classroom information via a newsletter and class website
c. Participating in professional development opportunities that focus on communication strategies with students' families
d. Scheduling conferences with students' families to discuss the education program, listen to their concerns, and collaborate in developing a plan to support the students' academic achievement

44. The sixth-grade team at a middle school has decided to host an open-house night in which they meet students' families, discuss curriculum, display student work, and let families ask questions and provide input regarding the education program. Which of the following will be the most likely result of this open-house event?

a. Families will feel encouraged to actively participate in decision-making related to the education program.
b. The sixth-grade teachers will be able to establish and maintain frequent communication with students' families more effectively.
c. The school administration will encourage other grade-level departments to host similar open-house events.
d. The sixth-grade team will be able to collaborate more effectively to meet their students' learning needs.

45. Every Friday, Ms. Garcia sends students home with a packet with resources related to content learned in class that week. These packets include extra practice activities, relevant websites and book titles, and activities that can be done at home to reinforce new concepts. She also posts this information on the class website each week. Which of the following best describes how this strategy will encourage students' families to reinforce learning at home?

a. Students' families will be able to evaluate their children's understanding of new concepts learned in class.
b. Students' families will be able to refresh their memories on the content in order to more effectively help their children.
c. Students' families will be more inclined to support their children's learning at home because they will have access to relevant resources and suggestions for helpful activities.
d. Students' families will be able to help their children prepare for upcoming assessments.

Answer Key and Explanations

Diverse Student Populations

1. C: Mr. Morris's efforts to get to know his students and their families establishes a foundation for open, positive communication that gives him insight into the backgrounds, experiences, interests, and learning needs of his students. This allows him to plan effective instruction that is tailored to his students' individual differences for maximized learning. In addition, by implementing team-building strategies, Mr. Morris promotes a positive classroom community focused on inclusiveness and acceptance of differences.

2. B: Communicating through a variety of means helps to ensure that important classroom updates, events, assignments, and information regarding students' progress is accessible to families of diverse circumstances. This creates a sense of inclusiveness that encourages families to become involved in their children's education, thus establishing a positive learning environment and increasing the likelihood that learning will be reinforced at home.

3. A: Encouraging students to share elements of their own culture's contributions to society fosters personal connections to learning that strengthen engagement and understanding. This strategy also encourages students to appreciate the importance of diverse groups in shaping American society and culture by encouraging them to consider how contributions from various cultures influence their daily lives.

4. D: Providing gifted and talented students with meaningful opportunities to extend their learning allows them to progress at a pace that matches their abilities and learning needs. This helps to ensure that these students remain engaged in the classroom, deepens their understanding, and encourages them to continuously seek challenging learning experiences.

5. A: By reflecting on notes from formative assessments, Mr. Morris can identify successes within the lesson as well as areas of whole-class and individual student need. This strategy allows Mr. Morris to effectively adjust instructional strategies and implement necessary supports or modifications to accommodate a diverse range of learning needs, interests, and preferences. In doing so, Mr. Morris can deliver more engaging instruction that focuses on promoting achievement for all students.

6. B: Seeking professional development regarding methods for teaching students from diverse backgrounds demonstrates an awareness of the importance of cultural competence in effective instruction. Doing so will teach Mr. Morris best practices, instructional strategies, and culturally sensitive communication techniques for creating a welcoming, accepting learning environment focused on student achievement.

7. A: By incorporating these strategies into his lesson, Mr. Morris accommodates the needs of various types of learners. Delivering instruction through a variety of means makes instruction relevant and accessible to diverse learners. Opportunities for student choice allow students of various learning styles to demonstrate their findings in the way that best suits their needs and preferences. Scaffolds and supports throughout instruction allow for an equitable learning environment that is inclusive of students with varying abilities. In addition, in selecting student groupings, Mr. Morris can ensure that students in need of support are paired with others that can help.

8. B: By incorporating authentic examples of ways in which immigrants continue to shape American society and culture, Mr. Morris delivers meaningful, relevant, and ultimately more engaging instruction. This allows students to create personal connections and recognize the real-world applications of the lesson, deepening their understanding and enhancing the overall learning experience.

9. D: In assigning the groups himself, Mr. Morris was able to ensure that students had the opportunity to work with others that they may not have interacted with otherwise. This exposes students to different perspectives, opinions, and background knowledge, which promotes respect and appreciation for diversity. Exposure to diverse perspectives also strengthens students' understanding of a given topic and promotes a classroom environment focused on positive communication.

10. A: Varying instructional strategies and incorporating necessary supports or modifications to instruction helps make learning comprehensible, relevant, and accessible to students of differing abilities. Doing so establishes the equity necessary for all students to engage in the learning process to the greatest possible extent. This is integral to creating a safe, accepting, and inclusive atmosphere that promotes positive attitudes toward learning.

11. C: Mr. Morris noted in his diagnostic exam that a few students indicated below grade-level reading comprehension skills. These same students appeared bored and disengaged during the class presentation, which indicates they may not have fully understood some of the text on the slides. Mr. Morris could have provided scaffolding by defining key terms and varying the complexity of the language within his presentation to ensure students of all abilities remained engaged.

12. Sample answer:

Mr. Morris's unit on the experiences and contributions of early and recent immigrants provides ample opportunities for him to strengthen students' appreciation for diverse groups of people. Mr. Morris already provides authentic and relevant examples of ways in which immigrant groups have shaped American society and culture. Another way he could strengthen students' appreciation for different immigrant groups is by incorporating diverse individual perspectives from early and recent immigrants throughout history into instruction.

There are several strategies Mr. Morris could implement to illustrate the diversity of experiences and contributions between individuals within specific immigrant groups. One method would be to give students examples of individual accounts from the perspectives of women, people of various age groups, and immigrants from different religious backgrounds.

Implementing this strategy would deepen students' appreciation for diverse groups of people by providing them with multifaceted accounts of the actual experiences and contributions of individual immigrants to the United States. This creates a more personalized learning experience while allowing students the opportunity to compare and contrast how individuals within the same immigrant group had different experiences. In addition, providing students with varied perspectives increases the likelihood that diverse groups of students will relate to aspects of the immigrant experience, which creates an engaging and authentic learning experience that highlights the importance of diversity throughout history.

English Language Learners

13. B: Compound bilingualism refers to equal exposure to two languages within the same environment. When children grow up equally immersed in two separate languages, they typically develop equal levels of proficiency in both. Coordinate bilingualism refers to the learning of two languages in separate environments (e.g., learning one language at home and one at school), whereas sub-coordinate bilingualism refers to learning a second language through the lens of one's native language. Late bilingualism means learning a second language in later childhood, after the period in which learning a language is natural.

14. C: By assigning student groups herself, Ms. Fisher could have ensured that students of lower English language proficiency levels were paired with others that could provide clarification and assistance throughout the activity. This would have given lower-level ELL students the linguistic support necessary to fully engage in the group activity and may have prevented these students from becoming off-task.

15. B: Giving the school ELL teacher upcoming lesson plans allows him or her to effectively work with individual or small groups of ELL students to discuss important vocabulary, concepts, and ideas prior to beginning instruction. This will help establish a framework for understanding when the new lesson is introduced, which increases the likelihood that these students will be able to actively engage in the learning process. This will also allow the school ELL teacher to determine individual language acquisition goals for ELL students and effectively measure their progress.

16. A: According to the Every Student Succeeds Act (ESSA), all students must be given equal access to education and learning opportunities. Therefore, linguistic aids are necessary for giving ELL students the necessary support to fully engage in the learning process and achieve academic success. Doing so scaffolds instruction so that learning is tailored to their linguistic abilities while giving them the tools necessary to master new skills and concepts.

17. B: Literacy development in the native language is integral to establishing the foundation necessary to properly develop literacy skills in a second language. Many literacy concepts learned in the primary language can be applied to the secondary language. Thus, limited or interrupted formal education in the native language results in inadequate literacy development that impedes ELL students' ability to acquire literacy skills in the second language.

18. D: Ms. Fisher immerses her students in English language literacy by incorporating word walls, lists, anchor charts, and a library into the classroom. Doing so continuously exposes her students to elements of the English language while encouraging them to interact with a variety of literacy materials. Such exposure is also beneficial in developing ELL students' knowledge of content-specific academic language. Accompanying instruction with visual representations, body language, and English-Spanish dictionaries provides necessary linguistic aids to help with clarification. Incorporating scaffolds such as graphic organizers, modified texts, and Spanish translations promotes comprehension. Applying research- and evidence-based strategies is integral in giving ELL students of varying abilities the support needed to develop English language proficiency.

19. A: For a variety of reasons related to developing English language proficiency skills, ELL students often have difficulty demonstrating their learning through traditional assessment methods. Authentic assessments are typically more performance-based and allow students to demonstrate their level of mastery of a skill or concept in a relevant context. Allowing students to create a product that demonstrates a given theme allows them to apply their learning in a meaningful way. This ultimately strengthens students' understanding while allowing the teacher to evaluate individual students' progress and identify areas in which instruction may need adjustment to provide additional support.

20. D: While the scaffolds, modifications, and linguistic aids within Ms. Fisher's lesson are necessary for effective instruction in an ELL classroom, lower-level ELL students with limited literacy skills likely still struggled with comprehension. As the lesson progressed, students' confusion likely compounded, causing them to disengage and become distracted. Conducting strategic formative assessments throughout the lesson would have given these students clarification to help maintain their engagement. Ms. Fisher should also consult the school ELL teacher to discuss further strategies for giving these students linguistic support.

21. C: When ELL students feel their native language is valued in the classroom, it contributes to creating an accepting and inclusive learning environment in which these students feel encouraged to build upon their English language proficiency skills. In addition, incorporating Spanish into the lesson demonstrates how literacy skills in their native language can be applied when learning English, strengthening their understanding and promoting English language acquisition.

22. C: Letting students practice delivering their presentations in English ahead of time would have helped ease their anxieties regarding speaking English in a whole-class setting. Doing so would have let ELL students ask for clarification, receive constructive feedback, make corrections, and develop their oral proficiency skills prior to speaking in front of the class. This would have also promoted students' confidence in applying English language skills in an academic context.

23. C: Ms. Fisher's set of task cards included passages of varying levels of complexity in which students were asked to identify the theme. While this was somewhat beneficial in scaffolding instruction, lower-level ELL students likely still had difficulty comprehending more advanced passages within the task card set. Similarly, native English speakers and advanced ELL students may have found the modified passages too easy. By creating three versions of the task card sets to accommodate beginner, intermediate, and advanced skill levels, Ms. Fisher could have more effectively promoted English literacy for ELL students at all stages of literacy development.

24. Sample Answer:

Ms. Fisher takes a variety of measures to accommodate her students' varying linguistic abilities in the classroom. Along with consulting the school ELL teacher, she includes several linguistic aids, scaffolds, and modifications in her lesson to ensure her students have the necessary support to learn effectively. Ms. Fisher could further support her ELL students' English language acquisition and academic achievement by establishing positive communication with their families.

There are a variety of methods to establish and maintain positive communication with students' families, despite potential language barriers. According to the Every Student Succeeds Act (ESSA), important information regarding classroom updates and student progress must be translated as necessary into families' native languages in order to provide equal access. Ms. Fisher could create a weekly class newsletter or website that includes information in both English and Spanish. To discuss individual students' progress, Ms. Fisher could invite families in for conferences with an interpreter present or communicate via email with the help of a translator. Hosting an open-house night with an interpreter present would also be valuable in creating a welcoming atmosphere that encourages students' families to engage in communication.

Frequent communication with students' families is highly beneficial in promoting academic achievement. With ELL students, establishing such communication would contribute significantly to promoting English language acquisition, and as a result, greater academic progress. Doing so would give Ms. Fisher insight regarding students' home lives, prior experiences with learning English, and individual learning needs, which would allow her to plan and implement the best possible instructional strategies. In addition, frequent communication between the school and home increases the likelihood that families will reinforce learning at home. By communicating with families, Ms. Fisher could offer beneficial resources and strategies to promote English language acquisition and academic progress at home, strengthening students' overall learning experience.

Students with Disabilities and Other Special Learning Needs

25. B: Teachers spend a great deal of time with their students and are often the first to notice when one of them is experiencing difficulties. If a teacher suspects that one of his or her students has a disability that hinders the quality of learning, the teacher has the ethical responsibility to consult the school administration and special education department to discuss his or her concerns. Doing so will result in further evaluation of the student to determine his or her qualification for special education services. If the student meets the criteria, the special education department will develop an educational plan that provides the necessary supports and accommodations to facilitate equitable access to learning.

26. A: According to the Family Educational Rights and Privacy Act (FERPA), student records, including academic, behavioral, or medical records, may only be disclosed to designated members of a minor student's family except in specific authorized situations. This extends to details regarding special education services, IEPs, and 504 plans. Therefore, Ms. Patel must keep all information related to her students' disabilities confidential to protect their right to privacy. This includes storing students' IEPs and 504 plans in secure spaces, discreetly providing accommodations and modifications, and refraining from discussing her students' special education services except in authorized situations.

27. D: Response to intervention (RTI) services differ from special education in that they are designed to improve the performance of students struggling in a given academic or behavioral area by providing varying degrees of support. Specifically, Tier 2 interventions give students extra support in a small-group setting in addition to their general education instruction. This is intended to develop these students' skills to a grade-appropriate level. While RTI services can influence decisions related to special education, they do not address specific disabilities and do not give students additional accommodations or modifications to classroom instruction.

28. D: According to the Individuals with Disabilities Education Act (IDEA), all students are legally entitled to a free and appropriate education in the least restrictive environment. Therefore, students with disabilities or other special needs must receive accommodations or modifications specific to their individual needs so as to provide equitable access to learning opportunities. In her lesson, Ms. Patel recognizes her students' individual needs and adapts instruction accordingly by providing enlarged print, graphic organizers, preferential seating, and access to speech-to-text technology to ensure all students are able to fully participate in the lesson.

29. B: Ms. Patel is conscientious in providing Maya with the necessary accommodations to sustain her focus in class, including preferential seating for reduced distractions, redirection, a graphic organizer, and a stress ball to prevent fidgeting. However, Maya's underdeveloped literacy skills, as well as her tendency to rush through her work, are likely to cause Maya difficulty when attempting to express her ideas in written form. Ms. Patel should continue to monitor Maya's progress in literacy development to determine whether further RTI services are necessary.

30. A: Positive Behavioral Interventions and Supports (PBIS) is a three-tiered program intended to promote positive behavior among students. Ms. Patel implemented a Tier 1 approach in her classroom by creating a system for all students in which they could redeem tickets received for positive behavior in exchange for prizes. This strategy can be highly motivational for producing desired behavior in the classroom, and especially beneficial for students with academic or behavioral goals.

31. B: Michael seems to struggle with interpersonal relationships and is therefore likely to struggle during the collaborative portion of the lesson. Ms. Patel spoke with Michael privately and redirected his attention when he began to lose focus during this activity. Further strategies to support him could have included a more targeted PBIS approach or adapting the assignment to more effectively meet Michael's learning preferences. Ms. Patel should address this behavior when discussing her observations of Michael with the school administration and special education department.

32. C: Providing Jordan with accommodations to support his visual impairment demonstrates that Ms. Patel recognizes areas within her lesson in which accommodations are necessary to facilitate his full participation in learning. Enlarging the font for printed activities and allowing him to type his conclusion using speech-to-text technology illustrates her awareness of how to effectively implement appropriate supports to create an equitable learning environment for Jordan.

33. D: In a classroom of students with varying abilities, strategic selection of student groupings can provide students in need of extra support with others that can assist. Doing so scaffolds learning by allowing struggling students to build upon their partner's knowledge for increased understanding. Maya, for example, may have been paired with a student that Ms. Patel knew could help her stay focused and organize her ideas for the conclusion essay.

34. B: While Ms. Patel accommodates Jordan's visual impairment by providing enlarged print and access to speech-to-text technology, his physical position in the classroom is not specified. Since Jordan often struggles to see words on the board or projector screen, he should be granted preferential seating at the front of the room to help him see pertinent information during instruction. Doing so would help ensure that Jordan is provided the support necessary to facilitate his full participation in the learning process.

35. Sample Answer:

Ms. Patel included a variety of accommodations in each component of her lesson to support her students' individual learning needs, particularly those of her students with disabilities. However, her delivery of instruction and subsequent activities often used only a single approach. In order to make learning more accessible to her students and increase engagement, Ms. Patel could have differentiated her instruction more effectively.

There are several components of the lesson that would have benefited from more effective differentiation. Rather than presenting the new concept solely through direct instruction, Ms. Patel could have created learning stations. Learning stations often incorporate several modalities for learning and would have let students explore the new material in a student-led setting. For students that struggle to focus during direct instruction, such as Maya, this strategy would have provided opportunities for movement and hands-on learning to increase engagement and focus on learning. In addition, Ms. Patel could have differentiated the second partner activity by letting students choose how they demonstrated their learning, rather than instructing all students to write conclusion essays. For example, since Michael is interested in drawing, he may have been more engaged in learning had he been able to demonstrate his understanding by creating an infographic rather than typing an essay. Allowing opportunities for student choice is a valuable strategy for differentiating instruction in that it allows students to engage in and demonstrate their learning in a way that is tailored to their individual needs.

By differentiating her instructional strategies and activities more effectively, Ms. Patel could have appealed to her students' varying learning styles, skills, abilities, and preferences for a more student-centered, and therefore, more engaging, learning experience. Differentiated instruction can yield significant benefits when working with students that have disabilities, as it allows the teacher to adapt learning to meet students' specific needs, thus encouraging their active participation.

Teacher Responsibilities

36. B: All students have the right to a free public education. As such, every student has the right to due process when a school administration is considering expulsion or long-term suspension, typically longer than ten days. While exact details regarding disciplinary processes may vary across school districts, due process entails the right to notice of a formal hearing at the school board of education. This allows the student to present and defend his or her case in an effort to avoid suspension or expulsion.

37. A: Students protected under the Individuals with Disabilities Education Act are entitled to an equitable testing environment with the supports necessary to allow them to properly demonstrate their mastery of a skill or concept. Modifications to the assessment and/or testing environment must be made in accordance with specifications outlined in the students' Individualized Education Program (IEP). Doing so is necessary to ensure that the students' disabilities do not hinder their performance on the assessment, thereby providing accurate and objective results.

38. D: When teachers suspect that one of their students is being abused or neglected, they have the legal responsibility to report their suspicions immediately to Child Protective Services or another appropriate agency, such as social services or the police department. Teachers can typically access the necessary information for making such reports via the school guidance office. In some districts, teachers may be required to inform the school administration of their report.

39. C: As teachers spend a great deal of the school day with students, they are often highly attuned to their individual needs, and therefore can serve as powerful advocates. Doing so helps ensure students' needs are heard and that they are provided the support necessary to facilitate success in learning. By addressing his concerns with the school administration and special education department, Mr. Green seeks the proper professionals to advocate for his student. This will ensure that the student receives adequate evaluation to determine the need for additional support.

40. D: The teacher's response to parents significantly impacts the nature of the interaction and ultimately can impact the student's success in learning. By engaging professionally and respectfully with the student's parents, Ms. Douglas validates their concerns, fostering an environment that facilitates positive communication. This increases the likelihood that the student's parents will be willing to participate in productive collaboration with Ms. Douglas to develop a plan that supports the student's needs for academic success more effectively in the future.

School-Home Responsibilities

41. B: For a variety of reasons, students' families may be hesitant to initiate communication with their children's school. This reticence could be due to work and lifestyle factors, previous negative encounters with the school system, or lack of confidence in their ability to become involved in their children's education in a meaningful way. By initiating and maintaining communication with students' families, the teacher establishes a welcoming environment in which families feel included as active participants in their children's education. As a result, family members feel encouraged and empowered to contribute to their children's learning both within and outside of the classroom, strengthening student development and achievement.

42. C: Communicating important classroom information through a variety of methods demonstrates responsiveness to the varying needs of students' families. Several factors may influence families' ability to access and maintain communication with their children's school, including differences in work schedules, living arrangements, and access to technology. By providing multiple avenues for communication, the teacher can effectively accommodate varying needs and facilitate communication with all students' families. This helps create a positive environment that encourages family participation in the education program.

43. D: Family conferences are a valuable opportunity for teachers to learn about their students' individual needs, learning styles, and preferences. Conferences that are conducted in a professional, respectful, and welcoming setting facilitate productive collaboration between teachers and families. In such an environment, families feel encouraged to share information regarding their child that will be beneficial to their learning and development. This gives teachers valuable insight regarding the most effective instructional strategies to implement for supporting each student's academic achievement.

44. A: Hosting events such as an open-house night establishes a welcoming learning community in which all students' families feel accepted, respected, and included in the education program. Encouraging families to ask questions and provide input regarding school-related topics validates their ideas and concerns, which encourages them to continue actively contributing to decisions related to the school and their children's education. This ultimately strengthens the connection between students' school and home lives, which also strengthens their support for academic achievement.

45. C: Reinforcing education at home has significant implications for strengthening students' learning and development. However, students' families are often unsure of how to extend their children's classroom learning at home in a meaningful way. By providing relevant resources and strategies to support learning at home each week, Ms. Garcia effectively encourages students' families to actively engage in supporting and reinforcing their children's learning outside of the classroom.

NYSTCE Practice Tests #2 and #3

To take these additional NYSTCE practice tests, visit our bonus page:
mometrix.com/bonus948/nystceeas

How to Overcome Test Anxiety

Just the thought of taking a test is enough to make most people a little nervous. A test is an important event that can have a long-term impact on your future, so it's important to take it seriously and it's natural to feel anxious about performing well. But just because anxiety is normal, that doesn't mean that it's helpful in test taking, or that you should simply accept it as part of your life. Anxiety can have a variety of effects. These effects can be mild, like making you feel slightly nervous, or severe, like blocking your ability to focus or remember even a simple detail.

If you experience test anxiety—whether severe or mild—it's important to know how to beat it. To discover this, first you need to understand what causes test anxiety.

Causes of Test Anxiety

While we often think of anxiety as an uncontrollable emotional state, it can actually be caused by simple, practical things. One of the most common causes of test anxiety is that a person does not feel adequately prepared for their test. This feeling can be the result of many different issues such as poor study habits or lack of organization, but the most common culprit is time management. Starting to study too late, failing to organize your study time to cover all of the material, or being distracted while you study will mean that you're not well prepared for the test. This may lead to cramming the night before, which will cause you to be physically and mentally exhausted for the test. Poor time management also contributes to feelings of stress, fear, and hopelessness as you realize you are not well prepared but don't know what to do about it.

Other times, test anxiety is not related to your preparation for the test but comes from unresolved fear. This may be a past failure on a test, or poor performance on tests in general. It may come from comparing yourself to others who seem to be performing better or from the stress of living up to expectations. Anxiety may be driven by fears of the future—how failure on this test would affect your educational and career goals. These fears are often completely irrational, but they can still negatively impact your test performance.

Elements of Test Anxiety

As mentioned earlier, test anxiety is considered to be an emotional state, but it has physical and mental components as well. Sometimes you may not even realize that you are suffering from test anxiety until you notice the physical symptoms. These can include trembling hands, rapid heartbeat, sweating, nausea, and tense muscles. Extreme anxiety may lead to fainting or vomiting. Obviously, any of these symptoms can have a negative impact on testing. It is important to recognize them as soon as they begin to occur so that you can address the problem before it damages your performance.

The mental components of test anxiety include trouble focusing and inability to remember learned information. During a test, your mind is on high alert, which can help you recall information and stay focused for an extended period of time. However, anxiety interferes with your mind's natural processes, causing you to blank out, even on the questions you know well. The strain of testing during anxiety makes it difficult to stay focused, especially on a test that may take several hours. Extreme anxiety can take a huge mental toll, making it difficult not only to recall test information but even to understand the test questions or pull your thoughts together.

Effects of Test Anxiety

Test anxiety is like a disease—if left untreated, it will get progressively worse. Anxiety leads to poor performance, and this reinforces the feelings of fear and failure, which in turn lead to poor performances on subsequent tests. It can grow from a mild nervousness to a crippling condition. If allowed to progress, test anxiety can have a big impact on your schooling, and consequently on your future.

Test anxiety can spread to other parts of your life. Anxiety on tests can become anxiety in any stressful situation, and blanking on a test can turn into panicking in a job situation. But fortunately, you don't have to let anxiety rule your testing and determine your grades. There are a number of relatively simple steps you can take to move past anxiety and function normally on a test and in the rest of life.

Physical Steps for Beating Test Anxiety

While test anxiety is a serious problem, the good news is that it can be overcome. It doesn't have to control your ability to think and remember information. While it may take time, you can begin taking steps today to beat anxiety.

Just as your first hint that you may be struggling with anxiety comes from the physical symptoms, the first step to treating it is also physical. Rest is crucial for having a clear, strong mind. If you are tired, it is much easier to give in to anxiety. But if you establish good sleep habits, your body and mind will be ready to perform optimally, without the strain of exhaustion. Additionally, sleeping well helps you to retain information better, so you're more likely to recall the answers when you see the test questions.

Getting good sleep means more than going to bed on time. It's important to allow your brain time to relax. Take study breaks from time to time so it doesn't get overworked, and don't study right before bed. Take time to rest your mind before trying to rest your body, or you may find it difficult to fall asleep.

Along with sleep, other aspects of physical health are important in preparing for a test. Good nutrition is vital for good brain function. Sugary foods and drinks may give a burst of energy but this burst is followed by a crash, both physically and emotionally. Instead, fuel your body with protein and vitamin-rich foods.

Also, drink plenty of water. Dehydration can lead to headaches and exhaustion, especially if your brain is already under stress from the rigors of the test. Particularly if your test is a long one, drink water during the breaks. And if possible, take an energy-boosting snack to eat between sections.

Along with sleep and diet, a third important part of physical health is exercise. Maintaining a steady workout schedule is helpful, but even taking 5-minute study breaks to walk can help get your blood pumping faster and clear your head. Exercise also releases endorphins, which contribute to a positive feeling and can help combat test anxiety.

When you nurture your physical health, you are also contributing to your mental health. If your body is healthy, your mind is much more likely to be healthy as well. So take time to rest, nourish your body with healthy food and water, and get moving as much as possible. Taking these physical steps will make you stronger and more able to take the mental steps necessary to overcome test anxiety.

Mental Steps for Beating Test Anxiety

Working on the mental side of test anxiety can be more challenging, but as with the physical side, there are clear steps you can take to overcome it. As mentioned earlier, test anxiety often stems from lack of preparation, so the obvious solution is to prepare for the test. Effective studying may be the most important weapon you have for beating test anxiety, but you can and should employ several other mental tools to combat fear.

First, boost your confidence by reminding yourself of past success—tests or projects that you aced. If you're putting as much effort into preparing for this test as you did for those, there's no reason you should expect to fail here. Work hard to prepare; then trust your preparation.

Second, surround yourself with encouraging people. It can be helpful to find a study group, but be sure that the people you're around will encourage a positive attitude. If you spend time with others who are anxious or cynical, this will only contribute to your own anxiety. Look for others who are motivated to study hard from a desire to succeed, not from a fear of failure.

Third, reward yourself. A test is physically and mentally tiring, even without anxiety, and it can be helpful to have something to look forward to. Plan an activity following the test, regardless of the outcome, such as going to a movie or getting ice cream.

When you are taking the test, if you find yourself beginning to feel anxious, remind yourself that you know the material. Visualize successfully completing the test. Then take a few deep, relaxing breaths and return to it. Work through the questions carefully but with confidence, knowing that you are capable of succeeding.

Developing a healthy mental approach to test taking will also aid in other areas of life. Test anxiety affects more than just the actual test—it can be damaging to your mental health and even contribute to depression. It's important to beat test anxiety before it becomes a problem for more than testing.

Study Strategy

Being prepared for the test is necessary to combat anxiety, but what does being prepared look like? You may study for hours on end and still not feel prepared. What you need is a strategy for test prep. The next few pages outline our recommended steps to help you plan out and conquer the challenge of preparation.

Step 1: Scope Out the Test

Learn everything you can about the format (multiple choice, essay, etc.) and what will be on the test. Gather any study materials, course outlines, or sample exams that may be available. Not only will this help you to prepare, but knowing what to expect can help to alleviate test anxiety.

Step 2: Map Out the Material

Look through the textbook or study guide and make note of how many chapters or sections it has. Then divide these over the time you have. For example, if a book has 15 chapters and you have five days to study, you need to cover three chapters each day. Even better, if you have the time, leave an extra day at the end for overall review after you have gone through the material in depth.

If time is limited, you may need to prioritize the material. Look through it and make note of which sections you think you already have a good grasp on, and which need review. While you are studying, skim quickly through the familiar sections and take more time on the challenging parts.

Write out your plan so you don't get lost as you go. Having a written plan also helps you feel more in control of the study, so anxiety is less likely to arise from feeling overwhelmed at the amount to cover.

Step 3: Gather Your Tools

Decide what study method works best for you. Do you prefer to highlight in the book as you study and then go back over the highlighted portions? Or do you type out notes of the important information? Or is it helpful to make flashcards that you can carry with you? Assemble the pens, index cards, highlighters, post-it notes, and any other materials you may need so you won't be distracted by getting up to find things while you study.

If you're having a hard time retaining the information or organizing your notes, experiment with different methods. For example, try color-coding by subject with colored pens, highlighters, or post-it notes. If you learn better by hearing, try recording yourself reading your notes so you can listen while in the car, working out, or simply sitting at your desk. Ask a friend to quiz you from your flashcards, or try teaching someone the material to solidify it in your mind.

Step 4: Create Your Environment

It's important to avoid distractions while you study. This includes both the obvious distractions like visitors and the subtle distractions like an uncomfortable chair (or a too-comfortable couch that makes you want to fall asleep). Set up the best study environment possible: good lighting and a comfortable work area. If background music helps you focus, you may want to turn it on, but otherwise keep the room quiet. If you are using a computer to take notes, be sure you don't have any other windows open, especially applications like social media, games, or anything else that could distract you. Silence your phone and turn off notifications. Be sure to keep water close by so you stay hydrated while you study (but avoid unhealthy drinks and snacks).

Also, take into account the best time of day to study. Are you freshest first thing in the morning? Try to set aside some time then to work through the material. Is your mind clearer in the afternoon or evening? Schedule your study session then. Another method is to study at the same time of day that you will take the test, so that your brain gets used to working on the material at that time and will be ready to focus at test time.

Step 5: Study!

Once you have done all the study preparation, it's time to settle into the actual studying. Sit down, take a few moments to settle your mind so you can focus, and begin to follow your study plan. Don't give in to distractions or let yourself procrastinate. This is your time to prepare so you'll be ready to fearlessly approach the test. Make the most of the time and stay focused.

Of course, you don't want to burn out. If you study too long you may find that you're not retaining the information very well. Take regular study breaks. For example, taking five minutes out of every hour to walk briskly, breathing deeply and swinging your arms, can help your mind stay fresh.

As you get to the end of each chapter or section, it's a good idea to do a quick review. Remind yourself of what you learned and work on any difficult parts. When you feel that you've mastered the material, move on to the next part. At the end of your study session, briefly skim through your notes again.

But while review is helpful, cramming last minute is NOT. If at all possible, work ahead so that you won't need to fit all your study into the last day. Cramming overloads your brain with more information than it can process and retain, and your tired mind may struggle to recall even previously learned information when it is overwhelmed with last-minute study. Also, the urgent nature of cramming and the stress placed on your brain contribute to anxiety. You'll be more likely to go to the test feeling unprepared and having trouble thinking clearly.

So don't cram, and don't stay up late before the test, even just to review your notes at a leisurely pace. Your brain needs rest more than it needs to go over the information again. In fact, plan to finish your studies by noon or early afternoon the day before the test. Give your brain the rest of the day to relax or focus on other things, and get a good night's sleep. Then you will be fresh for the test and better able to recall what you've studied.

Step 6: Take a Practice Test

Many courses offer sample tests, either online or in the study materials. This is an excellent resource to check whether you have mastered the material, as well as to prepare for the test format and environment.

Check the test format ahead of time: the number of questions, the type (multiple choice, free response, etc.), and the time limit. Then create a plan for working through them. For example, if you have 30 minutes to take a 60-question test, your limit is 30 seconds per question. Spend less time on the questions you know well so that you can take more time on the difficult ones.

If you have time to take several practice tests, take the first one open book, with no time limit. Work through the questions at your own pace and make sure you fully understand them. Gradually work up to taking a test under test conditions: sit at a desk with all study materials put away and set a timer. Pace yourself to make sure you finish the test with time to spare and go back to check your answers if you have time.

After each test, check your answers. On the questions you missed, be sure you understand why you missed them. Did you misread the question (tests can use tricky wording)? Did you forget the information? Or was it something you hadn't learned? Go back and study any shaky areas that the practice tests reveal.

Taking these tests not only helps with your grade, but also aids in combating test anxiety. If you're already used to the test conditions, you're less likely to worry about it, and working through tests until you're scoring well gives you a confidence boost. Go through the practice tests until you feel comfortable, and then you can go into the test knowing that you're ready for it.

Test Tips

On test day, you should be confident, knowing that you've prepared well and are ready to answer the questions. But aside from preparation, there are several test day strategies you can employ to maximize your performance.

First, as stated before, get a good night's sleep the night before the test (and for several nights before that, if possible). Go into the test with a fresh, alert mind rather than staying up late to study.

Try not to change too much about your normal routine on the day of the test. It's important to eat a nutritious breakfast, but if you normally don't eat breakfast at all, consider eating just a protein bar. If you're a coffee drinker, go ahead and have your normal coffee. Just make sure you time it so that the caffeine doesn't wear off right in the middle of your test. Avoid sugary beverages, and drink enough water to stay hydrated but not so much that you need a restroom break 10 minutes into the test. If your test isn't first thing in the morning, consider going for a walk or doing a light workout before the test to get your blood flowing.

Allow yourself enough time to get ready, and leave for the test with plenty of time to spare so you won't have the anxiety of scrambling to arrive in time. Another reason to be early is to select a good seat. It's helpful to sit away from doors and windows, which can be distracting. Find a good seat, get out your supplies, and settle your mind before the test begins.

When the test begins, start by going over the instructions carefully, even if you already know what to expect. Make sure you avoid any careless mistakes by following the directions.

Then begin working through the questions, pacing yourself as you've practiced. If you're not sure on an answer, don't spend too much time on it, and don't let it shake your confidence. Either skip it and come back later, or eliminate as many wrong answers as possible and guess among the remaining ones. Don't dwell on these questions as you continue—put them out of your mind and focus on what lies ahead.

Be sure to read all of the answer choices, even if you're sure the first one is the right answer. Sometimes you'll find a better one if you keep reading. But don't second-guess yourself if you do immediately know the answer. Your gut instinct is usually right. Don't let test anxiety rob you of the information you know.

If you have time at the end of the test (and if the test format allows), go back and review your answers. Be cautious about changing any, since your first instinct tends to be correct, but make sure you didn't misread any of the questions or accidentally mark the wrong answer choice. Look over any you skipped and make an educated guess.

At the end, leave the test feeling confident. You've done your best, so don't waste time worrying about your performance or wishing you could change anything. Instead, celebrate the successful completion of this test. And finally, use this test to learn how to deal with anxiety even better next time.

Review Video: Test Anxiety
Visit mometrix.com/academy and enter code: 100340

Important Qualification

Not all anxiety is created equal. If your test anxiety is causing major issues in your life beyond the classroom or testing center, or if you are experiencing troubling physical symptoms related to your anxiety, it may be a sign of a serious physiological or psychological condition. If this sounds like your situation, we strongly encourage you to seek professional help.

Additional Bonus Material

Due to our efforts to try to keep this book to a manageable length, we've created a link that will give you access to all of your additional bonus material:

mometrix.com/bonus948/nystceeas